THE MONTREAL FORTIES

BRIAN TREHEARNE

The Montreal Forties: Modernist Poetry in Transition

UNIVERSITY OF TORONTO PRESS
Toronto Buffalo London

Toronto Buffalo London
Printed in Canada

ISBN 0-8020-4452-2 (cloth)
ISBN 978-1-4426-1323-2 (paper)

Printed on acid-free paper

Canadian Cataloguing in Publication Data

Trehearne, Brian, 1957–
The Montreal forties : modernist poetry in transition

Includes bibliographical references and index.
ISBN 0-8020-4452-2

1. Canadian poetry (English) – Quebec (Province) – Montreal – History and criticism.* 2. Canadian poetry (English) – 20th century – History and criticism.* I. Title.

PS8159.7.M6T74 1999 C811'.5209971428 C99-930098-9
PR9198.3.M6T74 1999

University of Toronto Press acknowledges the financial assistance to its publishing program of the Canada Council for the Arts and the Ontario Arts Council.

This book has been published with the help of a grant from the Humanities and Social Sciences Federation of Canada, using funds provided by the Social Sciences and Humanities Research Council of Canada.

For Hilda W. Trehearne – 'Teach'

Contents

Acknowledgments

In the course of research for this book, I had the exceptional good fortune to meet P.K. Page and Irving Layton and continue my twenty years' conversation with Louis Dudek, and those encounters were its chief pleasures. I am particularly grateful to P.K. Page for granting permission to quote from her works in a letter so generous and richly reflective that it may itself one day require quotation. Irving Layton was kind enough to visit my classrooms three times as I formulated these ideas of his poetry with my students, and to debate them rigorously with me at his home. I owe Louis Dudek immeasurably for his keen-sighted and generous response to the manuscript in draft form – and for many of my intellectual compulsions as well. I am also grateful to Mr Orlando Gearing, Mr Sandor Klein, and Mr William Toye for their generous permission to quote from works in copyright by Patrick Anderson, A.M. Klein, and A.J.M. Smith. Without the confidence and ready help of all these individuals, this book could not have been published.

In the long course of its completion, I have had encouragement and research support from more individuals than I can hope to number. The Social Sciences and Humanities Research Council of Canada let me begin this project with a Postdoctoral Fellowship and helped me to conclude it with a Standard Research Grant. The Webster Postdoctoral Fellowship I held for two years at Queen's University was the vote of confidence my project needed in its first stages, and I am grateful to the members of the Webster administrative committee for their endorsement, as for their patience. The Faculty of Arts at McGill University granted me a sabbatic leave at a crucial moment in the manuscript's development. During and after that leave, I enjoyed the efficient and helpful services of several research assistants, to whom I am particularly indebted: may David Mazoff, Mark Cohen, Dennis Denisoff, and Matt Bergbusch (who wields a wicked paintbrush in off hours) find their labour and enthusiasm echoed in these pages. My editors at the University of Toronto Press, Emily Andrew, Jill McConkey, Frances Mundy, and Darlene Zeleney, have been particularly supportive, enthusiastic, and tactful in their management both of the manuscript and of its author, and Beverley Beetham Endersby copy-edited the manuscript's failings with scrupulousness and its idiosyncracies with generosity. I also thank the reference librarians and archivists who patiently guided me to and through the scholarly resources pertinent to my research: staff at the Public Archives of Canada and at McGill University's MacLennan Library and Department of Rare Books and Special Collections have been indefatigable on my behalf, and their company in this process has been truly appreciated. Finally, the McGill Institute for the Study of Canada, and its director, Desmond Morton, have provided me with a congenial intellectual home, and I valued the Senior Associate Fellowship with which they honoured me as my project moved towards completion.

Without the learned example of David Bentley, *il miglior fabbro,* this book would be less sound than I hope it is; without him as a friend, life would be less happy altogether.

With exuberance like his and even less shame do Nell, Caddy, Pip, and Calypso deny me a life spent all in the mind: saviours.

Maggie Kilgour, my wife, intercessor, and *genius loci,* lived through this book as surely as I did, though with better grace. More than I knew, I borrowed her ideas as freely as her sympathies; she shows me, in fact, that they can be one.

On a recent visit to Bradner, British Columbia, with my mother, I saw the single-room school in which she taught six grades simultaneously – after lighting the woodstove in the back at 7:30 a.m. – while across Canada the poets of Montreal were changing our literary history for ever. Two of her children became teachers in their turn. I dedicate this book to her inspiration of us all.

THE MONTREAL FORTIES

Introduction: Reading the Forties Poets

Modernist Histories

During the latter half of the Second World War, a group of young and unknown Canadian poets converged on Montreal and, in a few short years of little-magazine and small-press publication, rewrote the story of modern English-Canadian poetry. Patrick Anderson, from England by way of Columbia University in New York; A.M. Klein, Louis Dudek, and Irving Layton, from Montreal; P.K. Page, from Alberta via New Brunswick; and John Sutherland, from New Brunswick via Kingston and Queen's University: these poets were among the period's fascinating literary figures. Banding together in various personal and professional relations, they generated one of the most fruitful rivalries Canadian poetry has ever enjoyed – between the little magazines *Preview* and *First Statement* (1942–5), a contest still echoing in our literary theatre more than half a century later. Passionate participants in and defenders of the cultural modernism that had swept the Western world after the Great War, these poets argued with equal exuberance over the potential of an emphatically Canadian modern writing, and as they struggled over the war years' ideas and challenges, they left a rich documentary record of Canadian poetry in its great modern transition. This book offers an exegesis of that record, a grasp at some new, broad, and reliable truths about the compelling, rapidly changing poetry at the decade's heart.

It is the poetry that matters, obviously, not the colourful personalities, nor the European-American metropolis of their youth. My method is nevertheless inescapably literary-historical. I read a good many literary documents closely, and in selecting these with a particular interest and asking a sustained set of questions of them, I inevitably construct a partial narrative of Canadian poetry's transition during the 1940s. What's more, when you are dealing with poets whose writing lives have been as vivid as these, there is no way to keep 'readings' of those lives entirely distinct from readings of poems – nor would it be desirable to do so. Instead, the most pointed questions I ask of the poets in my study have to do with the connections between their images and conceptions of personal identity, of 'selfhood,' and their discoveries of poetic structure and style in that decade. I will shun, however, those models of literary history (now, at any rate, long superseded) that see the critic's first business as the narration of literary events – private relations, settings, the stuff of the 'scene' – in a colourful story of Canadian modern poetry's early years. In this sense, at least, no 'history' unfolds in what follows.

I suggested in my 1997 article 'Critical Episodes in Montreal Poetry of the 1940s' that our regrettably unanimous literary-historical narratives of Canadian poetry in that decade are impoverished by an emphasis on scene, as well as by a polarizing sensibility among the period's critics which has left us still largely fixated on the rivalry between *Preview* and *First Statement*, the dominant little magazines of the war years. A body of discussion almost wholly dependent on generalizing contrasts between the two – a fixation I referred to as the 'myth of the little mag' – persisted for forty years by opposing the (claimed) cosmopolitan, internationalist, Anglophile, upper-class, academic, reactionary, exclusive, politically doctrinaire, and formalist poetry of *Preview* to the (claimed) native, nationalist, Americanophile, working-class, proletarian, progressive, inclusive, politically flexible, and experimental poetry of *First Statement*. The degree to which such binaries were weighted, muted, or nuanced in any given survey of the Montreal period in question did little to shake the power of this founding myth, and nothing to rebut the critical neglect – at times, disparagement – of *Preview* and the poets who published there. As I concluded, there is still no strong alternative to the binary, scenographic consensus on the decade's poetry.

Perhaps the sharpest irony of this critical situation is that the editor and poets of *First Statement* who foisted the schism upon us in the first place have lately been caught in its reverberations. Determined in his attempt to steer critical attention away from the poets of the twenties – and successful in disenfranchising the *Preview* poets, if we are to judge by their collective silencing in the years from 1953 to 1955 – John Sutherland can hardly have imagined that the terms and stances of his engagement with the earlier generation would become key to a late-century inattention to his own poets and their achievements as well. *First Statement*, from whose pages emanated the earliest charges in Canada against a modernism that had apparently become orthodox, formalist and aestheticist, politically authoritarian, and canonically exclusive, is now as little discussed, its poets as infrequently analysed, as is *Preview*.

The consequences of 1940s caricature for *Preview* editor Patrick Anderson's reputation have always been clear: his poetry has received little critical attention, and much of what has passed for Anderson commentary has been defensive and apologetic; this for a poet whose work in the early and mid-1940s may be thought superior to that of Layton and Dudek in the same period, and of Sutherland and Raymond Souster in any period. His recent recuperation in a gay-studies perspective[1] is very well (he would not himself have welcomed the attention to his sexuality, as will be seen in in the second part of this introduction) but largely fails to reflect the complexities of 1940s poetry, of which he is such a stark exemplar. A similar neglect of his colleague Page's poetry has recently been ameliorated by a welcome feminist recovery of her poems and poetics, but the critical products of that recovery remain few,[2] and criticism of her poetry through the unifocal lens of gender has ironically concealed her central place among male poets in Canadian poetry's 1940s transition, a place made plain in chapter 1. As for the *First Statement* cohort, Dudek has received – this lamentation is a commonplace, though nothing changes – a fraction of the attention his output, both poetic and critical, would seem to require. It is unconscionable that a lifelong poet who showed such dedication and received such acclaim from confrères should be accorded the kind of scholarly attention reserved for the most minor of poets without prior proof of his deserving such neglect. But it is perhaps the case of Layton that is most revealing of the motivations and conditions of the neglect accorded Canadian modernism today. The boom-and-bust parabola of his fame's comet speaks directly to the success of *First Statement*'s inflated self-appraisal as well as to the trenchant revision of modernism's *sui generis* canon. In the process, a true Layton criticism never fully emerged.[3]

In the retrospect of the eventual *rapprochements* between the rivals, these consequences seem dishearteningly needless. The famous story of the magazines' amalgamation into *Northern Review* in 1946 is usually recounted as preliminary to the subsequent schism between the ex-editors of *Preview* and those of *First Statement* over Sutherland's rude, uncritical, hilarious review of Robert Finch's *Poems* and the Governor General's Literary Award, but the merger still signals the poets' sense of shared problems and need for a common front. As the editorial-board rupture died down, the reconciliations continued, with a series of minor ironies that serve to make *First Statement*'s self-election look shabby: especially in Sutherland, who followed his hurtful hints at Anderson's homosexuality with a long, favourable article in 1949, having published a book of Anderson's with First Statement Press in the interim, and who decided in 1951 that A.J.M. Smith had been substantially right in the 'religious' interpretation of Canadian poetry for which Sutherland had ridiculed him six years earlier.

Meanwhile, Dudek was increasingly attracted to F.R. Scott of *Preview* and his circle; that Dudek would eventually become an academic (though not necessarily an 'academic poet,' one of the disparaging terms he used to distance *First Statement* from both *Preview* and the older modernists), after passing through a period in his own poetics of obscurity and formalism much like that he had disliked in *Preview,* really underscores the degree to which he had been projecting his own aesthetic anxieties in his noteworthy contributions to the devaluation of *Preview.*[4] His departure for graduate studies at Columbia University coincided with the article's appearance; he was presumably making his own decision on academic life with a degree of ambivalence as he wrote the critique. Had they been read and understood positively by literary historians, such realignments might have signified the emergence in the 1940s of a Canadian modernism more capacious and mature, and invited research into the poets' common purposes. But they reveal more tellingly how posturing and superficial the antagonisms of the 1940s had been, how insubstantial must be the ground they offer contemporary critics. If 1940s criticism has languished, surely it is in part because the broad terrain has been so uninterestingly and emphatically charted.

Of course, it is not only the modernists of *Preview* and *First Statement* who are suffering from contemporary inattention. In the course of the 1980s, Canadian modernist studies more or less withered. Writers who dominated criticism of Canadian literature through to the late 1970s – Grove, Livesay, Smith, Scott, Layton, Purdy, Buckler – have effectively gone marginal in the current recentring (not decentring) of the discipline. Robert Kroetsch once famously remarked that Canadian literature had passed straight from Victorianism to postmodernism;[5] nothing significant had intervened, in effect, between Archibald Lampman and his own generation. Such simple erasures should be benign, least damaging because most obviously self-interested, but the view is apparently not without force. The dwindling of scholarship in the area since 1980 is telling.[6] Substantial editorial projects supporting the reputations of E.J. Pratt and A.M. Klein have kept their poetry in plain view and under fairly regular scrutiny, but an article favourable to the poetry of F.R. Scott or A.J.M. Smith now strikes one as a quaint rarity.[7] New studies of minor but once-valued modernists like Robert Finch or Raymond Knister hardly seem imaginable. In my view, the swing of taste away from the Canadian modernists has been extreme and suggests either that their early appraisal was grossly inflated or that their present eclipse is careless. There are still-harsher modernist realities: as I write, major poets Smith and Scott are out of print. Patrick Anderson remains out of print. John Glassco was out of print until Michael Gnarowski reissued his *Selected Poems* in 1997; much of his work remains unavailable. The major poems of Irving Layton are now unavailable for purchase: neither his collected nor his selected volumes have been sustained of late by McClelland & Stewart, though a few small and idiosyncratic 'selecteds' remain on the market. In these startling facts we have, I think, firm indications of disciplinary slackness, at least where our own modernism is concerned.

The sources of such scholarly neglect are too manifold to identify here, but, in Canada at least, we will have to admit that they include, ironically enough, *First Statement*'s critique of rival *Preview* and the outmoded modernism for which it supposedly spoke. *First Statement*'s polemical characterizations of *Preview* and an earlier Canadian modernism of which it was (they claimed) too reminiscent set the terms for many familiar if unreliable attitudes to modernism as a whole in this *fin-de-siècle*. A particularly favoured tactic was the assertion of *Preview*'s apparent rejection of contemporary social and cultural life. In Patrick Anderson's 'Dramatic Monologue,' Sutherland says, '[t]he distortion of the language, restricted to an improperly focused analysis of special aspects of the self, and unable to escape into contact with people and things as they really are, must be just as apparent as the distortion of the content.'[8] Dudek complained that 'our leading modern poets do not accept the universe: the universe of the contemporary social scene,' a failure of nerve he finds 'rampant in *Preview* magazine.'[9] Dorothy Livesay blamed A.J.M. Smith for writing poetry with a 'lack of range' that 'speaks to a coterie' – 'the poetry of an exile ... in a retreat.'[10] Irving Layton reached farther as he harangued the poets of the 1930s – 'Auden and Co.' – for 'a poetry of social criticism and frustration,' 'expressing their own maladjustments': they were 'hostile to their society and rejected it' by fleeing into 'desiccated coteries.'[11] When Sutherland blamed early modernist critics for their 'fear of contemporary life and thought,'[12] could he have envisioned a latter-day critical atmosphere in which the whole modernist project, his own included, would routinely be so characterized?

Astradur Eysteinsson's *The Concept of Modernism* (1990) is essential reading in this regard, particularly his third chapter, 'Reading Modernism through Postmodernism.' There he shows that contemporary and postmodern treatments of modernism continually replicate (unwittingly, of course) the *First Statement* claims. Among such commentators are Alan Wilde (for whom modernists 'impose on the world "a form, a frame, that resembles the mediating order of art, thereby confirming their estrangement from the life they seek"' [qtd. p. 128]), Iris Murdoch ('"What is feared [in modernism] is history, real beings, and real change, whatever is contingent, messy, boundless, infinitely particular"' [qtd. p. 123]), and Linda Hutcheon (who remarks on '"the naiveté of modernism's ideologically and aesthetically motivated rejection of the past"' and '"its inability to deal with ambiguity and irony"' [qtd. p. 121]). I need not deal here with Eysteinsson's brilliant refutation of such claims; it is their consonance with *First Statement* polemics that is of immediate interest.

If the poets of *First Statement* have been as broadly ignored in the last fifteen years as those of *Preview*, it is in part because we continue to think that modernism *was* bifurcated, that its aesthetic radicalism could *not* be reconciled with a direct engagement with the social world: an illusion for which we owe ironic thanks, at least locally, to the brilliance of *First Statement* militancy. But Eysteinsson has shown that a concept of modernism so divided between formalist aestheticism and political-historical engagement – unable to reconcile the demands of art with the demands of the actual – is in the direct interest of contemporary culture's claims for distinctiveness and accomplishment. Thus it is hardly surprising under a broadly postmodern dispensation to find the *Preview–First Statement* debates persisting in approximate critical tropes that tell the same limited story – or go altogether ignored while a cognate critique of modernism in general unfolds. Eysteinsson remarks that 'we need to ask ourselves how the concept of [formal] autonomy, so crucial to many theories of modernism, can possibly co-exist with the equally prominent view of modernism as a historically explosive paradigm' (p. 16), because he wishes to reveal the insufficiency of such polarities for a reliable critical construction of modernist activity. After comparing my own 'Critical Episodes in Montreal Poetry of the 1940s' with those literary-historical revisions exposed by Eysteinsson, I see two facts emerge in close relation: the critical narrative of 1940s poetry abiding to this day has solid roots in the self-fashioning of the 1940s poets themselves, and much of the dogma of the decade anticipates postmodern readings of modernism like those of Wilde, Murdoch, and Hutcheon. Facing these facts, I conclude that the roots of the current neglect of Canadian modernist studies are in modernist polemic itself, a paradox that will not surprise those accustomed to the arrogation by postmodernism of the most radical innovations of modernist theory and practice, or to the multiplicity and complexity of modernist thought.

There is little evidence that the force of argument in Eysteinsson's *The Concept of Modernism* and the fundamental questions of modernist representation it raises have reinvigorated Canadian modernist studies of a more comprehensive and approbatory viewpoint. This is hardly surprising. Canadian poets and writers of fiction of the early and middle twentieth century have usually been studied in nationalist isolation from pressing critical questions beyond the borders. The most significant inspiration of the *McGill Fortnightly Review* would still seem to have been the Canadian Authors' Association; of *First Statement*, *Preview*. The placement of Canadian writing against the backdrop of international modernism is very rare. Sandra Djwa's articles on the modernists and her biography of Scott are among the prototypes of such a better criticism, but her imitators are few. Frank Davey's good study *Louis Dudek & Raymond Souster* helps to underscore the Americanization of Canadian literary culture that the growth of these two poets involved. Brief articles also take up the international contexts of Canadian cultural change: an example to be called on later is Erwin Wiens's 'From Apocalypse to Black Mountain: The Contexts of Layton's Early Criticism' (1985). But this situation of Canada in world modernism remains eccentric to a critical tradition that has yet to renounce fully its founding cultural nationalism.

Any modernist study of the 1990s must speak to its position within such frames and propose counter-measures. Not to do so would signal either indifference or tacit surrender to present-day caricatures of its subject. My concerns are poetic style and poetic structure, but as I pursue these a rejoinder to the above claims for modernism's 'fear of contemporary life and thought' will certainly emerge, especially since I suggest that the transition in Canadian modern poetry in the 1940s is in part a strong reaction to acute historical pressures on poetic and individual identity. I make no further address to the theoretical issues of modernist representation; instead, I presume that a sound and detailed scholarship will offer the best possible elaboration of my own 'concept of modernism.'

Thus there are three methodological grounds to my argument. The first is plain: it is time that Canadian modernist poetry be discussed, dismissed if it can be, defended, in light of current international conceptualizations of modernism, and that it be recognized to be caught up in that context, as I shall show it was, indeed, in the conceptualizations of modernism current in its own time. We may not pay much better attention to our modernists afterward, but at least there will have been a debate. Second, we should now cancel our interest in the colourful squabbles of the period, with their resultant fragmentation of the decade into camps. If our narratives of wartime Montreal poetry are insufficient, it is in part because we have not been able to focus attention on a more profound set of issues and practices that characterize the decade as a whole. In our delight with the cartoons of fine polemicists, we have ignored the apparently commonsensical idea that the poets of a given era must necessarily face some common inheritance of influences, aesthetic confusions and opportunities, and sociopolitical events that shape – even if ignored – the poems they choose and choose not to write. Third, any attempt to improve the critical fortunes of Canadian modernist poets will have to separate three discourses from one another: (1) what we have habitually said about them; (2) what they said about themselves and one another; and (3) the poems they actually wrote. One can summarize the critical history thus far by noting that (1) and (2) have been in almost perfect alignment for half a century, but that neither (1) nor (2) bears any clear relation to (3). So it is with (3), their poems, as is my inflexible preference and pleasure, that I will chiefly preoccupy myself in this book.

We have not been really interested in the experiences that bound these poets together, only in those that alienated them. A better cultural history lies in an articulation of the *questions* a given selection of artists asked of themselves. Our interest to date in the *answers* they provided as personalities was briefly fruitful as a first-round report on an exciting period; but I now want to ask, what did all these poets, with their dissimilar backgrounds, disparate educations, and diverse ethnicities and political affiliations, face in common? Can we isolate a few opportunities of cultural experience in the 1940s and build a larger critical understanding upon them – one that evokes new commonalities and sees through the local animosities of the period? I have the privilege in this book about English-Canadian poetry of the 1940s of pursuing such questions, and I hope to register in it the excitement of re-creation in a period study, the documents of which are at increasing distance from us and subject to some scholarly neglect. I mean in the process to probe and display the breadth, complexity, and courage of Canadian modernism's 1940s transition. I will draw my contexts of discussion from as wide a range as possible by connecting the English-Canadian poetic tradition to the currents in other modernisms, primarily English-language, by which it was shaped. My appeal to Eysteinsson was only the first of a number of extranationalist gestures.

Canadian modernist poetry benefited during the 1940s from contact with a global abundance of schools, publications, and poets not commonly included in the mainstream narrative of American and English modernism. To name Imagism among these is perverse, not only because of its canonical status as modernist *ur*-concept, but also because its story for Canada is familiar, beginning with A.J.M. Smith's visit to England in 1918 and continuing through the *Newfoundland Verse* of E.J. Pratt, the *Laconics* of W.W.E. Ross, and the long-unpublished lyrics of Raymond Knister. But the only study to take Imagism as a context beyond the Canadian thirties is Bernhard Beutler's *Der*

Einfluss des Imagismus auf die Moderne Kanadische Lyrik Englischer Sprache (1972), in which the poetry of Dorothy Livesay and Louis Dudek, among others, is placed in the Imagist tradition. The book was never translated, and its impact has been minimal on a community presumably unable, like myself, to read it in the original. But the legacy of Imagism was felt in Canada and elsewhere well into the early 1940s, and its later permutations were to have an empowering and constraining effect on mid-century Canadian poetry and to engineer its advances well into the 1950s. Some charting of that process and its relation to the more familiar narratives of forties poetry will be crucial here.

The Imagist path to 1940s Canada was multiple, reaching not only directly from Ezra Pound and Amy Lowell to P.K. Page and Irving Layton, but also indirectly from original Imagism through the 1920s and 1930s, in both mainstream (Eliot, Auden, Spender, always over-cited for their influence on *Preview,* at least) and subterranean channels. In the latter category are some of the most exciting possibilities for fuller contextualization of Canadian poetic development. Chief among these are Surrealism, not only the French led by Andre Bréton with its well-known impact on John Glassco, but also the English offshoot, led by David Gascoyne and centring for historical purposes on the English Surrealist Exhibition in London in 1936; and Mass Observation (MO), a sociocultural (and briefly literary) experiment coinciding with the Surrealist impact in England. The aesthetic implications of Mass Observation are clarified largely through the experimentation of Charles Madge, an MO enthusiast and minor poet whose transmission of the image-gathering method to a group of undergraduates at Oxford led to the so-called Oxford Collective Poem. The whimsy of its highly thirties-ish project aside, the Mass Observation movement and its inquiry into the relation between collective historical truth and the individual's interested or eccentric image of it will prove suggestive for the elucidation of forties poetic experiment in Canada, especially on the part of P.K. Page, and add to the later history of Imagism in England. In turn, Surrealism's family resemblance to MO experiments in image and society will help to situate Irving Layton's early poetry in clearer relation to Page's and articulate a distinct 'forties period style' in both.

The Canadian decade profiting from these poetic experiments is also seen too little in relation to its defining catastrophe, that is, seen too little as a war period whose every exigency circles back to the questions of global conflict that defined individuality for the decade. The early cry 'Where are the war poets?' was not answered by the Canadian poets we continue to take seriously, but war was definitive for each of them: for Page, whose stenographer colleagues waited 'taut' for news of their 'boyfriends of blood'; for Klein, in horrific postwar consciousness of atrocity; for Layton, in the enlistment years of 'Drill Shed' and 'Petawawa'; even for Dudek, unable to serve for reasons of health.[13] Their poetry more usually brackets than faces war, but their placement against that backdrop is vital to a recognition of their conflictual self-representations as groups and as individuals. The pressures on identity that are an implicit (and, in the case of Klein, explicit) subtext of the commentaries that follow cannot be conceptualized independent of this fact of war.

A consequence of war-consciousness for Canadian as for so many English and American poets was a revival of romanticism, or at least a revival of romantic pressure to bear individual witness to the age. One of the most striking formulations of these new identifications lies in the now little-known New Apocalypse in London (England) in the early years of the war, a group consciousness spoken for by such figures as Henry Treece and M.J. Tambimuttu. When Irving Layton looked at English poetry in the war years, he remarked the Apocalyptics as the most promising new development. The implications for Layton studies are powerful. But equally powerful are the consequences for P.K. Page and Patrick Anderson, whose negotiations with the romantic revival were more painstaking and sceptical. The neo-romanticism of the Canadian forties needs substantially more discussion, linking up, as it does, not only with war-consciousness, but also with possible responses to the Imagist dilemma, and to the opportunities of Surrealism that Layton would seem to have seized upon only in the 1950s.

I perceive in such contexts a fruitful expansion of the 1940s literary-historical archive, since poets on either side of the long-standing *Preview–First Statement* chasm figure mutually and reciprocally in their Canadian expression. In the aggregate these contexts will lead me to the articulation of a 'forties period style,' as well as to a partial explanation of the emergence of modernist lyric in the early 1950s. My attempt to supersede the little-magazine alignments so familiar in the period is not, then, as I said from the outset, a rejection of Canadian literary history, only of one of its prominent and least compelling narratives. And this is perhaps the place to acknowledge flatly that I accept and welcome a number of long-standing predicates of traditional Canadian literary history. Chief among these is my belief, shared with every critic of the period, that the Canadian 1940s were a pivotal decade for our modernist poetry. Behind that lies my typically twentieth-century conviction that decades have special characters worth arguing about: moreover, that the characters of 'decades' are only rarely confined to the chronological period associated with a particular multiple of ten. Just as the 'sixties' of current connotation did not emerge until the 1960s were under way and did not cease until the 1970s had begun – choose your own closing date – so I discuss in this book on the 'forties' the years from 1942 to 1954 and regularly justify those bookends. The period encloses the birth, rise, and fall of the two journals chiefly discussed, and all but a few months of *Contemporary Verse*; it allows for at least two volumes of poetry from each of the major poets in the study; and it takes three of the poets of *Preview* to their various forms of silence, while allowing the poets of *First Statement* the measure of their 1950s dominance with the publication of turning-point volumes by Dudek and Layton.

Second, the Montreal focus of this study willingly endorses a Laurentian thesis of Canadian literature in the period prior to 1960 and, perhaps worse, flies in the face of a number of commentaries suggesting how badly we need to expand our forties horizons for Canadian poetry beyond Montreal: as Joan McCullagh would have us do by recognizing the significance of Alan Crawley's *Contemporary Verse*,[14] as Lyn Harrington would have us do in the form of greater respect for the influence of the Canadian Authors' Association and its *Canadian Poetry Magazine*,[15] and so on. But I persist in thinking, and this book tries to demonstrate, that critical choices as to the direction of Canadian poetry in the forties and fifties were made primarily in the names of *Preview* and *First Statement* by their poets and editorialists, and that the subsequent growth of Canadian poetry into a number of vital styles may be traced more or less directly to those choices. Nevertheless, there is no real and dramatic sense in which this study is interested only in two Montreal magazines; it is interested in six 'Montreal' poets of note, most of whom published in *Contemporary Verse*, and some in *Canadian Poetry Magazine* and *The Canadian Forum* as well, and two of whom had no prolonged affiliation with the city. Still, in so far as Montreal provided the meeting-ground for their confluence of ideas, this study is narrowly but appropriately defined by a city.

Finally, 'poets of note' is a signal of another theoretical acceptation of this book: there is a fairly familiar 'canon' endorsed here. It is true that little detailed work has been done on the writing of Sutherland and Anderson, and in the second part of this introduction I lay out a number of the book's broader arguments by comparing their editorial and 'personal' styles; but, those two apart, I have made little attempt to expand and refine a canon whose principals have been so little attended to as to suggest that there is no 'canon' at work in Canada at all. It may perhaps be more urgent than I think it to suspend work on the traditional canon while canon revision is under way, but I see no inherent contradiction between the two critical actions: it may even obtain that revised interpretation of already-sanctioned poets encourages the recuperation of figures at present on the margin by virtue of their shoring up, or usefully antagonizing, new readings.

In the abstract, these determinants suggest a history of Canadian modernist poetics of a traditional nature, and perhaps that is a fair description of what follows; but innovation, especially in criticism, cannot always be the result of historic discursive and paradigmatic shifts. Indeed, it can only very rarely be so categorical, and never, I would claim, in the hands of a single critic. So there is nothing radical in the paradigms of critical research that subtend this study. Such newness as the findings offer is more muted, practical, finite in implication. If I am successful, I hope to suggest to my students, whose ideas during ten years of seminars on Canadian modernism are not readily separable from the findings of this book, how slight may be their theoretical innovation, and how useful still their labour to the literature they serve.

Case Histories: The Two Editors

In 'Critical Episodes in Montreal Poetry of the 1940s,' I exposed the remarkable degree of consensus in forties criticism, despite one or two helpful dissenters and the recent waning of activity in the area, and I contended that such consensus depends largely from the little-magazine polemics of the *First Statement* editors, especially John Sutherland and Louis Dudek, as they worked to distance themselves from the (to them dominant) *Preview* poetics characterized by the work of Patrick Anderson and P.K. Page. Fifty years of criticism of 1940s Canadian poetry, based largely on the exaggerated antagonisms of *Preview* and *First Statement*, will not, however, be set aside for good by a brief rejoinder. As I open my discussions, I feel the weight of that vestigial tradition, and with it the need for further rebuttal. It is perhaps especially important, in light of recent claims for John Sutherland's homophobia and its severe consequences for Patrick Anderson's poetry and reputation, more radically to undermine our still-powerful tendency to make antitheses out of persons, and thus out of the little magazines with which they were involved.

For such reasons I mean now to look simultaneously at the two primary editors of *Preview* and *First Statement*, not chiefly to recapitulate the article's findings, but rather to test their value for forties criticism and to establish the kinds of reading I pursue later. There can be no doubt of the sharp differences between the two editors, and I have no interest in a harmonious portraiture accomplished by the blunting of their edges. On the other hand, there has been no critical effort to grasp what Anderson and Sutherland might have shared. I'll juxtapose them and try to see – if only as the Imagist might – what insight, what *tertium quid*, glimmers between them. The effort should help us look back to what Robert K. Martin refers to as 'a time before the lines of the official history of Canadian modernism had been drawn' (p. 111).

The comparative neglect of Anderson and centring of Sutherland in the forties narratives make little sense: neither figure dominates a retrospective view. Anderson published his last Canadian collection, *The Colour as Naked,* with McClelland & Stewart in 1953. He had left the country for good by 1949. John Sutherland left Montreal in January 1955, three years after his break with Dudek, four months after his conversion to Catholicism, and eighteen months before his death. Anderson entered a prolonged silence as a poet, which he made up for with various genres of professional writing – travel, memoir, literary journalism, and children's instruction – until a bucolic and Wordsworthian incarnation of his poetic Muse returned *circa* 1967.[16] Sutherland published his own poetry for the last time in late 1948 and replaced his abortive gift with increasingly reactionary criticism and isolated editorship. One after the other, his contemporaries had to distance themselves from him: Layton by 1948, Dudek and Souster by 1952. Yet it is Sutherland, of the two editors, who emerged as a central figure in the forties narratives. When Seymour Mayne reassured Anderson in 1973 that 'a whole chapter has developed around the myth of Patrick Anderson,' Anderson responded correctly, 'Well I can hardly believe that.'[17]

Certainly Mayne's kind claim had no basis in the published record. Apart from the recognizable misrepresentations of Anderson in Wynne Francis's 'Montreal Poets of the Forties' (1962) and the odd sardonic reference in an interview with an ex–*First Statement* partisan,[18] only Christopher Ringrose's 'Patrick Anderson and the Critics' had appeared to justify Mayne's assertion.[19] Sutherland, on the other hand – the clearly *miglior fabbro* of Francis's article – was canonized rapidly in the course of the sixties, least critically but perhaps most visibly in the dedication by Dudek and Michael Gnarowski of *The Making of Modern Poetry in Canada* 'to the memory of John Sutherland.' Anderson can hardly be blamed for complaining of

> ... the treatment of *Preview* and its whole question of attitude to life which occurs in the Dudek–Gnarowski volume about the making of modern Canadian poetry where on the whole about 85 to 90 per cent of the emphasis is always given to the *First Statement* group and so little real attention is paid to what *Preview* is trying to do.[20]

Close on the heels of Dudek and Gnarowski's elevation of Sutherland came Miriam Waddington's edition of his *Essays, Controversies and Poems* – his thirty-three poems, by the way. Waddington justifies the book in her introduction by referring to Sutherland's 'brilliant and original essays' and 'authentic critical talents'; she says that 'he was the single stable element in a situation filled with variables.'[21]

Comment on Sutherland after Waddington's establishment of his canon maintained the reverential tone. Indeed, Neil Fisher's *First Statement 1942–1945: An Assessment and an Index* (1974) had an introduction so favourable to Sutherland that Dudek himself, ironically, was uncomfortable with the eulogy.[22] Frank Davey extended the Sutherland hagiography in his study *Louis Dudek & Raymond Souster*: 'Although a year younger than Dudek and only two years older than Souster, [in early 1943 Sutherland] was already through his editorship of *First Statement* forcing Canadian letters to accommodate him.'[23] The Sutherland legend was intact enough in 1992 to justify ECW Press's publication of Sutherland's letters, notwithstanding the fact that most of them show at best the drudgery of little-magazine editorship, as editor Bruce Whiteman candidly admits. No such reconsideration – certainly no such investment by a publisher – has been afforded Anderson.

Of course, a few years' compensatory emphasis on Anderson would merely maintain the opposing of the two. Indeed, recent Anderson studies have required Sutherland as heteronormative antagonist and, to that extent, confined us in shopworn paradigms of opposition and rivalry. But what if, instead, we go in search of collaboration and similarity? Comparison of their editorial styles is, I take it, self-evidently desirable. Their poems, too, can be mutually illuminating: though Sutherland's few are perhaps justifiably neglected, the light they cast on the exemplary impact of Anderson's modernism is compelling. Comparison of their personalities is in one sense beyond my expertise, and in another beyond my reach except through cold documents; but I will attempt this as well. My reasons are various. I want to dispel still-prevalent assumptions of their enmity that have loomed large in the period's skewed criticism; I want to suggest that a criticism attendant to personalities need not be binary in implication; and I want to prepare the ground for the chapters to follow, in which images and crises of poetic structure are often figured – by the poets themselves – as correlative to images of identity and psychic coherence.

I will start with the last of these, attempting to clear the highest hurdle first: the broad dissemination of an implicit critical portraiture that has starkly opposed the two personalities. No major revelations are imminent. I am more interested, in fact, in their daily than in their existential lives, and hope only to nuance, not to collapse, our keen sense of their difference. Both men, for example, dealt continually with a sense of secret physical damage or disease, and figured themselves as lifelong convalescents. Before arriving in Montreal in fall 1941, Sutherland had been hospitalized with tuberculosis and, after the removal of a kidney, had kept to his bed for three years under doctor's orders. He had lost his mother to the same disease at the age of seven.[24] As we shall see, the loss of vital years (*aet.* eighteen to twenty-one) in a recuperation he later came to think unnecessary[25] made the theme of convalescence the prominent motif of his writing. Elspeth Cameron remarks retrospectively that 'as the forties came to a close ... John Sutherland was slowly dying,'[26] but few appear to have noticed Sutherland's ill health at the time: most registered his drive and energy instead, though the return to illness in the summer of 1955 – the cancer that killed him – suggests that his constitution was never robust.

The most literal parallel to the theme of convalescence and illness in Patrick Anderson's history occurs in the year he and his wife spent in Saint-Sauveur-des-Monts in the Laurentians (1946–7). Whitney gives a serene account of Anderson's year, noting his receipt of the Harriet Munro Lyric Prize from *Poetry* in the fall, his trips to Montreal during the winter for a lecture series 'Art in Society' sponsored by McGill University, and his evening lectures to 'a group of enthusiastic students.'[27] These activities are in contrast to the more intimate record of the year, however, in letters concerning the preparation for publication by Ryerson Press of Anderson's *The White Centre*. The situation was perhaps aggravated by the offhand remarks of Lorne Pierce, Ryerson's director, probably distilling Earle Birney's original report on the manuscript:

> Very often the poem seems to depend entirely upon metaphor. The result is that whatever thought or point the poem has seems to become submerged or over-elaborated.[28]

> [Anderson] shows more possibilities than any other of the younger Canadian poets ... obscurity, metaphor for its own sake at the expense of coherence ... straining after effect ... at his worst he is drunk with words and lost in a juvenile gaudiness.[29]

Anderson had perhaps heard enough of such remarks from Sutherland and Dudek. Birney's positive recommendation survived these demurs, fortunately for Anderson, and they were muted in his subsequent review of the volume.[30] Nevertheless, Anderson wrote querulous, irritable, and neurotic letters to Pierce regarding the manuscript from the point of its acceptance in August 1945[31] until its appearance in the winter of 1946–7. These were at first fairly routine dispatches: Anderson wanted the last verse of his poem 'Education' to stand as an epigraph to the volume; his publisher objected to words like 'pus' and 'gangrene' in the stanza.[32] Once such matters had been settled, however, the rhythm of Ryerson commitments kept the book from appearing until well after the Andersons' departure for the Laurentians. Anderson did not take the delay well, and a spate of letters was exchanged in which the Press tried patiently to reassure him of their commitment to the volume and Anderson proved unreassurable. At one point of emotional crisis, Peggy Doernbach, his wife, sent a telegram to Pierce, demanding a firm date for the book's appearance and claiming that the delay had aggravated Anderson's 'already serious nervous illness.'[33]

Indeed, it is likely that the sabbatical of 1946–7 was medically motivated. Anderson wrote to A.J.M. Smith prior to the year away (the letter is undated, though the *Northern Review* letterhead suggests late 1945 or 1946) to complain of his not having been included in a Smith survey of Montreal writers for the Montreal *Herald*. He acknowledged that he was perhaps overreacting to Smith's neglect: 'As you probably know I am suffering from a nervous illness and this in itself makes it difficult for me to get personal things straight.'[34] In February 1946 he wrote to lawyers in England regarding a small inheritance, and remarked, 'I am now negociating [*sic*] with regard to giving up my job in order that I may both take the rest my doctor deems nevessary [*sic*] and have more time in which to write ...'[35] Clearly the year in Saint-Sauveur-des-Monts was arranged as a period of convalescence for the unnamed, and perhaps indefinite, nervous illness that Anderson had had diagnosed as early as 1945. It cannot be controversial at this point to suggest that the 'nervous illness' of which Anderson complained must have been related to his ongoing suppression of his homosexuality; within a year of the sabbatical's end, he had met Orlando Gearing, with whom he was to spend the rest of his life.[36]

Anderson had also had his childhood illness: after a bout with rickets during eighteen months in Russia in infancy, he had 'had to wear leg-irons day and night for several years.'[37] One can hardly compare the force of such a trial with Sutherland's early experience of death and illness, but it seems not unlikely on balance that both editors felt their health uncertain, and hypothetically possible that some of their mannerisms – in particular, their shared verbal aggressiveness and petulance, of which more later – were compensatory to such a self-image. Sutherland would predicate most of his creative and much of his critical imagination on the theme of convalescence. A number of poems have at their centre a figure alone in bed, or in a room, or otherwise convalescent, the surrounding walls often destabilized in the intense and surreal imagery his delirium calls forth. In prose, Friedrich Nietzsche is chiefly interesting to Sutherland as one who spent a significant part of his life in literal or figurative convalescence. The two articles 'Wagner and Zarathustra' and 'Convalescence and Writing' see all of Nietzsche's career in symbolic relation to a pivotal period of convalescence before the drafting of *Dawn of the Day [Morgenröte]*, indeed suggesting that, for Nietzsche, the alternation of composition and rest was identical to the rhythm of robustness and convalescence. Sutherland also ties the fact of convalescence to Nietzsche's alienation from others: 'the years of convalescence constitute the long uphill climb against a social opinion that bears witness to one's own unimportance and inferiority.'[38] That these remarks are at least in part projections of Sutherland's own anxieties onto the figure of Nietzsche is indicated by his largely autobiographical, though pseudonymous, sketches 'Why George Left College' and 'Why George Smokes a Pipe.' In the former, 'George for three years had been an invalid ... As an invalid, he played a castrated part.' One result is paranoia: 'when he walked in the corridors he felt as if heads were turned aside from him in rebuke and disgust.'[39] In the latter sketch, George 'often argued [that] it is in a state of sickness, or at the best of convalescense [*sic*], that all great art is produced.'[40] The collocation of these fragments makes plain that Sutherland reads Nietzsche in a manner that will redeem his own experience of convalescence; it is also apparent that 'George' is John.

Anderson wrote nothing comparable on the fact of his 'nervous illness.' Despite frequent and sometimes disturbing homosexual musings in his adolescent journals from the 1930s,[41] he attempted a heterosexual orientation by marrying in 1940.[42] The marriage was short-lived and apparently costly, splitting Anderson sharply between a private imaginative sexuality and a public masculine role. As Robert Martin has shown, a good deal of Patrick Anderson's poetry of the little-magazines period takes its energy and tension from homoerotic undercurrents, usually symbolic, that are never thematically acknowledged in the poem.[43] However different the 'illnesses' involved, both he and Sutherland show this recurrent need to explore their bodily unease in pseudonymous or impersonal literary gestures. Moreover, the weakening of Anderson's poetic inspiration coincides closely with his acceptance of his homosexual desires. As noted, he began travelling with Gearing in 1948; he was divorced in 1950. Only when he ceased to medicalize his sexual preference did his hidden sense of 'illness' subside; a journal entry in spring 1949 sports a new tone of reconciliation and self-understanding that appears to have been perceptible to others:[44] 'To some extent I know what I want: to live in profitable interesting work (such as I have now) with a beddable male, whom I like personally, who likes me personally, and who strikes some sort of balance between beauty, imagination, intellect ...'[45]

At the end of the 1940s, for Anderson, lay a reconciliation of social and private identifications that would coincide with his departure from Canada and more or less from poetry. The new affiliation was not much publicized: to a correspondent of 1972 who sought permission to include some of his poems in 'an anthology of contemporary male gay poetry,' Anderson responded with an emphatic 'No!' scrawled across the bottom of the request.[46]

Sutherland was to close his 'forties,' of course, with a conversion almost as dramatic. In 1952, Sutherland began to make favourable notebook entries about the resurgence of Christian faith; in 1954, Whiteman says he 'took instruction, and in October of that year he was admitted to the church.'[47] Catholicism played no such baffling subterranean role in Sutherland's life as homosexuality had in Anderson's, although his remark to Anne Wilkinson that he had 'no beliefs that could be accurately described as "religious",'[48] contemporary with the notebook pieties of 1952, suggests a degree of reticence or embarrassment about his increasingly orthodox faith. Still, the language of religion has a strange currency in Sutherland's criticism from the start. According to Waddington, 'Sutherland became a Catholic when Canadian literature failed him as a source of belief.'[49] The connection is not unambiguous, but the fact remains that religious faith is a predicate of Sutherland's thought from the first *First Statement*:

> The religious ceremonies which thrived many centuries ago must have arisen from a belief in the newness of living and the youth of the race. What had happened seemed rare, and it was not certain that it would happen again. Bread was broken to express the hope that bread would be granted again. We intend to go through the ceremonies, in our Canadian literary youth.[50]

In 'On a Story Published in Preview Magazine,' in the same inaugural issue, Sutherland claims that, '[b]efore an artist has any other creed, he has a religious faith towards words.'[51] Defending Louis Dudek against a riposte from one Mrs Murray in April 1943, Sutherland asserted 'the validity of religious poetry' and tried to distinguish good examples (he notes recent poems by Anne Marriott and Dorothy Livesay) from 'the religious vulgarity of minor Canadian poetry.' Mrs Murray had made no allusion whatsoever to religion in poetry, having merely sought to distinguish what she called 'the physical' from 'the spiritual eyes,' that is, the imagination. Sutherland used her remarks to his own ends.[52]

His quarrel with A.J.M. Smith pivoted, in Sutherland's mind anyway, on the validity of religious expression in poetry. His first remarks on Smith offered, ironically, a defence of the older poet against John Coulter's radio assessment of Smith as landscape poet. To Sutherland, on the contrary, 'Mr. Smith has appeared from the beginning as a religious poet, and he has concerned himself with the ascetic mind.'[53] He would retain a religious reading of Smith well after his attitude had turned from defence to ridicule: 'Bishop Smith' is pilloried in Sutherland's incendiary 'Introduction' to *Other Canadians* for his 'hilarious catholicism' and 'that pure aestheticism which, properly understood, is nothing less than the history and tradition of the human spirit wrapped in a papal bunnyhug.'[54] The remarks had great currency in subsequent critical discussion and initiated the steady decline in Smith's reception over the next several decades until his death. Nevertheless, Sutherland repudiated them in early 1951, in a much-less-remarked response to Smith: 'I criticized Mr. Smith, the editor of *The Book of Canadian Poetry*, for his religious emphasis ... Well, I take it back. I still think Mr. Smith was forcing matters at that time, but events have shown that he was substantially right.'[55] Sutherland goes on to remark religious dimensions in the work of Kay Smith, James Wreford, Miriam Waddington, and P.K. Page. His own remarks on the resurgence of Christian belief follow within a year, his conversion to Catholicism – presumably not 'hilarious' – within three.

The rhythm of these remarks suggests a young man given in childhood a conventional religious outlook from which he lapsed enthusiastically in late adolescence, perhaps during the years of convalescence. The language of his Christian education remained functional for him, however, in the secular vocation of editorship and criticism, and its significance to his moral development is ironically indicated by the hysteria with which he repudiated such terms by projecting them violently onto Smith (who privately called his religious poems, by the way, the exercises of an unbeliever).[56] His vague return to a religious identification in his early thirties coincided with his adoption of increasingly conservative critical views that had become reactionary by the time of his literal conversion in 1954. What he had been in and to the forties he had largely to reject, for whatever complex of reasons, if in his own judgment he was to retain a functional identity and role as the decade came to an end. The same is true of Anderson; indeed, as I shall show in the chapters that follow, the same is true in some degree of every major poet of the Montreal forties.

Perhaps related to their suppression of these eventual identifications is the two editors' shared tendency to abrupt verbal aggressiveness. Although Anderson did remember him as 'gruff and bluff,'[57] Sutherland was chiefly belligerent in his critical prose, not only at the heights of his invective (as in the attack on Smith noted above), but in his first essay, 'On a Story Published in Preview Magazine,' which opens in revealing self-projection: 'This man uses words in the way one uses fists to clip people on the jaw.'[58] Not long after, he would 'use his fists' on a Kay Smith poem published in his own magazine: 'The poem is so bad on the point of obscurity that its merits are spoiled' ('A Criticism'). When he sneers at Smith for politely approving an early review of Charles Heavysege's *Saul: A Drama* ('who the devil would be interested enough in Heavysege's "Saul" to start offering "explanations"'),[59] he shows a gleeful brusqueness so needless as to demand a psychological interpretation. Waddington says that in conversation Sutherland expressed his 'original' ideas 'diffidently';[60] if he did, it can only be because he successfully sublimated their persistent belligerence in his rough prose. Anderson had the more genteel prose tone; even in responding to a letter attacking his criticism, his voice is measured and thorough.[61] On the other hand, he had, in his own estimation, a conversational manner as edgy as Sutherland's written style. He refers to his own 'unfortunate tactless but self-defensive tendency towards aggression' in a letter to A.J.M. Smith,[62] and the correspondence with Ryerson during the period of his 'nervous illness' suggests a defensive, irritable, and reactive personality. This persona contrasts with the poised raconteur who shows up in Louis Dudek's memories of the period, but Anderson's 'mellifluous and hyper-eloquent manner of speech (that overwhelmed our literati) ...'[63] is not hard to reconcile, after all, with an intermittent nervous brusqueness.

Both men had understandable difficulties with personal relations, perhaps partly as a result of their largely defensive aggressions. Sutherland's gradual isolation of himself from Layton, Dudek, and Souster has been remarked upon. The aggravations were obviously mutual: Layton wrote the cruel 'Goodbye Bahai' at Sutherland's expense. Dudek would later call him 'dead as a doorknob' and a 'sluggard.'[64] Waddington puts it that, 'except for his wife, Audrey Aikman, [Sutherland] remained a detached figure, at times surrounded by friends and editorial associates, at other times not';[65] the transition from centrality to isolation was more linear than Waddington acknowledges. Anderson had similar difficulties with his *Preview* confrères, though he avoided dramatic and clear ruptures. His journals of the mid-1940s speak tellingly of his sense of alienation from those we now tend to imagine as his literary intimates:

> I used, when Pat Page was still here, to remind myself of the time someone wrote a letter calling PREVIEW *my* group. During her year of apartments Pat never invited either of us once. She was always going out with the others. I rather pinned my hopes on her. I wanted her approval most. She liked a good deal of my stuff but that only made our personal malaise more irritating. As for the Surreys [Phillip and Margaret] and Neufville Shaw and Bruce [Ruddick] – I never felt natural and I am still disappointed. I realised that I was actually glad when Pat left a few months ago.[66]

After Anderson's own departure from Canada, the tenuousness of his *Preview* relationships must have been driven home to him; by 1955 he sent a circular letter to each of them in search of contact and correspondence. Only the 'disappointing' Neufville Shaw continued to exchange letters with Anderson.

Anderson's relations with A.M. Klein give an indication of the complexity with which his friendships were fraught. Usher Caplan, Klein's portraitist, remarks the cordial but distant friendship the two men maintained.[67] Anderson himself wrote cautiously (and privately) of Klein, 'I have nobody with whom I can discuss my poetry, except Abe who is serious and competent and friendly but scarcely up my emotional alley.'[68] Sadly, Anderson let his political commitments outweigh the possibility of a deeper intimacy with Klein: as a committed Communist he worked actively, albeit ambivalently, for the Labour Progressive candidate Fred Rose against Klein in the latter's abortive bid for the Cartier riding in 1944.[69] Klein, as we know, withdrew from the election. Surely he felt some sense of betrayal by Anderson; at any rate, he wrote thereafter to A.J.M. Smith with a hilarious sneer at Anderson's political depth:

> I, as you know, have resigned from the teaching staff of McGill. Patrick, I think, is to take my place. There was some question of his Communistic affiliations, but he wrote, I am told, a complete letter of recantation, informing the authorities that he is no longer a Communist sympathizer, that he never really was, and that as a matter of fact, he is now writing several poems and a short story to prove this. I am telling you this because I want you to laugh too.[70]

Anderson, who seems by Whitney's account to have caught himself routinely between political and personal commitments, should hardly have been surprised to lose touch rapidly with Klein after his departure from Canada.

Anderson's slightly forced remarks on Sutherland are telling, though, of his eagerness to reconcile such damaged relations. The homosexual libel notwithstanding, Anderson felt himself 'a friend of John Sutherland':

> Apart from publishing my first book, he wrote a very perceptive and extremely long article about my work after myself and the others had left *Northern Review* and when I was teaching at McGill, and I prize this article though it was pretty critical about some of my earlier work, about which I am also critical. It did praise the more recent poems which appeared in what I considered to be my best Canadian book, *The Colour as Naked*, and it also printed several poems to go along with his article. So that particular *Northern Review* is almost exclusively a Patrick Anderson issue. And I

can't honestly see how people could imagine that I am the bitter enemy of a man who does that for me.[71]

The minor friendship of the two men having been utterly obscured by the critical urge to polarization of *Preview* and *First Statement*, only Anderson's retrospective generosity gives us a glimpse of the two editors in a brief mutual kindness. A similar responsiveness, whether to Anderson or others, is harder to find in Sutherland's case, largely because so few intimate documents remain. It is apparent, nonetheless, that his manner was in the 1940s at least more compelling than abrasive to those around him – enough so to generate a prolonged critical misreading of his rival editor and professional 'friend.'

The shared consciousness of ill health, periods of convalescence, and tendency to sublimate these in their writing, the two end-of-the-forties conversions, their differently wielded verbal aggression, their difficulty in separating personal and political relations – keeping in mind the political dimension of Sutherland's exposé of Anderson's homosexuality (and see below, in reference to Page) – show that Anderson and Sutherland had some interesting personal commonalities. To these might be added their comparable vacillation and lightness as thinkers, a suggestion better defended in regard to their styles of editorship, and their shared contradictory impulses towards self-revelation and self-concealment. In Anderson's case, these latter terms will be readily understandable; as noted, he wrote a great many poems whose visual and emotional energies stem from concealed homoerotic desire. Analogously, he was concerned to hide his Communist affiliations when in the Selwyn House School ethos and vice versa; Whitney particularly evokes this embarrassment in Anderson's personae.[72] Sutherland, less loudly affiliated politically and little given to intimate records, was nevertheless persistent in his use of scholarship and editorializing to establish a resonant self-image: his appropriation of Nietzsche on the theme of convalescence is a fine example of self-revelation by indirection and projection. The 'George' sketches – with their depiction of a young ex-collegian who had spent three years in bed – would have been readily read back into Sutherland's experience by his literary friends. So much so, in fact, that one wonders what the point of the name change in the sketches really was.[73]

These personal correlations do not take us far into our subject, but they do encourage more mutual readings of the two editors, and we can begin to see possible alignments between matters of private experience (self-representation, in effect) and literary outlooks – as well as the occasional confusion of these. Anderson's and Sutherland's similarities and differences as editors and critics help us pursue these alignments and hear some unfamiliar resonances of the poetry of the 1940s. Sutherland's 'critical' remarks on Anderson's homosexual past in 'The Writing of Patrick Anderson' readily evoke such complexities. He urged Anderson to be more candid about his sexual experience, in fairly neutral language:

> At the same time, while I have no desire to make an exposé of Anderson's personal life, I surmise that the distinction between the 'frightened boy' and 'the hero who sings of joy' [in 'Montreal'] could be traced back to some period in the writer's childhood, when there occurred a sexual experience involving two boys, one of whom was frightened and the other demonstrated his joy.[74]

While Sutherland's references to Anderson's sexual experience as 'of a kind not normal' are homophobic in Martin's sense, Sutherland does affirm that Anderson's 'message is not wrong in itself, but his method of arriving at it, and his manner of stating it, make his poem appear like a wholesale falsification.'[75] Foolhardily, Sutherland seems to have imagined that Anderson, if pushed, would write a better poetry by representing homosexual desire more freely.[76] Anderson, nearing the end of his cautious Selwyn House employment and beginning to manifest the 'nervous illness' that would take him on a year's sabbatical, threatened libel action: the casually toned Sutherland remarks were obviously made at severe cost to his deliberative image.

Sutherland would write three subsequent criticisms of Anderson: a letter of defence to *The Canadian Forum* rebutting A.J.M. Smith's review of Anderson's *The White Centre*,[77] a series of more or less sceptical references in the 'Introduction' to *Other Canadians*, and the long 'The Poetry of Patrick Anderson' that Anderson himself remembered gratefully two decades later. These pieces make evident that Sutherland valued Anderson as friend and poet sufficiently to want to affirm his gifts occasionally. He accorded no other poet of either little-magazine cohort such sustained critical attention. Arguably, Anderson provided Sutherland with an emblematic version of the modern poet: 'the personality of the modern poet' is to him, for example, that of 'an individual too honest for his own advantage,'[78] a phrase that tellingly echoes Whitney's assessment of Anderson's rigorous self-criticism: 'Anderson was relentless, even brutally honest, about his faults.'[79] Sutherland often refers to Anderson as modern type elliptically, as when he misquotes Anderson's 'Love Poem' in order to praise Dudek's poetry: '[Dudek] does not say, as one of our modernist poets does, "You are as tall as Europe, I as Asia"';[80] or chides 'certain obscure poets' for their image-mongering without naming his clearly local object of scorn ('On Certain Obscure Poets'). When Sutherland claims in 'The Great Equestrians' that modern literature, while 'strictly impersonal in theory,' is 'wholly personal – or perhaps I should say, wholly selfish – in its practice ... [that] In its most distant reaches, it never escapes the chilling touch of the author's ego,'[81] he works up a dichotomy that was a predicate of his original attack on Anderson: 'After a deep dive into introspection, the poet has a contrary mood, in which he tries to correlate his "private circus" with some general trend or feeling.'[82] On the other hand, as we have seen, Sutherland also projected his own experience into his essays: the modern poet in the Prufrock mode 'begins to entertain two ideas about his character: one that is founded on the unflattering opinion that other people are bound to have of him; and another one that provides consolation by putting him in a romantic light.'[83] Compare this generalization with the self-estimate in 'Why George Left College': 'He began to regard his own smallness as gigantic and his own greatness as monstrously inferior.'[84] Sutherland's critical and his private evaluations were easily confused.

Indeed, a tendency to confuse the personal and the critical is characteristic of Sutherland, not only in the Anderson libel: P.K. Page appears to have been offended on similar grounds. In 1947 he wrote to her in a defensive mood: 'I said [in 'The Poetry of P.K. Page'] that I "suspected" you were not satisfied with your early poems, and that you were "probably" not happy about the novel: I thought those lies might help to keep the essay on an impersonal level. I did not want it to seem that I had "consulted" the author ...'[85] Indeed, Sutherland routinely based his critical remarks on Page on private information: not only in the *Northern Review* article that occasioned this letter,[86] but in his earliest responses. In 'P.K. Page and *Preview*' he concludes that she feels 'some emotional discomfort with [her] subject-matter';[87] in 'Earle Birney's "DAVID"' he remarks that 'she wrote for years of almost nothing but the first trillium on the hills,'[88] which he can only have known because of their personal relations, the trillium poems remaining unpublished; in his review of *Unit of Five* he said that 'Miss Page appears to be in the throes of an effort to make up her mind.'[89] (That these personal remarks had their effect on Page will be apparent in my discussion of 'After Rain'; see chapter 1.) Clearly, Sutherland was indifferent to the ethics of exploiting private information in public comment; the Anderson article is only the most blatant example of the habit. And as we have seen regarding Klein, Anderson showed a parallel lack of angst over his own confusion of personal with political obligation.

Sutherland's conflicts of personal and critical interest are closely linked to the editorial belligerence I remarked earlier. His bravura inclusion of 'A Criticism of "In League With Stones"' in the same issue with the Kay Smith poem itself was obviously meant to send a message about *First Statement*'s rigour and readiness to debate. The gesture may be usefully contrasted with one of *Preview*'s early indications of its own honesty and inclusiveness. After Anderson had written 'Stephen Spender and the Tragic Sense' for *Preview* 7, the little magazine received an acerbic letter from Allan Anderson, attacking the piece and its author: 'such a poor performance as a critic,' in fact, 'that ... one is bound to suggest he content himself with the private circuses which constitute his own poetry.'[90] Patrick Anderson had no obligation whatever to include the snarling piece in *Preview*; that he did so, and provided a quite moderate reply to its criticisms, gives a good indication of that little magazine's sense of a responsibility to various perspectives. It is an interesting coincidence that Sutherland published his 'A Criticism of "In League With Stones"' in the next issue of *First Statement*.[91] The most significant matter, however, is that Sutherland tried to dramatize his little magazine's inclusiveness by attacking one of his own poets; Anderson made the parallel attempt by printing the attack on himself.

Anderson's self-effacement in this instance was as typical as his occasional aggressiveness in speech. In the 1970s he wrote a few memoirs of the forties, and they have in common a charming, and perhaps slightly deceptive, tone of self-critique. In his introduction to the *Preview* reprint, for example, he remarks, 'I sometimes think that my usefulness to *Preview* ... lay in the fact that in my nervously compulsive way, I wrote far too much and so shamed my colleagues into increasing their output to keep pace with me.'[92] In 'A Poet Past and Future,' he notes that the *Preview* 'editors declared themselves anti-fascists, but only I, who became entangled in the far-left, deserved Professor [Wynne] Francis's term "doctrinaire".'[93] Sutherland did not live long enough to write such retrospective self-critique; there is little evidence that he was given to it, however, despite the vacillations and occasional retractions of his critical views. As I concluded in 'Critical Episodes,' his editorial personality was decidedly negating and antagonistic: he wanted for *First Statement* a degree of distinction and uniqueness that could be obtained only by a good deal of polemical attack. Anderson showed no comparable interest in divorcing his or his *Preview* confrères' practice from the work of other journals or other generations. On the contrary, he noted with pleasure in the fourth issue positive comments on the little magazine from the editors of *Poetry*, *New Directions*, and *Horizon*, evidently with no interest in distinguishing *Preview* from their example. His greater sin may have been that he did not seek distinction from *First Statement*; rather, he assumed it. From the *First Statement* perspective, this meant that '*Preview* ... pretends to have put its face to the wall and turned its back on us';[94] Sutherland's resentment at being taken insufficiently seriously is very adolescent, but his caricatures of *Preview* have become common enough.

Thus far the evidence suggests that Anderson and Sutherland were very different in editorial style, and in important ways this is true, a number of them arguably to Anderson's credit. They had more editorial methods in common, however, than the above would suggest. Both men, with the help of their editorial boards, were full of fertile ideas for keeping their little magazines fresh and imaginative. Sutherland's decision with the others to 'go to print' with the purchase of a press is the best indication of his expansive editorial imagination, but he had been similarly inventive from the earliest issues of the magazine. In the third issue of *First Statement,* he established a rate of pay per word (one-half cent) that would be the same for prose as for poetry; in the fourth, he inaugurated a *First Statement* supplement with a long story, 'Gerontion,' by R.G. Simpson, one of the editors (the idea did not last); by the fifth issue, he had merged with a Western literary journal, *The Western Freelance,* incorporating their subscribers and contributors; the twelfth issue was a special poetry issue, containing the work of Dudek, Layton, and Kay Smith, and introduced by a lengthy Sutherland commentary; and so on. The ambitious fertility of his editorial imagination is self-evident. But Anderson's little magazine shows a not dissimilar creativity: the sixth issue (only six were projected) included a questionnaire to readers regarding their reactions to the little magazine's format, inclusiveness, and literary value; the eleventh was called 'Some Aspects of the War: A Civilian Report' and tried to blend *reportage* with poetic observation; the fifteenth announced in a 'Note' *The Victory Broadsheet,* a subsidiary publication containing 'poetry of a simpler, more popular kind ... to bring poetry to the people'; *Preview* 21 was 'An Explanatory Issue' in which the poets were to append brief comments helping to elucidate their poems; and so on. My impression, given the chronology of the issues' publication, is that Sutherland's constant innovations spurred the *Preview* group to their own editorial changes, an important note for the 'who was first' fan but little relevant to criticism of the two little magazines.

The two editors may also be likened for their equally indefinite intellectual gifts. Anderson, who was briefly a visiting professor at McGill University and was invited to return to work there at the time of his departure for Singapore,[95] must have had the more apparent credentials, his Oxford baccalaureate standing up ironically well against Sutherland's two abortive semesters at Queen's and McGill. Temporal distance, however, has helped us to see, as emotional distance helped A.M. Klein to see, the shallowness of Anderson's political analyses. The privileged young Oxonian who could move from an apparently 'progressive' Conservatism to communism in the space of three years – assisted in the 'skin deep' conversion, Anderson says, by his 'wife [, who], having, you know, once been a methodist, became very ideologically left-wing for a while and I was supposed to tag along'[96] – was not a profound political thinker, and his utter repudiation of communism eight years later was perhaps the more genuine gesture. Sutherland's parallel flightiness of intellect has already been suggested by his extreme but unstable attitude to A.J.M. Smith on the question of religious poetry, but the intellectual instability was broader in import. A typical polemicist, he was less concerned to find a consistent alternative to Smith's views, or to *Preview*'s, than he was to caricature those views to establish *First Statement* on a more prominent footing. As I show in 'Critical Episodes' (pp. 42–4), his first remarks on Smith's native–cosmopolitan dichotomy indicate the idea's value; his next, its inability to account for the *First Statement* poets; his next, the idea's worthlessness, since all good poetry will necessarily partake of both native and cosmopolitan characteristics. (Smith and Sutherland make a good case for a study of 'the anxiety of influence,' as Philip Kokotailo has suggested.)[97] A similar inability to settle might be remarked in his critical relations with Anderson, of course. Not only on the question of 'the motivation of Mr. Anderson's poetry' ('Retraction'), by the way: the poet he would later pigeonhole for his British idioms had, in Sutherland's first remarks, a bad 'habit of using words with a slang twist which he acquired in America.'[98] His general sponsorship of a nationalistic Canadian writing throughout his career is similarly contradicted by a late comment to Desmond Pacey: 'I am not sure that Canadian writing – as distinguished from individual Canadian writers – is a proper subject for extensive critical discussion ... Personally, I would not have the heart to re-read Sangster or Lampman or Anderson, or the vast majority of Canadian poets.'[99] And yet at the same time he was critiquing Katherine Mansfield in familiar nationalist terms for 'the slavish trend of consciously or unconsciously imitating the English writer,' a complaint that raised the disaffected Dudek's ire.[100]

The latter issue is more than complicated by the transparent nationalism of a number of Anderson's poems, such as the well-known 'Poem on Canada'[101] and the less familiar 'Canadian Scene.'[102] Such inversions of the forties consensus become commonplace, however, after a survey of the period criticism and a perusal of the magazines themselves. The consensus would have us see Anderson, for example, and dismiss him, for the intense formalism and stylism of his poetry; Dudek's memory depicts him as a bit of a dandy, and it would not be straining too many readers' imaginations to align him with the Aesthetic strain of Canadian modernism I have identified.[103] But the comparable

Aestheticism of John Sutherland's criticism and editorship is unremarked and will contradict those who associate him too easily with the *First Statement* realist orthodoxy (in Frank Davey's words, quoting Sutherland): 'a growing commitment to the temporal, phenomenal world, to "fundamental realism," use of the natural speaking voice, attention to local experience as a source of subject matter, and ... breaking down of "the dividing wall between the author and the people," to ensuring that "poetry is coming into contact with the ... environment".'[104] Sutherland's Aesthetic taste is visible variously and most tellingly in the poets he chose to include in *First Statement* before Dudek and Layton had their impact on editorial policy. Among these were P.K. Page and Patrick Anderson, prominently so for the first several issues, as well as Leo Cox, erstwhile chair of the Canadian Authors' Association's Montreal Branch. Anne Marriott, Norma E. Smith, and the Kay Smith whose obscurity of metaphor so exercised Sutherland round out a collection of highly formal and/or stylized poets, only Anderson among them showing the interest in locality that is supposed to ground the distinctiveness of *First Statement*. It is no doubt partly on account of such inclusions that Dudek came to think Sutherland 'really a Preview-ite at heart ...'[105]

Sutherland inaugurated his *First Statement* with a 'gesture ... a display of activity': 'Someone will say that we will be talking in a vacuum, to ourselves alone, and be making gestures that have reference to nothing' ('Editorial' *FS* 1.1). He does not resent the imputation. Indeed, in his imminent attack 'On a Story Published in Preview Magazine,' he would insist that words 'are not mechanical, not utilitarian, not even a modern convenience. They are not intended always to present the blank, gray facades of factories.' Instead, '[i]t happens that words, when touched by a keenly pointed pen, begin to glow. They glow with a brilliance, without being opaque. There are suggestions, hints, glimmerings ...'[106] Fascinating, surely, to see Sutherland deny the social-realist function and insist that words, far from being 'utilitarian,' chiefly refer to one another. The premises are only vaguely Aesthetic (Walter Pater's 'hard, gem-like flame' is not far away), but it is easy to see why this editor should find the poetry of Anderson and Page attractive. To be sure, this is Sutherland juvenilia, and he would abandon such pretentious prose soon enough, but the Aesthetic principles would only be uncomfortably suppressed. In 'P.K. Page and *Preview*' five issues later, Sutherland projects his own Aestheticism onto *Preview*, in which he finds 'a beauty that has an element of strangeness about it,' the conjunction of 'strangeness' and 'beauty' a typically Aesthetic premise; but he still disdains Page's tendency to socialist and social poetry, and he speaks as we have seen of her 'discomfort' in the mode. His own discomfort with social poetry would persist: as late as August

1944, long after he had begun sparring with Smith, Sutherland would insist that while 'the political context of the work of poetry or prose is of course a fascinating study ... the final criterion of judgment is still the standard of art itself – good taste, which derives its authority from a long tradition ... This, and nothing else, decides whether 'social significance' will be artistically valid or not' ('Editorial,' *FS* 2.8).This after a March 1944 editorial in which he had affirmed, 'We ourselves believe that an author is free to write upon any subject he chooses. His subject-matter seems to us less important than his ability to deal with it' ('Editorial,' *FS* 2.5). 'There is no such thing as a good or a bad book. Books are well or badly written, that is all,' remarked Oscar Wilde. Obviously it need not be proven here that Sutherland's persistent discomfort with social realism and defence of purely artistic standards is indeed Aesthetic in any reliable historical sense. Suffice to say that he is in such comments both distinct from the *First Statement* stereotype and at the more aestheticized end of the scale running between literature *engagé* and the literature of artistic detachment. At the time, this Aesthetic leaning in *First Statement* policy was visible. Anderson chided the fellow magazine for establishing 'First Statement Groups' in early Canadian literature: 'Is he [the artist], like the First Statement Group, going to content himself with study circles to ponder the platitudes of Lampman and Carman? Or is he going to plunge boldly into the progressive movement ...?'[107] Perhaps Sutherland's Aestheticism seemed demanded by a period in which poetry was so constantly called to utilitarian service: to war, to revolution, to faith.

Because of views like these, Dudek found Sutherland's 'conservative view of literature' so consistent that if he, Sutherland, 'had never met Layton etc. he would never have passed through a radical phase between his earlier criticism and his later critical conversion to E.J. Pratt and Roy Campbell.'[108] The same latent conservatism in Anderson, not to mention the other coincidences of their editorial styles, may well have given the men the basis of a rivalrous friendship reflected in the healthy competition between their respective little magazines. The two magazines have never been commented on interleafed, according to now fairly reliable dating, but the results can be fruitful. *First Statement* published its first issue after six of *Preview*; the *Preview* editors had only agreed to a run of six issues, so it seems likely that one motive for the establishment of *First Statement* was a sense of the imminent loss of the 'rival' journal. The two editors had a competitive attitude to quantity: when *First Statement* went to a typical twelve from a typical eight pages, *Preview* followed suit in its next issue (or vice versa, exact date of issue being uncertain).[109] Six months after *First Statement* went to print with their purchased press, a *Preview* 'Note' 'reminded' readers of the $100 target of their own

'Preview fund,' purpose unclear. Earlier noted exchanges, such as that between Page and Sutherland over *First Statement*'s 'policy of inclusion,' help to confirm that the two magazines were very much engaged with one another, that the legendary *Preview* indifference to their rivals is a myth. Anderson and Sutherland had much to gain from one another; their editorships were more mutual, and far more parallel, than has been clear.

It will probably do little to weaken further the consensus over *First Statement* and *Preview* to demonstrate that these affinities of personality and intellect between Sutherland and Anderson have their corollary in the poetry of the two men, but the task is worthwhile anyway. After all, Sutherland is not remembered as a poet and Anderson scarcely so, largely as the 'superb mannerist' George Woodcock damned with faint praise after his death in 1979,[110] or as the 'tea-drinking Dylan Thomas' of Milton Wilson's famous sneer,[111] or more recently as a closeted gay poet. That the two editors should in fact prove similar poetic stylists may help us to see Anderson's 'mannerism' as less eccentric to, than exemplary of, the poetic mainstream in Canada during the forties, and Sutherland's creative limitations as at least historically typical.

In 'Critical Episodes' I argued that the only *aesthetic* distinction the *First Statement* polemicists offered between themselves and *Preview* was the overuse by Anderson and Page of compact, obscure, and dense images and metaphors, a mannerism to which the *First Statement* poets claimed, in Sutherland's phrase, to offer a 'more wholesome,' more colloquial, alternative ('Two Schools'). I will not re-create here my full survey of Sutherland's and Dudek's remarks on the matter, but, rather, canvas three exemplary versions: Sutherland's claim that the *Preview* poets' 'metaphors may be drawn from everyday things, but they are grouped together in an intense word pattern to produce a novel effect';[112] Sutherland's view of Dylan Thomas's poetic, in which 'a few good metaphors can become the equivalent of a poem,' but 'the unity of the poem begins to suffer';[113] and Dudek's view that the work he associated with *Preview* was all 'word-patterns rather than poetry,' or, more snidely, that it was full of 'polyglot displays.'[114]

In the article's context such a refrain seemed entirely strategic, a local antagonism in a minor key. In my next chapter, I will show, on the contrary, that the Canadian debate echoed analogous disputes among English and American poets over the function of the powerful single image in the search for a new conception of the 'whole' poem. In fact, that one concrete criticism levelled by *First Statement* at *Preview*, replicating as it does a fundamental mid-century modernist debate over poetic structure and style, cues the readings of this book, although I turn its descriptive force as fully on two *First Statement* poets as on two of *Preview*. Setting the original polemical purposes aside entirely, I contend that a style in which brevity, density, and difficulty of metaphor are central to a poem's soundness of structure, or lack of it, is so dominant from 1942 to 1954 as to be called the 'forties period style' – in part because Sutherland, and Dudek and Irving Layton at one time, pursued it themselves, with idiosyncratic but not substantive difference from its *Preview* manifestation. The *First Statement* poets who would offer a genuine alternative to that period style – Layton and Dudek – did not do so convincingly until 1953–4, a year of creative change that I will repeatedly assert to have been paradigmatic for Canadian poetry's transition. Anderson and Sutherland had both lapsed as poets by that time (although the former's *The Colour as Naked* of 1953, like Page's *The Metal and the Flower* of 1954, may have suggested a more robust poetic drive than he was in fact sustaining), but we find the dominant style readily in their forties poetry.

Anderson does manifest an elaborateness, obscurity, and intensity of metaphor and image in most of his poetry from Canada, more so, to be sure, than any other poet of the period:

> Boy, was I born beaumont to the bone!
> naked, and the servile doctor wrapped me in a coat of arms,
> a stripling and I wore the Garter on my select muscle,
> married cecils in cathedral Mays below
> history and the sky's bulging blue eye of victoria:
> then we rode our passionate hunters after the fox of love
> and were blooded at midnight: o the little lord
> for Eton and Christchurch by his moaning mother
> pre-destined – news to cottagers for miles.
>
> ('English Fantasy')

Few of the metaphors are radically uninterpretable ('married cecils' gives me trouble), but they are all clearly intended to challenge readerly complacency in a typically modernist way, and their intensity – which I will often characterize in the chapters that follow as a kind of ratio, the number of metaphors or images per line – is undeniably striking. There has been no discussion of persona in Anderson's poetry, so the 'fantasy' aspects of the style here, the obvious distance between the poet and the aristocratic speaker, and the irony at the persona's expense with which the poem is governed, would not be remarked by his typical detractors, nor likely by his critical friends. (Rhythm, too, is beautifully handled, though the judgment remains subjective.)

When Anderson's purpose is less satiric, it is not uncommon for him to reduce the intensity of metaphor, in a concomitant interest in scene:

A pastoral country, and the quiet window
is flounced to the view like a lady;
the pony sunlight buries its nose in her hand
while the farms crack smiles and snap their laborers' muscles ...
Violence intervenes to rust the violet
and fish alter the flowers,
the anchor plows the field - in the iodine lane
the villagers see me freed by the art of drowning.

('Three Storms')

Formulations like 'the pony sunlight' and 'the iodine lane' are typical, and upon closer examination of them in the poetry of P.K. Page I will assert their roots in Imagist principles of juxtaposition. Anderson does pick up from Thomas the habit of juxtaposing two nouns around 'of,' like the 'blue eye of victoria' and 'fox of love,' 'the art of drowning' in these passages, a tic so common to the poets of *Preview* and of *First Statement* that I shall have to refer to it short-hand as the *'a of b'* formula. This, too, suggests the survival of Imagist prescriptions in reified form well into the 1940s. But perhaps the deeper fact of Anderson's style is the potential for verbal clutter, poetic structure subordinated to the metaphorical imagination, that the reader might well experience in such poems. In simpler terms, they might strike some as overworked, overwritten, even neurotic in their desire to accumulate as much of the poet's imaginative residue as possible without quite failing as poems. It is important to keep this possibility conditional: to say that a failure of this kind is endemic to Anderson's poetry is to move too quickly from local to general conditions, and few have read him thoroughly enough to sustain the claim.

Anderson's poetry is not highly enough thought of to make such subjective considerations compelling, but they will arise again in regard to P.K. Page, for whose early poetry they are fundamental, perhaps injurious. In this preliminary survey what matters chiefly is that Sutherland's poetry offers no profound response to the Anderson stylistic challenge. From 1942 to 1953 (the dates of his publication coinciding ideally with the parameters of the 'forties' I will rely on), Sutherland was to deploy metaphors and imagery with an intensity and opacity not much reduced from Anderson's:

Objects, obsequious when he walked among them,
His flexing body like a whip of motion,
Crouched low on the earth as animals,
Hide in the twilight safety of their skins:

Or, with a counterfeit of motion, gained
From his scythe limbs, that, mowing the tall light,
Shed them like thistles on the travelling wind,
They seeded in a farther valley for him.[115]

The '*a of b*' formula is operative in 'whip of motion,' 'counterfeit of motion,' of course, but the deeper commonality with Anderson's style is the desire to get in a vivid metaphor per line. The third line is in fact exemplary: 'His body' is first linked by metaphor to something that can 'flex,' then (a second metaphoric instance) compared to 'a whip of motion,' which itself contains a third metaphor, the '*a of b*' noted. Proceeding with such a positivist response, I count fourteen metaphors in these eight lines: the effect is again of crowding, a potential exhaustion of poetic structure by the creative will to accumulate and juxtapose. Sutherland's specific comparisons are not as difficult as Anderson's can be, but he makes up for it with various stylistic ambiguities and ineptitudes, like the slippage into present tense in the fourth line quoted, the unclear antecedent of 'They' in the eighth line, or the clumping rhythm with which the octave closes ('The Master' is indeed a sonnet – Sutherland favoured the form).

Sutherland also evidently found attractive the surrealized landscapes, or, in his case, room-scapes, for which he had upbraided Anderson:

Not lulled by sleep's pretenses, when I see
The star above me in the cave of night
Wink dimly at the zero sign of being,
I rise to force my image on the room.

Glad as I walk to feel my blundering form
Trample on shapes of things that, during day,
Like snakes raise threatening heads to strike, and now
Drop their defenceless shadows on the floor ...

Afterwards iron stillness. But I stand
Not moving, while unceasing swarms of light
Crawl slowly on their heavy wings, and hive
Their honey in the white comb of the walls ...

('Triumph')

If it is a fault that 'In Patrick Anderson's writing, the confusion of self with outer reality ... is physical as well as mental. The spatial relationships between his body and external objects is [*sic*] not clearly estab[lished],' as Sutherland would have it,[116] it is no less a fault here. I would prefer to remark though (as I would of Anderson's work) the rich interpenetration of self and scape in 'Triumph,' one of Sutherland's most effective pieces. Perhaps Irving Layton agreed: the image of Sutherland's seventh line would recur in Layton's composition soon after of 'The Swimmer,' where 'snakeheads strike / Quickly and are silent.' Sutherland's surrealism, formalism, and once again the '*a of b*' formula stand in to remind us that the two editors were men of a given period, and that their relation to period styles was at least as powerful as their occasional antagonisms.

Sutherland rarely varied from this manner: he made gestures towards Imagism ('Astral Journey,' 'Girl in Spring,' perhaps 'Snowless Moment') and satire ('Guide to the Canadian Poets') but returned in the end to the formal conservatism that was dominating his criticism as well. There is little to distinguish him from Anderson in such brief explorations and, of course, Anderson himself explored a variety of manners quite distinct from the 'beaumont to the bone' playfulness seen above. One helpful distinction lies in the syntactic styles of the two poets: it may be expressed roughly as a magnetic pull towards parataxis in Anderson's poetics, and towards hypotaxis in Sutherland's. Compare the elaborate subordination and complex-compound structure of Sutherland's sentences in 'Triumph,' above, to the more accumulative syntax of Anderson's 'Soldier (An Attempt),' in which an unnamed civilian strips for a conscription medical:

> Casts clout and cancels place
> diminishing like clothes,
> untying like a shoelace
> the lights on the picture-palace,
> loses like handkerchief
> friend's hanky panky face,
> the lemon gloves of summer,
> the shrunk pyjamas of flowers,
> the jacket of 'class' and the snap
> brim of the private dream,
> and the Sunday suit of a girl
> that made one beautiful.

The accumulation of parallel clauses, in an anaphoric passage that typically suppresses any pronoun or noun that would identify the subject of all these predicates, is to say the least intensive. The five successive '*a of b*' instances bring the passage and the poem as a whole to a point of structural enervation at which we might well ask, what is the principle of inclusion here? What tension of creative judgment has the poet enacted that made him cast away some phrasings and incorporate others – or was there none? If some such scepticisms as these may be thought to subtend a 'typical' response to Anderson's poem, they imply our sense that good poems have a form of structural coherence and boundedness that the force of accumulation here vitiates. The daring of accumulation in the passage – and it is daring, a wilful pushing at the edge of syntactic incoherence – forces us to imagine a vanishing point at which the poem collapses into an ironic entropy, its energy played out in a world that cannot, after all, be included *in toto*. Sutherland's hypotaxis reduces such risks, and the effect it creates of a ruminative consciousness constructing the poem – assisted, to be sure, by the sonnet form – perhaps helps to mute any sense we might have of a similar accumulative collapse incipient in his poetics.

The nicety with which such a distinction might be made is suggestive of the proximity of Sutherland and Anderson in poetic style. Further alignment *and* distinction of the two poets would certainly be desirable. For now I want to survey a few surprises of subject-matter in the two poets and conclude this synoptic survey with a brief discussion of the way their careers as Canadian poets ended. First of all, a complete lack of 'social realism' is already apparent in Sutherland's work. His poems do not 'come into contact with the environment,' as he says significant poems should do,[117] nor do their central figures often make such contact. On the contrary, a core of Sutherland's poetry shows protagonists – usually rendered, in a 1930s mannerism, in the third person – in interior settings, often closed rooms ('With Expert Tailoring,' 'The Flood,' 'Triumph') that are hard to keep separate from our images of Sutherland's prolonged convalescence. 'On Thomas Wolfe' is an interesting adjunct: like Nietzsche, Wolfe is figured as a convalescent in a surreal interior, 'struggling to remove / The bandage of his dream around his eyes.'[118]

Sutherland's tendencies to surrealism, formalism, and a vague psychologism are sufficiently evident and make it easy to agree with Anderson's ironic assessment near the end of his life that 'the free-form verse fashionable in Canada today and sometimes claiming an ancestry in Ezra Pound, William Carlos Williams, the Black Mountain school, etc., bears little relation to the verse published by Sutherland.'[119] Sutherland's latent critical Aestheticism is also surprisingly confirmed in a few poems:

Her twined body
Angular but full,
Had the crooked beauty,
And the whiteness of her face
And the redness of her cheeks and lips
Twined the rose and pearl
Of the swan.

('Girl in Spring')

A.J.M. Smith would have welcomed the piece two decades earlier for his *McGill Daily Literary Supplement,* where his own poems of beauty and swans are prominent.[120] Sutherland's poetic world is generally a place of stylized retreat enforced upon the convalescent or chosen by the aesthete. It is certainly not the recognizable urban world so habitually associated with *First Statement* innovation. It is not surprising, then, that Sutherland should have been reading the poetry of Auden, Spender, and Thomas as vigorously as had Anderson.[121] We recall that a commonplace of forties criticism would have only the *Preview* poets under their influence;[122] the similarities of the two editors' poetic worlds should help to deter further renditions of that old saw.

It may be my tactical error to suggest that Sutherland's surrealism and aestheticism help to liken him to Anderson, for there is just as much in Anderson to reverse the period orthodoxy. I have already remarked the blatant nationalism of some of his Canadian-period poems: an association of Smith's 'cosmopolitanism' with *Preview* and 'nativism' with *First Statement* is much problematized thereby. Equally surprising will be Anderson's ability to represent the urban and social world that is a supposed predicate of the *First Statement* accomplishment:

Where old men mumble in decrepitude
or fallen over tables lay their loose cheeks
on grained pine wet with beer that spills
and drips for them:
in taverns easy as swing doors
off the disastrous streets where grinding gas
and shouting newsboys stuff the unseen hole
of the unfillable and ultimate zero ...[123]

It is not Anderson's *métier,* no, but he routinely attempts the downtrodden urban setting for which Sutherland had no apparent taste. Also to be noted in

Anderson is a continual subjectivism: it is in fact Sutherland who is the more doctrinally impersonal of the two, even given Anderson's obvious desire to hide the most intimate areas of his experience. Anderson poems like 'Three Storms,' 'Love Poem,' and 'Winter in Montreal' rely on the establishment of a highly perceptive persona for the coordination of their dense metaphors, and while none of them is frankly self-revelatory, they are lyric in their emphatic interplay of perception and imaginative emotion. The quality is too little considered in discussion of Anderson.

Perhaps in the isolation of their endings do the two poetic careers seem most poignantly alike: both men had lost all contact with their fellow 1940s poets by the time of their creativity's waning. By the end of 1953, Anderson had published his last volume of new poetry in Canada, and Sutherland had seen his last poems published in *Poetry*. Anderson entered a prolonged dry spell that was not to break until the late 1960s, when news of the renewed Canadian 'interest' in his work seems to have spurred a fresh start in a different vein. Both men left Montreal, Sutherland, sadly, just before falling ill with 'cancer complicated by tuberculosis'[124] and entering another and finite period of convalescence. Anderson himself died of cancer before his sixty-fourth birthday.[125] The poems he wrote from the mid-1960s until the end had lost most of the tension, and with it much of the energy and vividness, of his early work; to borrow a typically self-effacing phrase from the late 'Winter in the Sticks,' the poems had 'no fire left but filigree.'[126] The two departures from Montreal and from vital poetic expression help us again to see, as will the prolonged middle silence of P.K. Page, the end of A.M. Klein's poetry in a tragic mental distress, and the mutual rejuvenation of Louis Dudek's and Irving Layton's poetry during 1953–4, that for these poets the 'forties' unconsciously extended, whatever the internal rhythms of the decade, from the inauguration of the two little magazines in 1942 until roughly 1954, and that is why my term 'forties' refers to that vital dozen years, '1940s' signalling a more literal reference to the decade.

These affinities and new articulations of distance between Patrick Anderson and John Sutherland should do more than confirm Dudek's description of the latter as 'a Preview-ite at heart.'[127] On the contrary, they help us break through the surviving binaries of forties criticism and look again at the field. They enjoin upon us a more fruitful model of forties literary exchange than the essentializing methodology of little-magazine study has made possible – a model I will now pursue in reading their more powerful contemporaries. If the positive thrust of my argument has rested too openly with Anderson, that is largely because he has needed more corrective attention than has Sutherland, whose reputation is more apparently secure. But I should not want to be thought to have contended for Anderson's superiority to Sutherland, other than as poet. I hope instead to have helped to neutralize the kind of debate that seeks to hierarchize the fascinating men and women who lived their youth as poets in Montreal in the 1940s. We have more to gain from their friendships than from their squabbles. 'In Canada,' says Milton Wilson, 'nothing is more tedious than literary quarrels in which the opponents try to date one another – the sort of quarrel which you win by pretending to react against your opponent's reaction.'[128] Forty years later, I share Wilson's view, adding only that there is nothing tedious in the Montreal forties that we have not made so.

1

Imagist Twilight: Page's Early Poetry

Page before 'After Rain'

The status of 'After Rain' in P.K. Page's *oeuvre* has something of the inevitable about it. Written in 1954,[1] on the brink of her prolonged middle silence, Page's personal *summa* is, on the one hand, an engaging self-criticism whose contexts are literary-historical, aestheticist, feminist, religious, and psychological, while, on the other hand, exemplifying with careful irony the very poetics for which the poet and persona – in this case largely overlapping voices – chide themselves. It engages the criticism and reviews the poet had until that time received; it evokes the aesthetic skirmishes between *Preview* and *First Statement*, in which Page served as both favoured target and skewer; and it is one of the few subjective poems she had written to that time. Very shortly after its composition – despite the success of her then recent volume, *The Metal and the Flower* (1954), winner of the Governor General's Literary Award – Page, out of the country, stopped writing poetry for ten to a dozen years. Could her critics have asked for a more loaded text for explication and contextualization?

Rosemary Sullivan has shown how usefully this poem raises the aesthetic issues of Page's early poetic development.[2] Her reading of 'After Rain' is exemplary if basic, honouring, as it does, the persona's own vision, recorded primarily in the last two stanzas, of a new poetics. The speaker prays by way of closure for a 'heart' that will remain 'a size / larger than seeing, unseduced by each / bright glimpse of beauty ...,'[3] thus implying – as indeed the whole poem implies – her too great tendency to see beautiful phenomena and to translate them as if without choice into poetry, excluding possibilities of sympathy and community signalled here by her inappropriate remoteness from her gardener, Giovanni, whom she keeps 'beyond [her] rim.'[4] This prayer is more obscure, however, than Sullivan notices; it is only a prayer, after all, to the birds in her garden, and it relies on a typical Page neologism in which the noun 'choir' is verbed: 'O choir him, birds, and let him come to rest ...' It is also a prayer relying heavily on abstraction; after the precise images of the first five stanzas, a sudden rush of words like 'heart,' 'beauty,' 'whole,' 'meaning,' 'pure' does not give the closure much conviction or purpose.

I emphasize these ambivalences because, strikingly, the prayer not only preceded Page's poetic silence – thus calling into question the worth and profundity of the conclusive aesthetic vision – but ended, even in this poem, with its own self-contradiction. The ostensible fruition of her desired escape from 'seeing' – from what she would elsewhere call 'the tyranny of subjectivity'[5] – is an improved poetics, in which

> ... the whole may toll,
> its meaning shine
> clear of the myriad images that still –
> do what I will – encumber its pure line.

But the ironic helplessness with which she concludes her prayer signals the frustration of this apparently preferred alternative: 'do what I will' is a self-surrender that more powerfully anticipates imminent creative collapse than does the vague revisionary promise of the invocation to the birds. The poet's sympathy with Giovanni is again elided by this conclusion, his briefly recorded dolours having merely provided an occasion for her persistent aesthetic fixation. This more disturbing matter makes 'After Rain' the complex, inverted manifesto it is, and provides the key to an interpretation of Page's creative crises in the period concluding with its composition.

Page's choice of words here is striking and provides me with some crucial concepts. The distinction she urges between the 'whole' poem with its 'pure line' and the images that 'encumber' its 'meaning' is fascinating, in that both *image* and *line* are embodied in the same elements – words chosen – and in that sense indistinguishable from one another. (She is clearly not speaking of the 'line' in a metrical or rhythmic, but in some vaguely referential, sense: 'line' as outline, as evocation.) For some reason Page is concerned to conceptualize images quantitatively – as things that can be counted (a 'myriad'), of which there can be too many per 'line' – and poems qualitatively, as declarations demanding wholeness and purity. This is a courageous self-assessment in keeping not only with a wide range of discussion of English poetics in the 1940s and 1950s, as I shall demonstrate, but also with the view of her early poetry I want to elucidate.

This ironic reading of the poem's conclusion echoes the skilful dialectics and ironies Page deploys in earlier stanzas. The poem's title implies not only the destruction of a garden – gorgeously visualized – but also a washing of the eyes: 'I see already that I lift the blind ...' One of the poem's dichotomies is between seeing and blindness, but this polarity will be complicated when it becomes apparent in the fourth stanza that seeing may be itself a kind of blindness, a condition from which we should pray to be released. Another such opposition is energized between male and female, not only in the different reactions of the female poet and her male gardener, Giovanni, to the ruined garden, but also in the speaker's intense self-consciousness about her own femaleness: she 'lift[s] the blind / Upon a woman's wardrobe of the mind.' Because she has seen the 'cabbages' and 'choux-fleurs' as, variously, 'lace,' 'broderie anglaise,' 'chantilly,' and 'tulle,' she upbraids herself for 'female whimsy,' anticipating perhaps the more practical and apparently male responses of Giovanni, but also – I would argue – evoking ironically and perhaps undermining the association by Page's male reviewers of her intensely imagistic poetics and her gender.

This skilful and muted feminist meditation gives rise to another of the poem's central dialectics, between the fluidity of delicate fabric and the rigidity of geometry. Having established her tendency to transform vegetables punctured by devouring snails into various kinds of 'lace,' the poet appears 'in gum boots pac[ing] the rectangles' of her garden, now a 'garden abstracted, geometry awash – / an unknown theorem argued in green ink.' Her imagination spills these images until she arrives at 'Euclid in glorious chlorophyll, half drunk' and then aligns herself with him, for she, too, is 'none too sober.' A polarity emerges between the 'flimsy' fabrics she has conjured out of cabbages, and the rigid and angled lines of the measured garden. The stunning image of the soaked clothes-reel in the third stanza, mocked by a dripping spider's web, 'its infant, skeletal, diminutive,' hanging from it, closes on the same dichotomy, for the web is 'sagged with sequins, pulled ellipsoid.' This play of 'wardrobe' and geometric forms anticipates the later tension between 'the myriad images' of the poet's creative habit and the 'pure line' she wants to maintain.

The brilliance of these images and their skilful interpenetration is a major part of the success of 'After Rain.' Without them we would lack the intense visual engagement with the phenomenal world that earns Page the right to abstract her themes at the end. But the poet does not share our satisfaction. In the fourth stanza the self-consciousness that earlier motivated a chagrined remark of 'female whimsy' becomes metapoetic and threatens the entire verbal construction:

I suffer shame in all these images.
The garden is primeval, Giovanni
in soggy denim squelches by my hub
over his ruin,
shakes a doleful head.
But he so beautiful and diademmed,
his long Italian hands so wrung with rain
I find his ache exists beyond my rim
and almost weep to see a broken man
made subject to my whim.

What is the speaker's 'hub,' though? What is her 'rim'? The two obscure images fix for the persona (and for the poem) a centre and a circumference; they create a within and a without; and they divide two people whose mutually disappointed labour in the garden might be uniting them. Once again the poet chides herself for 'whimsy,' for what one might call 'Imagist whimsy' in fact, the tendency to fix her imagination on 'glimpse[s] of beauty' – as the last stanza has it – at the expense of sympathy with suffering and loss. A larger dialectic now takes over the poem, between the image-making power of the poet and the depths of her experience not amenable to such a manner. The poet remains ambivalent about the tension: she 'almost weep[s],' but does not weep; nor does she leave her place in the centre, at the 'hub' of the image. Of course, to say that this dialectic of image–manner and sympathy functions on a metapoetic level is not to sublimate its powerful resonance with the dichotomies of fabric and geometry, male and female that enrich the first stanzas, nor its anticipation of the 'image' and 'pure line' tension that will be called upon to close the poem.

We have arrived, then, at the crux of a poem that lends itself to dramatic readings of the Page career as a whole. After opening this daunting gulf between the poetics of her first decade and the necessary sympathy with human suffering demanded by the figure of Giovanni, Page will seek closure in a prayer, as we have seen, whose deities are garden birds and whose operative term is an obscure neologism. The turn to prayer for closure is itself an evasion of the question, of course, granting poetic agency to a transcendent power and, incidentally, diverting attention from her own lack of sympathy for her gardener. Although the first stanza of prayer seeks 'a heart that knows tears are a part of love,' this heart has no clear possessor; it may be Giovanni's, the poet's, or no one's: who will feel the granted sympathy? And if that first request is unclear, its possible effects rootless, how are we to judge the efficacy of prayer in the final stanza, in which the poet seeks a revision of her poetics? The abashed 'do what I will' of the final line is clearly a surrender to the inevitability of 'whimsy' in her poetry; if the 'birds' do not 'choir' her appropriately, she in turn can do nothing for Giovanni – at least, not in writing. There is a desire for some more comprehensive poetics, but a concomitant sense of helplessness wins out.[6]

It is now easier to see precisely how 'After Rain' anticipates the imminent silence of Page's middle period. Although the poem enacts a subjective poetics that might have represented a major advance in her own career, it does so within a paradigm of binary pairs that cannot be reconciled, despite their interpenetrative resonances. The poet's abashed acknowledgment of her various failings in the poem – her 'whimsy,' her inebriation, her 'shame,' her lack of creative sympathy – portends no ethical or aesthetic change. The poem's splendour and remarkable candour are its chief enduring virtues. The poet remains at her 'hub' in the 'ruin[ed]' and 'primeval' garden, a fallen creator whose acute sense of poetic error leads to no real release. If the poem can be imagined in which 'the whole may toll, / its meaning shine,' it cannot be enacted by her. For reasons not really made clear, she is caught in her unsympathetic poetics, 'slipping in the mud' of the 'myriad images' that she cannot convert into wholeness. 'After Rain' gains its poignancy because it is in this sense a final testament from a lapsing verbal creativity; the Page who resurfaced in the mid-1960s was a stylistically different poet, most of these formal tensions buried in Giovanni's garden.

The questionable connection grounding my reading of 'After Rain' – between a biographical phenomenon, a period of creative silence, and a literary one, a single poem – needs some interrogation. It will become apparent that a prime irony of forties literary history is the inescapability of biography in a decade of largely impersonal poetics; indeed, a constitutive irony for most poets of the period lay between their innate and historical urges to self-affirmation and self-expression, and their stylistic compulsion to modernist self-erasure. The validity of such biographical reference in Page's case will serve as a precedent for subsequent treatments, and particularly for my interpretation of A.M. Klein, for whose critics the tragic biography must surely loom largest over the best efforts at his poetry's depersonalization. Page's life has been less dramatic (at least on public record); nevertheless, her own creative crisis tempts scrutiny and demands brief theoretical reflection. First of all, is her middle silence so striking as to be *necessary* to a full discussion of Page's development? Second, some obvious biographical contexts can be tendered for Page's silence (her departure from Canada and a sustaining literary community, her duty-entailing marriage to an ambassador); why not let biography itself explain biography? Third, is the middle silence pertinent to readings of her early poetry – that is, should we read backward causally, hoping to 'explain' the silence by showing that prior poetics anticipated it? Fourth, is the biographical oddity sufficient context for readings of 'After Rain' (as my so-far thin contextualization implies)?

These questions have answers that justify – indeed, that demand – a full consideration of Page's period of silence in relation to the poems she wrote before. To the first question, I would reply that Page's silence is especially striking, given the success of her early career (publication while young, a prompt Governor General's Award) and its coincidence with some other notable silences of the period. It was during the early 1950s, as we shall see, that A.M. Klein also gave up the composition of poetry after a shattering nervous collapse; Patrick Anderson's poetry evaporated at about the same time, after his departure from Canada and acknowledgment of his homosexuality. Thus, between 1953 and 1954 the three major contributors to *Preview* stopped writing poetry. John Sutherland of *First Statement* abandoned creative work, as well as Montreal and most of his friendships, at the end of the latter year, while, between 1952 and 1954, Louis Dudek and Irving Layton undertook profound creative developments that changed their poetics substantially from forties incarnations (as chapters 3 and 4 will show). That generational pivot seems to me a phenomenon broad and deep enough to demand attention to its manifestation in Page. To the second question, I would reply that, if departure from Canada could explain creative silence, it would also have to explain creative renewal (as in the case of Dorothy Livesay); as for marriage, would such explanations be offered of a male poet? The third question demands caution. I think it highly likely that later creative frustration will be anticipated to some extent in poems written earlier, but I reject linear causal analyses which would point *all* effects of *all* poems forward to that *lapsus;* each poem's more immediate contexts have to balance and contain such determinist readings. I therefore answer the fourth question in the flat negative: the silence is not a sufficient context for readings of 'After Rain.'

To it we must add a number of components of the literary-historical nexus in which Page's poetry was nurtured and matured: the doctrine of 'impersonality,' receiving so much current sceptical interrogation; the collaboration and strife between *Preview* and *First Statement* during the 1940s; the Aestheticism of the early Canadian modernist program; and, most important here, the legacy of Imagism, the 'rhetoric' of which (to use John T. Gage's striking phrase) has so permeated Page's version of her poetry in 'After Rain' as to be almost imperceptible. By exploring Page's creative difficulties in relation to these larger forces, I hope to illuminate not only the Canadian poet, but the contexts themselves, particularly the contradictions of Imagist practice and inheritance that still engaged poetry of the 1940s in English. Thus I want to re-create the living complex of aesthetic choices available to new poets in the 1940s, in a spirit of inquiry best summarized by Samuel Hynes:

> It is only when a period has passed that it solidifies and becomes history, and we begin to think of it as a set pattern of events, forces, and consequences. At the time, history feels fluid and uncertain, the forces that time will eventually confirm don't yet know that they *are* the significant ones; in studying the past, we must try by an act of imagination to recover that sense of fluidity.[7]

Hynes's caution is valuable to the literary historian, though this is no place to argue with those who would call into question the entire project of literary history. There remain better and worse renditions of the past. In the words of Astradur Eysteinsson, 'every discussion of an author is an act of literary history: any approach to a particular work is bound to involve its implicit placement, its inscription into literary history.'[8] The following merely attempts to make a virtue of necessity.

First Statement and Page's Style

The situation of Canada's poets in the early 1940s was at once like and unlike that of their contemporaries in the United States and England. The sense of a generational shift was similar. The new war gave to younger poets on both sides of the Atlantic an urgency of aesthetic and political debate from which the previous generation had by then largely absconded. But poets of the 1940s in England had, dauntingly, two previous generations of modernists against whom to define themselves: in the near past, Auden and his contemporaries, and behind them (but perhaps not far enough) Eliot and his. This predicament of originality was paradoxical, in that such precursors commanded indubitable respect yet had discredited their own poetics and politics variously. As A.T. Tolley remarks,

> [f]ew literary events have been so dramatic as the collapse and dispersal of the literary movement that dominated the thirties. Left-wing, nostalgically critical of the dominant middle class from which most of its writers came, ironic and preoccupied with the actual, it lost cohesion and direction when the war brought an end to any hope of a peaceful, political defeat of fascism. The departure of Auden and Isherwood for America, the closing down of *New Verse* and of *Twentieth Century Verse* and the temporary cessation of *New Writing*, reinforced the disorientation these writers felt.

Yet the forties were to see them consolidate their position as the literary establishment of their day.[9]

With slight alteration, Tolley's summary of the British situation could be applied to the paradoxes of Canadian poetry in the same period, the significant difference being that the prior generation of Canadian modernists – Smith, Scott, Livesay, Glassco, Kennedy, Klein – could as yet claim nothing remotely like the achievement and precedence of the Auden generation.

To the young poets beginning to write and publish in Montreal in the early 1940s, the achievements of their national predecessors must have looked thin indeed: yet the forties are, without question, the decade of modernist consolidation in Canadian literature. The best example of this paradox is A.J.M. Smith, who, when *Preview* and *First Statement* began to appear, had yet to publish a volume of his poems, but who would dominate forties discussion of Canadian poetry and its canon in a way few have been able to do since. He and Leo Kennedy were both by this time living by professional exigency in the United States;[10] Kennedy's slim volume of 1933, *The Shrouding*, was the climax of his poetic career, which had waned substantially by the beginning of the 1940s. F.R. Scott had also lost much creative enthusiasm throughout the 1930s; he was in desperate need of the encouragement of the *Preview* group to develop. A.M. Klein had, of course, published his first volume, *Hath Not a Jew ...*, in 1940; in that achievement he was remarkable, as was Dorothy Livesay, who had published two volumes before the new decade began. Neither poet was to emerge as a dominating influence on forties verse, Klein for reasons I will consider in chapter 2, Livesay for her prolonged Marxist propaganda, and no doubt her sex.

When the forties poets looked back to these Canadian modernist predecessors, therefore, they did so largely through the lens of *New Provinces: Poems of Several Authors*, the anthology of Canadian modernist poetry published tardily by Smith and Scott in 1936 (Livesay's exclusion having been commanded by Scott's opinion of her politics). Louis Dudek records his and Irving Layton's reaction to the volume soon after they met in 1941:

We thought it was very lukewarm stuff as far as modernism was concerned. We laughed at some of the experimental gimmicks in there, words running down the page – superficial and silly forms of modernistic poetry. We would want something much more energetic, more visceral than that. From that moment, and probably before, there was a considerable rivalry between ourselves built into the whole situation of ourselves as the younger generation.[11]

This attitude to the older poets was not exclusive to those of *First Statement*: Bruce Ruddick of *Preview* also remembered a feeling that forties poets 'didn't have a history in poetry to go back to ... that none of [them] had great admiration for previous Canadian poetry.'[12] The reaction is not just a matter of brash youth mocking orotund age; F.R. Scott's own preface to *New Provinces* admits the Canadian modernist movement was 'frustrated for want of direction,' and the volume does indeed project a certain diffidence.[13] So did its sales, which never reached a hundred copies.[14] Later perspective would allow Dudek to see the weaknesses of *New Provinces* experimentation as part of a larger pattern of revolt and hesitation in the precursor generation: 'The Scott–Smith generation were labouring under severe limitations. They were rebels against their own class, still deeply attached to the culture which they attacked.'[15] (Compare Tolley's remark above that the thirties poets of England were 'nostalgically critical of the dominant middle class from which most of its writers came.') It was inevitable that the poets of the forties should move beyond the tentativeness of their precursors by ridicule, but it is also true – as Tolley's version of events in England implies – that they must have felt keenly the embarrassment of having such apparently exhausted modernists take control of the critical codification of their own revolutionary impulses.

So the ironic distancing from modernist precursors in England in the 1940s was also visible in Canadian poets, although it was largely unrestrained in this case by a necessary awe. Indeed, the peculiarities of early Canadian modernism must have exaggerated this generational consciousness, especially the Aestheticism that characterized early Canadian modernist poetry, an influence I have charted in detail.[16] An intriguing consideration here would be how far poets of the forties recognized – and really rejected – the Aestheticism of their precursors. John Sutherland was alert to the Aestheticism of A.J.M. Smith, using it satirically against the older poet in his introduction to *Other Canadians* (1946), though his own vague Aesthetic tendencies must have helped him to the identification (it takes one to know one). Sutherland's first attack on *Preview* similarly implied that magazine's Aesthetic and formalist leanings, its search for 'a beauty that has an element of strangeness about it'; not to simplify, however, we should remember that Sutherland himself spoke for Aesthetic ideals at times, and also that *Preview*, too, attacked Smith for the 'glittering inconsequentials' of his style.[17] Without necessarily recognizing the historical implications of their views, a number of forties poets seem to have intuited that early Canadian modernist poetry had had a formalist and Aesthetic bias that their generation both inherited and hoped to supersede. This was to prove an energizing insight, a favoured tactic of *First Statement* in the period's poetomachia being the representation of *Preview* as a recidivist organ of the 1920s generation.[18] The polemical tactic has had a persistent impact on the way we read Page's poetry, though: by emphasizing the decorative and formalist stylistics of Anderson and Page, Sutherland could imply an Aesthetic continuity in Canadian modernist poetry from Smith to Page, against which *First Statement*'s poets could then define themselves.

The *First Statement* treatment of Page was from the start condescending. As indicated by the title of the first attack, 'P.K. Page and *Preview*,' a common tactic was to blur the distinction between general remarks on the magazine and specific criticism of the poet. Thus other *First Statement* polemics against *Preview* could always be read as specific to Page's poetics. In 'P.K. Page and *Preview*,' for example, immediately after remarks on *Preview*'s Aestheticism, Sutherland adds,

> P.K. Page joined PREVIEW after the appearance of the first issue, and she has been particularly influenced by their general policy. To write of people in general appeals to the humane side of her nature. It serves her as a relief from introspection ... She has been like a field worker for the magazine, making a special poetical report on the lives of stenographers.[19]

Sutherland's customary deceptiveness is in place: Page joined *Preview* for the second issue, but Sutherland would have it that her late-coming (by one month!) gave the journal time to develop a dominant aesthetic, an interest in 'people in general,' that influenced her powerfully. It would be more correct to remark, of course, that *Preview* had no central aesthetic unless one were exemplified in common by Page and Anderson; and, as for concern with 'people in general,' Page's interest is so obviously the exceptionality of people, their eccentricity, that Sutherland's remark was fatuous. His approval of 'the humane side of her nature' is a cool pat on the head, to be followed by a sneer at her self-consciousness: she presumably seeks 'relief from introspection' because of a failure of existential nerve. In the more 'positive' comment following, he implies that she had written 'The Stenographers' over and over – lacking, presumably, other talents or inspiration.

In subsequent remarks Sutherland takes up patriarchal language that is by now familiar in criticism of women's poetry, especially modernist.[20] Page is to be praised in that '[o]ne feels the emotional sincerity of what she is saying, but one also feels that the subjective element has not been erased' (p. 8). A beautifully deployed double-bind: the poet is to be praised for a particular emotional proclivity, then chided for her apparent inability to control that essential quality of her gift. Needless to say, such talent as she has must then be attributed to the influence of a male poet: in lines following Sutherland remarks 'the influence of Patrick Anderson of the PREVIEW group in her style ... [her] heavy round alliteration is like the full-throated phrasing of Anderson's lines' (p. 8). The paragraph continues by adducing five further examples of Anderson's inspirational power over Page's sensibility. (As we know, Sutherland's dispute with Anderson was also largely determined by the former's inability to clarify a distinction between poetic style and the poet's gender; for Sutherland, Anderson's implied homosexuality was utterly determinant of his poetic decisions.)

Sutherland's criticism was both enabling and undermining of Page's further creativity. The essay was prominently placed after two Page contributions to *First Statement*, so it was intended to flaunt that journal's comprehensiveness and free exchange of ideas. Page, it is clear, ought to take the remarks in a tough spirit and be better for it. A closing crumb of praise seems meant to inspire such a reaction, but Sutherland cannot sustain the generosity and concludes with high-schoolish abruptness:

> she writes now with greater fluency and more power to create an abundance of images. But as one feels that the emotion is overwrought and becomes subjective, so one feels that the phrasing is too overwhelming to be entirely true. There is lack [*sic*] of complete ease in the style and there is some emotional discomfort with the subject-matter. (p. 8)

Obviously, in the context of *First Statement*'s constant remarks about the *Preview* weakness for 'an abundance of images,' even Sutherland's concluding sop to Page should be construed as a good chiding. His avuncular tone cannot mask the self-revelations latent in his own language, however: he stands, for example, *for* objectivity and believes that emotion must be impersonalized, a bias which militates against the subjectivist and neo-Romantic leanings associated with *First Statement*. He also says that Page '*had been* developing in the general direction of Auden and Spender' but that 'under PREVIEW's influence she took a considerable step forward' (p. 8; emphasis added); note there the contradiction of the persistent historical view that *Preview* embodied the Auden poetics slavishly, whereas *First Statement* led Canadian poetry past that enervating influence.

No subsequent attack on *Preview* was to be so explicitly aimed through Page, but *First Statement* polemic made frequent theoretical appeals to verbal simplicity, visceral power, and virility, at the expense of delicacy, stylization, and eccentricity. That these terms are gendered is obvious. A typical exchange occurred in April 1943, when Patrick Waddington wrote a long letter attacking Irving Layton's short story 'A Parasite.'[21] A closing editorial note says that Waddington was a member of the Toronto 'First Statement Group' and adds that his view of *Preview* had been no more sanguine. In printing the letter Sutherland excised Waddington's disparaging remarks on that journal but now felt compelled to quote them anyway: 'There are, of course [Waddington remarks], many writers now whose printed stuff is worse than Mr. Layton's. Without Mr. Layton's prolixity, I feel Neufville Shaw's work in another and worse sense pretentious, superficial and self-conscious. And Pat Page, with a defter hand, yet more defective, neurotic, strained.' One wonders how the 'defter hand' can be 'more defective,' but there is no mistaking the import of Waddington's last two adjectives, with their imputation to Page of a female neurosis that ruins her (presumably marginal) aesthetic gift. In such a context even a 'deft hand' may be a failing suggestive of prestidigitation, deceit.

Sutherland himself became more positive in tone with time, but he could not for the life of *First Statement* alter his tendency to speak of Page as of a weak and dilatory mind:

> Miss Page appears to be in the throes of an effort to make up her mind. When she allows herself a statement of faith it has the appearance of a tag, affixed with a dutiful blessing, but not much hope, to the end of a poem. She resembles the character in her poem *Cullen*:
>
> 'He knew there was a reason, but couldn't find it,
> and marched to battle half an inch behind it.'
>
> Yet Miss Page has unquestionable talent, and she has written several of the most striking poems in the book [*Unit of* 5]. She will produce even better work if she can succeed in joining her creative powers with a more exacting principle of selection.[22]

In a projection we know to be typical, Sutherland finds his own anxieties in Page: I have exposed in the introduction his own trouble making up his critical mind on a number of issues. He is about to turn on A.J.M. Smith, for example, in *Other Canadians*, a derision he would later retract. But the force of his criticisms for Page should not be underestimated, especially since the 'principle of selection' enjoined upon her by Sutherland appears later in her own self-scrutiny as a chief failing of her poetics. It is hardly surprising that she did not again publish poetry in *First Statement* after the appearance of 'P.K. Page and *Preview*' in November 1942.[23]

Sutherland's remarks often play subtly and conflictedly on his intimacy with Page, and I have shown such conflicts of critical and private interest to be at the root of his critical practice. Page's possible responses to Sutherland's patronizing criticism must have been further constrained by declarations of love he sent to her in a series of undated letters, probably from the period of his Birney essay, with its allusion to her early 'trillium' poems.[24] Page's answers to the letters are not available. This private matter need not be dwelt on, but it does cast ironic light on Sutherland's later critical language regarding her inability 'to make up her mind.'[25] Such a tendency in his judgment of her poetry can hardly be separated from the powerful emotions he had experienced from the inception of their editorial relationship. As for Page, the male critic's inability to distinguish the roles of editor-critic and intimate mentor-confidant must have played some part in her tendency to internalize received criticism and redirect it more powerfully against her own particular gifts – of which I shall have more to say later.

Sutherland's conflicts of critical interest aside, his treatment of Page is connected to his more general project of associating *Preview* with the 'failed' poetics of an earlier Canadian modernism. This tactic is already evident in the Birney essay, for example, when he alludes to Page's early poetry of nature in order to demonstrate in her more recent work a rejection of nature allying her to the (supposedly) urban modernism of 'Scott, Smith, Klein and Kennedy': she is his first example 'of those recent writers who have a kinship with them.'[26] Her rejection of her early naturalism is clearly held against her in subsequent remarks that work to Birney's credit, and the implicit identification of Page's artificiality is in keeping with the drift into Aestheticism Sutherland claimed to have isolated in the *Preview* pages.[27] Indeed, the broad *First Statement* emphasis on Page's and Anderson's 'polyglot displays,' 'intense word pattern[s],' and 'group[s] of vivid metaphors'[28] is an attack on a principle of Aestheticism afoot in their style; the connection is more visible if we remember Paul Bourget's original definition of Decadent style: 'A style of decadence is one in which the unity of the book is decomposed to give place to the independence of the page, in which the page is decomposed to give place to the independence of the phrase, and the phrase to give place to the independence of the word.'[29] But for its polished style, Bourget's definition might slip unnoticed into any of the *First Statement* commentaries on the problem of *Preview*. Thus, when Sutherland went on to attack Smith's Aestheticism in his introduction to *Other Canadians*, his remark abetted his ongoing attempt to set *Preview* aside from the significant literary continuity of his decade. Hence some of the language in *First Statement* writings on Page: her work is 'overwrought,' 'overwhelming' because of an 'abundance of images'; Waddington adds 'defective,' 'neurotic, strained.' Although Sutherland would eventually see himself as Page's champion, defending her, for example (with typically unwitting paradoxicality), from Smith's criticisms in *The Canadian Forum*,[30] he had set into play too strong a nexus of critical biases for her reputation – and perhaps her early poetry – to withstand. As Sutherland and his team forged their polarization of mid-century Canadian modernism into 'the Aesthetic twenties' against a realist-naturalist and finally *First Statement* forties, Page's work was caught in an untenable opposition from which it emerged only after a prolonged silence.

This identification of Sutherland's *tactics* need not, however, discredit his opinions of Page's work altogether. Too many others, among them Page herself, found something to agree with in Sutherland's assessment of her early poetry. Milton Wilson noted in 1958 that both Page and Anderson produced 'decadent pastorals' that were 'dominated by the common assumption of those years [the forties] that the degree of metaphorical extravagance is the measure of poetic success,' but he importantly – and perhaps too subtly – distinguished the two by remarking that Page's poetry 'wears better' because of 'an underlying *integrity* of imagery or principle.'[31] Wilson correctly notes, with a critical fairness to Page that Sutherland rarely achieved, that although she and Anderson shared a predilection for metaphorical and imagistic accumulation, their practice and degrees of success had been different. Wilson's identification of an 'underlying integrity' in Page's poetry provides a distinction of the two forties poets and helps us towards a renewed assessment of Page in the decade; the term is impressionistic and value-laden, but it strikingly echoes Page's own desire for a poem in which 'the whole may toll' and be 'clear of the myriad images' of her early style. Integrity and wholeness were favoured terms of forties poets as they struggled under the visual and structural implications of high modernist Imagism. Sutherland had recognized Page's chief formal difficulty, even if he lacked the detachment to appreciate her poems' vivid and energetic responsiveness. Throughout the 1940s, Page's poetics visibly negotiate the relation between the local image – 'that which presents an intellectual and emotional complex in an instant of time' – and the integrity of the whole poem, and we must first appeal to that broader context if we wish to understand her difficulties in the 1950s.

Imagism and the Forties Search for *Integritas*

According to the editors of the *Imagist Anthology* of 1930, Imagism had passed in 1917.[32] They refer of course to the Imagism of Ezra Pound and Amy Lowell and to the handful of group collections published by that year.

As such a coherent movement or school, Imagism was indeed over by the middle of the First World War. To seek a later date for its demise is to fiddle the concept: there were many groups, periods, and practitioners of poetry in subsequent years whose poetics were imagistic, or who attempted to build on the Imagist legacy, but the 'school' proper was quickly dispensed with.[33] On what grounds, then, might one claim a connection between the poetics of Page in the 1940s and the pre-war English mannerism?

The fate of the original Imagism that Pound and Lowell had shaped is not in fact so easy to describe. In the purest sense it might have ended by 1917, but in looser formulation it might not have been clearly defunct until 1950, as David Perkins seems to suggest.[34] He notes that by the 1920s Imagism had found its way into the 'graduation yearbooks,'[35] certainly not a sign of aesthetic vitality, and by 1925 American practitioners had reduced 'the charged, compressed objectivity of Pound in 1912' to 'a short, free verse impression of some object, scene or happening,' including 'a few carefully selected and vividly rendered details and metaphors, with understated emotion and maybe a mute, musing implication of further meaning.'[36] In the 1930s 'young poets had not experienced the moment of Imagist advocacy. Pound's ... maxims [were] of no force for them.'[37] But this gradual desiccation of the original Imagist impulse is outweighed by the number of poets Perkins locates under the Imagist sign: not a single major modernist escaped its evident impact. This is the paradox of Imagist history, its quick death as coherent doctrine, its striking power over future innovation. Louis Dudek remarked in 'The Theory of the Image in Modern Poetry' (1979) that 'Imagism held the key to modern poetics ... the idea underlying Imagism has poured into the poetry of each generation that has followed the beginning of modernism' (p. 265). Gage affirms that 'if we are to consider the ideas for which the name [Imagism] stands, we have to stretch our chronological limits somewhat.'[38]

The broader Imagist influence is harder still to chart, for it involves not only the assertion of unitary influences (Imagism to Eliot, Imagism to William Carlos Williams to Raymond Souster), but influences among movements of ideas. Graham Hough in *Image and Experience* noted that 'even in its longer flights Imagism is a small affair. But as a centre and an influence it is not small. It is the hard irreducible core of a whole cluster of poetic ideas that extend far beyond Imagism as a movement.'[39] Hough argues that Joyce's 'epiphany' and Eliot's 'objective correlative' gained much of their momentum as literary concepts from their subliminal echo of Pound's Imagist doctrine and concludes that Imagism 'connects itself easily with other speculations and manoeuvres which start from a different point.'[40] This seems a useful method for the extension of the Imagist example forward into the century, and one can hazard a guess at some of the stepping stones between 1917 and the Second World War.

Eliot and Pound shared general doctrinal power over poetic innovation well into the war years. By 1920 Pound had worked out much of the idea of the *Cantos* if not its later variations; *The Waste Land* demonstrated in 1922 – via Pound's precise laceration – some of the ways in which Imagist juxtaposition could be used to structure longer texts. These powerful examples, especially Eliot's, were to weaken somewhat during the 1930s, however, as geopolitical and economic urgency moved younger poets – inspired and ambivalently led by W.H. Auden – to a more discursive and historicist manner than Eliot's early critical ideas of aesthetic autonomy and impersonality, codified, had made possible. But Auden would not therefore escape the Imagist legacy, despite his evident discomfort with the fragmented and asyntactic structure it demanded. During the 1930s his characteristic treatment of scene and mood accepts Imagist methods of dissonant juxtaposition, and his practice was certainly crucial to the forties search for fresh renderings of the phenomenal world – a particular concern of *First Statement* editorials, as of *Preview* practice.

'High' modernism in its relation to Imagism has been fully charted by Gage in his *In the Arresting Eye: The Rhetoric of Imagism*. But the danger of my invoking such powerful exemplars as Eliot, Pound, and Auden is that a 'great men' emphasis can cut us off from the byways of literary development, often more telling for local and particular traditions like the forties Canadian. Other phenomena which helped to develop Imagist doctrines into the war years are less clearly canonical but perhaps more suggestive. I refer to three coincident literary-cultural fashions of 1936–7: English Surrealism, a brief phenomenon spearheaded by poet David Gascoyne and the Surrealist Exhibition in London in 1936; the meteoric rise of Dylan Thomas, whose vehement denial of Surrealist influences suggests their power in his development; and Mass Observation, especially in its enactment in the Oxford Collective Poem of 1937. The sudden popularity of three new visions of the image's relation to the whole poem suggests – even in a year of international war consciousness and dread – that such issues were not remote from but vital to the new directions of modernist poetry in the 1940s.

English Surrealism was, to be sure, a minor moment in the country's literature, and even in Gascoyne's, and no English Surrealist poet was to enjoy the extended influence of André Bréton, the French movement's originator and theorist. But Gascoyne remained well read by young poets in the 1940s and provided in both poetry and theory a Surrealist conduit to Page's generation. Surrealist, like Imagist, doctrine quickly lost its prescriptive power once the boundaries of 'the surreal' in verbal and visual art were pushed outward from the core principle, in this case, of creative automatism (in poetry 'automatic writing'), until conscious artistic control had been reinstated. But the similarity of Surrealist and Imagist poetics is striking, particularly in their fusion of images and theoretical subordination of the artist's conscious role in their generation. Paul C. Ray calls that force which brings two previously unlinked visualizations or thoughts together 'objective chance,' its function in the Surrealist artwork strikingly like the function of Pound's binary Image:

Every real encounter, then, involves a convergence of two series of events: one which results in the existence of the object and its being in the right place at the right moment, and the other in the need for just that object in the seeker and on his being in the right place at the right moment. The fulfillment of all these conditions produces the flash of revelation that is the sign of objective chance, of the reconciliation of the subjective with the objective, of the world answering the mind's desire on the plane of the surreal.[41]

Compare this model of 'convergence' with the force of juxtaposition in Imagist poetics, with the Imagist effort to elide the subjective ground of the poem's structure, and with Gage's proof of 'the impossibility ... of distinguishing the objective from the subjective in imagist poetry.'[42] The Imagist and Surrealist poets arrive at these similar premises from opposite directions – the one in effect by refreshing the eyes, the other by closing them – but their mutuality of purpose is apparent. We can therefore add to Hough's list of 'other speculations and manoeuvres which start from a different point' from Imagism and arrive at similar aesthetic premises the Surrealist enterprise, especially as it was adopted in England by poets already aware of Imagist demands. The impact of Surrealism on the forties – in Canada or in England – is largely unstudied, but for present purposes we need merely note that a very recent school of English poetry offers a possible renewal of Imagist implications for the decade of Page. (That Anderson was in England at the time of the Surrealist fashion may suggest a readier conduit to hand; Layton, too, would show the Surrealist effect, for which see chapter 3.)

Another relation among Imagism, Surrealism, and the Canadian forties emerges if we reconsider Dylan Thomas's protests that he was not a Surrealist poet.[43] Thomas's stunning poetics took the mid-thirties by storm, incorporating and renewing the rediscovered rhythms and diction of Gerard Manley Hopkins, the lapsing faiths of thirties intellectual aspiration, and Welsh bardism. Although Thomas rejected, like Auden, the structural demands of early Imagism, his verses move forward by a juxtaposition of striking and exaggerated metaphors that draw deliberate local attention:

Foster the light nor veil the manshaped moon,
Nor weather winds that blow not down the bone,
But strip the twelve-winded marrow from his circle;
Master the night nor serve the snowman's brain
That shapes each bushy item of the air
Into a polestar pointed on an icicle.[44]

The reader choosing to respond to this by 'making sense' of it must begin within the individual line, guessing at relations between polestars and icicles, bushes and air, and so on. The task is very similar to that which we face with Pound's 'In a Station of the Metro,' except that the Imagist juxtapositions are here so multiplied that the leisure of reason is taken away. Beyond that phrasal reaction one must make syntactic as well as Imagist sense of the relations among lines and thence among stanzas. Thomas generated, *contra* the analytic discursiveness of Auden, an explosive and impacted poetics incorporating the automatism of Surrealism with the Imagist dicta of juxtaposition, subordination of the perceiving consciousness, and radicalization of metaphor. If Thomas's example was as important to the poets of the forties as most accounts suggest, these structural implications of his poetics are another part of the general period influence of Imagism.

A third – more minor but equally useful – link between Imagist practice and the forties is the brief phenomenon of 1936–7 (coincident with English Surrealist activity and Thomas's emergence) known as 'Mass Observation,' briefly remarked in the introduction.[45] Hundreds of Britons were asked to record each day the image they had found dominant in their visual experience; the resulting archive was meant to be one of the most complex and faithful records of English social history ever conceived (and can still be consulted at the University of Sussex.)[46] Half anthropological speculation, half epistemological ideology, Mass Observation was

an attempt to take Socialist Realism back to a point beyond style and even subject matter, to its sources in proletarian consciousness. Since in Mass-Observation that consciousness is *mass*-consciousness, there is also an implied shift of the basis of artistic creation from the individual to the mass, and this provides both a theoretical foundation and a collective method for a new revolutionary art.[47]

The literary implications of Mass Observation are exemplified in the 'Oxford

Collective Poem,' printed with an introductory note by poet Charles Madge in Geoffrey Grigson's *New Verse* in 1937 to coincide with 'Mass Observation [Coronation] Day,' 12 May 1937. A dozen undergraduate Oxford poets were enlisted to perform largely the same kind of daily visual recording, but their particular purpose was to distil the hundreds of resulting images, debating their virtues by committee, into a single 'collective' poem:

> Believe the iron saints who stride the floods,
> Lying in red and labouring for the dawn:
> Steeples repeat their warnings; along the roads
> Memorials stand, of children force has slain;
> Expostulating with the winds they hear
> Stone kings irresolute on a marble stair.[48]

The style of this passage is strikingly similar to that of Thomas's 'Foster the Light,' quoted above, with which it is contemporary. The connection between the Oxford Collective Poem and Imagism is also apparent, for it, too, juxtaposes strongly visual phrases to create meanings whose interpenetrative resonance is the force of 'meaning' in the poem. (It also invites comparison with the poetics of Patrick Anderson, president of the Oxford Student Union during its compilation; he was not, alas, seconded by Madge.)[49]

Poet and literary historian Kathleen Raine considered the Oxford Collective Poem more than a campus idiosyncracy. She read it as an ironic reflection of poetic experiments in England at the time, linking it, for instance, with the Surrealism of Gascoyne. The attempt to forge a relation between the individual creative vision and the 'objective' phenomena of mass experience strikes her as essential to 1930s poetic effort:

> This conception made possible a kind of poetic (or pictorial) imagery at once irrational and objective ... Thus the poet re-assumes the ancient role at once of national prophet and reader of the auguries; not from entrails or yarrow-stalks, but from (literally) the 'writings on walls,' the seemingly fortuitous recurring images in the daily records. Anything and everything speaks to the augur attuned to its meaning. The two apparently irreconcilable opposites are in such poetry brought together: imaginative inspiration, and a realistic objectivity.[50]

Such investigation of the boundary between subjective imagination and objective pictorialization was a major if implicit goal of the Imagist doctrines enunciated by Pound in 1913. (Indeed, I shall contend that this search for a fusion of subjective and objective modes was constitutive of Canadian poetic development well into the 1950s.) The connections that thus emerge among Imagism, Surrealism, Thomas, and Mass-Observation suggest powerfully the extent to which Imagist consciousness generated or coincided strikingly with poetic experiment right up to the Second World War.

Avant-garde British modernisms of the pre-war focus suddenly, then, and tellingly, on new ways of generating, expressing, and incorporating the image, as the period of Canada's modernist maturity took shape. If from this insight from eccentric literary history we return to the obvious transmission of Imagist principle *via* mainstream figures such as Eliot, Pound, and Auden, not to mention Smith and Scott, we can reasonably acknowledge the power of Imagist doctrine well into the Canadian forties. Page herself acknowledged such a history when asked by Michael Heenan if 'the work of Ezra Pound and the Imagists [has] influenced your aesthetics and poetry':

> I don't think that Pound and the Imagists have had any direct influence on my work. To say that they have had no influence would be absurd. A figure like Pound who, in his *Cantos*, spilled so much gold into the air we breathe, could hardly have not had an affect [*sic*] in one way or another. He must have changed the whole poetic body and as a minor part of that body, I must have been affected by him.[51]

As Page recognizes, a given poet's indifference to Pound's Imagism will not necessarily entail rejection of the Imagist essentials: visual emphasis, fragmentation, decontextualization of objects, juxtaposition and subjective–objective inquiry. Such is the paradox and force of the Imagist legacy.

All of the texts I have mentioned in relation to that legacy manifest the challenge of building on powerful autonomous images in the move to longer and more discursive structures. Once original Imagist poetics had deteriorated into impressionistic, subjective, and often sentimental[52] verse, the Imagist motive required new forms that could embody and yet extrapolate from the primary doctrine. This project can be formulated, in retrospect, as a series of questions which Canadian poets felt it necessary to answer in the middle of the century. The most obvious of these had to do with the nature of the images appropriate to modern poetry. Once the binary energy of Pound's Image has been surrendered, there is a danger, as Graham Hough drily puts it, 'that the whole natural world offers to the poet a collection of bric-à-brac from which he takes selections to represent emotional states'[53] – that the Imagist legacy could be used to justify catalogued verbal snapshots without visceral energy, without what Pound called the 'goatish ability to butt.'[54] Indeed, several poems discussed in this book pursue such a potentially flaccid method. The relation between Imagist poetics and the 'real' world is an ambiguous one. On the one hand, the doctrine demands immediate and concrete language and visualization, but, on the other, it rejects passive 'recording' as its model of visual perception. Ignore that proscription, and the next crux in the debate is prompt: which – or whose – 'real' world to record. When, for example, *First Statement* posits its own attachment to the phenomenal world in contrast to *Preview*'s supposed refusal to do so, it really privileges a particular *political* view of the phenomenal world, a world in which the ugliness of poverty and despair are, to be frank, stylish. But that cannot mean that *Preview*'s 'world,' with brief pastoral glimpses complicating its occasional urban portraiture, is less 'real' than *First Statement*'s, just less locally fashionable. Such largely fruitless and transitory tastes would energize debate over image mannerisms well past the mid-century.

A second and more serious problem raised by the Imagist burden is the nature of poetic structure itself, especially in the longer experiments demanded, it seems, after the Great War. The most obvious means of producing such structures was the simple accumulation of brief images without governing paradigms of voice, theme, or conceit; as Gage has it, 'the simplest, though not the most frequent, means of creating longer imagist poems is simply to link short imagist poems end to end, with no transitions to provide the reader with a sense of necessity compelling a conclusion.'[55] Yvor Winters, one of Imagism's important dissenters, quickly identified the danger of such aesthetics in 'The Testament of a Stone, Being Notes on the Mechanics of the Poetic Image' (1924), its final section entitled 'Upon the Construction of the Poem, with Relation to the Image':

> Many poets have entirely omitted any intellectual sequence from one image to the next, depending upon an emotional unity ... Other poets have attempted to carry the method even further, omitting all intellectual (syntactical) sequence within the image, or trying to, attempting to create aesthetic relationships from broken words and phrases ... The difficulty ... is that, having cast out all other thought from their minds, they cannot cast out the clichés, the very old sentimentalities, which seem to be so deeply rooted as to be almost mental reflexes. Their poems become, then, desperate efforts to conceal those clichés under a broken exterior, which is evading the question.[56]

Winters hits upon the problem of coherence that dogs Imagist development. He notes the tension between the fragmented surface of post-Imagist style and its underlying sentimentalism, but he fails to perceive that the urge to sentimentalize may itself be the result of the accumulative aesthetic's desperation for unity at any cost.

Without some such grounding, the post-Imagist poem has neither beginning nor end, neither subjective nor objective truthfulness. It could be extended if the poet simply draped an eye over yet another phenomenon, and the poem would be largely unchanged by the addition. It would be slavish in its photosensitivity, but aggressively egotistical in the poet's presumption that the phenomena of his or her world cast in his or her words were worth our attention. It would exclude history – the impersonal eye's experiences are not time-bound – and metaphysics, direct contemplation of the noumenal. A third question emerges: how might one render such a poem coherent without sacrificing its exemplary adherence to radical Imagist disruptions?

Joseph Frank, whose 1945 essay 'Spatial Form in Modern Literature' is among the shrewdest forties addresses to modernist form, took the problem to lie at the heart of contemporary poetry's potential and danger:

> [The Imagist] view of the nature of poetry immediately gave rise to numerous problems. How was more than one image to be included in a poem? If the chief value of an image was its capacity to present an intellectual and emotional complex simultaneously, linking images in a sequence would clearly destroy most of their efficacy. Or was the poem itself one vast image, whose individual components were to be apprehended as a unity? But then it would be necessary to undermine the inherent consecutiveness of language, frustrating the reader's normal expectation of a sequence and forcing him to perceive the elements of the poem as juxtaposed in space rather than unrolling in time.[57]

To deal with such issues, as Gage has shown, modernist poets had to renegotiate their negative responses to elements of traditional prosody eschewed by Imagist doctrine: personation, argument, narrative, syntax, abstraction, and so on. It becomes possible to conceive much modernist poetic development from this point of structural crisis forward as a cacophony of answers to the problem Frank later identified. It is not surprising in this sense that Eliot's confirmation as Anglo-Catholic, Pound's as Fascist, Auden's as Socialist occurred soon after Winters had identified the crisis of later Imagist practice in 1924. In each case the new meta-narrative offered (among other things) a means of subsuming fragmented cultural experience and restoring the 'wholeness' of vision that was to become such a pronounced *desideratum* of forties poetic debate.

In the preamble to 'Spatial Form,' Frank had remarked a curious inattention in the 1940s to the relation between the literary and the 'plastic' arts, especially 'at present [1945] when so many writers on aesthetic problems are occupied with questions of form.'[58] He would go on to offer an interpretation of modernist literary form which would account for its powerful dialectics of unity and fragmentation by comparing its wholeness with the spatial organization of signifiers in painting and sculpture. In so doing he signalled the 1940s' need for an account of modernism's dislocated formalism that would clarify its means of coherence and comprehensiveness, in a period in which objectivist image patterns would look dilettantish and indifferent to unprecedented global violence. Only a year later, in 1946, Cecil Day Lewis would deliver the Clark Lectures at Cambridge University on the subject 'The Poetic Image,' and he, too, would be keenly concerned to find a compelling account of modern poetic wholeness, to counter the unintegrated 'festoons of imagery'[59] dominating recent poetry.

Day Lewis, a poet apprenticed after all in the prolonged pre-war anxieties of the 1930s, grants that 'when a social pattern is changing, when the beliefs or structure of a society are in process of disintegration, the poets should instinctively go farther and more boldly afield in a search for images which may reveal new patterns.'[60] The concern of his lectures is clearly not that modern poets reduce the density or obscurity of their imagery but rather that they learn to discriminate *good* image-crowding from bad, and the key will be their generating an impression of what he calls 'wholeness,' a structural and thematic soundness that we can both intuit and reason about. Sadly, 'what the modern poet often sacrifices through his violent and inconsequent use of images is not consistency of impression so much as this wholeness ...'[61] Surveying 'After the Funeral' by Dylan Thomas, however, he notes that, '[t]hough the image pattern is most intense and closely wrought, the images are centrifugal. And yet I am very sure that it is a *whole* poem.' He finds his impression critically unaccountable, though: 'What is it, then, that has prevented this centrifugal strain from disintegrating the texture, as so often happens with contemporary verse of this *genre*, giving us instead of a poem a handful of whirling fragments?'[62]

Day Lewis clearly anticipates A.M. Klein's now well-known notebook entries of 1948 regarding 'centrifugal' and 'centripetal' forces in modern poetry (see chapter 2, p. 112); like Klein, he finds it difficult to visualize or articulate a poetics of limitation and containment for such forces. Day Lewis's attempts to engage this fundamental forties question remain obscure. In a New Critical inflection, 'wholeness' is a 'clear supremacy of theme over decoration and detail';[63] in a more suggestive but opaque formulation, '[w]holeness lies, surely, in imaginative statement which creates a pure imaginative response reaching out beyond the limits of a theme towards human experience on all sides, yet at the same time perfectly satisfied within those limits.'[64] Too close historically, perhaps, to the poetic problem he was attempting to resolve, Day Lewis cannot quite say what will constitute 'wholeness' for the forties poem; but he clearly enjoins a search for it upon his post-Imagist contemporaries.

Some exemplary critical minds were turning in the mid-1940s, then, to a reconfiguration of modernist poetics that would stress its accomplishment of aesthetic completeness, rather than its increasingly orthodox embodiment of cultural fragmentation. New poets of the decade were asking strikingly similar questions. One of the most powerful calls for structural 'wholeness' in modernist poetry – one might call it the forties 'coining' of the term, for it precedes Day Lewis's usage – is in the documents of the New Apocalypse poets in England, especially in the writings of G.S. Fraser and Henry Treece during the war years. Of preliminary importance here is Treece's acknowledgment of the antecedents of Apocalyptic doctrine:

> Poetry written with such a belief will make use of all forms, or no form; it will use music to elucidate meaning and sense to strengthen sound; its images will at times be as photographic as anything created by the Imagists, and at other times an adumbration of a world as yet unknown ... [here Treece quotes Fraser:] 'Apocalypse in a sense derives from Surrealism, and one might even call it a dialectical development of it; the next stage forward. It embodies what is positive in Surrealism. It denies what is negative – Surrealism's own denial of man's right to exercise conscious control ...'[65]

The Apocalyptics clearly wanted to acknowledge their descent from the Imagists (and in doing so endorsed the Imagist legacy I sketched through Surrealism), but they also clearly felt the lack in such poetics. Imagism had descended into the hands of 'picture makers' who sacrificed the sense of integrity in their poetic structures;[66] Surrealism had suspended the power of conscious will, a commodity at a premium in the struggle against the Axis. These Apocalyptic demurs from late Imagist practice engage a larger spiritual and psychological concern for humanity's well-being; according to Fraser, drawing on J.F. Hendry, 'the unnatural economic life of the present time has produced a split in man's mind, has made of him a half-conscious, half-living machine. For Hendry the first object of any art is therefore to restore the wholeness of man, to make him conscious once more of all his faculties ...'[67] Treece has it that 'Apocalyptic writing ... insists on the fusion of all elements of life and thought, at the highest pitch of intensity. It will teach man to aspire towards wholeness ...'[68]

This return to 'wholeness' in poetry and in selfhood was to be enacted, in part, by a new attitude to the relation between the individual image and the whole poem. As Treece puts it, '[t]he image must be reborn, then, to heart as well as to head, to sense as well as to sound, to health as well as sickness, to the world invisible no less than to the world of objects. In short, to a new WHOLENESS.'[69] Therefore, '[c]riticism of Apocalyptic writing will, I think, ultimately be based not on the writer's selectivity, but rather on his ability to combine, to fuse into a justifiable whole, his several sets of experience ...'[70] This important turn from the hidden subjectivism of Imagism – which lies in its *unacknowledged* selection of 'random' images – was never enacted with particular success by the Apocalyptic poets. Indeed, the school is far more significant for its enunciation of some key forties doctrines than for any poetry it produced as a result. But its relevance to the Canadian context is assured by the catholic reading of Irving Layton at that time. In his 'Politics and Poetry' in *First Statement* (August 1943), he recommends the Apocalyptics, especially Treece and M.J. Tambimuttu, to his Canadian readers as a corrective of the thirties preoccupation with doctrinaire politics and artificially abstract diction. (A derivatively Apocalyptic poem by one Paul Halley, entitled, indeed, 'Apocalypse,' appeared in *First Statement* soon after.)[71] Treece's emphasis on poetic 'wholeness' had reached the Montreal *cénacles* in some form soon after its emergence in England.

Therefore, when John Sutherland completes his attack on Ralph Gustafson's 'rows of dead verbs like stone pigeons' by claiming that *First Statement* will reveal 'a more wholesome trend' ('Two Schools'); when he claims that the poetry of Louis Dudek and Irving Layton is 'much more honest and wholesome than that of our modernist school' ('Editorial,' *FS* 1.12); when he speaks in broader Apocalyptic language of Anderson's 'failure to distinguish between the self and reality ... a personal incapacity that accounts for ... the excessively metaphorical style, that destroys the unity of his poems,'[72] or of Page's 'lack of selection and unity' in presenting 'metaphors which depend on the confusion of the body with an inanimate thing, and which spring out of ... fear,'[73] he continues more or less unwittingly a debate about the relation between local image and poetic 'whole' that was contemporary and vital. In this context *First Statement*'s attacks on the manner of metaphor accumulation in *Preview* are far more intelligible, as a generational conflict reflective of international literary debate.

A historical contextualization of the *First Statement* attack on *Preview* is valuable (and I hope there will be others), but I have surveyed these materials at length for another reason. In my readings of Canadian forties poetry, I find this desire for a new wholeness for modernist poetics – and its inversion, a fear of formal incoherence, a gift for striking images left insignificant and unimpactful – to bind the Montreal poets in a common undertaking far more profound and interesting than their repetitive distinction by little-magazine affiliation has been. It's true that John Sutherland and Patrick Anderson seem merely to replicate the problem of a hyper-imagistic style without showing much sensible concern with its implications, and I have exploited their poetry in brief introductory remarks intended merely to dramatize the possibility of a common *Preview–First Statement* location in poetic history. But P.K. Page, A.M. Klein, Irving Layton, and Louis Dudek, all of whom pursued an image-dense, accumulative, and arguably incoherent poetics at some period in their development, display with equal force the difficulty of sustaining such a modernism, the cost of its impersonalist grounding to the poet's self-expression and self-realization, and the possible routes forward.

Their chief difficulty lay in the integrity of their modernism: none of the four was interested in a regression to the traditional poetics, to old forms of lyric or narrative framing, that had been critiqued and superseded by the first dislocating wave of modernist experiment. On the contrary, in poem after poem they sought new principles of structural coherence that would really be predicated on, that would not seek to override, the essential fragmentation, obscurity, and formal violence that in their view still constituted the vital gains of modernist poetics. So much so, in fact, that their desire for a new wholeness in their poems is often visible alongside, and simultaneous with, a steady raising of the stakes of poetic integration and soundness, as the poem seeks to incorporate more, and more intense, images of the phenomenal world. In a collective vision that makes sense of Eysteinsson's claim of the modernist's 'aesthetic heroism,'[74] mid-century poets intuited a dual pressure to offer still more random and disjunctive styles and yet to create ever more subtle though powerful forces for the poem's structural stability.[75] The poets who avoided this conundrum – the early accumulative Anderson, arguably, at one extreme, and Raymond Souster's minimalist simplicity at the other – miss, in this sense, the decade's fundamental opportunity of poetic growth and accomplishment.

In Day Lewis's handling, this wholeness is largely a thematic unity: the Thomas poem can be praised for a 'counterpoint and cross-reference of image' that we can work up into a good New Critical reading, one which will establish a 'clear supremacy of theme over decoration and detail.'[76] I have no strenuous objection to such an understanding of the critic's task, but its failings for my purposes here are its thematic emphasis and its presumption that poetic coherence, seeking 'supremacy ... over decoration,' is somehow distinct from, and opposed to, poetic complexity, an idea the modernist *poets* particularly subverted. The forties poets were not looking for a new thematic unity so much as a new idea of structural stability, an arrangement of aleatory particulars with enough artistry that a strong impression of the poem's coherence is granted the reader even before its thematic comprehensiveness is certain. To use a metaphor of my own, they would be interested more in the surface tension that sustains the shape of a bead of water than in the symbolism of such a drop, or its temperature, or its chances of quenching our thirst. They sought a concept of wholeness that would not struggle against multiplicity and particularity but rather be in some way identifiable with the things contained – images, concepts, and so on – as is the water bead's surface tension with the water itself.

Before I try to put flesh on these bare conceptual bones in readings of Page's early poetry, I want a better term than 'wholeness' (and better than 'unity') for the structural energy that makes aleatory or image-accumulative modernist poems forcibly complete. 'Wholeness' is valuable – obviously forties commentators found it so – because it asks us to think not so much of internal self-reference as external completeness, a perimeter or skin bounding and defining the poem's powerful accumulative energies. Still, its easy shading into 'wholesomeness,' Sutherland's preferred antonym to 'modernist,' is undesirable. 'Coherence' is similarly contaminated by its opposite, 'incoherence,' a term that has surrendered almost all reference to lack of structural soundness and has instead come to suggest inarticulacy and verbal slurring. Without pretending to a stark differentiation from 'coherence' and 'wholeness' but wishing to negate their connotations, I henceforth call this quest-object of forties poetry, after Aquinas but chiefly *via* Joyce's Stephen Dedalus, *integritas*. Stephen's appropriation of Aquinas's idea in his delicately fraudulent enunciations in *A Portrait of the Artist as a Young Man* summarizes ideally, if ponderously, the nature of art's projection of self-sufficiency, the stability of structure, and distinctness of inclusion so desired by mid-century poets:

> The first phase of apprehension is a bounding line drawn about the object to be apprehended. An esthetic image is presented to us either in space or in time. What is audible is presented in time, what is visible is presented in space. But, temporal or spatial, the esthetic image is first luminously apprehended as selfbounded and selfcontained upon the immeasurable background of space or time which is not it. You apprehend it as *one* thing. You see it as one whole. You apprehend its wholeness. That is *integritas*.
>
> – Bull's eye! said Lynch, laughing.[77]

With the accuracy of Stephen's rendering of Aquinas, as with the degree of irony mediating his ideas in Joyce's handling, I am unconcerned (although my inclusion of Lynch's boisterous answer is an indication of my leaning on the latter question).

The passage is worth raiding rather because Joyce's aesthetics had an exemplary force in discussions of modernist poetics, and particularly so in the period of interest to this study.[78] Edmund Wilson's *Axel's Castle* of 1931 was an early but still powerful example of the tendency of modernist commentators to make levies on Joyce's aesthetics for the elucidation of the modernist project. Joseph Frank's 'Spatial Form in Modern Literature' with its exemplification of modern formal practice through *Ulysses* appeared in 1945; he shares Stephen's interest in the difference between art forms apprehended in space and those apprehended in time. A.M. Klein's own obsession with *Ulysses* in the late 1940s was such as to threaten his personal coherence, as we shall see in chapter 2; he would reconceive the Aquinian triad (*integritas, consonantia, claritas*) in his 'Marginalia' in 1948. I take these exploitations of Joyce's ideas as evidence of their centrality to the period I am interested in and think it fair to borrow Stephen's term, and most of his definition, for my own purposes.

Certainly that definition, however I may wish to avoid Joyce's layered ironies, embraces many 1940s concerns regarding poems' energy and wholeness. Indeed, Stephen's translation of *integritas* as 'wholeness' is the common one. To *integritas* read as 'wholeness' one may add other nuances of connotation, such as 'completeness, soundness,' as well as 'purity, correctness,'[79] all more or less pertinent to the kind of structural firmness the poets were after. The echo of and important distinction from the word 'integrity' is also useful: the echo because it reminds us of the inescapable connection between conceptions of personal and of poetic wholeness, looming large in this book; the distinction because 'integrity' bears moral and ethical resonances I am happy by this means to avoid. I will also have regular need of Stephen's idea that we must perceive the boundary that marks off the work of art from the world to which it refers in order to enjoy its *integritas*: the accumulative post-Imagism of the forties period style risks blurring precisely that boundary, as its incorporative method projects a vanishing point in which the whole world has been catalogued, in what Louis Dudek will much later call 'the infinite poem' (see chapter 4, pp. 252, 278).

In this sense, the force of *integritas* is inseparable from the poem's field of reference. While flaunting their incorporative power, modernist poems create their structural boundaries, in part, by including so much, and not more, of the fragmented world to which they refer. In this sense they project a second-order 'real world'– different in degree but not in kind of aleatory complexity from *the* real world – which is sufficient to their interpretation. All poems supply some such outer sphere of sufficient reference: when we read a lyric poem, for example, we consider that all utterances in the poem are referrable to the mind and experience of a single speaker. When we face interpretive cruces in our readings of the poem, our answers may vary, but they will all have to be commensurable with that single governing consciousness that is fundamental to the poem's references. When a modernist poem abandons the construction of a single speaker, and when it further heightens the rapidity and obscurity of verbal concatenations, it invites us to appreciate its randomness, its freedom from traditional constraint, but it is free to do so only because it has adopted other, less familiar forms of constraint that we try to articulate. Among these is the projection of a sufficient sphere of poetic reference to which we may appeal, a world we trust to have some coherence of its own. And in a surprising number of modernist poems, we intersect that referential sphere with the plane of a single consciousness, as Hugh Kenner did in dealing with Pound's 'In a Station of the Metro': 'The "plot" of the poem is that mind's activity, fetching some new thing into the field of consciousness.'[80] What a single mind, however learned or eccentric, *can* believably refer to is among modernist poetry's new models of limitation and containment.

As the 1940s progressed, this connection between the mimesis of fragmented consciousness and the representation of an object-world would become more apparent to the Montreal poets, as to poets elsewhere. Perhaps the most enlivening idea of the Apocalyptics, visible too in Sutherland's criticism, is their insistent connection of the disintegration of psychic life, 'the split in man's mind,' under the impact of modernity with the disintegration of poetic form under the Imagist line of modernism. Poetry cannot be healed, Treece insists, without attention to the 'wholeness' of personal life. The recognition will prove fundamental to the Canadian forties search for *integritas*. We have already seen its debased form in Sutherland's personally inflected criticisms of Anderson and Page: their reactions suggest an understandable desire for an inviolable boundary between poetic styles and psychic life. But Page had admitted their inseparability as early as 1946 in 'If It Were You': there her persona challenges a (probably male) interlocutor scornful of those for whom the self's incoherence renders the images of the object world inarticulable, cluttered, and confused:

If it were you, say, you
who scanning the personal map one day knew
your sharp eyes water and grow colour blind,
unable to distinguish green from blue
and everything terribly run together as if rain
had smudged the markings on the paper ...

and if you became lost, say, on the lawn,

unable to distinguish left from right
and that strange longitude that divides the body
sharply in half – that line that separates
so that one hand could never be the other –
dissolved and both your hands were one ...
would you call help like a woman assaulted,
cry to be found? (*GA*, p. 38)

This 'garden seems to emblematize poetic vision run amuck,' as Laura Killian notes,[81] and Page's opposition of 'sharp eyes' and a world 'rain / had smudged' into indistinct forms and colours powerfully anticipates her eventual self-critique in 'After Rain.' Here the condition is projected onto a helpless other, although the speaker's angry insistence that it's 'you bewildered – not me this time' suggests that the argument has in the past had charged personal implications.

Page's intuition here that poetic *integritas* has a frightening but inescapable connection to psychic wholeness was prophetic of a decade's work in Canadian poetry that lay ahead, but it was not, not even for her, very helpful. The poets of the period continued to work in the forties with largely impersonal and image-accumulative styles, at occasional cost, as I shall suggest, to their creative confidence. The correlation of mental and poetic dissolution was dramatic in the career of A.M. Klein, of course, whose body of poetry would be more or less complete two years after Page's poem appeared; and in his poems of those two years the relation of a meaningful and coherent world to a sense of psychic soundness is a stark longing. When Louis Dudek and Irving Layton moved forward in the early 1950s from these problems of forties poetic expression, they did so in the conviction – now historically understandable – that a return to representations of the self was essential to a renovation of poetry. All share with the Apocalyptics an intuition, not entirely welcome, that the new exigencies of mid-century social and political life would impose dramatic new demands of self-conception and self-revelation. Apart from historical forces urging self-sacrifice, from the outbreak of civil war in Spain to the end of the Second World War, and apart from private circumstances of ethnicity and gender that made self-revelation a complex matter, for Anderson, Page, and Klein, as for Layton and Dudek, there were modernist dicta of regulatory force to be challenged only uneasily at the time – a nexus of forces that helps to explain why the overwhelming majority of poetry written in the Canadian forties was impersonal in manner and matter.

The conceptual ground on which the forties poets struggled to differentiate themselves from early modernist strictures they were finding untenable, T.S.

Eliot's various doctrines of 'impersonality' would dominate poetic debate well into the 1950s. Recent discussions of the concept by Maud Ellmann and Astradur Eysteinsson have shown that Eliot was little concerned to give the idea a consistent sense and have suggested, as had Gage, that impersonality and subjectivism are hardly such separable concepts in poetry as some modernist dogma sought to imply. Eliot's own highly personal poetry is the best exemplification of the contradiction inherent in the doctrine, as his critics have long recognized. Eysteinsson's argument about Joyce's *Ulysses* is similar:

> In *Ulysses*, for example, it is near impossible to detect a narrator or narrative perspectives that can decidedly be said to represent the author. In that limited sense, the text might be called antisubjective or impersonal (and Joyce was indeed a spokesman of a 'poetics of impersonality'), but at the same time we experience in the work radical modes of subjective representation of reality, to the extent that outside reality comes to lose its habitual, mimetic reliability. But so does the 'reality' of individual experiences mediated through the text, and in this respect the effect of such 'subjective' methods is clearly related to that 'loss of self' or the 'erasure of personality' that exhausts many characters in modern fiction ... This foregrounds a decisive point: what the modernist poetics of impersonality and that of extreme subjectivity have in common (and this outweighs whatever may separate them) is a revolt against the traditional relation of the subject to the outside world.[82]

In Eliot alone, as Maud Ellmann remarks, the 'personality' extinguished in the objectivity of great art involved, variously, 'the theological soul ... the philosophical subject, psychological consciousness, legal individual, or grammatical first person.'[83] Caring little for the theorization of poetics, Canadian poets tended to identify only the last of these for suppression, perhaps convinced that its absence would guarantee the elimination of all other subjectivisms.

By the 1940s, their ambivalence over the device was palpable. Page's first poem for *Preview* may be, ironically enough, in the first person, but only so as to be loud about the speaker's impersonal devotions. In 'Desiring Only ...' (1942) the persona expresses an unambiguous desire for her eroticized addressee but wants 'only the bone on the Mount of Venus'; any attached subjectivity will be unwelcome:

> pass me no hand, then, as an offertory,
> no, nor sound of your voice.
> Keep silent and do not touch me,
> even the air on my face is an effrontery ...

Desiring only the bare soles of the feet
pacing triumphantly the ultimate basement ...
pass me no thick-carpeted personal contact ...

Some will psychologize and suggest that a constitutive irony in 'Desiring Only ...' makes plain the speaker's (or Page's) suppressed *need* for 'personal contact,' but the poem's closing sneer at shows 'of pity and understanding' is too convincing to my ear to support the argument. Eliot's idea still made for powerful orthodoxy in 1942; Perkins says that 'the prestige of high modernist style was such that departures from it caused misgivings of conscience, and poets feared they could overcome the modernist isolation of poetry only by diluting the modernist artistic achievement.'[84]

Such dogma remained powerful in Canada throughout the period of Page's most prolific activity. Their force is apparent, albeit by a curious inversion, in Henry W. Wells's *Where Poetry Stands Now,* published by the Toronto scholar with Ryerson in 1948 (along with Klein's *The Rocking Chair*). In Wells's argument, 'personalism' is poetic solipsism: the poet manipulates the difficult symbols of a private world for her own aesthetic pleasure while expressing little of the coherent force of personality that might help to contain or translate those symbols for a readership. He calls 'impersonalist' that lyric, subjective and direct poetry in which the poet sets aside his own private symbolism in favour of self-expression in a poetic language that all his readers might value in common – an unselfishness that stresses the poet's duty to communicate as simply as possible with an audience. In this formulation the impersonality of Page, for instance, with its concomitant idiosyncrasy of symbolism and reference, makes her a 'personalist.'

Wells is chiefly arguing against the polarization of the two kinds of poetry, since 'good poetry is that which most equally and successfully combines personal and impersonal qualities' (p. vii), but the eccentricity of his terminology suggests some of the decade's difficulties in grappling with the force of modernist impersonality in an era demanding intense personal commitments. Eliot himself recognized the inevitability of the decade's poetic change in his coincident 1948 lecture 'From Poe to Valéry':

I believe that the *art poétique* of which we find the germ in Poe, and which bore fruit in the work of Valéry, has gone as far as it can go. I do not believe that this aesthetic can be of any help to later poets. What will take its place I do not know. An aesthetic which merely contradicted it would not do. To insist on the all-importance of subject-matter, to insist that the poet should be spontaneous and irreflective, that he should depend upon inspiration and neglect technique would be a lapse from what is in any case a highly civilised attitude to a barbarian one.[85]

Eliot's tone is wistful, and it is a measure of his continued perspicacity that he should so accurately forecast the immediate future of English poetics even as he tries in a gentlemanly way to pre-empt likely excesses. To consider his negative anticipation here of the Layton poet-persona of the early 1950s is to note how close to the fulcrum of forties poetic change his mind remained, his increasing rejection by young poets notwithstanding.

It should now be apparent that still-persistent ideas of adherence to impersonality in *Preview* or to lyric in *First Statement* avoid the real complexity of forties poetic discourses. The value of impersonality did indeed dominate the transition in Canadian poetry in the years between P.K. Page's first two volumes. The poets of both Montreal little magazines *were* fighting through the forties a battle over the status of the subject in modern poetry – but fighting not so clearly with one another as within themselves, and within their art; so much so that *Preview*'s rivals at *First Statement* were themselves largely impersonal poets throughout the decade. That battle is their Canadian version of the broad modern search for a new *integritas* that would permit poetry's adherence to *and* growth beyond late-Imagist accumulation: the coherent force of the poem would become by the mid-1950s the delineation *through presence or absence* of the poet's speaking voice, whether we think of Dudek's itinerant intellectuals in Europe, Layton's egoistic *Übermenschen* or Raymond Souster's urban diarist. Page and Anderson, still largely committed to the impersonality that regulated the poetry of the 1940s in Canada, found it impossible to accept that new subjectivist *integritas* but could find no alternative equally convincing, and both fell silent for many years after 1954. It is in the context of that post-Imagist search for new means of coherence and 'wholeness' that their poetry reads with the most resonance, Page's in particular because it makes so many vivid gestures of *integritas* before painfully admitting a first defeat.

Image and *Integritas* in the Early Poetry of Page

Thus far I have tried to revivify a few of the interwoven literary and cultural forces at play in Page's apprenticeship. Without insisting that she was critically aware of or creatively inspired by these forces, but that her era was, we can now turn to her forties poetry with a fuller body of historical reference and a worthwhile hypothesis. First: that the basic structural unit of the early

Page poem is the post-Pound Image, not declaration, not clause, not the verse line; second, that the relation among her images in the forties is dominantly accumulative, with relatively little subordination or linear progress explicit; third, that her adherence to the rigours of impersonality made that accumulative energy challenging to her poetry's structure and coherence; fourth, that the alternatives of *integritas* she explored provide her early poetry with vital aesthetic tension; and finally, that she was herself aware of structural difficulties in her poetry's development but only found them crippling in the early 1950s, when her versification grew stiffer and uninnovatively formal, her obligation of impersonality clashed with her now stronger instincts of creative sympathy, and her imagery grew more sharply private. This reading of her creative development coincides apparently and usefully with contemporary currents of literary and poetic debate.

The surreal and decorative flair of Page's early manner – and its notoriety – has obscured her indirect absorption of Imagist poetics. This can be recovered if we shatter the poems and extract some basic units:

> Let us by paradox
> choose a Catholic close
> for innocence,
> wince at the smell
> of beaded flowers
> like rosaries on a bush.
>
> ('Poem in War Time,' *GA*, p. 17)

> For all your brass
> reflected the tall suns
> of the season of green corn
> and I saw above your battlements of stone
> Orion –
> glittering scabbard at his groin.[86]

In such fragments it becomes clear that the Page image-manner shares the binary tendencies of early Imagism. These passages work largely on the juxtaposition of two categories of image, latent affinities between them producing visual and intellectual resonance. I have chosen fragments in which linearity and narrative are at a minimum to make my point, but if our passivity in the face of Page's virtuosity is ruptured, most of her early poems may be recognized to rely on such an Imagist extrapolation.

On a minimal level this tendency of juxtaposition can be seen to operate in one of her most characteristic early mannerisms. I refer to the '*a of b*' formula: Sutherland says she learned it from Patrick Anderson,[87] who in turn had adapted an effect of Dylan Thomas's. The formula's popularity may suggest a generation of writers and readers who not only wanted their vivid Imagist juxtapositions but wanted them as compact and frequent as possible; the value of the Imagist currency having fallen, one must bring more and more images to the market to procure the same degree of poetic surprise and difficulty. The pattern is extreme in Page's most canonical poem, 'The Stenographers,' with its 'bivouac of Sunday,' 'forced march of Monday to Saturday,' 'snow-storm of paper,' 'mid-sun of temper' (all these from the first four-line stanza; *GA*, p. 22). In 'The Bands and the Beautiful Children' are 'strings of sun,' 'auditorium of light,' 'dome of drums,' 'yellow of imagination,' and 'limits of distance' (*GA*, p. 3). The mannerism is not uncommon in forties poetry, and Page's fondness for it is not eccentric; her persistence with it probably explains A.M. Klein's sudden use of the formula in the mid-1940s (see pp. 152–3). The '*a of b*' formula relies on a principle of unmediated juxtaposition between two previously unconnected concretes: '*a*' and '*b*' are usually nouns, '*b*' without an article, so the odd construction mimics the swiftness of juxtaposition in the Imagist poem. Effects on this phrasal level may be intense *and* minor, of course, but when they help to gel the fragmented images extracted above they give a sense that Page's genius worked, as it were, from the briefest of Imagist gestures outward to fuller poetic structure.

The categories of visual phenomena in Page's poetry are not central to my argument, but one or two patterns in her selection of visual material are worth noting. The first of these is her tendency to rely on imagery from the natural world, vaguely but suggestively pastoralized, in her elucidation of contemporary issues, social or psychological. It was to this tendency Milton Wilson referred when he spoke of her 'decadent pastorals,'[88] but I am more interested in the habit's inflection of the 'phenomenal world' usually claimed by *First Statement*'s quasi-realists. To return to 'The Stenographers,' for example, much of the poem's force is earned by its contrasting the taut visuals of the stenographers' day with a world of childhood and memory, evoked in images of the sea, of 'the scatter-green vine,' 'wasps' nests on water' and 'the sand and the leaves of the country.' Whether or not such imagery is indeed pastoral, its juxtaposition with images of the urban capitalist world in which Page herself lived and worked is innovative and suggestive. This yoking of modernity and pastoralism is common in her early poems; it is visible in 'The Permanent Tourists,' 'Reflection in a Train Window,' 'Journey Home,' 'No Flowers,' 'Generation,' and 'Cullen' (all in *GA*). In these poems an ironic dissonance is generated when Page's characters or themes – modern, sociopolitical, perhaps feminist – are set against finite images or looser conceits stemming from nature, particularly of the sea and water,[89] and playing on greenness as a metaphor for freshness, youth, hope, and naïvety.[90] This exposure of urban alienation is the real function of the 'pastoral' in her early poetry, and it reveals once more the juxtapositive and binary nature of her visual imagination.

An interesting offshoot of these habits of imagery is a surrealism of effect that is often worth remarking. The manner is achieved with a feeling of accident, Page's quirky painterly imagination occasionally producing juxtapositions of the Bréton or Salvador Dali flavour:

In streets where pleasure grins
and the bowing waiter
turns double somersaults to the table for two
and the music of the violin is a splinter
pricking the poultice of flesh; where glinting glass
shakes with falsetto laughter,
Fear, the habitué, ignores the menu
and plays with the finger bowl at his permanent table.

('Some There Are Fearless,' *GA*, p. 20)

Perhaps it is not surprising that such an early poem (July 1942) should show the effects of the Surrealist fashion that had briefly won English poetry in 1936–7, especially if Treece and Fraser were correct in their location of Imagism and Surrealism in a common lineage. It is not typical of the later-forties Page, who works less with the surreal than with decontextualized fragments of the apparent real, but some touch of it may be seen to persist in the ironically 'nude' travellers 'in any café' of 'The Permanent Tourists' (1948); the hauntingly distanced swans, hunters, and silver liquor of 'Stories of Snow' (1945); or the apocalyptic imagery of 'The Event' (1952):

The keys all turned to that event
as if it were a magnetic lock.
A rush of streams flowed into it
thundering from the great divide
while numberless and hidden heads
like flowers leaned out to feel its light.

(*GA*, p. 60)

Perhaps the Surrealist flavour here is nothing more than the cumulative effect of Page's esotericism; it is not important to label the mannerism. But (what I at least consider) her occasional inspiration to Surrealism is useful in relating her work to the post-Imagist contexts of English poetry discussed earlier, as well as surprisingly to the poetry of Irving Layton, to whom the Surrealist experiment remained exemplary well into the 1960s.

Such imagistic mannerisms show us the uniqueness of the Page style in her first decade. They suggest the larger structural issue, in fact raised by Page in 'After Rain': that is, the appropriate density of such images in her poems and the challenge of their integration within a coherent 'whole.' The extreme crowding of imagery in a typical early Page poem does not often allow the leisure of visual contemplation:

> And now that the tunnel of trees was done, his eyes
> sprinted the plain where house lights in the dusk
> fired pistols for the race that led him on.
> He shed the train like a snake its skin; he dodged
> the waiting camera which with a simple click
> could hold him fast to the spot beside the track.
>
> (*GA*, p. 33)

(Sutherland's style is worth comparing to Page's in this poem, 'Journey Home': see his 'The Master,' quoted on pp. 34–5, for good reason to think Page's manner his inspiration and example. Page is of course the better maker. Her rhythms rush us through the spools of metaphor, while Sutherland's remind us of the manner's potential heaviness.) The range of imagery in Page's poem incorporates the roughly recognizable ('tunnel of trees') as well as the frankly surreal ('house lights ... / fired pistols'). The task of reading is made deliberately onerous. After a possible intuitive response to verbal music and the flash of imagery on first reading, one presumably begins to negotiate the images one by one, trying to understand their juxtapositions. Page is not as difficult here as all that: eyes that 'sprint the plain' presumably sweep across it; 'house lights' that 'fire pistols' are instead *like* the flash of a pistol fired at night, the simile phrased curiously as literal action; and the camera 'holds him fast' because of its ability to fix an image of things – a by now conventional postmodern symbol of entrapment by representation. But however successfully we translate the images, they accumulate at breakneck pace, and their individual interest or value is quickly subsumed by our responses to the broader manner.

Perhaps more than those of other poets, Page's career invites such evaluative reflexes from the reader, not only because of the judgments of 'After

Rain,' not only because Page herself tended for a while to disdain her 'extraordinarily bad work ... in Preview,'[91] but also because she so openly rejected this style when she returned to poetry in the mid-1960s (see below, pp. 103–5). The questions to which one is invited are, did 'Journey Home's' purposes as I or another reader interprets them – and I am clearly not after a 'reading' here – need such a plethora of difficult imagery to evoke intellectual excitement, and if so, is a purely stylistic excitement satisfying to the mind? Is the pleasure of modernist self-reflexivity as art-about-itself sufficient motivation for our effort? And is Page's metaphoric exuberance a style we should now – having thrown off the reductionist dogma of modernist hygienics – reconsider and applaud? Or is there a sense in which 'Journey Home' dissatisfies still because of this very tendency, whether we are reductionist modern or play-loving postmodern readers? A relativist absconding from these questions (as in, each reader will draw the line between 'excess' and 'exuberance') is too obvious to be of much intellectual value. A more telling consideration is that the evaluation I move to in such a case will have to do with my sense of the poem's having earned such exuberance by an inclusiveness, exclusiveness, and tautness of outline that work structurally, in the organization and deployment of its images. That is the current of creative energy I have called *integritas*: the limits of reference and structural tension that stabilize a rich crowding of images and make submission to their density a pleasure rather than a frustration.

Before advancing a discussion of the sources of *integritas* in Page, I want to know more about this fragmentary density that typifies her early image-manner. No Page poem merely adduces imagistic fragments without attempting their integration – as Winters, Frank, and Gage hypothesized the obvious post-Imagist poem might do – but a similar aesthetics of accumulation is central to her sense of poetic structure. It is inherent in her structural consciousness to push the poem forward by extending a catalogue of images in parallel relation, whether syntactically or conceptually, to some primary statement or concept with which the poem opened. 'Personal Landscape' of 1942 exemplifies the manner:

Land is
love, round with it, where the hand is;
wide with love, cleared scrubland, grain
on a coin.
Oh, the wheatfield, the rock-bound rubble;
the untouched hills
as a thigh smooth;

the meadow.
Not only the poor soil lovely, the outworn prairie,
but the green upspringing,
the lark-land,
the promontory.

(*GA*, p. 1)[92]

Note that the passage asserts its central metaphor ('land is love') immediately and then extrapolates from that metaphor a series of subordinate images that justify and slightly complicate it. After the bardic 'Oh,' four noun phrases are listed in parallel construction; after a subsequent 'Not only' (with intermediate 'but'), five more. The passage is thus an accumulation of visual fragments depending from a central intuition. No thematic need would have prevented its extension (or truncation), and there is no obvious determinant of the number of images appropriate to the poet's vision. Gage earlier called this determinant of post-Imagist poems 'a sense of necessity compelling a conclusion'; he said most lacked it. Page's poem at least raises such questions. What is the principle of image-exclusion or closure in 'Personal Landscape'? At what point could such a list of images be known to have ended justly – that is, other than by the poet's arbitrarily setting down her pen? Page's own conclusion is both rhythmically disruptive and highly self-reflexive and suggests her wish to put a point to the poem's momentum: 'A lung-born land, this, / a breath spilling, / scanned by the valvular heart's / field-glasses.'[93]

Albeit with more intervention in their arrangement and coherence, most of Page's poems make forward progress within this accumulative aesthetic. Hers is not a poetry that proceeds through logic, expansion of emotion, or unfolding of narrative; rather, it extends the range of the subjective eye through a constellation of images that are more or less dependent on a single central metaphor, abstraction, portrait, or initiatory incident. 'Personal Landscape' is not typical early Page, of course, but only because its euphonies are excessive, its abstractions close to sentiment. It appeared in the first issue of *First Statement*, in tandem with 'Poem ["She was dime-dead ..."],' similarly exemplary of her early accumulative aesthetics:

... and where the spoken word sounded or the leaf
scratched stucco or the boy
slung the strap of his bag on a bony shoulder
and shouted down lighted avenues
she was a shadow.

Under the arc of drawing rooms
or bending on the crooked black arm
she was quick as money ...

'Poem' shows the reliance on parataxis that seems demanded by the poet's desire to conjoin as many images as possible in the least verbal space. I remarked the same effect earlier in Anderson. The 'impersonality' of 'Poem' lies thus in the poet's suspension of her power of creative choice: there is not, clearly, one true image for each perception, but several equally valid images, between which the disjunctive 'or' is the only possible grammar of organization. For some time the accumulative method was sufficient to Page's needs; its chief development lay in her growing interest in emotional and psychological dislocations that could be especially well articulated in such verse, as in 'The Sleeper,' of *First Statement*'s seventh issue:

Close the shutters of this open-faced house on a main street
so the webbed bat swings in the cornea of the eyes
and the spark of the mouth sags to a summer furnace
while still, in the back garden, garrulous neighbours lean
elbows on the weak fence – their voices high
tents pitched below eye-level on the plains of the epidermis.

As with the slightly later 'Waking' on a similar theme, discussed later, the style here is clearly asked to represent by mimesis the disorientation and rush of sensory stimuli that occur on the margins of waking and sleep. There is a greater interest in hypotaxis: 'so' and 'while' work to suggest logical and temporal sequences in the poem's visualizations and thus coordinate the heap of images more effectively than could the haphazard 'or' of 'Poem.' This conjunction of image accumulation and psychological interest helped Page to some of her best poems by mid-decade.

Certainly the same accumulative mechanisms function to organize poems of middle length and more representative style, like 'Stories of Snow'; even though a recognizable syntax continues to assert itself, the collocation of narrative fragments and surrealist images is especially powerful in her evocation of the unreality and dream-likeness of northern landscapes:

While tethered in the wind like sleeping gulls
ice-boats wait the raising of their wings
to skim the electric ice at such a speed
they leap jet strips of naked water,

and how these flying, sailing hunters feel
air in their mouths as terrible as ether.
And on the story runs that even drinks
in that white landscape dare to be no colour;
how flasked and water clear, the liquor slips
silver against the hunters' moving hips.

(*GA*, p. 42)

Nevertheless the superficial effects of syntax and temporal structure here ought not to obscure the essentially accumulative nature of Page's style. The clauses are again paratactic, joined only by 'ands' and commas. There is even a certain self-consciousness about this very technique: 'and on the story runs' seems to signal a desire to appeal to some external literary model as a justification for the 'running on' of her own bright visions.

It's readily apparent that part of the acceptability of 'Stories of Snow' to anthologists was Page's relative curtailment of the idiosyncratic density of her earlier image-manner. The accumulative principle expands more gradually here, from the cluttered compilation of difficult juxtapositions, '*a of b*' gestures and brief phrasal images to the gathering up of longer and more syntactically complex visualizations; in the above passage, for instance, there is a new tendency to let each 'image' extend over a pair of lines. This is perhaps why in Page's finest and best-known poems a drift into accumulation has not been remarked. Nevertheless the very titles of some canonical Page poems indicate her tendency to choose generic subjects which permit extended visual catalogues: 'Photos of a Salt Mine,' 'Stories of Snow,' and 'Images of Angels' are titles that suggest loose accumulative structures in which a genre of interest is first defined, and the stanzas and images then provide variations on the central theme. This is especially striking in 'Images of Angels' (from which I will extract dramatically to emphasize the points at which new variants emerge):

Imagine them as they were first conceived:
part musical instrument and part daisy
in a white manshape ...

Not children, who imagine them more simply,
see them more coloured and a deal more cosy ...

More easily, perhaps, the little notary
who, given one as a pet, could not

walk the sun-dazzled street
with so lamb-white a companion ...

Perhaps, more certainly perhaps, the financier.
What business man would buy as he buys stock
as many as could cluster on a pin? ...

The archaeologist with his tidy science ...

Perhaps only a dog could accept them wholly ...

Or, take the nudes of Lawrence and impose
asexuality upon them ...

Or a child, not knowing they were angels ...

(*GA*, pp. 82–4)

The title is appropriate: this poem works by compiling 'images of angels' and placing them in aleatory relation to one another. Its closure (of which more later) emerges only when the poet has had enough; nothing in the poem's inner consistency demands it. Page's tendency to such catalogues (and we might add poems with titles like 'Sisters,' 'Young Girls,' 'Puppets') is strong in her first decade.

Even Page's longer poems thus reveal an accumulative habit which clearly will have its attendant risks: swift but then sagging intensity, apparent indifference to tautness of structure, subordination to the visual at the expense of other senses, abruptness or inexplicability of inclusion and closure. These dangers are self-evidently not impossible to overcome; 'Stories of Snow' and 'Images of Angels' are evidence of the rich possibilities of the manner. But the dangers were not eased by Page's strict impersonality in the period, since explicit subjectivity would have offered a means of integrating otherwise loose and random structures by providing a locus of organization and reference, the imagination of the persona, who 'speaks' and is therefore outside – framing – the poetic construct. In Page's case impersonality also enforced a rigorous detachment from her early subjects. This is most evident in 'The Stenographers' (and is perhaps responsible for its prompt canonization); although the speaker's personality *is* to an extent signalled by the sympathetic images she chooses in which to render the plight of the women in her office, she is nowhere a 'subject' until the poem demands closure. At that point a single personal pronoun looms: 'In their eyes I have seen / the pin men of madness in marathon trim / Race round the track of the stadium pupil' (*GA*, p. 23). The lines appear to involve the speaker with her subjects, but this should not blind us to the distance she retains. She remains an acute observer, able to spin arcane imagery for the 'madness' she feels in her peers; her low-key personation is in tension with the poem's accumulative energy. 'The Stenographers' is poised on the edge of incoherence; that is precisely part of its vividness.

Page's characteristic early distaste for complex syntaxes is a second exacerbation of the risks of accumulation in her poetry. While her circumvention of sentence logic is not precisely cognate to the suppression of syntax in the Imagist poetic, it does create some of the same jarring. Her most striking tendency in the forties is to suppress referential pronouns. She parallels a series of verb phrases to a single prior pronoun, as in the parataxis of 'Summer Resort.' After the initial 'They lie on beaches,' thirteen lines accumulate parallel clauses:

> Search out the trees for love, the beach umbrellas,
> the bar, the dining-room; flash as they walk,
> are pretty-mouthed and careful as they talk;
> send picture post-cards to their offices
> brittle with ink and soft with daily phrases.
>
> Find Sunday empty without churches – loll
> not yet unwound in deck chair and by pool,
> cannot do nothing neatly, while in lap,
> periscope ready, scan the scene for love.

(*GA*, p. 26)

'Summer Resort' appeared in *Preview* 16 (October 1943); poems from adjacent issues confirm the habit as a distinct phase of her style,[94] as does 'The Permanent Tourists,' perhaps the best known poem in the manner (*GA*, p. 66). Such anaphora plays handily into the aesthetic of accumulation I have remarked. The elision of personal pronouns is related to the impersonality of her method, as it deflects attention away from subjects onto actions – actions that can be more effectively rendered in brief images than can persons.

The techniques I have noted – from the binary and juxtapositive nature of Page's imagery through its accumulative aesthetics, minimal syntax, and firm impersonality – clearly presented her with the problem of *integritas*, of finding sure methods of binding the juxtapostions and accumulations together in ways that produced tension, energy and irony. It was perhaps in recognition of this difficulty that Page so often turned to vigorous and resounding closure as a method of asserting the unities of her vision. We have already seen that in 'The Stenographers' closure demanded a sudden and unique first-person pronoun. 'Images of Angels' closes ambiguously with invocation of 'the angelic word' that releases all the imaged angels into the sky, and a sudden descent of winter ('cold / and snow') onto the 'warm and sunny avenue' conjured up by their presence. 'The Permanent Tourists' requires a rather unearned and flaccid abstraction to signal its closure: the ironies of the tourists realized in the first five stanzas suffer when we are told at the opening of the last that they are 'Yet somehow beautiful' (*GA*, p. 66). It is in fact remarkable as one scans Page's early work how often she required sudden abstraction in order to make an exit from the exuberance of her image-manner; Tolley has remarked this typical facet of forties poetry, in which escape from the quasi-Imagist 'direct presentation' of the poem proper is possible only by retreat to 'a worn rhetorical gesture,'[95] though Page's closures are rarely so tired.

Having now attempted to elucidate a few of the structural challenges Page faced in the development of her poetics during her first decade – and having asserted perhaps contentiously that one of her favoured means of responding to those challenges, by way of dramatic closure, was occasionally forced – I now want to examine the kinds of *integritas* she developed in that same period. The most accessible of these is stylistic: Page's complex prosodic effects figure large in her attempt to incorporate and subsume the density of her visualizations. A typical passage, from 'Waking' of May 1943, will suffice to note the relation:

Invalid, I –
and crippled by sleep's illness,
drowned in the milk of sheets
and silk of dreams,
I rise and write the rising curve of day
with mercury of the smashed thermometer
and trouble the silent mirror, who have been
pale in suspension on the oval bed.[96]

Note the prevalent '*a of b*' formula and the cluttering and obscurity of some of the imagery. The poem is remarkable for its personation, an extreme rarity in her first volume *As Ten As Twenty* (1946). But rhythmic and phonic gestures also contribute to the images' integration: among them, assonantal long vowels, sharp in the opening ('sleep,' 'sheets,' 'dreams') then slower ('I rise,' 'write,' 'rising'); intense liquids ('illness,' 'milk,' 'silk,' 'pale,' 'oval'; 'rise,' 'write,' 'rising') and nasals ('mercury,' 'thermometer,' 'mirror'); alternation of line length (the truncated 'I,' the emphatic echoing in the third and fourth lines); and mimetic effects of rhythm (the crowding of incidental syllables after the fifth line's careful iambics, mirroring the flurry of mental and sensory activity after waking). Clearly, Page was already a virtuoso stylist, to the advantage of a poem whose vision might otherwise seem solipsistic.

Euphony offers perhaps a fairly superficial *integritas*, risking as it does some of the same hypertrophy with which the imagery itself could be charged. A more unifying and less decorative *integritas* lay with her pronounced tendency to verse portraiture, especially of eccentrics and outsiders whose idiosyncrasies invite imagistic curiosities. The most candidly named of these is 'Portrait of Marina,' but if one counts the number of poems in the early Page collections which portray eccentric individuals the phenomenon becomes remarkable. 'Only Child,' 'Boy with a Sea Dream,' 'The Landlady,' 'Man with One Small Hand,' 'Blowing Boy,' 'Paranoid,' 'Sailor,' 'Freak,' and 'Mystics Like Miners' (all in *GA*) all claim structural coherence by positing an odd individual in the title as a referent for the poem as a whole, and then meditating in more or less random imagery upon his or her condition. In 'Portrait of Marina,' this tendency to accumulate the details of a single portrayed consciousness is somewhat hidden by the appearance of narrative; a loose temporal structure seems to explain the succession of images of Marina, as we learn about her surrender of identity to the eccentric domestic demands of her seafarer father. But the narrative structure is very little developed; articulated in lines 5–10, the father–daughter relation really only provides an occasion for Page's superb Gothic imaging of Marina's psychological pain:

> Slightly off shore it glints. Each wave is capped
> with broken mirrors. Like Marina's head
> the glinting of these waves.
> She walked forever antlered with migraines
> her pain forever putting forth new shoots
> until her strange unlovely head became
> a kind of candelabra – delicate ...
>
> (*GA*, p. 51)

The passage obviously invites our sympathy for Marina, although we might well ask – as Page eventually would in 'After Rain' – whether such a precise aestheticization of suffering bespeaks much sympathy in the observing poet.

'Portrait of Marina' seeks to contain its visual density with a number of other gestures of coherent force: the poem is divided into sections, for example, according to different distances of the sea from the land: 'Far out the sea has never moved ... Slightly off shore it glints ... But where the wave breaks ... And where it moved in shallows ...' This progress from 'full fathom five' to the shore's edge – emphasizing inversely the poem's accumulative structure – is actually more successful in integrating the complex of imagery than is the story of father and daughter. But the poem's deeper *integritas* is our recurrent reference of its rich metaphors to an equally complex tenor, the damaged and delicate mind of Marina. We do not thereby reduce the poem's energy, but we do have a full intimation of its restless coherence.

Marina – or the 'Only Child,' or the 'Paranoid' – is thus the outer sphere of meaning to which all Page's images, however obscure, however impacted, must refer. The point is more than thematic: before we even begin to dispute theme we seek assurance that the poem's vortex of images has a structural stability in which the idea of a unitary theme is indeed worth seeking. In this sense, the very frequency of portraiture in Page's first decade bears a likely relation to the intensity of accumulation she intuited and eventually condemned in her own style. But this is not to say that the decision on portraiture is a *sufficient* response to the imagistic energy and risk-taking of Page's creativity. The verse-portrait does not *per se* guarantee coherent structure; as it does not necessitate moderation of image accumulation, one might still write portrait-poems in which the problems of *integritas* remained unresolved, the images incoherent, quantitatively as well as qualitatively excessive.[97] 'Portrait of Marina' does not then gain all of its *integritas* from its status as portrait but from visual and thematic resonances among its images as well (the more traditional matter of its New Critical 'unity'). The poem also provides a helpful perspectivism, by invoking expansive time-structures – Marina's father is both 'Father' and 'great-great-grandpapa' in the poem's multiple perspectives – and generational dissonances. Narrative, temporal perspective, and portraiture need not coincide (Page's portraits often have the atemporality of the still life about them), but she wrote a number of middle-length poems in which portraiture seeks to include such temporal structures.

Typical of these are 'Round Trip' and 'Cullen,' both early poems that borrow the mere superficies of narrative poetry as a means of organizing Page's accumulated images. In 'Round Trip' a generic 'passenger' boards a train; the poem that follows is a rich visual gallimaufry recording his internal and external responses to a trip that leaves him at the end back at home, aware 'that nothing's changed, that everything's the same' (*ATAT*, p. 7). Despite such circularity, the poem seeks the effects of narrative with phrases like

'Now he removes his hat' (p. 2), 'The train devours its track' (p. 3), 'Trees pass and pass,' and so on. In between these rare fictive lines are rich catalogues of images:

In such sweet rain his ears and armpits grew
flowers and humming birds were part of him –
hanging jewels upon lapel and hat.
At night the oranges and lemons cut
small amber caves from darkness where he sat
and the mercurial rivers found their seas
at any spot he bathed.

(*ATAT*, p. 5)

It becomes apparent that narrative, the representation of action within time, is largely incidental to 'Round Trip.' The poet wished to paint a variety of transitory emotional conditions in such colourful images as she could subsume within the poem's central conceit of a train ride, and the thrill of those representations is the major source of its energy. The effect again is accumulative, and in this ironically atemporal structure (given the 'round' nature of the trip) any greater or lesser number of images might have been included: narrative here proves more an occasion for imagistic enthusiasm than an *integritas* that sustains it.

In 'Cullen' a fuller narrativity is immediately obvious. The eponymous archetypal young man of the Depression and war years trips through splintered scenes of urban and pastoral life before marching off to a war he does not understand. The 'narrative' is handled in very broad strokes; temporal shifts are deliberately obscure, and periods of Cullen's experience are again rendered for the most part in cryptic images accumulated with relatively little syntactic or temporal coherence:

Summer grew foliage to hide a scar,
bore leaves that looked as light as tissue paper
leaves that weighed as heavy as a plate.
Fall played a flute and stuck it in his ear,
Christmas short-circuited and fired a tree
with lights and baubles; hid behind Christ; unseen
counted its presents on an adding-machine.

(*GA*, p. 15)

So the poem proceeds, with a clear but casual interest in passing time ('Summer,' 'Fall,' 'Christmas') while image after image conveys the purposelessness of modern life as it is handed to passionate youth. Page's creative *instinct* here was the accumulation of fragmentary images. The more conscious effort of narrative offers a dissonant *integritas,* a rough perimeter for her imagery's energy, but narrative cannot really contain this degree of exuberance. The structural principles in this longer poem are largely the same as those informing the other poems examined so far. Her habitual compilation of more or less surreal images made her seek the *integritas* available in portraiture and narrative, but such wholeness as those modes provided was not always able to prevent the stylistic overdetermination, the 'myriad' images, that she eventually came to regret.

A more complex coherence was gained for Page's image-manner by her frequent desire to capture abstract emotional conditions through visual correlatives. The method is especially prominent in the later 1940s work that fills *The Metal and the Flower* (1954) but is visible earlier in less sophisticated forms. Although the precise emotion represented is often ineffable, partly because Page is interested in emotions beyond denotation, the effect on her accumulative style is noteworthy. Because the pleasure of reference in such poems is directed to our eventual identification of 'the' central emotion, her ability to compile striking images no longer seems the point: there is an external determinant of the number and nature of images incorporated. An example of the manner is the title poem of *The Metal and the Flower,* originally called 'Intractable Between Them Grows':

> Trespassers have wandered through
> texture of flesh and petals.
> Dogs like arrows moved along
> pathways that their noses knew.
> While the two who laid it out
> find the metal and the flower
> fatal underfoot.
>
> (*MF,* p. 44)

The garden of this poem is a tangle not only of metal and flowers but of images and abstractions, emotions, and actions. By no means is the emotion it wishes to evoke straightforward, although each of us could now begin the compilation of details that might point to a successful symbolic reading. Although a tendency to accumulate curious juxtapositions still dominates the poem's image-manner ('flesh and petals,' metal and flower), the poetic structure as a whole is sound, taut, and determined without static conventionality, because each image is so apparently subordinate to a purpose – evocation of the emotion – beyond its own splendour.

This impression is not merely an effect of the piece's relatively traditional stanzas. A freer versification in 'Failure at Tea' does not lessen the structural soundness engineered by the poet's desire to evoke a requisite emotion: rather, the poem's crowded and confusing images are integrated by the title's reference of their ambiguity to a social *faux-pas*. The difficulty of our readerly task is less significant than the reference's impact on the accumulation of imagery:

> Plates rattled somewhere in the porcelain ear
> and vicious as a drug our words became
> quick nickels pushed in broken slot machines.
> No jackpot rang,
> no Petty blonde undressed,
> the little guy who should have made a goal
> stood as he was –
> inanimate under glass.
>
> (*ATAT*, p. 37)

Whatever the eccentricities of representation here, the effect of random accumulation is lessened by the deflection of the reader's attention from rapid-fire imagistic brilliance to emotional suggestion. Without necessarily claiming 'Failure at Tea' as one of her successes, I would claim that along with 'The Metal and the Flower' it reveals one of Page's functional means of shaping her accumulative aesthetics, by opening the poem's referential boundaries to experiences beyond the pleasure of technical display. The interpenetration in such poems of powerfully felt emotion and the cool detachment of aesthetic complexity is typical of Page's best work – one of the signs, in fact, of Margaret Atwood's affinity with her poetics.[98]

Indeed the tension between the compulsion to aesthetic brilliance and the force of experiential sympathy is central to the development *and* to the crises of Page's early poetry. Upon it the success of the last *integritas* I wish to consider is predicated: that is, the socialism that hovered over the early vision, ideas and methods of her poetry. Especially in a number of poems from *As Ten As Twenty*, a loosely socialist perspective sustains verbal excess by subordinating individual desire, including aesthetic desire, to a larger social judgment, condemnation, and compassion. The precise link between Page's politics and the styles and structures she develops is difficult to pinpoint (even without enlarging upon 'socialist aesthetics' *per se*, a different matter), but her socialist education during the *Preview* years gave her the intuition of an alternate *integritas* that might help to contain the exuberance of her more interior and solipsistic mannerisms, by testing their usefulness in imaging the suffering of others. The intuition is fitting: both the poet and her poems found new directedness and vocation in a widening and theorizing of sympathy, Page in political, the text in aesthetic and referential, terms.

Page's socialism cannot be narrowly defined, and its registration as a more general humanist compassion is usual in her poetry. Despite *First Statement*'s drive to categorize *Preview*'s socialism as 'doctrinaire,' there is nothing systematized about the vague suggestive leftism of the poems in *As Ten As Twenty*. The requisite thirties liberal references are visible, to the 'cities of Europe,' to 'Spain,' and to 'Guernica.' There is a general interest in society's unattended outcasts, the exploited 'Stenographers,' the emblematic convict-lovers in 'The Condemned' (*GA*, pp. 58–9). There is also the curious pamphleteering of 'Election Day,' in which the speaker makes her left-wing vote against the 'gentle overlords / propped by their dames' who run the Canadian political system (*ATAT*, p. 30). But there is no party-political doctrine *per se* in any of these poems.

Despite this rather indefinite liberal context 'The Stenographers' remains a powerful indictment of the despiritualization of labourers in the capitalist economy. It gains conviction from its treatment of a category of workers whose exploitation is psychological rather than physical. Although their less concrete hardship prevented the stenographers' inclusion among the Socialist emblems of labour popular during the thirties, Page restores their centrality in a vision that is (characteristically) both political and private. The political matter is relatively suppressed. The employer is reduced to a disembodied 'voice'; the conditions of the stenographers' labour are portrayed through their effects on the women rather than narrative statement. But these implications are direct enough that any reading of the poem which ignored its political matter would have no very deep explanation for the despair of the women portrayed.[99]

In what sense does this political undercurrent in 'The Stenographers' help to organize its imagistic and structural complexity? In the first place socialism has encouraged Page to treat a class or community of persons in their socio-economic relations, thus avoiding the revelling in private eccentricity that motivates her individual verse-portraits, as well as the delight in fantasy – the angels, puppets and swans – of her other generic catalogues. It is not possible when dealing with such a group to extrapolate particularities *ad libitum*, since the point of the treatment is to locate more broadly based characteristics of the group as a whole – a limited range of possible images. Second, it has encouraged a forward motion for the poem based loosely on the stenographers' periods of work, divided into morning and afternoon, the intervening 'inch of the noon' when they take their lunch breaks, and the hours of bad sleep when their dreams are fretted by memories of the office. This imposes on the poem's imagery a stronger sense of temporal limitation (compare the apolitical 'Round Trip,' in which the vague circularity of its narrative permits infinite detail); Page's politicized anger at the stenographers' lives encourages a fruitful restriction in her own aesthetics. Third, it has encouraged ironic juxtapositions among her images, so that her pastoralism, noted earlier, jars painfully with the urban and economic milieu of the poem. Such dissonances complicate and contain her image-manner rewardingly, each image taking on self-reflexive ironies often missing in her other early poems. But perhaps most significant, because of this political dimension Page's images of the stenographers are not important solely for their autonomous brilliance; the imagery's political reference is obvious enough that her technical virtuosity is usefully stabilized. The poet submits her images to an authority and a veracity larger than her own aesthetics, and the result is the kind of *integritas* we associate with most masterpieces.

'Generation' shows perhaps even more explicitly the way in which the projection of political undercurrents in a poem can contribute to the integration of its imagery. Here the individual images are more accumulative and idiosyncratically difficult than those of 'The Stenographers':

> Tragically, Spain was our spade;
> the flares went up in the garden.
> We dug at night;
> the relics within the house
> sagged.
> Walking down country lanes
> we committed arson –
> firing our parent-pasts;
> on the wooded lands
> our childhood games grew real:
> the police and robbers
> held unsmiling faces
> against one another.
>
> (*GA*, pp. 18–19)

The centralizing of the Spanish Civil War establishes clearly the leftist context in which the speaker attempts to portray her generation. The generalizing consciousness is active again, in that she wishes to describe not an individual but an entire generation and must not be too interested in the idiosyncracies of eccentrics. Once again a progress is implied from the poem's outset; as in 'The Stenographers' the work-day enforced the poem's parameters, so here the maturing of a generation offers firm but ambiguous closure. The political and military contexts of the poem locate its images in experiences and conflicts that refer outward well beyond the poet's private aesthetics. The images 'make sense' sufficient to the achievement of structure, because that larger context is clearly invoked and each one may be read in relation to it. When such a larger context is absent, the *bizarreries* of her imagery cannot be so readily pointed and may serve as little more than irritants to the reader's desire for meaning. It is in this sense that Page's brief engagement with political subtexts provided a temporary *integritas* for her early poetry: not because of the profundity or complexity of her leftist vision, but because it offered an extra-imagistic commitment with attendant conventions to which the difficulties of her early style could be referred for some immediate sense of clarity. Such poems attempt a free exchange of ideas with the world beyond poetry; and poetry that refuses such an exchange in sole adherence to interior aesthetic dynamics and standards risks the kind of entropy that Page's poetry eventually manifested – to her discerning eye in 'After Rain' at least.

I have claimed that Page's poetry in this period, like much poetry of the post-Imagist decades, works by the accumulation and juxtaposition of brief striking images; that her simplest structures at the time are little more than such accumulations, without subordination or linearity; and that she delimited such accumulative aesthetics by adopting various styles and frames productive of *integritas,* including euphony, portraiture, narrative emotional suggestion, and political commitment, some more and some less successful in containing her imagistic flair. In these qualities she is little different from other poets of her generation, and we are not much closer to an explanation of her middle silence, although the historical contexts of her own self-critique have given us a better understanding of her motion towards that lapse. It remains to suggest a reading of her silence after 1955 that depends from these interpretations of her creative problems, and that can best be set in motion through a preliminary juxtaposition of her first two volumes in relation to the structural questions I have raised.

In *As Ten As Twenty,* the various kinds of structural integration I have sketched above are in suspension, all offering potential routes for a young poet's further development but none dominating the others. The poems range from the simplest accumulative catalogues to the complex structures of

'The Stenographers,' from Aestheticist formalism to socialist engagement, and in so doing supply a full sense of Page's youthful promise. In that context of *potential* mannerisms, the artifice of her post-Imagist method seems a promising exuberance whose fruition and discipline await future work. *The Metal and the Flower* does not follow up on this variety and promise, however, and its retrenchment may be described in relation to problems of *integritas* that Page had diverted or failed sufficiently to address during the late forties and early fifties.

The image accumulation certainly persists in the second volume, its difficulties exacerbated by the increasingly obscure referents of many of the images gathered. But the socialist or socially conscious context is largely dispensed with, the exception being 'Photos of a Salt Mine' (generally acknowledged as one of Page's strongest poems). As a result the quasi-pastoralism of the earlier poetry, previously balanced by social vision, is allowed to take over and become common, indeed to cast up new favoured symbols whose Aestheticism is conventionally marked, like the lilies of 'The Event,' the swans of 'Green Little Corn,' and the peacock of 'Arras.' At the same time the 'world of the poem' reaches less and less into the recognizable world of her readers; it is increasingly a private formal garden into which the concerns of 'The Stenographers' and her 'Generation' cannot enter. Although as I suggested earlier the poems' attempt to correlate ineffable emotions is functional in their accomplishment, we are still dealing with poems whose chief reference is to an interior symbolism: if we are frustrated with the difficulty of a particular Imagist juxtaposition, we can try to accept its typicality of the idiosyncratic mood of the poem, but we may still feel entrapped in a *mise-en-abyme* of self-reflexive gazing. This epistemological claustrophobia is also risked by the high proportion of verse portraits in the later volume. A full third of the book's poems present an individual through a more or less inchoate catalogue of images. It is as if the method had proven its integrating force too well in successes like 'Portrait of Marina' and become quickly conventionalized: missing in many of this book's portraits is the tension of imaginative self-delight and controlled sympathy that Page's best effects required. The new convention also makes plain that Page felt the need, typical of the early 1950s, to look for an aesthetics of selfhood, but she remained unwilling to risk the self-revelation that might have better served to justify and deepen the range of her eccentric eye.

This aesthetic remoteness is enforced by a much decreased range of verse forms. Most of the poems in *The Metal and the Flower* reach for or have achieved a rigidity of versification that was not apparent in *As Ten As Twenty*. The experimental versification of the earlier volume has here hardened into a formalist propensity for more consistent line and stanza lengths. Rich euphony in the earlier work has already shown Page's tendency to draw on prosody in order to unify imagistic catalogues; the stiffened versification of her second volume indicates a similar need to contain and delimit her running image-manner by conventional means, perhaps exacerbated now by the abandonment of some of her more successful experiments with *integritas,* and the conventionalization of others.

Thus the imagistic obscurity and accumulative structures of Page's early work are evident and enervating in *The Metal and the Flower* but have at the same time fewer sources of *integritas* available for their containment. The volume's urges towards formality and portraiture contribute to the impression of a gallery of eccentric images projected without substantial engagement with the world shared by poet and reader. In this sense it is Page's more 'academic' volume, fulfilling retrospectively and sadly the decade-old *First Statement* attacks on her image-manner for a lack of engagement with the phenomenal world, and perhaps explaining the Governor General's Literary Award it earned in 1954 – as that honour had gone chiefly until that time to poets whose intellectual and formalist training superseded romantic or political visions. Considering these features of the volume's accomplishment, 'Arras,' the closing poem, is all the more remarkable a masterpiece that seems to point a route out of the predicament in which Page found herself. It sacrifices none of the imagistic richness of her best early work; rather, its 'peacock,' 'candelabra,' and 'jewels and silk' confirm the decorative tendencies of this second volume. The whole vision however is successfully subsumed within a new and unique ironic-personative manner:

> The peaches hang like lanterns. No one joins
> those figures on the arras.
>   Who am I
> or who am I become that walking here
> I am observer, other, Gemini,
> starred for a green garden of cinema?

(*GA*, p. 90)

The curious detachment and instability of selfhood visible in Page's persona makes 'Arras' another of her poems that anticipate some of Atwood's most characteristic effects. As she had done so brilliantly in 'After Rain,' with which it is contemporary, she projects into 'Arras' the problems of her poetics, speaking at once as disturbed visionary and constructing poet confused among her own creations:

Voluptuous it came.
Its head the ferrule and its lovely tail
folded so sweetly; it was strangely slim
to fit the retina. And then it shook
and was a peacock – living patina,
eye-bright, maculate!
Does no one care?

(*GA*, p. 91)

The result is another masterpiece perched on the edge of silence, incorporating many of the ironies of 'After Rain,' though arguably more sophisticated than that masterpiece in its ambiguous half-portrait of an ironic speaker. The images are as evocative, and indeed the euphony as artificial ('retina' / 'patina'), as in the past, but the rare acceptance in both poems of a necessary cautious subjectivism has provided a means of grounding those qualities in a striking new *integritas*.

Why though did that brief eccentric subjectivism of the early 1950s not open up a new period in Page's poetry, instead of signalling the beginning of a pronounced silence? Perhaps she found the personative mode functional only in self-reflexive poems in which she attempted to critique her own poetics, a degree of intense Aestheticism she was not prepared to endorse. Perhaps, too, she was not ready to develop in lyric poems her need for a sympathetic identification with others: Giovanni remains 'beyond [her] rim' in 'After Rain,' and in 'Arras' her fellows are the uncaring *bourgeoisie*, 'folding slow eyes on nothing,' unmoved by the peacock of her renegade vision. We could invoke as well commonly noted biographical details – departure from Canada and so on – as other facets of a comprehensive portrait of Page's creative crises in the period, and add that her poetry had always suppressed such materials. But the *aesthetic* dimension of her crisis is now I believe articulable and pertains to the difficult relation between part and whole, between image and *integritas*, that Page's early poetry rather urgently negotiates, even as it proves that an engagement with that dilemma lay at the heart of the most characteristic – and much of the finest – poetry written in the forties.

Criticism, Sympathy, Silence: 'Cry Ararat!'

My strongly worded judgment of *The Metal and the Flower* will not be endorsed by many. The Governor General's Award it won suggests that the second Page volume spoke clearly and successfully to at least one cadre of readerly opinion at the time, and it would obviously be possible to re-create that historical criticism to arrive at fuller praise. Milton Wilson, who earlier supplied some key perceptions of Page's poetic difficulties, nevertheless felt that the poems of *The Metal and the Flower* had 'new severity and intensity,'[100] and the asceticism of his critical metaphor in 1958 suggests the persistent authority of an astringent modernist aesthetic in Canada. A.J.M. Smith, chief bearer of that aesthetic well into the 1950s, was early on and remained a champion of Page's poetry, notwithstanding his strictures of 1948 that had roused John Sutherland to her defence. He would continue to remark her excellences long after it became apparent that *The Metal and the Flower* had been the end, not the beginning, of Page's early 'metaphysical' gift.[101] By 1961 the trends of critical judgment had changed sufficiently that Desmond Pacey could remark of Page's *The Metal and the Flower* that 'the general impression is of a talent that has worked itself out.'[102] Indeed, Pacey had been the prophet of Page's *lapsus*; as early as 1954 – surprisingly, the year of her noted second volume and its major award – he remarked that Page, who had once been poised to become the 'leading poetess of Canada,' whose work was 'more complex and sophisticated' than that of the *First Statement* survivors, had more or less failed her potential: 'Unfortunately Miss Page has published very little during the last five years: it will be a great pity if her very subtle talent is lost to our poetry.'[103] Pacey's remarks are oddly compelling, flying as they do in the face of institutional opinion while nevertheless striking eerily close to the truth of Page's predicament.

Page's self-criticism should no longer be taken merely to *coincide* with remarks like Wilson's and Pacey's, however, nor with Sutherland's earlier polemics, nor with the currents of late-Imagist aesthetic debate I have briefly surveyed. I would contend instead that she formed some of her judgments of her own poetry by internalization of those critiques, a process in which persistent strictures voiced over her poetry – interpretable by the way, given their gender-consciousness, partly as attacks on her private self – precipitated in her mind in *self*-critiques that she either assumed were or came to think of as authentically her own. It hardly matters whether this was a conscious or unconscious process, but the latter has more evidence than the former, for Page has never noted, in print at least, the similarities of her own and of her critics' views of her early poetry. Page received no more, nor less, nor less fair, criticism than most female poets of her day (Sutherland's manipulative rhetoric of editorial intimacy notwithstanding); while it is certainly possible to hear the condescension of a masculine literary ethos when Sutherland or Pacey refers to her as 'Miss Page,'[104] and such conventional politenesses cannot be separated from the gendered force of their critical assumptions, there was little in the criticism of Page to suggest dismissiveness or invective. Next to each male critic who might be condemned for such a tone and its attendant avuncularism is another who might be praised for a more even-handed and judicious response to Page's artistic particularity.

Nevertheless the force of *First Statement* critique of *Preview* and of Page had initiated a relative univocality in the reception of her work, and the little magazine's emphasis on the image-mongering in her style was certain to find its seconders. The *First Statement* opinion of her metaphorical *richesses* was shared for example by an anonymous reader for Ryerson, who nevertheless recommended acceptance of her manuscript collection 'The Untouched Hills' in late 1945:

> I find this poetry interesting and most striking in general but it is extremely – almost exhaustingly – indirect. It rather wafts between the very beautiful and the very prosaic and there is always a good observation decorated profusely in metaphor and simile, the cleverness of which I find I can only take in limited quantities.[105]

Page no doubt received these remarks and must have found them much in keeping with the opinions of Sutherland and Dudek. The theme was a commonplace: Henry Wells in *Where Poetry Stands Now* of 1948 praised her 'cooler tone' largely because it helped to constrain her occasional 'romantic enthusiasm' of style;[106] he, too, had argued, by the way, a connection between an elaborate 'personalist' style and a poet's gender,[107] and Page's poetry, though it 'is largely limited to the feminine sphere of a criticism of manners, and lacks the dignity and scope of a religious, social or historical view of the world, within a narrow field ... enjoys a high perfection.'[108] Wilson, as we have seen, compared her favourably with Patrick Anderson for her 'underlying integrity of imagery or principle,' but thought both poets 'dominated by the common assumption of those years [the 1940s] that the degree of metaphorical extravagance is the measure of poetic success ...' She was, like Anderson, 'extremely insulated,' in need of fresh air; their 'anxious sense of social responsibility contributes a sinister, deliquescent atmosphere, but no poetic means of escape.'[109] The formalist tenor of all these comments suggests that Page's critics were unstimulated by her themes of eccentric individuality, social alienation, and diffident pastoralism, but it is noteworthy that most of them, Sutherland and Wells most obviously, allowed formalist comment to shade, by loaded vocabularies, into thematic disapproval.

Page offered no reactions to such critics. Unlike Irving Layton, whose tendency to pre-emptive manifestoes antedated his first book of poems, she was not looking to exchange invective. She may have held self-criticism – defensive explication of her own artistic purposes – in a degree of disdain. The

'Explanatory Issue' of *Preview* (21; Sep. 1944), for example, was intended (probably by Patrick Anderson, who wrote the enthusiastic headnote) to provide the hapless *Preview* reader with 'short explanatory passages' in which the poets were to comment on their meanings. Anderson, Bruce Ruddick, and A.M. Klein (the last named commenting on 'Montreal') complied; F.R. Scott's 'explanation' was provided for him by Anderson; Page's 'Children' was the only poem to go unexplicated in the issue. Anderson's headnote implies that the *Preview*-ites had a difference of opinion over the idea of self-review,[110] and Scott's and Page's mutual silence is noteworthy. Despite increasing reputation in subsequent years, Page never broke that self-critical silence until after her return to Canada, perhaps preferring – as an adherent of impersonality – to suppress any explicit acknowledgment of her conscious subjective control of her poetics.

In the context of her later silence, though, Page's strict dissociation of poetry from criticism suggests not so much superior indifference to critique as alarm at its stultifying potential. She was hardly so slight a poet as to fall silent solely *because of* such criticism – that would be a cheap rendering of a concept of internalization anyway – but it appears to have supplied the *terms* of her struggle, and the terms had strong endorsements. Certainly the audible critical consensus on her intense deployment of metaphor had a part in her conviction by the mid-1950s in the inadequacy of her early poetics, a conviction so profound that she eventually remarked in a letter to Patrick Anderson in 1973 that the bulk of her contribution to *Preview* was 'extraordinarily bad work ... I wonder that I wrote it or that anyone ever agreed that it was publishable.'[111] The harshness of this self-castigation – which Page must have later recanted if she allowed *Preview* material to reappear in *The Glass Air* and the recent *The Hidden Room* – suggests a curious resentment, apparently of her own early work but also of those whose original approval encouraged her in those mannerisms. 'After Rain,' then, rests on the fulcrum of various contending judgments, keenly alert to the prevailing reaction to her style but unable to surrender the Imagist intensity on the basis of which she had been published and praised throughout the forties. 'After Rain' is in this sense a brilliant poetic *mea culpa* to the judgments of her critics to that point; but its real resonance lies in a more profound self-assessment, only glancingly related to her critics' chorus. Page saw more deeply into the ethics of metaphor than had her reviewers and was troubled, for she had recognized the dissonance between an elaborate verbal style and desire for human sympathy and solidarity, a tension noted in 'The Stenographers' and 'Portrait of Marina,' and I believe found their incommensurability an utter impasse to her verbal creativity's continuation at that time.

Page's accounts of her silence are few and often cryptic. 'Questions and Images' is her most extended 'explanation' of what happened to her poetry in the 1950s; it emphasizes her visual and imaginative transition to the tropics (Brazil in 1956) and suggests that sudden *being* in another language revealed to her the alarming fluidity of her articulate selfhood. Her descriptions of her situation at the time to correspondents are less usefully introspective, but they do make plain that the crisis began long before the move to Brazil: to Floris Clarke McLaren in early 1955 she noted 'at the root of this excessive uncertainty that has held me – Australia perhaps, and the current poetic idiom so different from my own';[112] to Cid Corman, editor of *Origin*, in early 1953, she was naturally less revealing: 'The excuses for not writing are a not too distant move to Australia, and all the business attendant upon such a move.'[113] Two features of these offhand remarks are striking: first, that Page was aware of a distinct shift in critical taste *circa* 1953–5 as one of the factors isolating and perhaps stifling her poetry, and second, that she had an acute sense of her poetry's lapsing as early as the winter of 1952–3, prior to her departure from Canada. The remark to Corman is quoted, to be fair, in a letter in which she thanks him for suggestions that she had found invigorating for her poetry; it is nevertheless true that she published only two new poems in literary journals after 1952 ('After Rain' and 'Giovanni and the Indians').

Indeed, Corman's intervention in Page's development in the early 1950s is worth pursuing, because he pinpointed better than any other contemporary observer – and in terms that she would herself adopt in 'After Rain' – the transition she had to welcome if her poetry was to grow. He had initiated the exchange with a letter asking her to submit poems to *Origin*, and her response of 16 January 1953 was blunt in its self-assessment: 'I am writing so little and so badly that I don't think I have enough for any kind of a spread without drawing on work which has already appeared in Canadian little mags.' While he declined to reprint old material, Corman responded freely to her embarrassed tone and recommended to her poetry a warmer contact with the uniqueness of others, and only secondarily praised her own eccentric eye: 'a more logical development in work like yours would seem to be an opening awareness of others, others specifically, in terms of their personal dilemmas, etc., and so of your own perceptive accomplishments.' Corman's remark was offhand, but Page's response registers its impact:

Thank you for your letter. This is not a conventional opening – I really mean, thank you for your letter. It has been enormously helpful to me, really made me take a good look at the bruises. Proud flesh is perhaps a better phrase ... But better still, I have been writing, and at a time when excuses for not writing are very real. Goodness knows what the work is like. I have very little idea.[114]

Page had been writing her impersonal portraits of eccentric 'others' for some time, so clearly she took Corman to have demanded something more radical. Page's tone suggests that Corman had made articulate to her a direction for her poetry that she had already intuited but more or less suppressed, or dismissed, or felt beyond her. There are no clear records of the new work she spoke of so exuberantly to Corman; by the evidence, the composition of 'After Rain' was at least a year away, but it is hard now to keep its themes quite separate from the insights he offered.

The brief Corman–Page correspondence thus triggers new biographical narratives of Page's middle silence and reminds us that the causes of her temporary surrender of poetry lay in personal convictions regarding the latent exclusionism of modernist style as much as in the constantly fluctuating literary-historical contexts of her peculiar development. There was in Canada in the 1940s a persistent idealization of complex metaphor and a concomitant faith that the activity of reading such poetry could lead to an enlightenment that would carry over into the reader's adjudication of social and political issues. The characteristically politicized poet of that decade remained convinced that a difficult and sometimes obscure poetic style was in ideal keeping with the need to see society's complexity and potential anew; such styles did not belie the poet's human sympathy because such sympathy was with classes, or groups, or catalogues of persons rather than with individuals – it was a sympathy from above or outside. But in the course of the forties a transition of political and with it poetic taste was completed (attested to in a limited way by the increased emphasis on persons in Page's poetry), and a gap opened between the abstractions of poetic style and the increasingly eccentric particularity that then seemed demanded in the representation – that is, the defence – of humankind.

For Page, a poet who after all began her training in the 1930s, the transition towards a greater creative sympathy with individual others was natural and compelling, but the more difficult transition – away from an impersonal poetics that in her view at least obscured such sympathy – was to be so challenging that a prolonged period of personal silence was necessary to its undertaking. Perkins summarizes the broad dilemma precisely:

... whatever direction [mid-century] poets take, their way is thickly beset with fears and guilts. On the one hand, they feel themselves threatened with self-consciousness, loss of direct emotion, isolation from an audience and from ordinary reality, the futility of the esoteric. Yet perhaps the other way [a return to subjectivism] leads inevitably to a bad conscience as a writer and the contempt of one's peers. The self-conflict is even more bitter for the many poets who have or want to have feelings of solidarity with the poor, the victimized, and the oppressed. What can our complicated, elitist art present them? How can it cry aloud in confronting those moral, political, and social issues in which feeling ought to be complex?[115]

Perkins's remarks on British poetry of the 1930s are applicable over the whole length of modernist development in Canada. (In Milton Wilson's famous phrase, 'one of the advantages of a poetry less than a hundred years old is that all the things that couldn't happen when they should have happened keep happening all the time.')[116] Cid Corman appears to have given Page a statement of this broad intuition in blunt and immediate form; his remarks briefly stimulated new attempts at poetic change, but they may also have formulated the question too effectively and made a specific 'answer' seem too requisite to her poetry's continuation.

Amid such choices and frustrations 'After Rain' was written, in a spirit of self-'chastisement,' as Page remarked in a letter to Floris Clarke McLaren of early 1955.[117] McLaren had earlier suggested that the draft version, then entitled 'Kitchen Garden,' be retitled and surrender its present final stanza, which she found 'to drop in poetic level ... dangerously close to women's magazine emotion and thinking. (And that's something you've never been guilty of).'[118] Apparently not only male critics emphasized the gender of Page's stylistics. McLaren's suggestion was set aside, luckily, and the final stanza left intact, to clarify not only the poet's sense of helplessness but also the poem's broader examination of her thin sympathy with her gardener's plight, as well as her 'encumbrance' of the emotion with her relentless image-making. It is now clear that Page was pushing in 'After Rain' at the edges of her and her age's aesthetics, at the very least intuitively aware of their constitutive contradiction and eager to articulate a resolution and move on. Since she was unable to do so, we are invited to conclude that the contemporary possibilities of poetic renovation in the 1950s, with their new emphasis on the subjectivity of the poet and of those she portrayed, as well as on the transparency of a new 'natural' (meaning American) idiom, were sufficiently antithetical to her own art that she could not embrace them.

The terms of this argument have done little, though, in their turn, to recreate with sympathy the suffering of Page herself in this period of creative loss. We can recover some of the poignancy of her drift into silence if we juxtapose 'Arras' and 'After Rain' with a third poem of 1954, 'Reflection in a Train Window,' that once again foregrounds the relation among images and their *integritas*, their perceiver's ambivalent sympathy with others, and the opaque poems she fears she writes. I read 'Reflection' highly speculatively, as a moment of painful self-revelation[119] in which the poet acknowledges the personal erasure involved not only in her own impersonal aesthetics, but in her humble resignation to their contemporary insufficiency. The visionary woman in this poem is a haunting palimpsest whose suffering is curiously aesthetic and real at once:

There is a woman floating in a window –
transparent –
Christmas wreaths in passing houses
shine now in eye and now in hair, in heart.
How like a saint with visions, the stigmata
marking her like a martyr.

(*GA*, p. 47)

The woman's transparency of identity permits the phenomena of the world external to the train to enter the poem, passing from her 'eye' to her 'heart.' This visual penetration casts her as 'martyr,' a lovely touch of irony that modulates the poem's lamentation into clear self-criticism. The pane of glass that divides her from experience becomes a figure for the poem itself, in which the images are focused only at the cost of personal effacement, yet the glimmer of personality remains in their selection. But the cost is real: the loss of self, the silencing of private feeling and the submission to her own 'image' are a source of isolation and grief:

She without substance, ectoplasmic, still,
is haloed with the reading lamps of strangers
while brass and brick pass through her.
Yet she stirs
to some soft soundless grieving and tears well
in her unseeing eyes and from the sill
her trembling image falls, rises and falls.

The poet is 'haloed' by those who 'read' around her, but her own 'image' fluctuates. The violence of this strange insubstantiality is revealed in the 'brass and brick' that continually invade the boundaries of her 'body.' The poem takes its closure when the 'image' she has tried to sustain has 'fall[en]' one last time. The tyrannous 'eyes' that had controlled her way of thought are now 'unseeing,' and only their 'tears' remain.

'Reflection in a Train Window,' which I have taken as a subjective poem despite its third-person superficies, helps to convince me that Page was keenly aware of the various forces I have identified as key to her development and eventual silence. Her later wry references to abandonment by the Muse ('"Why did you stop writing?" "I didn't. It stopped."')[120] are to my mind conscious or unconscious attempts to project these practical creative crises onto an external and more powerful agent, a tactic we saw her exploit with the birds of 'After Rain.' The three poems I have taken to deal with those crises make clear her conscious recognition of her place – and her fear of a lack of place – in a history of modern poetry. I would contend against her pessimism that those three poems reveal more clearly than any of her others her precise place in that history, presenting as they do the best of her early poetics, the frustrations of those poetics, and the needed subjectivist alternative.

'Cry Ararat!,' the first major poem of Page's return to her work a dozen years later, is explicit in its retrospection on these issues:

> The bird in the thicket with his whistle,
> the crystal lizard in the grass
> the star and shell
> tassel and bell
> of wild flowers blowing where we pass,
> this flora-fauna flotsam, pick and touch,
> requires the focus of the total I.
>
> (*GA*, p. 100)

Accumulation remains fruitful, and images are still deliberately artificial; but they cannot now be conceived separate from the unique experience of selfhood that moves her visionary eye. Not that this need imply a first-person, or even loosely lyric, poetics. 'Cry Ararat!' sustains many of Page's usual diversions from self-revelation: definite articles replace possessives ('the dream,' not 'my dream,' 'the fingers,' not 'my fingers'), first-person plurals replace singulars ('the dream that haunts us when we wake'), and private experience is projected onto abstract figures ('sometimes there is one / raw with the dream of flying'). At the same time, however, a new intimacy with our speaker is available:

> First soft in the distance,
> blue in blue air
> then sharpening, quickening

taking on green.
Swiftly the fingers
seek accurate focus ...

(*GA*, p. 97)

She allows us to see Ararat with her eyes; what's more, her eyes are not now so startlingly different from our own, since she too needs binoculars and can fail to focus. Of course, our sharing this vision of dry land – and it's worth keeping in mind that that's what Ararat offers the swamped poet, a regrounding – involves us in her pain when vision is lost. In this sense Page establishes new sympathies among her persona, her readers, and her fellow artists; we too are speaking as the 'one / raw with the dream of flying' laments her new limitations:

'Must my most exquisite and private dream
remain unleavened?
Must this flipped and spinning coin that sun
could gild and make miraculous become
so swiftly pitiful?'

(*GA*, p. 99)

The 'focus of the total I' is not, therefore, a reinscription of first-person point of view but rather a deep recognition of the I-ness of all perception – her reader's, her subject's, her own – and of her obligation to bridge those remote lookouts: as the dove must, who 'believed / in her sweet wings and in the rising peak / with such a washed and easy innocence / that she found rest on land for the sole of her foot ...' (*GA*, p. 99).

The poem's search for a new sympathy of viewpoint is prominent and yet not contradictory of Page's painful register of loss and alienation when vision falters, at which we 'cry Ararat!' in despair. If 'the total I' experiences both Ararat and flood, focus and blurring, sympathy and alienation, the poem will have to be equal to her bifurcated expression. Whereas in 'After Rain' Page's awareness of the contradiction between her sympathy for Giovanni and her visionary eye could not be resolved with conviction, here she recognizes that the two can coexist, not cancel each other. The poetic image may still be so intense as to blind us to its own significance; *or* it may capture the noumenal wholly and ideally: 'A single leaf can block a mountainside; / all Ararat be conjured by a leaf' (*GA*, p. 100). The effect depends, perhaps, on the 'focus of the total I,' the punning phrase immediately preceding these binary closing lines.

Page's willingness to leave the poem at this indeterminate point is a signal of substantial new confidence and a reconciliation to her own poetic gift. The two lines typify much of the poem's juxtapositive and fragmentary nature: 'Cry Ararat!' is full of such swift transitions in image, implication, and, above all, tone, so that we can leap in a single line from the agonized cry of 'Ararat!' to the 'washed and easy innocence' of the dove completing her circle, 'a green twig in her beak' (*GA*, p. 99). Page has not reduced, in other words, the fragmentary and combinatory drive of her early poetry, although she certainly has reconceived the relation of 'image' to 'line.' Here she is willing to set the joy of visionary experience side by side with the suffering of its daily loss – with minimal mediating comment – and to presume that in a handful of fragmented stanzas recording their tension, a powerful *integritas* will be palpable. Although she may appear to have lowered the stakes of modernist form by adopting a more direct and colloquial imagery, she has, on the other hand, raised those stakes conceptually, leaving us as she does hovering at the moment between ideal vision and its grim loss – and then leaving the poem outright. When I intensely experience this poem's *integritas,* I am enjoying a superlative tension between fragmentation and wholeness (not one or the other) that lies at the heart of Page's modernist poetics: a poetics of sympathy and identification called for, but not accomplished, when she wrote 'After Rain' near the end of her apprenticeship to the styles of the forties.

The extent to which the urgent questions of forties poetic history have been carried over by 'Cry Ararat!' to Page's most recent writing is beyond the scope of this book,[121] and it is enough to have suggested that her work on either side of the middle silence engages ideas of poetic wholeness that were vital and broadly shared, in Montreal and elsewhere, during the *Preview* and *First Statement* years. Though perhaps no closer to the causes of Page's middle silence, I have a better account of its anticipation in her early poetry, and of that poetry's situation in the transitional decade in which it was chiefly nurtured. Page has always seemed eccentric to our narratives of the forties, at first because a *First Statement*–authorizing criticism of the decade cast her as faulty poet, but equally now, when recovery and acclaim have come in largely feminist terms inattentive to her historical centrality. Though others would meet – and suffer – more fully than she the mid-century call for new lyric models of modernist selfhood, in her career-long search for a 'heart a size / larger than seeing' and a 'pure line' of formal intensity, Page remains the exemplary poet of the Montreal forties.

2

The Poem in the Mind: The *Integritas* of Klein in the Forties

Integrity, *Integritas*, and the Distinctness of Klein

Page's poetics reflect a larger effort that was definitive of the forties experience: the search for sound new bases for collectivity, identity, and wholeness, not only on the level of idiosyncratic poetic style, but on that of (what one might call) mental style as well. The mannerist impersonality on which her poetry of the period insists cannot properly be conceptualized without recourse, as we have seen, to metaphors whose resonance lies in the psychological dimension. An 'impersonal' poem will suppress content that would alert the reader to a particular poet whose private experience made her say these things in verse; and the suppression of such individuality in the poem requires, obviously, some loosely analogous suppressions in the creating mind, however temporary: whether of private experience, or a private idiom, or of ineffable emotions explicable solely in relation to her being precisely and inescapably who she is. We may figure such impersonality neutrally and think it no more than a poetic effect achieved with conscious skill by a poet who chooses what and what not to include; or we may, at the opposite extreme, imagine a mind in which the rigour of impersonality is achieved at great cost, by a poet whose dedication to it jars with an equally forceful experience of the representativeness of his selfhood and its right to expression. In either case we presume analogies between poetic style and mental style: that they share impulses of admission and suppression; that their mutual task is the configuration of the particulars of a sensibility; that the goal of both is a representation of stability and order sufficient to the recognition of the poem, or the personality, by another who encounters the poet.

In Page's case, a rigorous determination to exclude personality from her range of *integritas* contributed to an intense stylization of her poetics and had something to do with the lapse in her verbal art from the early 1950s to the mid-1960s. While this situation was doubtless distressing to her, perhaps intensely so, there is little basis for claiming a connection, like those routine in the doctrines of the New Apocalypse, between the frustrations of her poetic style and such challenges as she may have undergone to her personal and psychological integrity. Whatever her nadirs of mood during her middle silence, she clearly maintained a forceful identity, finding expression not only in private and public life, but in a shift to visual artistry as well, and when the poetry returned in a more subjective and less idiosyncratic manner, no radical change in that stable private selfhood was apparently required for its renewal. In short, I felt no need to explore the recesses of mind in elucidating the growth, interruption, and renewal of Page's creativity. But the case of A.M. Klein is obviously sadly otherwise. Indeed it reverses Page's situation: in Klein's poetry there has been no such talk of a stylistic crisis, of a struggle for new *integritas*, or a fear of subjectivism in verse, while the vividness of his personal and mental withdrawal gives urgency, and delicacy, to the language of 'wholeness' and 'integrity' that has engaged us so far.

There are good reasons to remain silent on Klein's breakdown, the most profound pertaining to critical ethics. Respect for Klein's privacy as an individual should form some part of our treatment of him as a poet; sympathy with his suffering, however little we know of it, should probably curb our inquiring too closely into its causes and manifestations; politeness alone makes us sensitive to the feelings of his family and friends when the matter of his later life is raised. But Page's case also makes it clear that we cannot, with rigour, choose to ignore creative lapses whose consequences for our criticism are apparent. If *her* middle silence has proved helpful in reading poems as early as 'The Stenographers,' then Klein's final silence – although psychological as well as poetic – should be examined on the same grounds. Whether that can be done with respect and sympathy will surely test my, and perhaps my audience's, ethics of criticism.

Klein's experience will show us that the dilemma of the forties poets was not only aesthetic, but individual and existential: that the problem of unifying intense images of the world, to create poems, or of one's self, to achieve identity and authenticity, was broad and deep and *can* help us to understand the complexity of literary culture in the period. What's more, we can expand this *topos* to include another of the decade's impulses to cohesiveness: that of individuals forming literary collectives (*Preview* and *First Statement*, for example, and those two merging in *Northern Review*), struggling at cost to maintain their unity, and experiencing their eventual breakdown. Indeed even the energy of generation-identification in Sutherland's and Dudek's

First Statement polemics was claiming coherence and collectivity for a group of poets whose real solidarity was to prove – very shortly – surprisingly fragile. In the midst of this general oscillation of the decade, into and out of coherent collectives and shared identities, Klein's crisis proves acutely relevant to and representative of the decade of his greatest accomplishment.

During the forties Klein's poetry was to undergo a marked revision of style and subject that bore the inarguable imprint of his exposure to the poets of *Preview*. Nevertheless, the careful nature of his affiliations in the local 'little mag' culture suggests the impressive elasticity of his group commitments. He did not appear as an editor of *Preview* until the nineteenth of twenty-three issues, two years after the magazine's inception. While hesitating, he maintained a consistent relationship with *First Statement*, by regular appearance in its pages as well as his friendship with Irving Layton. He showed alertness to the loose editorial tastes of the two magazines, sending his more sardonic and impersonal work to *Preview*, his more lyrical and explicitly Jewish poetry to *First Statement*.[1] Curiously, the journal with which he finally affiliated himself suffered more of his sarcasm, as this fragment of a letter to A.J.M. Smith makes plain:

> I did see the [Neufville] Shaw manifesto in Preview, and felt the same way about it as you, and this despite the disarming comment on myself, and told both Page and Anderson so. The truth is that that kind of criticism both sickens and enrages me; these people think that having discovered that bread is vital, they have found the last word in human thought ... My only consolation lies in watching them jump through the hoop every time the party changes its line. The punishment is Dantesque.[2]

Klein's antipathy was focused, as we have seen, on Patrick Anderson, whose work against him in the Cartier riding election of 1944 may explain in part Klein's scorn for his political depth. That *Preview*'s inspirational leader should receive such sarcasm, while the rival journal's editors are treated with remarkable silence in the letters, shows Klein's tendency to distance himself from collectives of which he formed a willing if nominal part. But it is that very tendency in Klein that makes him so invaluable to renewed study of the 1940s, for he denies easy generalizations about the two magazines' differences even as he undermines clear generational categories for the modernisms of the 1920s and the 1940s.

Klein's involvement in the literary culture of the forties was characterized then by his ambiguous position both at the centre and on the margins of that activity. An established 'twenties' poet with a susceptibility to forties innovation, a *Preview* poet with scorn for its editors and friendship for its rivals, a lawyer on the bohemian fringe, Klein construed his own poetic identity in ways that complicate criticism and at the same time attract it powerfully. The ambivalence of his commitment to his own literary milieu will be a minor theme in what follows, and in choosing that modernist context I am deliberately paying little fixed attention to Klein in his most familiar double agency, as a Jewish poet of the English language. Zailig Pollock's *A.M. Klein: The Story of the Poet* is the most recent and comprehensive work to mine that vein; he has surveyed Klein's conflicted relations to his own Jewishness so thoroughly that I cannot hope to improve on – but I can gratefully exploit – his findings in what follows.

Still, the broadest purpose of Klein's profoundly syncretic genius was, obviously, the expression of his relation to Jewish tradition *in contemporary English verse*. The task situated him, typically, between two powerful contending forces, with Klein the gifted mediator whose heroic powers of reconciliation made him the pivot on which the Hebraic and English cultures could meet. Thus a situation of Klein in the context of the forties transition in Canadian modernist poetry – a situation still little sketched – has direct bearing on our grasp of his vocation as a Jewish poet.[3] Klein's effort to embody such widely disparate fields of image and idea, by experiment in poetic style and structure; the contemporary and traditional styles he rifled and fused; his hesitant affiliation with more single-minded coteries; and his eventual silencing in the crucial years 1953–4 (compare Page, Anderson, and Sutherland), speak to his moving representativeness in the forties – even if the precise terms in which each of these problems emerged for him *are* particular to his Jewish experience. And the ambiguities of self-identification generated by his dual allegiances are, I would argue, very much in keeping with that broader matter of forties literary culture I am asserting: the pressure towards the establishment of new collectivities, new wholes, and the counter-pressure that makes that effort costly, whether to the poem's soundness, or to the personality's.[4]

Thus, Klein's involvement, as a North American Jew of the 1940s, in a period of modernist consolidation in Canada did much to determine and to problematize his poetic choices. In the context of varied challenges to his creative and at times personal selfhood, an injunction like the demand for impersonality in modern poetry – however thinly theorized in the Canadian literary community – must have seemed ironically forceful. Much of Klein's sense of creative purpose depended on his ability to conjoin a particular and different personal heritage with an 'alien' English tradition demanding of contemporary poets a rigorous exclusion of the 'merely' personal. Klein did not understand this injunction in the absolute terms that seem to have conditioned Page's early poetics, and he may perhaps have had a more subtle grasp of Eliot's varied meanings in 'Tradition and the Individual Talent' than she; but it remains true that a *general* obedience to the demands of impersonality is one of the conditions of Klein's broader synthesis of the two traditions he revered. That such a condition should be accepted by a poet whose public life came to a dramatic conclusion in an 'extinction of personality' bitterly echoing Eliot's ideal is a final irony of Klein's ambivalent modernism, and a necessary object of inquiry in what follows.

The Holocaust and Klein's *Integritas*

The above remarks moved too freely between an aesthetic and a psychological diction, and although Klein's career invites such slippage, the relation between them needs to be stabilized. I want to show, first, that Klein's aesthetic theories *circa* 1948 participate tellingly in the forties address to poetic *integritas* that I remarked in the poetry of Page, and, second, that it was Klein's own habit in that pivotal year to base conclusions about the language of poetry on intuitions about the grammar of the mind. I will then make claims for the applicability of *integritas* to a description of Klein's psychological life. I hope thereby to ground a reading of the poems of *The Rocking Chair* in their embodiment of both the daunting comprehensiveness and the exhausting urge to objectivity of Klein's poetic mind, and to suggest that the internalized violence of the Holocaust enforced in those poems a suppression of personal experience that is itself the mark of a mental integrity under acute historic pressure.

Klein never elaborated a sytematic aesthetics, and indeed, when asked for a statement of his poetic convictions, he tended to reply with more or less mild sarcasm.[5] In the second half of 1948, however, he jotted a series of notes, apparently to himself, in which he sketched aesthetic ideas about the coherence of poetic structures and the energy of verbal juxtaposition.[6] These 'Marginalia' constitute as much of an aesthetics as Klein desired explicitly to record. Coinciding as they do with the beginning of his near-obsessive work on Joyce's *Ulysses* (of which more later), it is no surprise that Klein's remarks should have a Joycean flavour, and moreover echo powerfully the conceptions of *integritas*, figured through Joyce's *Portrait*, that were potent elsewhere as he wrote.

Perhaps a danger of my 'coinage' of *integritas* is its derivation through Joyce from Aquinas, whose definitions of beauty were fundamentally determined by his estimation of the mundane world's spiritual significance. In regard to Klein, however, such a linkage is appropriate, for Klein's literary art participated in a tradition which (because denied the expression of devotion through images and idols) focused its evocation of divinity on the potential of language to body forth the ineffable.[7] Certainly he shows no anxiety in the 'Marginalia' over the divine resonance in the beautiful 'artifact,' which he first qualifies in his own terms and then legitimates in those of Aquinas: an object's vividness consists of

> (a) form, (b) content, (c) light. By the last one must understand internal light – radiance; external light is already assumed in the concept of form.
>
> It was from his God, therefore, that the Angelic Doctor learned that 'Ad pulchritudinem tria requiruntur: integritas, consonantia, claritas.'
>
> (*LER*, p. 182)

This fragment of the 'Marginalia,' 'Towards an Aesthetic,' does nothing to define Aquinas's terms, nor does Klein draw further parallels between his three (modernist) components of beauty and the 'Angelic Doctor's'; but he does seem to want to confirm the affective drift of Aquinian aesthetics, and his attention to 'radiance,' 'internal light,' suggests a particular concern with the force of representation and clarity crucial to the work of art.

Klein's citation of 'integritas' affords no particular connection to the forties concept of *integritas*; it is difficult to know how he might have developed these ideas, and their sketchy form may indicate that he saw nothing in them to develop. But 'Towards an Aesthetic' was composed in the 'Marginalia' notebook between two statements of aesthetic that nudge Klein's reference to Aquinas in contemporary directions useful to the current study. The first of these is only apparently whimsical. Entitled '$x^2 + 2xy + y^2$,' it shows Klein doodling mentally with the nature of verbal juxtaposition and its relation to creative power:

> Successful is the poetic statement only then when each of its constituent words acquires through juxtaposition a significance equal to at least the square of its value in isolation.
>
> Let a̲ and b̲ represent any two words in dictionary isolation. It is contended that when juxtaposed (a+b), they do not become poetry unless such juxtaposition effects a raising of their power to $(a+b)^2$; i.e. juxtaposition must give them the value $a^2 + 2ab + b^2$.[8]

Klein's concern is clearly that the startling juxtapositions of words and phrases in modernist poems have poetic value, that the meaning and beauty elicited in such a technique be sufficient to justify its strangeness. The algebraic formulae to be fulfilled, playful as they are, seem to work ironically, to suggest that there is indeed no *quantifiable* power in good poems, but also that good poems should be much concerned with the degree of power they achieve in return for their – perhaps laboured – techniques.

The fragment immediately *following* 'Towards an Aesthetic' in the 'Marginalia' dossier also borrows the language of the sciences to distinguish poetic kinds, in this case, kinds of excellent poetry. 'The Poem as Circular Force' is the best known of the 'Marginalia';[9] Bentley employs it in his reading of 'Portrait' to ground an optimistic rendering of the poem's concluding section.[10] The distinction of 'centrifugal' from 'centripetal' poetry that Klein offers[11] is not at the moment so interesting to me as the image both words ask us to work with: of the poem as an atomic structure, with a kind of nucleus (perhaps of meanings) surrounded by orbiting particles (ideas, images). This imagination of the poem as a field of 'force,' or energy, is particularly resonant in the context of '$x^2 + 2xy + y^2$,' with its interest in the kinetic value of verbal juxtaposition, and it suggests the character of Klein's interest in 'radiance' (the equivalent of *claritas* in Aquinas). Klein's imagery and language also strikingly echo the spatial metaphor employed by Joseph Frank in his 'Spatial Form in Modern Literature' of 1945; like Frank, Klein found it helpful to speak of modernist poetics as a structuring of atomic fragments under subtle forces of containment, a tendency illuminated for both men by Joyce's *Ulysses*.[12]

The atomic model of poetic energy implied in 'The Poem as Circular Force' has analogues in other pieces from the 'Marginalia': especially in 'The Poem of the Age,' in which Klein's image of the poetics his age demanded gave 'atomic' its second, more explosive meaning:

> What will this great poem of the future look like? If we knew, we would write it. We venture, however, the formula for a minuscule exemplar. Take the word: *Love*, and proceed first of all by chain-reaction. What two other words does it suggest? Put them down. Then what two words does each of love's suggestibilities bring to your mind? Put them down. You will advance, thus, in a geometric progression, simulating, on your way, the repercussions of the chain-reaction, invoking, as you go along, the associational promptings of our common psychology – and you will be surprised to what a point you will come.
>
> (*LER*, pp. 190–1)

Nowhere else does Klein endorse the automatist methods of Surrealism. A broad irony is likely. Such a vision of poetic renewal begs the question underlined by '$x^2 + 2xy + y^2$': how can we be assured that such a radical poetics of juxtaposition will lead to verbal force? To answer, Klein intuits the poetic structure's analogy with the psyche ('our common psychology'), but the point goes undeveloped. Still, the positivistic leaning of Klein's aesthetic language suggests how vital it was to him at the time to find new images of poetic structure and energy, and how concerned he was that such new ideas not be allowed to set aside the principles of verbal organization, unity, and power that poetry had taught him to seek.

The concatenation of Klein's references adumbrates, then, my formulation of *integritas*. He sketches the atomic model of poetic structure that modernist *integritas* implies, considers the enticements and implied dangers of an aesthetic of accumulation, and reveals a late-career concern with the sources and kinds of poetic energy. The echoes between his intuitions and the challenges faced by Page, for example, are clearly audible in his extension of the idea of 'centrifugal' poetry: 'Up to this point [the poem's end] the poet confined himself to images which could be kept within the limits of his stanzaic canvas; here release takes place; and the mind, too, is set winging with the swallows in the skies' (*LER*, p. 184). As in Page's 'After Rain,' we have a quantitative relation between 'images' and the 'limits' of poetic inclusion (for her, the 'pure line'); and, perhaps fortuitously, another representation of birds, to whom the persona of 'After Rain' utters her prayer for a heart 'a size larger than seeing,' that associates them with a level of significance beyond the constraints of poetic structure. It is newly clear that the aesthetic speculations of the forties poets, and of the period's critics, cluster suggestively around a handful of key structural ideas.

The tone of Klein's aesthetic fragments is consistently positive. Nowhere does his assertion of the atomic, juxtapositive nature of modern poetry or of the limits of its 'circular force' openly reflect a reading of his own poetry or anxiety about its *integritas*. He does want to show, however, that the concepts of poetic structure he jots down are implicitly analogous to concepts of mental structure; witness the allusion above to 'the mind set winging with the swallows' as one effect of the centrifugal energy of good poetry. Indeed, the major interest of 'The Poem as Circular Force' is the effect of poems' atomic energies on the reader's mind: is it drawn in by the poem, or thrown outward? In 'The Poem of the Age,' immediately after remarking that 'atomic is the era's word,' he adds, 'Nor can the writer of the future afford to ignore the new psychological frontiers of the mind; the truth is that the manner of most contemporary writing has already established it as a truism that no author can approach the criticism of life without a Freudian-et-al. apparatus' (*LER*, p. 190). And we have already noted his remark later in the same piece that the 'chain-reaction' of juxtapositive verbal automatism is akin to 'the associational promptings of our common psychology.' While such remarks hardly make a Klein interpretation of mental structure clear, they do reveal his own 'associational' habit of referring to the workings of the brain shortly after remarks on the workings of the poem, in ways that emphasize their symbolic affinity.

Bentley has read this association of mental and poetic structure in Klein in fairly positive terms, at least in so far as the stanzas of 'Portrait' are concerned:

> Klein's sixains certainly provide evidence of their author's ability to perceive and to project order in a world that is superficially chaotic and insane: their composed, artful and balanced structure is a manifestation of his mental composure, of his control over his subject matter, and of the sense of balance which differentiates him from many inhabitants of the modern world ...[13]

It is only with the first of these three claims for Klein's mentality that I would want to take issue, for there can be no guarantee of a particular 'mental composure' in Klein's ability to complete stanzas or poems. Indeed it is possible that, as Dudek remarked in *First Statement* of Emile Nelligan, 'had he been a normal man, he would not have written these poems.'[14] We do not need the evidence of Klein's later breakdown to demur, but it does seem likely that there was more conflict between Klein's poetic 'composure' and his mental life than Bentley suggests. To what extent may we apply, though, Klein's coincident interest in *integritas* to *his* mental life?

A brief intuitional survey of the Klein *oeuvre* and biography do seem to justify the manoeuvre. We need not have looked too deeply to discern Klein's remarkable embodiment of an enormous variety of cultural experience and his persistent desire to widen the nets of his consciousness so as to increase the comprehensiveness of his contact with other classes, races, religions, persons. Born into a Jewish household whose daily life was lived in Yiddish but whose devotions required his study of Hebrew, Klein went on to gifted expression in English and intimacy with French. A child of Ukraine who grew up in English and French Canada and dreamed fondly of a restored Israel, he drew his poetic subjects from the emblematic persons of all four cultures, and gave voice to individuals fictional and historic by setting aside his own keenly felt intensity and uniqueness. The son of struggling immigrants in the cloth trade who briefly considered the rabbinate before becoming a lawyer, Klein would add to his circle of colleagues professors of literature, copy-writers, Marxist neophytes, and multimillionaires – the last named despite his concurrent electoral bid for a socialist party. A narrowing of our focus to the literary-historical would allow this pattern to extend, so as to remark (for example) the Keatsian poet who became modern, the *Preview* poet who admired *First Statement*, and so on, but it is sufficiently apparent without doing so that a good narrative of Klein's life would emphasize its tendency to juxtaposition, sometimes to synthesis, and, sadly, sometimes to fragmentation and collapse.

The chief value of such a catalogue is that it urges us to admire the consciousness of Klein for its astonishing concatenations, for his ability to sustain a field of memory, idea, and feeling of unexampled complexity. That he should at the same time have found various forms of self-effacement congenial, whether in the multivocality of his poetry or his glum persistence in a low-profile legal career, not only highlights a compelling dichotomy of his mental life, but also justifies the evocation of *integritas* as a model of that dichotomy. If the modernist poem may be figured as a forceful and energetic structure delimiting a wide range of kinetic images and ideas unified often by no more than their juxtaposition in a single *consciousness* – their 'association,' to use Klein's Hartleian term – the mind may be similarly represented in the language of poetic structure: especially if we want to capture the energy and inclusiveness, the associative genius and comprehensive breadth of image and reference, in a mind like Klein's. To speak so is to return to the etymological missing link that allowed 'integrity' to move from its Latin resonances having to do with structure, soundness, and the like to its current and perhaps reductive English usage as a term descriptive of moral probity. For Klein was a 'man of integrity' in his ability to sustain widely disparate ranges of knowledge, points of mental view, articles of faith, and languages of human experience. In this reading the creative mind, too, has its centrifugal and centripetal energies, moving us simultaneously *beyond* the known limits of our selves and deeper *within* our selves as we grow and create. One figure of Klein's late mental breakdown emerges if we see this tension lost: if we recognize a point in his mental life when the outward motion of selfhood was suddenly withdrawn, leaving the force of inwardness lamentably unchecked.[15]

I want to consider, then, that the pressures on Klein's mental integrity may be akin to the pressures working against poetic *integritas* in the forties; indeed, to force the connection, I refer to both as *integritas* henceforth. Moreover I believe that by charting the mental corollaries of *integritas* and disintegration, by inquiring into the nature and causes of Klein's nervous breakdown, we will be learning something useful about the causes of poetic breakdown, and poetic transformation, in the period. But such an inquiry is hampered quickly, partially by a weak taboo I sense as I write, but more strongly by our almost complete ignorance of the causes and conditions of Klein's trouble – an ironic ignorance, since we are so keenly aware of the breakdown itself. Lacking new 'facts' to add to the Klein dossier, I propose a review of the knowledge we do have, in hope that the current context will reconfigure our information in useful ways. My method takes its cue from Klein's own recognition of the link between poetic structure and the associations of the mind, to seek a 'reading' of the compulsive silence of his later years.[16]

Caplan's *Like One That Dreamed: A Portrait of A.M. Klein* remains the best narrative of Klein's life from the exhausting lecture tours of the early 1950s to his death of a heart attack in his sleep in 1972, and I draw on it extensively. Pollock deals only in the most oblique and laconic way with Klein's breakdown, having chosen a different perspective on the ethical questions I tendered earlier; he nevertheless contextualizes a number of Caplan's uncited documents in ways that nuance their impact, and I refer to his biographical asides on occasion. Caplan's treatment is judicious, sensitive, and evocative, passing quickly over the electroshock therapy and suicide attempts of early 1954 (p. 205) to give more detailed attention to the pathos of Klein's gradual withdrawal from all public life (pp. 210–13). His most poignant images of Klein as recluse emerge in accounts of late visits by fellow poets, such as Abraham Sutzkever, who during a 1959 meeting with Klein 'ventured to ask what he was working on most recently. In response, Klein simply nodded to his desk, which was completely bare' (p. 210). The image of Klein inactive is wrenching enough, but his non-verbal, indifferent way of conveying his creative incapacity to Sutzkever is especially unhappy. A.J.M. Smith's story of a late visit to Klein, quoted at length by Caplan, captures the glacial remoteness of his personality, the refusal to be touched by those outside the hermetic home:

> My *Oxford Book of Canadian Verse* was published that year [1960], and I had dedicated it to Pratt and Klein. I'd sent a copy of it to Abe and never heard from him, so I called him on the phone and asked if he'd received it. I didn't know how ill he had been. There was a long pause and he said nothing. I said, 'I dedicated it to you and Pratt.' A pause again, and then he said, 'Thank you' ...
>
> So I went with my wife to see him at his house. She and Bessie sat talking in the front parlour, and Abe took me into the library. He poured me a good stiff slug of Scotch, though he took nothing himself, and I talked to him. I asked if he was writing anything. He answered only in monosyllables, he said no. I said, 'Did you see Steinberg's article on *The Second Scroll*?'– it had come out just a while before in *Canadian Literature*. He said, 'No, I didn't read it.' So after a few minutes of talking to him and getting polite but distant monosyllables, I decided that I had to go. It was very, very sad, and that was the last time I saw him. (qtd. uncited, p. 210)

Smith emphasizes, not surprisingly for one who loved his poetry, Klein's withdrawal from verbalization, the long pauses and brief monosyllables of their final conversation. Caplan adds that '[t]owards the end, Klein's conversations with his own family were usually limited to very short responses. Sometimes he would remain completely silent for days at a stretch' (p. 211). Although during the Sutzkever visit a year earlier Klein was 'unusually receptive and conversed affably' (p. 210), the Israeli poet's allusion to Klein's own work could only be acknowledged in sardonic silence.

A second prominent feature of Klein's distress was a paranoia 'about any unfamiliar item that was brought into the house from the outside' (p. 211). This was so pointed a condition that it led to his refusal to accept any payments for royalties on his books, despite financial strain (p. 213). The terse refusal of inquiries from former colleagues and friends is in keeping with this desire for a clear and fixed boundary between himself and the unpredictable events of the world outside the home. Caplan's use of 'A Psalm of Abraham of That Which Was Visited Upon Him' to anticipate Klein's breakdown[17] opens up the suggestive connections between Klein's early alertness to the invasion of mental disease and the imagery of a home broken into:

A prowler in the mansion of my blood!
I have not seen him, but I know his signs.
Sometimes I hear him meddling with my food,
Or, in the cellar, poisoning my wines ...

I know that he has breached my household peace,
I know that somehow he has let him in.
Should I then run to a window, and shout *Police*!
I dare not. He is of my kith and kin.[18]

Despite its composition well before the period of Klein's mental illness, this 'Psalm of Abraham' is especially resonant for its anticipation of that crisis. Its remarkable prefiguration of Klein's paranoia about the boundaries of his home, its strange pronomial reflexivity that briefly suggests the prowler is, like the speaker himself, a doubled agent ('he has let him in'), and its contamination of one of Klein's early group titles for poems celebrating his Jewish heritage ('of kith and kin' here being an acknowledgment of family relation to a criminal) indicate that we cannot understand the configuration of Klein's later disturbance without some recourse to his earlier writings.

More interesting at the moment, though, is the way in which the lapsing into literal silence and the paranoia regarding invasion from without reflect and illuminate one another. To psychologize loosely, we might say that a fear of allowing entrance to some unwanted or dangerous force external to the carefully guarded home (or mind) is the obverse image of a decision not to allow any mental energy from within to be wasted outward in verbal form. Both fears indicate an extreme concern for an impenetrable boundary between the safe world of private unarticulated experience and the unpredictable world of intimate verbal exchange. There is no more poignant rendering of this obsession with the boundaries of house and self than Klein's decision to sit *shiva* for his wife alone at his home while all other family members gathered at his son Sandor's house (Caplan, p. 212). The purpose of *shiva* being communal acknowledgment of grief and beginning of healing through daily prayer, Klein's inability to perform that service in company suggests how badly the rituals of verbal exchange frightened him and how essential the refuge of the home was to his mediation of intimate emotion.

Speakers at Klein's own funeral resolutely made no reference to his poetry (Caplan, p. 213): there was some will, clearly, to erase from his narrative the vocation that had motivated his life's only real work. To see the funeral's suppressions in their fullest possible light, though, we are compelled to return to the 1940s – to a period in which no sign of Klein's mental illness was visible to others, a period to which we might naturally be hesitant to apply for an interpretation of his later mental life. Caplan appends, silently, a fragment from Klein's papers, 'Journal, 1945,' to his narration of Klein's funeral. Pollock clarifies that the passage is drawn from a 'fictionalized diary' (p. 126) forming part of the 'Raw Material' dossiers in Klein's papers, probably drafted in 1943. He takes Klein at the word of his dossier label and reads the material as a draft novel, 'The Inverted Tree,' rather than for its autobiographical force (though he does highlight at the same time Klein's own remark that '[n]o thing happens but it is autobiographical' [p. 126], of which I will have more to say later).

The passage is written in a manner that suggests the recounting of a dream, though 'Kay,' Klein's typically permeable persona in the novel, seems merely to be daydreaming (Pollock, p. 126). Kay is attending his sister's funeral: he remarks the reasons for his shedding no tears, and observes the other mourners, until 'suddenly it is I who lie there in that box.' Now living out the familiar fantasy of attending his own funeral, 'Kay' notes with satisfaction the bereavement felt by his family, appreciates his own eulogy, and concludes,

> From behind my tears, I watch the entire ceremony, a stranger at my own funeral. Among the dead, I am beyond pain and pity, and am unmoved by the ululation which

I have so unintentionally caused. But I feel a certain glow of mild satisfaction. Here, my whole biography has been recounted, but nobody mentioned the fact that I was a poet.

I have kept the secret well. Now, no one will ever know of what I died. (p. 215)

Once again we see Klein doubled, both observer and observed – or tripled, if we want to maintain the strict illusion that this is fiction, 'Kay's' fantasy only. More tellingly, however, we see Klein's actual funeral pre-enacted, and his poetic life a 'secret,' like so many others, *not to be verbalized*. The acknowledged 'satisfaction' at this suppression seems to indicate that Klein conceived of his vocation as a burden on his well-being long before the years in which such mental stresses became apparent. '*Seems to* indicate' because the status of the excerpt, hovering between 'diary' and 'fiction,' remains unclear, and it may have been composed in a mood of dark whimsy that would serve to undercut dramatic interpretations of its images. Still, Pollock himself refers to these writings at one point as 'thinly disguised autobiograph[y]' (p. 114).

We have now seen enough to feel sure that an important stylization of behaviour functional in Klein's breakdown was an anxiety about speaking and writing that mirrored an equivalent anxiety over the admission of strangers and strange messages into the Klein home. This connection is especially convincing if we recognize the increasing identification of bodily space and domestic space suggested by the ever-diminishing distances he would travel when he left the house in later years (Caplan, pp. 210, 212–13). My purpose in highlighting this pattern is not to ground a new claim for the nature of Klein's illness; rather, by clustering some of its more obvious gestures, to suggest its profound relation to the vocation as a poet that had defined an identity for him for thirty years. It seems reasonable to suspect that his late antagonism to self-expression reflects a harsh negative relation to an earlier public life whose every feature was determined by the power of language, whether for legal, corporate, or artistic ends. And it seems, as a consequence, essential to return to the documents of that earlier life with an awareness that we are treating the materials of a selfhood that Klein too vehemently rejected: to recognize that we *must* look to the poems for further insight into his disorder and, in turn, that they to some extent anticipate a mental life in which words themselves could eventually become aggressors against whom one had to defend the walls.

The most obvious such prefigurations in the poetry have been well canvassed. Pollock lists the best-known references to 'madness' in Klein's poems, the 'Prayer of Abraham, Against Madness' of 1941, the 'prowler in the mansion' psalm quoted earlier (pp. 107–8); Caplan adds the 'some go mystical, and some go mad' of 'Portrait of the Poet as Landscape' and remarks that 'hindsight ... now accentuates these clues' (p. 181). And hindsight might add others: the 'little cherub' of 'A Psalm of Abraham, Concerning That Which He Beheld Upon the Heavenly Scarp' who, 'glimpsing God's work flaw'd, / Went mad, and flapped his wings in crazy mirth' (*CP*, p. 531), has always seemed to me a figure of Klein himself, for whom the flaws of God's dispensation were early visible and soon destructive of his childhood faith. The identification is assisted by the word 'little,' on which Klein of course punned elsewhere in a gesture of self-disclosure and self-disguise.[19] 'The Break-Up' of 1946 purports to depict the cracking of the ice in spring in Montreal's harbour, but its closing image is of a horror surfacing uncontrollably:

> ... from their iced tomb
> the pyramided fish, the unlockered ships,
> and last year's blue and bloated suicides.
>
> (*CP*, p. 647)

No doubt my earlier use of the word 'glacial' to describe the condition of Klein's personality in his last interview with Smith was governed in part by the power of this image for me; but the poem *was* written not long after Klein's funeral fantasy in 'The Inverted Tree,' and his drafting of another piece of 'raw material' for that novel dealing extensively with the different means of suicide,[20] and it is suggestive at the least of the poet's sense of a disturbing self-destructiveness lurking beneath the frozen surface of daily routine.

Such poems do indeed leap to our notice if we are thinking about the later crisis: like Keats's line 'I have been half in love with easeful Death,' they offer the comfort of linearity and determinism, as well as the clairvoyance of genius, as we think about poets cut off too soon. That very linearity, however, is also their chief weakness as documents of Klein's mental life. Caplan concludes his catalogue of such passages with useful caution: 'That Klein of all people would one day succumb to mental illness was certainly the last possibility that any of his friends or family could have imagined' (p. 181). P.K. Page's remarks second Caplan's conclusion: 'I never saw him moody or angry. He was the last of the *Preview* people whom I could have imagined having a breakdown. Any of us, I could have thought, might have had before Klein' (qtd. uncited in Caplan, p. 98). We need an image of Klein's consciousness in the forties which can make the poetic harbingers of later disturbance coherent with the genial poise registered in remarks like these. The psychic pressures particular to the late 1940s and early 1950s that divide Klein's confident prime from his later crisis can be surveyed to clear up Page's bewilderment, but none of those immediate triggers of breakdown satisfies as an explanation of the events of 1953 and 1954. I consider other causes of Klein's crisis to lie deeper and earlier in his experience, despite his earlier public urbanity, and I believe we have a way of speaking about such apparent contradictions in my metaphor of mind as *integritas*, the urge to wholeness of selfhood that holds conflicting mental data together without imposing ego's sameness on them – sometimes to one's own cost.

Caplan suggests that Klein endured a number of situations productive of mental stress from 1949 on. He cites with special emphasis (supported by Colman Klein, the poet's son) the frenetic pace of travel and speech-making following his return from Israel in 1949 and the publication of *The Second Scroll* in 1951 (p. 182). The humiliating election defeat of 1949 was clearly a severe blow to his sense of himself as a representative of the Jewish community of Montreal: despite the apparent success of his speeches and rallies, Klein's 'favourite son' candidacy came in a distant third, failing even to overtake the Labour-Progressive (Communist) candidate, despite that party's unquestioned involvement in the Soviet espionage leading up to the Gouzenko affair (pp. 157–61). At the same time Klein's 'darkening view of western civilization,' with its roots surely in the Holocaust but with more immediate manifestation in the postwar leniency shown to Nazi war criminals (p. 115), gave him little sustenance for a battered humanism and a near-obliterated faith. And his writing gave him, apparently, less and less recompense for these other burdens: despite the Governor General's Literary Award he received for *The Rocking Chair and Other Poems* and the positive notices and sales of *The Second Scroll*, Klein persisted – in a mood that seems to have been established during the difficult publication of *Poems* (1944) by the Jewish Publication Society of Philadelphia (Caplan, p. 91) – in the belief that his work was misunderstood and little appreciated. (On the other hand, he was receiving substantial corporate acclaim and reimbursement for the writing he performed in the employ of Samuel Bronfman and Seagram's, a kind of public success with which he was persistently uncomfortable and which must have given him a jaundiced reverse image of the notice he desired from his real constituencies.) Related perhaps to his own desire for critical attention was his obsessive scholarly work on Joyce: 'finally,' Caplan remarks, 'there remained but a short step from his over-reading of *Ulysses* to the delusions and illogical perceptions of paranoia' (p. 185).[21] In the Joyce work we can see the connections, perhaps dangerous, between the fetishization of literary style and the increasing fixation of Klein's mind.

Such circumstances as these can certainly help us to understand why the breakdown should have been triggered in the early 1950s. It is difficult, however, to list such incidents and feel that we have come close to a possible first cause. In so far as a first cause can never be known (and anyway we cannot re-create Klein's childhood with much accuracy), we are forced to rest among circumstances; but we can, if we choose, look at the greatest and most profound of these, even if in doing so we are taken back to that period of Klein's life when he seemed to those around him particularly well adjusted. I refer here to the years of the Holocaust, and to the slim religious belief with which Klein faced the news of that disaster to his people. Despite advances in the theory and practical criticism of Holocaust literatures, remarkably little attention had been paid to the Holocaust's impact on Klein's poetry prior to Pollock's *A.M. Klein,*[22] perhaps because it does seem difficult to reconcile the period of his greatest public success with a horror so tangible to his consciousness and conscience. In what follows I do not imply that the late war years, and therefore most of the 1940s, were periods of undocumented mental crisis for Klein, but rather that the emphatic mental well-being he projected to his contemporaries during that period is in itself alarming and suggests patterns of psychological survivalism that could not be sustained once the further burdens of the 1950s set in.

The wavering of Klein's Judaism was not *per se* a dimension of his breakdown.[23] A more stable faith would not have remotely reduced the horror he felt as the news of the European Holocaust began to reach North America in the second half of the war. On balance, he responded to the genocide more powerfully as an attack on people than on a faith *per se*: the pogrom in Ratno, the dehumanizing slaughter of Kamenets, and the stench of the Casablanca *mellah* in *The Second Scroll* are far more concretely evoked than the apparent restoration of Melech Davidson in his faith just before his murder in Israel. The guilt of the Holocaust survivor, however, which Klein felt as fully as any, might well have been made keen rather than blunted by an earlier abandonment of the Jewish religion: not only had the North American Jew escaped the hell of Europe by accident of birth, but the weak believer survived where the faithful had been swept away. Within this larger context, Klein's breakdown becomes all too familiar: the postwar witnessed the suicides and attempted suicides of many Jewish writers who could not possibly come to creative terms with their visceral knowledge of the Holocaust but also could not go on in life without coming to such terms. To remark the similarity of Klein's case to this pattern is not to reduce the particulars of *his* distress in the 1950s, but rather to see that distress as having some of its sources in an internationally felt phenomenon that prolonged the Nazi destruction well into the second half of the century. The suicide of Jerzy

Kosinski in 1991 is only the most recent and public example of this horrific cultural *thanatos*.[24]

It hardly seems necessary to 'prove' that the Holocaust contributed substantially to Klein's later breakdown: any demur would depend on an untenable reading of mental illness as perfectly *sui generis* and autonomous from the deepest circumstances of the mind it ravages. But the pattern of Klein's responses to the Holocaust seems to confirm not only the reading of his mental life I offered earlier, with its stylized anxieties of speech and seclusion, but as well the polarization of testimony and silence that has so long frustrated the attempts of Jews to tell the needed and dreaded story of their collective nightmare.[25] His prompt public responses might be characterized as urbane: the editorials in *The Canadian Jewish Chronicle*, always highly rational and brilliantly written, on the 'situation in Europe,'[26] and the composition from 1942 to 1943 of *The Hitleriad*, Klein's best-known failure in poetry. If there is a consensus on its weakness, it must pertain to the curious clash, first noticed by Irving Layton in his prompt review, between Klein's Augustan satirical remoteness and the evident sense of outrage and horror that motivates his response. It is as if a compulsive objectivity occasioned by his painfully immediate involvement in the genocide had got out of hand in the face of the enormity of emotion it had to control; the result is a poem in which so much articulate speech seems always to deflect the loss felt most deeply.

That conceptual gulf at the heart of *The Hitleriad* can also help us see why, as the news of the camps became more regular and detailed in 1943,[27] Klein's poetic output should have dropped off so remarkably. To be sure, *The Hitleriad* was a substantial exploitation of his gift, but Pollock in the *Complete Poems* notes only three other poems in the year: 'Actuarial Report,' which would eventually appear in *The Rocking Chair* and sounds remarkably like an attempt to imitate E.J. Pratt's 'Come Away, Death' in its rendition of contemporary violence; 'And in That Drowning Instant,' to which I shall return in a moment; and 'Not All the Perfumes of Arabia.'[28] The last named poem treats the olfactory sense as terror's most powerful messenger, and then catalogues the odours of war and murder of the times. The murder of Jews is here one horror among many: a bitter, but not unique, viciousness. Noteworthy now is the first stanza's concluding remark that terror's stench, passing by nostril and 'stealthy vein,' eventually 'thrust[s] / Its cry of havoc into the haunted brain!' (*CP*, p. 610). Not only foreshadowing the undercurrent of paranoia in the 1950s, the 1943 poem also echoes the 'prowler in the mansion of [the] blood' of 1941, whose poisoning of wines 'in the cellar' is here figured in Claudius's murder of the elder Hamlet, as 'poison into the ears of royal Denmark.' Such images of bodily invasion also anticipate the nightmare ashes of the 'Elegy' of 1947, the eventual 'Gloss Beth' of *The Second Scroll*:

> O through a powder of ghosts I walk; through dust
> Seraphical upon the dark winds borne;
> Daily I pass among the sieved white hosts,
> Through clouds of cousinry transgress,
> Maculate with the ashes that I mourn.
>
> (*CP*, p. 673)

The force of horror here comes from the speaker's inescapable inhalation of the ashes of his lost kinsmen; in all three poems such a sense of helpless contamination paralyses the invaded speaker. This six-year motif in Klein's poetic utterances suggests the continuity of his later collapse with the stresses on his mental *integritas* throughout the forties: the anxiety over bodily/domestic invasion is not new to the fifties, but rather newly acute.

Though 'Not All the Perfumes of Arabia' lacks the visceral intimacy with the Holocaust registered in 'Elegy,' it might well have inaugurated a period of composition in which Klein struggled, however pathetically, to bring his outrage for his shattered people into the public sphere. Instead it appears by Pollock's chronology to have been his last poem referring to the decimation of the Jews for three or four years: indeed, the Jewish people, their language and traditions, the massive violence done to them, face an eclipse as sudden in Klein's poetry as in Europe. 'Address to the Choirboys' of 1944 is a last, lingering evocation of the historic suffering of the Jews, but it is in truth an ironic attempt to shield young penitential singers from knowledge of the world's horror. From that poem until 'Meditation Upon Survival' of 1946, there is no reference whatsoever to his own people, though Klein was in one of his most prolific periods of composition. These are the years of the '*Suite Canadienne*,' the poems that would eventually form *The Rocking Chair*, well known for their intense detailing of Québécois life, but equally remarkable for their elimination of Jewish references from the rendition.[29] There is no escaping the disturbing fact that Klein's abrupt break from the tradition and context that had governed his creativity until the composition of 'Not All the Perfumes of Arabia' coincides exactly with the months in which the full horror of the death camps was reaching those in North America who were willing to hear.[30]

This 'coincidence' of events seems to me alarming. In that period in which the news of the Holocaust became inescapable for Klein and penetrated his mind with the utmost violence, a sudden silence about his own shattered people changed his poetry utterly. This juxtaposition has many other partial explanations, among them his great frustration over the preparation for publication and reception of his volumes of 1944, which he considered badly neglected by the very Jewish community with which he had so strongly identified his career as a poet. But having remarked already the later interplay of silence and anxiety over boundaries in Klein's mental life, I find it impossible to nuance the definiteness of his withdrawal from Judaica: especially since his speech continued elsewhere, while a rigorous silence forced an exclusion of the matter – of the very men and women – that had given his poetry its fabric for twenty years.

There can be no 'explanation' at the end of such speculations, no use in concluding – to put the matter nakedly – that he stopped writing Judaica and stopped expressing horror at the Holocaust because the enormity of the crime was too great for words. 'No poetry after Auschwitz,' Adorno insisted,[31] and Klein may appear to have felt so; but such a statement seems controverted by the gaiety and number of the Quebec poems, and by Klein's continuing mental robustness and increased public activity. But I *will* conclude that on some (perhaps very subliminal) level Klein's response to the Holocaust – lack of it, in poetry, at least – from 1944 to 1946 is the first disturbing sign of repression in the pattern of his private life and must be taken to some extent as the first nexus of those mental pressures that would eventually cost him his public selfhood.

These findings can be further refined to make them more particular to the case of Klein than general to North American Jewish trauma. Klein's very ability to sustain so many points of view, so many poetic personae, and to give expression to each through the gracious deferral of his own voice, is in times of communal celebration a source of his verbal richness, but in the teeth of the Holocaust may have multiplied his consciousness of suffering and given each murdered Jew a voice in his mind. This reading is indicated by those many self-portraits and portraits of others in which Klein interprets the individual Jew as the embodiment – in some cases very literally so – of the entire Jewish people from antiquity to the present. Klein's poetry is full of such figures, who become – often by persecution – the conduit of memory through which the dead remain vital and the as yet unborn become consequential. How anguished must such representative personalities be at a time when the extirpation of their entire people is possible – when not only the past must be held tangible in one's self, but the present, too, and millions in the present whose individual histories and futures have been wiped out? Such a sense of one's own representativeness and responsibility can hardly have been rivalled among the psychic pressures of Jews who survived the

Holocaust. Klein's motif of the self as conduit for the race addresses both extremes of the identification, from the joy of communal identity to the hell of absorption into the ashes of six million.

'A Psalm Touching Genealogy' (*CP*, p. 624) is the most positive of these treatments. Although it retains the images of bodily incorporation ('this / Body is residence' to 'the fathers,' 'They dwell in my veins,' 'In exit and in entrance all day pull / The latches of my heart') and a degree of paranoia ('they eavesdrop at my ear'), the ancestors of the speaker are clearly invited to enter and welcome once within. The poem is suffused with an implied responsibility: if 'there look generations through my eyes' then I must use my vision well and 'see' in keeping with their wisdom. 'And in That Drowning Instant,' later incorporated into *The Second Scroll*'s 'Gloss Hai,' continues the positive thrust of such identifications, although its strangely blurred relation of Jewish persecution requires vigorous overcoming (in the Nietzschean sense) by the speaker:

> the image of myself intent
> on several freedoms
>
> fading to
> myself in yellowed Basle-print
> vanishing
>
> into ghetto-Jew ...
>
> to show me in old Amsterdam
> which topples
>
> into a new scene
> Cordova where an Abraham
> faces inquisitors
>
> (*CP*, pp. 608–9)

The speaker is drowning throughout this soliloquy, but at the end, 'For the third time [his] body rises / and finds the good, the lasting shore!' The image suggests that the speaker is at first swamped by the sea of memories that constitute his race's history and risks his own swallowing up and self-loss in that flood, but its tidal force and depth eventually cast him up precisely where he wishes to be, at 'Jerusalem-gate and Temple-door!'

If a substantial and consistent part of one's imaginative self-identification includes such a relationship with one's racial and religious genealogy, what must be the impact of an international cataclysm whose effect is the expungement of six million of those in fellowship with whom one has constituted a self? 'Elegy' has already provided an indication, with its suffocating imagery of a speaker surrounded by the clouds, ghosts, and ashes of his people. Here it is guilt that urges forward the identification with the dead: 'The faces are my face! that lie in lime' (*CP*, p. 674), cries the speaker, in an attempt to forge again the links with the murdered. 'Meditation Upon Survival,' slightly earlier, speaks directly to the survivor's 'stuttering innocence' that is 'a kind of guilt' (*CP*, p. 663), and that guilt once again involves the horrific incorporation of the dead:

> At times, sensing that the golgotha'd dead
> run plasma through my veins, and that I must live
> their unexpired six million circuits, giving
> to each of their nightmares my body for a bed –
> inspirited, dispirited –
> those times that I feel their death-wish bubbling the
> channels of my blood –
> I grow bitter at my false felicity –
> the spared one – and would almost add my wish
> for the centigrade furnace and the cyanide flood.
>
> (*CP*, p. 663)

The 'stuttering' effect of the dashes in these lines suggests the speaker's desperate attempt to bring units of syntax together into a coherent meaning that will convey sufficient historical outrage. Perversions of meaning, however, undercut the effort: the 'six million' are blamed for a 'death-wish' that is more truly original with the surviving speaker, and the 'flood' that once cast the persona up at 'Jerusalem-gate and Temple-door' in 'And in That Drowning Instant' is here the flood of poison that annihilated them. 'Meditation Upon Survival' has no hope of surmounting these violent emotions: at the end the speaker 'recognizes' himself as 'the last point of a diminished race' and the next corpse, to be contained in 'the glass-case / some proud museum catalogues *Last Jew*' (*CP*, p. 664).

Such is the dual consequence of Klein's intense identification – and I am prepared to associate it with the poet and not only with his personae – with the history and all the individuals of his persecuted race. I think we gain from such poems an intuition – all we will ever have – of the dimensions of Klein's own psychological wounding as a victim of the Holocaust. A poet for whom the embodiment of the Jewish people and giving voice to others are constitutive suddenly finds his identification with others to be a melding with horror. Its wrenching impact on his vocation as a poet seems clear, not only in the sudden silence on Jewish suffering that follows closely on the heels of the news of the camps, but also because the very identification of himself as a conduit of race consciousness depends largely on his mastering the medium of poetry in which to express, to press out, that consciousness. The precise causation between this motif in the poetry and the sudden exclusive focus on Québécois life will not, I think, ever become clear – as, for instance, a matter of involuntary repression or wilful suppression – but that such a linkage is justified and profound seems undeniable. That the Holocaust impinged directly and powerfully on his mind and on his poetry, and that that effect is among the causes of his later breakdown and attempts at suicide is a conclusion that will not only force us to see the period of the forties as the beginning of a gradual straining of Klein's mental order, but also – and perhaps most valuably – help us to understand the poetry of that period as earning a part of its eminence and celebrity for his having overcome, poem by poem in effect, the most outrageous vicarious experience probably ever incurred by an individual.

I said earlier that the idea of *integritas* as a model of mental life might supply a means of reconciling the Holocaust horror with Klein's public well-being of the same period, and I want to return to that claim now. I have not thus pushed the darker content of Klein's breakdown backward into the forties in an effort to suggest that his poetry of the period papered over an abyss of horror or that it is itself the vestige of early mental illness: on the contrary. What seems remarkable to me *and* critically recuperable is the surprising wholeness he attained as a poet while under the kind of psychic stress I have been attempting to describe. This is my point of divergence from the findings of J.M. Kertzer, whose 'Personality and Authority: A.M. Klein's Self-Portrait' otherwise strikes me as among the finest and most thorough considerations of poetic voice and structure in Klein. For Kertzer has concluded that 'the Klein who is interpreted by his own work ... fails to define an authoritative, authentic, poetic self because he cannot accept the traditional religious, romantic or existential assurances of personality.'[32] To invert the phrase, I think it is precisely *because* Klein refuses such usual assurances of stable selfhood – for himself and for his poems – that a resonant self-creating 'personality' emerges in and among the poems, and I think that his ability to generate such authority despite the notable pressures on his emotional stability speaks to a degree of mental energy that I at least would want to associate with genius.

I characterize, then, the mind of Klein in the forties by his bringing into coherence, if not always expression, the full range of his experience, from the multiply joyous voices of the Chassidim to the routine of his uninspired legal career; from the sardonically experienced meetings with his fellow *Preview* editors to those of the text-loving discoursers of the Talmudic age; from the unfolding images of his family life in Catholic Quebec to the dying voices of those murdered in Europe. Klein's gift lay in his ability to contain so much of the world and of time, and his capacity for reverence was such that he felt it a sufficient calling to poetry to lay aside the expression of his own personality and reproduce the full range of his imaginative memory. The consciousness of Klein emerges as the field upon which all these forces impinge and the source of energy that both juxtaposes them and keeps them separate. I am implying that selfhood lay – for Klein at least – in this ability to incorporate, to synthesize, and to express a wealth of inherited perspectives, vocabularies, and personages; that 'he' is very much composed of 'whom' he has absorbed; that it was important to his sense of himself to be able to sustain such variety without continually intervening with the demands of a peremptory personality 'of his own.' In short – just as I have tried to shear poetic *integritas* away from the simpler 'unity' associated with New Criticism – a mental *integritas* in Klein emerged as a pattern of subtle coherence among disparate traditions, voices, and points of view that affirmed, not suppressed, their difference.

The Holocaust was an immediate challenge to the *integritas* Klein valued. Its initial entrance into his imaginative and mental life must have been predicated on its being seen as a fact, however extreme, among others: hence the curiously separable strands of satiric wit and exclamatory outrage in *The Hitleriad,* and the very relative treatment of Jewish suffering in 'Not All the Perfumes of Arabia.' But I suspect that the Holocaust, as the news emerged and was absorbed, took greater and greater energy to contain and keep separate in his mind, especially as it went on to poison his experience of so many of the other elements of his consciousness – a pressure that we can witness in the images of mental, physical, and domestic invasion that begin to resonate in the period. Throughout the struggle of realignment, Klein wrote a few poems of no special weight or depth of outrage about the persecution of his race ('And in That Drowning Instant,' 'Address to the Choirboys'), but at some unlocatable moment must have found it impossible to treat the Holocaust as one more relative powerfully stimulus to poetry. At such a moment the only recourse appears to have been a reduction in the comprehensiveness of his imaginative life, a turning of creative attention away from both the genocide and the people attacked, who could no longer be written of in any context other than their victimization. Here emerged the poems of *The Rock-*

ing Chair, in a style which, I shall shortly argue, suggested powerfully the effort involved in their diversion and narrowing of focus.

By what pattern of mental change Klein passed from this first attempt to hold off the force of the Holocaust in his mind to his eventual breakdown cannot even be guessed at. But I believe that Klein's turning away from the Jewish subject was a first deep admission that his mind was not sufficient to the synthesis of his experience, and that that admission was eventually to prove costly, precisely because it was of such value to Klein to see himself as one through whom the *entire* experience of his people could be conducted into voice. In the course of this struggle in his imaginative life, what remains remarkable is the duration to which he was in fact able to continue as a poet, even if at the expense of his identification with his own people, and to subsume vital new traditions and voices within the forceful verbal coherence of his poems. If he focused so abruptly on the Québécois, it must have been in part because he could continue his location of representative personae without encountering the spectre of their extermination. And it is not surprising that his decision on a 'new' subject should have been accompanied by a newly developed style: it is in the poems of *The Rocking Chair* that he most clearly shows his affiliation with P.K. Page, Patrick Anderson, and *Preview.* Although these changes of poetic manner coincide with what must surely have been a profound disturbance of his mental balance, they speak thoroughly to the creative force that persisted in his mind and work until the crisis came. 'Genius,' says Eugène Lampert, 'is a way out that one invents,'[33] and Klein moved outward brilliantly until the doors closed for good.

Anonymity, Inventory, and Vocation in *The Rocking Chair*

Klein's case endorses then an indissoluble connection between a poet's psychic life and identity, and the structures of poetic expression that he or she has recourse to as that selfhood is challenged. In 1942 he was himself prepared to admit the fundamentally personal aspect of all writing: 'No thing happens but it is autobiographical. The irreducible residuum of all literature – the diary, journal of the mind ... Even those ubiquitous bards – Ibid and Anon – Blind Ibid, mute inglorious Anon – are but ego in incognito dight and doubly proud.'[34] The fragment draws attention to an available index of Klein's attitudes towards the experience of 'personality' in poetic language: his shifting use of the favoured words 'anonymous' and 'anonymity' to describe the gifted creator's actualization in his or her art. Evoking as it does concepts ranging from modernist impersonality to the Adamic 'naming, praising' that are so important to 'Portrait of the Poet as Landscape,' as well as the more disturbing implications of a statistical anonymity visited upon millions of European Jews by the Nazis, Klein's term refracts a number of crucial ideas in his experience of the forties. That it also offers a useful means of illuminating Klein's aesthetics in *The Rocking Chair* poems helps to centre the term in a reading not only of Klein, but of the problem of 'personality' that engaged most of his contemporaries as well. The meanings Klein accorded 'anonymity' shifted largely in keeping with his reaction to the Holocaust, suggesting once again that modernist impersonality has to do with suppression of that personal content that we most fear to engage. Maud Ellmann says of T.S. Eliot's impersonality that 'the poet's reticence actually safeguards his identity, as if impersonality were the formaldehyde that preserves the self against dispersion ...,'[35] and the same self-protective attitude can be theorized for Klein.

In the period of his mature Judaica, Klein conceived 'anonymity' as an attribute of divine creation to be emulated by the mortal artist, as in the 'Shiggaion of Abraham Which He Sang Unto the Lord' of 1940:

> O incognito god, anonymous lord,
> with what name shall I call you? Where shall I
> discover the syllable, the mystic word
> that shall evoke you from eternity?
>
> (*CP*, p. 519)

To close the 'Shiggaion,' the speaker expresses his confidence in God's attentiveness, despite His anonymity: 'I do evoke you, knowing I am heard.' The closure implies a comfortable relation between a sacred ideal of aesthetic detachment and the inevitability of subjective expression in the practised arts. The equanimity of Klein's usage would be lost, however, in the later years of the war, as the news of Nazi atrocities made God's 'anonymity' and a chilling indifference to His people's fate harder to distinguish. In 'Portrait of the Poet as Landscape,' written early in the period I have identified for Klein's sudden silence on Jewish persecution, anonymity is certainly of much more ambiguous value, its meaning shifting from the early lament for the poet as an 'anonymous taunt / of the Gallup poll' (*CP*, p. 634, ll. 18–19) to the closing wish that the poet should 'by necessity and indirection bring / new forms to life, anonymously, new creeds ...' (*CP*, p. 639, ll. 155–6). To be 'without name,' without a recognized persona, is among the most feared consequences of a life of poetry in 'Portrait'; but to create namelessly, to press no petty ego into one's 'green inventory,' is a condition of the poet's survival as the poem concludes. Both meanings are present in the peroration, where the poet 'makes of his status as zero a rich garland, / a halo of his anonymity' (*CP*, p. 639, ll. 160–1). 'Portrait' thus shows the increased instability and weight of 'anonymity' in Klein's lexicon of aesthetic conditions *circa* 1944; the poem's ambivalent treatment of anonymity intervenes tellingly between the years of Klein's greatest propensity to lyricism and his period of most rigorous modernist impersonality.

The poems that would constitute 'The Psalter of Avram Haktani' had been written according to Pollock from 1938 through 1941, and whatever the containing ironies enjoined by the pseudonymous play of the title, the largely first-person lyrics evoke emotions and experiences very recognizably like those of Klein himself in the period of their composition. He had not indeed been so self-expressive since the earliest Romantic love lyrics to Bessie Kozlov in the late 1920s. Composition of the ambiguously anonymous 'Portrait' followed, and on the far side of that masterpiece are the dozens of poems cataloguing modern Quebec, in which Klein's careful self-erasure governs an impression of thoroughgoing impersonality from 1944 to the end of his poetic career, with few exceptions. The Quebec poems adopt a firm objectivity, less now like the benevolent anonymity of a trustworthy God and more like the codified exclusions of modernist impersonality. Indeed one may think it a weakness of the *Rocking Chair* poems that they reflect a far more rigorous polarization of subjectivism and impersonality than Klein elsewhere endorsed.

By 1948, when *The Rocking Chair* appeared – coincident with the creation of the state of Israel – Klein's flirtation with such a strict understanding of impersonality was winding down, and a desire for restored balance of subjective and objective expression is apparent in 'Towards an Aesthetic,' the source of his 'integritas' allusion earlier:

> ... if, in a poem, everything is as clear as daylight, it might as well have been written in prose; if, on the other hand, its moonlight radiance, shrouded in shadows, threatens to remain so forever, it is a light again unsatisfying; it thwarts the natural desire for clear and complete vision. The compromise consists in the alternation of the two kinds of light; one mystical, the other apocalyptic.[36]

As a result of this balance between revelation and concealment, the 'artist is a creator completely surrounded by mirrors'[37] who is always both present in and absent from the poem he creates. Sadly, Klein's poetic career was all but over as he wrote these lines;[38] the return to a more complex relation between the subjective and the impersonal elements of literature was to have its chief manifestation in *The Second Scroll*. By the time of that novel's composition, 'anonymity' had been rehabilitated for Klein and returned to something akin to its original function; it had also become more casually synonymous with 'impersonality' in Klein's lexicon.

When the (significantly anonymous) nephew-narrator of the novel concludes that the true poetry of the new Israel is not with the poets, but with the Hebrew-remaking people, he emphasizes the egolessness of such artistry: creativity is with 'the fashioning folk, anonymous and unobserved, creating word by word, phrase by phrase, the total work that when completed would stand as epic revealed!'[39] This same language motive is later called 'Nameless authorship' and 'the great efflorescent impersonality' (*TSS*, pp. 78, 79) and appears to stand in *The Second Scroll* as a sufficient discovery of meaning for the reconstitution of Jewry and of the narrator himself. *The Second Scroll* is not, however, as transparently affirmative a novel as the narrator's conclusions presume. After all, not a single Israeli *poet* is endorsed by the highly critical North American narrator: the new notion of anonymity would have cost Klein his vocation. The murder of Melech Davidson and the consequent loss of the nephew's longed-for *anagnorisis* then make it impossible for the narrator to claim a single affirmation of the hopes with which he set out on his journey. If the 'King' who is 'David's son' is indeed to the new Israelis 'a kind of mirror, an *aspaklaria*, of the events of our time' (*TSS*, p. 92), an interpretation on which Pollock usefully casts doubt (p. 250), we are forced at the end of the novel to watch as a decimated people lose their new sacral figure. Melech's 'anonymity,' maintained throughout the novel as in the incident of the multiply exposed photograph, is here as elsewhere perilously close to the statistical individual anonymity of the Holocaust's victims. Indeed, the body is soaked in gasoline and set on fire by the 'assailants, who were many against one' (*TSS*, p. 91). Such disturbing resonances powerfully complicate Klein's secular renewal of the anonymous ideal of his early career.

The effect of these remarks is a temporarily useful division of Klein's last creative decade. In most of his Judaica, Klein implies that the creator's selfhood may be affirmed in his art even when he takes on the voice and experience of some other, especially when that other is of his own disenfranchised race. Alternatively he may write highly subjective and personal poems, like many in the 'Psalter,' and yet maintain his objective distance from their content by gestures of self-concealment (as did 'Avram Haktani'). There was at the time no rigorous choice to be made, apparently, between subjectivism and impersonality: they were both essential to poetry. In late 1943 and 1944, however, during and after his absorption of the news of the concentration camps from Europe, this comfortable interpenetration of the two concepts became untenable, and it became important to Klein to find a new voice that would reify their relation into opposition: to adopt an impersonality defined more strictly by its elimination of personal and particular content. The poems of *The Rocking Chair* would seem to suggest that the personal could no longer emerge in Klein's poetry with the needed leaven of anonymity that he had counted on in the past, so subjectivism became inimical to the achievement of poetry, whereas a more dogmatic impersonality could still ground a genuine – a brilliant – verbal art.

Klein's unpublished fictions and diaristic notes make plain the strength of his desire for self-expression, for the affirmations of identity that underpin gestures of autobiography, so his broad dedication to an art of anonymity was not a simple matter of personal inclination, but an aesthetic and to some extent racial choice involving what must have been an at least intermittent consciousness of sacrifice. Even his pseudonyms, from his earliest publications a gesture towards anonymity, register more powerfully a desire to break free of self-disguise: how quickly 'A.M. Keats,' 'M.A.K.,' 'Antonius Mentholatum Kochleffel' (Caplan, p. 54), and 'Avram Haktani' could be resolved again into the well-known A.M. Klein.[40] The revealed interplay of self-revelation and self-concealment – the anonymity that suppresses the individual poet's voice in order to affirm him through his people – is a dualism that is highly typical of the decade in which Klein found his most memorable expression, and he was not the only one to suffer for his official allegiance to a poetics that denied him direct expression of his powerful sense of selfhood and uniqueness.

The Rocking Chair poems can be situated, then, in a period of some four years in which Klein's Holocaust trauma is reflected in a sudden turn away from Jewish subjects subtended by an uncharacteristic polarization of impersonality and subjectivity, two concepts whose mutuality had previously grounded his poetics, and a decision to pursue a more modernist, and less Judaic, understanding of the anonymity of creation. These changes were accompanied by a surprising stylization of Klein's poetic language, and by a newly felt need to emphasize through exclamatory vocalization the power of his vision and expression. The generally emphatic style of the poems in *The Rocking Chair* speaks in my view to the cost to Klein of such a dogmatic impersonality, as well as to the unease with which he felt his way into a new poetry after the Holocaust had called his former confidence of voice and manner into question. Most of the signs of this poetic stress are visible in the master-work of the period, 'Portrait of the Poet as Landscape,' and I will consider that poem before extrapolating from it a series of concerns that are motivational to Klein's creativity in *The Rocking Chair* as a whole.

'Portrait of the Poet as Landscape' is obviously evidence of Klein's acute awareness that the poet is disappearing 'from our real society,' and such a conclusion can hardly be divorced from Klein's own self-estimation. The emblematic poet of 'Portrait' is akin to those representative figures of his earlier poetry who had, similarly, been asked to stand in for a lapsed or lost tradition: he is to contemporary poets as Solomon Warshawer, for instance, is to Jews throughout history. Indeed, the Gothic ending of 1946's 'Meditation Upon Survival,' with its '*Last Jew*' catalogued by 'some proud museum' (*CP*, p. 664), has strong echoes in 'Portrait': the last Jew is one of 'a diminished race' that has gone 'the way of the fletched buffalo,' while the poet's craft is 'archaic like the fletcher's.'[41] Sombre parallels of this nature have much to say about 'Portrait's' conclusion, as well as the intense interweaving of Klein's Judaism and his poetic vocation in the language of extinction that darkens the masterpiece. These connections will be especially fertile if we remember the situation of 'Portrait' in the year following Klein's suppression of Holocaust themes and its coincidence with his public alignment (as editor) with *Preview*: much of the language of analysis here is lifted from the Holocaust context and applied directly to the Anglo-modernist situation with which he was increasingly affiliated.

If we stand back briefly from the poem's familiarity and try to state its project in general terms, we might note its broad strokes roughly as follows. First of all, its third-person narrative serves only officially to distance Klein from his own grievances as a modern poet: which is not to say that all content in 'Portrait' should be unilaterally applied back to Klein, but that obviously some substantial portion of its complaint derives from his own personal sense of his role and value in society. Second, much of what Klein condemns in 'Portrait' is feared rather than safely disdained: for all the irony of their presentation, the 'local tycoon ... so epical in steel' and 'the troubadour / rich and successful out of celluloid' (ll. 109–10, 113–14) are powerful threats precisely because they are such attractive alternatives to poetic isolation and loneliness. (Klein, for example, can hardly have referred to 'the local tycoon' transparently and without some degree of irony over his own co-optation by Samuel Bronfman.) Third, for all the poem's wit, stylistic power, and modern grace, its organization into sections masks the disjointedness of its observations: it is by nature a catalogue, not a narrative, not an argument, even though it leans on those discourses for some of its structural gestures. Fourth, all possibilities of solace in the poem – reserving comment for the moment on the crucial final section, of which I nevertheless believe this remark accurate – are undermined after their articulation: especially so vitiated are suggestions that the poet may find comfort in affiliation either with other poets or with an alternative audience. Thus the poem denies the poet the very act, successful expression by ink or tongue, by which he is constituted and offers no alternative means of self-identification. The effect of these general qualities of 'Portrait' is in my reading deeply disturbing, and its sombreness is only slightly penetrated by the ironic light of the final section.

Not surprisingly in such a secular poem and at such a period of Klein's emotional life, Judaism is carefully expunged from the record of 'Portrait,' its function confined to a single allusion early on, when the poet is lamented as one who once 'unrolled our culture from his scroll' – the evocation of Torah functioning here, as it will in 'Montreal,' to offer Klein's faith a minuscule point of entrance into the poem's images. Similarly controlled, as we have already seen, are the poem's references to mental crisis: although the two allusions to madness (ll. 13, 83) are telling, they are invoked in glancing asides that suggest the spuriousness of emotional disturbance as an explanation of the poet's condition. One of the more significant motifs of Klein's development in the forties is crucial to 'Portrait,' however: his tendency from as far back as 'A Psalm of Abraham of That Which Was Visited Upon Him' of 1940, as we have seen, to blur the boundaries between the physical body and the intangible forces that surround it and constitute or threaten selfhood. Here it is not only a feared 'prowler' that dissolves the boundary between bodily space and exterior forces, but also the holiness of poetic language itself: in the poem's conclusion, when the poet's works 'map, / not the world's, but his own body's chart!', but more vividly in the second section, when the young poet's recognition of language's beauty is eroticized into a first experience of pleasure in another's body. Although the passage clearly echoes Donne's 'Elegy XIX, To His Mistress Going to Bed' and contains language ('warm auxiliaries,' 'complexion,' 'dimple') more likely associated with women's sexuality at the time, Klein is careful to avoid giving the adored body a distinct sex, an ambivalence leaving open the possibility of a sexual objectification of his own male body: 'the act of conjugation at the climax of the passage is with a body which the poet recognizes as "his own",' as Pollock has it (p. 164). Klein's metaphor thus suggests the intensity of his identification with his function as poet, since he is a doubled body – both lover and loved object – that is coextensive with the energy of language:

> Then he will remember his travels over that body –
> the torso verb, the beautiful face of the noun,
> and all those shaped and warm auxiliaries!
> A first love it was, the recognition of his own.
>
> (ll. 41–4)

As the phrase 'his own' suggests, mastery of language is one with self-possession for the poet: and a crisis of poetic confidence will be tantamount to a shaking of identity as damaging as a rupture to the body.

The bodily identification with language is invoked as a potential compensation for 'moods' in which the generic poet is 'depressed to nadir' (ll. 35–6), and it does briefly help him 'zoom ... to zenith' (l. 53), but in the final stanza of this wishful section a gradual deflation occurs. An initial self-aggrandizement as 'Count of Monte Cristo' sags when the poet is transformed into an 'unsuspected heir' who has to prove his status 'with papers' rather than swordplay, and from there to the falsified death of 'the chloroformed prince awaking from his flowers' a further decline is palpable. When the section closes with the poet 'on parole,' the burlesque of the pun is unlikely to make up for the easily pierced inflations of the body of sexualized language. In fact this rhythm of false exaltation followed by gradual degradation is typical of the whole poem, although it is resolved into a gifted ambiguity – hardly celebration – in the final stanzas.

The location of a happy and joyous relationship with language in an idealized past underpins 'Portrait's' play on a dichotomy between a time of ideal, even Adamic, creativity, located either in lost youth or in a fantasized future, and a present-day lapsarian will-to-create that is routinely undercut not only by the social and literary forces determining the poet's freedoms, but by the internecine antagonisms of poets themselves. The latter theme is developed in Section III; here the connection between the beloved parts of speech and the delighted body that briefly energized Section II is still visible, but severely perverted: poetry's vitiation is incarnated in poets who have 'lost the bevel in the ear' and allowed a 'colon'– the pun on excretion is telling – to replace their 'eyes' (ll. 67, 70). Poets have mistaken revisions of style for renewal of substance: they 'mistake the part / for the whole, curl themselves in a comma, talk technics' (ll. 68–70), and the result is 'something convolute and cerebral' rather than poetry's prophetic truth, for 'the time they do not tell,' nor, clearly, the times. Klein's evident desire to distance himself from modernist excess is especially remarkable, given his then-recent editorial affiliation with *Preview*, but it is not atypical: easy as it is to apply some of these criticisms to the more extreme poetic practice in that journal, the lines also show his familiar tendency to critique the collectives of which he was a member.

Indeed the *Preview* context becomes quite explicit by the section's conclusion: while the 'fear ... of the platitude' (l. 73) might apply to modernists anywhere, their seduction by party politics in the fourth stanza powerfully echoes the sarcasm of Klein's letters to Smith regarding the political naïvety of *Preview*-ites like Shaw and Anderson. More tellingly perhaps, the lines also evoke Klein's first abortive bid for election under the Cooperative Commonwealth Federation banner in early 1944, about the time of his coming aboard *Preview,* and thus suggest another tactic active in 'Portrait': a tendency to project his own worst fears for himself onto his contemporaries. The last two stanzas move ever closer to a specific irony at Anderson's expense. The poet who 'courts / angels' is likely Rilke-influenced, as were both Page and Anderson (and Klein himself), and surely the section's ultimate condemnation of poets who 'are friendly, and then quarrel and surmise / the secret perversions of each other's lives' (ll. 93–4) alludes, at least in part, to John Sutherland's publication of Anderson's homosexuality in May 1943, perhaps a year before 'Portrait' was begun. If so, then earlier lines come into focus differently: the poet who 'courts / angels' does so because he 'fear[s] rebuff' everywhere else, as Anderson remarked himself to do in repeated diary entries; is Anderson also the one 'sick with sex' who 'doodles him symbols convex and concave,' whose tormented journals are decorated with stylized human figures, some of whom have in place of genitals some image of anger or violence – wounds, knives, lightning bolts?[42]

A definite object of Klein's sarcasm need not be located; we need chiefly to see that the effect of this second section is to eloign the archetypal poet from all the other poets mentioned in 'Portrait.' A modernist literary culture that suggests that the renovation of art is possible only if artists address themselves to the highest standards of their fellow artists – a culture in which Klein himself had to function – is here spurned. As Klein would put it in 'The Usurper' in 1949, the modernist avant-gardes had collapsed out of sheer solipsism:

> There is no more pathetic reading in the whole realm of literature than the dusty bound volumes of the 'little magazines' of yesteryear. As one thumbs these pages, hectic with manifesto and ever fretful like the porpentine, one's heart is heavied by this spectacle of rebellions which overthrew nobody but their authors, of world-shaking pronunciamentos recorded by no real seismograph, of new movements too soon paralysed ...
>
> (*LER*, p. 195)

Those 'Who live for themselves, / or for each other, but for nobody else' (ll. 90–1) can give the true poet no comfort from the opprobrium and disregard of a broader society. He is utterly alone, despite the opening's pious wish that he be 'not completely alone,' and the section's contribution to mood is an intensification of the poet's isolation to a point that makes 'madness,' so casually alluded to here, a more genuine possibility.

The interest of Section IV for the current discussion is its replication of Klein's forties commonplace of the invaded home in a language and imagery strongly suggestive of his later paranoia, and its conjunction of those anxieties with images that evoke faintly, but notably, given their suppression elsewhere in 'Portrait,' the persecution of the Jews that had its forceful impact on Klein's imagination in the months preceding the poem's composition. As Bentley has remarked (p. 29), the representation of the modern poet 'with special haircut and dress, / as on a reservation' (ll. 97–8) is too suggestive of the shaved heads, yellow stars and demographic 'concentration' of Klein's European 'cousinry' to be recorded innocently in 1944–5, and the section's later glimpses of 'the don who unrhymes atoms' and 'the chemist death built up' suggest that Klein's deep attention to the war and the emergent Holocaust threatens to disrupt the smooth detachment of 'Portrait's' surface here. Such dislocations add renewed force to the section's images of 'an impostor' who, 'having studied [the poet's] personal biography,' itself an invasion, 'is at home, and slippered, in his house' (ll. 101, 106). As so often elsewhere, the poet is here a doubled figure, a benign passive victim and an aggressive, sometimes criminal assailant who is so deeply identified with the speaker that his house-breaking is accomplished before a threat is even articulated. The juxtaposition of these images in Section IV confirms the heretofore subliminal link between the 'last poet' and the museum's 'Last Jew' in 'Meditation Upon Survival' and moreover seems to insist that Klein's compulsive return to images of domestic invasion, tied as they are here to intimations of Holocaust, is not a fortuitous but an essential image, for him, of the invaded consciousness that would surrender its own expression in the 1950s.

Not surprisingly after such gestures, Section V is the briefest and least developed section of 'Portrait.' Its interruption of the loose temporal continuity of the poem – from adolescence through marriage and parenthood to a future glorification – with a present-tense and generalized consideration of poetry's persistent motives might suggest that the disturbing content of the previous section has temporarily derailed the confidence of the speaker's *Künstlerroman*. Once again, the proffered salves to the poet's wounded sensibility are set up and dismissed one after another, particularly '*Fame,* the adrenalin,' presumably needed to regulate the 'thrombosis' of the previous section. Only a severely abstract and arguably forced concept is offered as a reliable impulse to poetry: 'stark infelicity' is supposed to account for the poet's compulsive creation, which is here rendered as insomnia and death-defying, indeed suicidal, strolls 'upon roofs and window-sills' (ll. 129–32); note that the latter image echoes the suspected intruder who alarmed the poet earlier. Pollock has it that 'stark infelicity' registers the poet's 'newly achieved dialectical transformation' (p. 166) and that his 'infelicity' 'has been a source of strength, not weakness, to him' (p. 167), but the reading rests too much on a vague phrase. I wonder, indeed, to put it bluntly, if we have been told anything significant in these lines; has the poet's 'stark' unhappiness helped to differentiate him from his inattentive readers and rival poets, busy with their own neuroses of insignificance and supplantedness?

When the poem's final section opens with 'Therefore,' we are asked to respond as if to a logical argument, but the section break makes the antecedent premise hard to locate. We have to assume that 'stark infelicity' is offered as the cause of the poet's 'seed[ing] illusions,' at least in the local logic, but the last section's attempt to perorate legitimates an alternate suggestion that the entire poem is the 'proof' which now enters its conclusive utterance. The instability of the reference, at any rate, gets the conclusion off to a forced start. To proceed from this point, I will have to acknowledge distance from Bentley's treatment of the section: he refers to 'the poem's mutedly triumphant closing section' (p. 11), cites 'the poem's insistence in its final section on the achieved equipoise of the poet' (p. 12), and remarks 'the sense of present hope and future potential at the conclusion of the poem' (p. 13). I agree that sentiments in this direction are present in the conclusion. They are rivalled, however, to my mind, by the containing irony with which the section opens and which governs its diction, and rendered doubtful, at times undermined, by the ambiguity of their expression. The conclusion is not therefore so much affirmative as wishful, and like all auditors of wishful thinking we are cast into irony the moment we recognize it.

First of all, a critical response to the entire section must be governed by its opening statement: 'Therefore he seeds illusions. Look ...' (p. 133). There is no way of containing the ironic force of this line, nothing in subsequent lines to close off its resonance, in a poem that has become predictable in its invocation and revocation[43] of a series of illusions under which the poet struggles. If we are attuned to this pattern, we are surely left waiting at the end for the inevitable hollowing out of this section's 'illusions' as well, and the ultimate sentence fragment provides it, as I shall claim later. Bentley's remark that 'seeds' echoes 'cedes' and therefore half-suggests that the poet 'surrenders' his illusions is excellent, not because it manages an evasion of the line's bitter containment, but because it balances the line's meanings on positive and negative poles that remain operative throughout the section. The phrase 'the nth Adam,' for example, not only suggests the poet's participation in a God-like naming of the visible world, but also pushes the acceptance of that task forward into an infinitely receding and variable future.

The Adamism of 'Portrait of the Poet as Landscape' is recognizably modernist, the spontaneity and innocence of Adam's coinages standing as the primary modernist fantasy of poetic innovation. For all the affective power of Klein's 'green inventory,' a phrase which has figured large in the poem's criticism, the stanza is indeed fantastic and illusory in its imagination of a 'world but scarcely uttered' (p. 135). The subtext in this longed-for Eden is a recovery of the freshness of metaphor (the freshness of language being unavailable): Klein's reference to 'the flowering fiats in the meadow' echoes beautifully a poetic fragment probably of the same period, from Klein's persistently fruitful 'Raw Material' file:

Fiat of metaphor, O silvered glass
Propelling out of the blank and shine of naught
Worlds, satellites, similitudes,
The planetary parables.
What is the x of which this world
is metaphor?[44]

Klein's language not only anticipates 'Portrait's' visions of 'another planet' viewed from God's perspective, but also picks up the decade's ongoing fascination with the near-sacred potential of metaphor itself. Indeed, the second stanza is aggressive with startling metaphors, the 'syllabled fur, stars aspirate, the pollen['s] sweet collision' (pp. 137–8), thus itself embodying the reinvigoration of language towards which the lines could otherwise only gesture.

Standing in for Adam through metaphysical conceit is no answer, though, to the issues with which 'Portrait' hitherto concerned itself – namely, the poet's isolation from an audience and lack of real function in a quotidian, not Edenic, world. I think this is why the next stanza ushers in a subtle desperation in the poet's language and syntax. Once again the body and the world are identified, but this time through a 'praising' that speaks of creation, not invasion:

   Until it has been praised, that part
has not been. Item by exciting item –
air to his lungs, and pressured blood to his heart. –
they are pulsated, and breathed, until they map,
not the world's, but his own body's chart!

(ll. 141–5)

The staccato rhythms enforced by the enjambments and excess punctuation are a mimetic signification of the world's own gradual emergence into being as the poet speaks, but they are also suggestive of stumbling and, in the bodily context, of a struggling for air. It's not surprising that the exclamatory punctuation that will become almost compulsive in *The Rocking Chair* breaks in here, with its reassurance of a significance the poet fears lacking in his 'new' vocation. Without commenting on the grandiosity of the poet's (redemptive?) task, I do want to remark the degree of pressure he places on himself when he takes on not only the power, but also the responsibility, of God. In this dispensation each word must be used with divine exactitude, for we are talking here not of words, but of things in their first, their essential, form. One slip spoils the fabric of the world: a consciousness that might well serve as inspiration but surely offers torment and despair regularly as well.

In case we had lost touch with the language of 'illusion' that continues to determine the visions offered in the section, the third stanza opens and concludes its vision of a poet confused with God with indisputable irony. The previously claimed identification between 'the world' and 'his own body' is not apparently sufficient godhead: 'now *in imagination* he has climbed / another planet, the better to look / with single camera view upon this earth' (ll. 146–8, emphasis added). Certainly suggestive that the earlier identification was illusory, the lines also border on the farcical, with their spatially surreal imagery (how does one climb a sphere?) and sudden appeal to a 'camera' for an image of ultimate insight. We return again to the obsession with a complete catalogue of the world: the poet will have to record 'its total scope, and each afflated tick, its talk, its trick, its tracklessness' (ll. 149–50),[45] and since such Adamism was pursued in the previous stanza without apparent closure its second prescription here suggests the recurrence of neurosis, as does the surely ironic over-alliteration. If these ironies are not sufficiently clear, the poem's narrator intervenes with one of his heaviest weighings-in in the whole of 'Portrait': 'and this,' he remarks scornfully, 'this he would like to write down in a book!' (ll. 150–1). Note once more the need for exclamation: nowhere in the poem is there a greater gap between the representative poet and the speaker who organizes his experience.

Klein was clearly unwilling to conclude the poem on such a dissonance, however, and he returns in the last two stanzas of 'Portrait' to a more neutral consideration of the chances for poetic persistence and growth in the 'real' world. Shunning the science fiction of the previous lines, he reminds us once again that the poet's is a 'déclassé craft / archaic like the fletcher's' (ll. 152–3), that 'his status [is] zero' (l. 160), that he 'lives alone' (l. 162). Nothing, in other words, has changed in the poet's relations with the public world: what the final section offers us, once it settles down from fantasy to function, is instead a new stoic attitude to the condition of isolation and ignorance that the poem has so brilliantly underscored. New aesthetic values emerge: apart from the double reference to anonymity already considered, it is clear that words such as 'function,' 'necessity and indirection' are intended to cue us to a new determination in the poet to ignore the ignorance of his social audience and to write, instead, Adamically, for the sake of 'praise' itself. Coupled with the sudden emphasis on poetic newness – the word 'new' appearing thrice in four lines – there is a distinct sense of change earned, and learned, by the poet. That these 'answers' are to questions the first 132 lines of the poem did not ask is easy to forget in the face of such apparent resolution.

This final section leaves us, then, in a decidedly ambiguous position. If we have felt the force of 'Portrait's' lament for the poet's largely *social* crisis, we will have to acknowledge that closure is achieved by means of a manoeuvre that slips our attention deftly to a purely *individual* resolution. To return to the word 'Meanwhile' that I remarked upon earlier, it seems clear that we should take these gestures as temporary measures until the social isolation of the poet changes by some means not guessed at. But the most distinct indication that Klein's peroration is ambiguous and ironic occurs in the final line, when an idiosyncratically placed period prevents our comfortable escape from the complexities raised earlier.

Meanwhile, he
makes of his status as zero a rich garland,
a halo of his anonymity,
and lives alone, and in his secret shines
like phosphorus. At the bottom of the sea.

(ll. 159–63)

The final image returns us, as we all know, to the Lycidas parallel with which the poem bitterly opened. But the fragmentation of the last sentence places particular emphasis on the poet's remaining, despite whatever triumph he has earned, washed out, drowned, silent in darkness. After all, had the period been withheld, as prose would demand, the final sentence's clear emphasis would have remained on the poet's 'shin[ing] / like phosphorus'; the additional prepositional phrase would clearly modify 'phosphorus' and do no more than tell us where phosphorus was. The phrase's actual function of locating the poet himself on the sea shelf might still be a faint *double-entendre* but would be clearly subordinated to the more practical meaning. Even were the period a mere comma, this emphasis would probably have been achieved. But the deliberative decision to prevent that smooth subordination of the last dark phrase by dramatically highlighting it as an independent thought makes of it a last reminder that whatever the poet chooses to do, whatever the luminosity of his record, his final resting place will be with the fishes and Lycidas, who was, after all, a dead fellow poet for whose works his original elegist, Milton, had little admiration.

A need to restore the balance of irony and scepticism has undoubtedly made me accentuate the negative in this review of 'Portrait of the Poet as Landscape.' Nothing will take away, certainly not the errors of one critic, from the poem's powerful representation of poetic crisis and struggle or from the moments of genuine reconstitution it *is* able to encompass. But I believe an emphasis on the poem's affirmative force not only flies in the face of its involvement in Klein's decisive turn away from Jewish matter in the repercussive months of the Holocaust, but also simplifies the doubleness and complexity with which he could hold contending ideas stable in his mind. The genuine affirmation of 'Portrait' is a highly ironic one, in which the speaker who resolves on affirmation is potentially in error, and the affirmation expressed is potentially inefficacious. That these fault lines are *potential* in the poem's conclusion means that Klein's gestures towards poetic newness and reconstitution are genuine and have force, but also that he was particularly aware of the gap between poetic resolution and poetic accomplishment. It is in the latter mood, I think, that 'Portrait of the Poet as Landscape' was composed *and* completed.

Like all masterpieces, 'Portrait' is itself 'a kind of mirror, an *aspaklaria*' (*TSS*, p. 86) of Klein's choices in the mid-forties, and its referents are remarkably sufficient to a further discussion of the poetics of *The Rocking Chair.* I want first to return to the poem's Adamism. When the speaker affirmed the poet's desire to go 'naming, praising' through the world, he added a daunting motive: 'Until it has been praised, that part / has not been' (ll. 141–2). I remarked the degree of pressure invited by such a formulation and may have seemed to be forcing a point, but Klein's fragmentary 'outline' for 'Portrait of the Poet as Landscape'– one of Pollock's many wonderful unearthings – manifests the deep-rooted anxiety contingent on the demand:

> The world diminished by the contents of my lungs – paid back.
>
> ***
>
> Describe being a poet. Who wants him in this age, the day of gasoline and oil.
>
> Cursed be the day I penned my first pentameter.
>
> What prompted me. Vanity, mimesis, afflatus
>
> But here it is. That's what I am. I have yet in me to do something. So many things still unpraised (See Natonek) still unlabelled by my words. My inventory has not yet been taken.

> Moreover I want more than discrete isolated visions, I want yet to see the world as a photographer on Mars, focussing all of the sunlit in the camera glimpse
>
> (*CP*, pp. 1000–1)

The brief reference to gasoline ghoulishly anticipates the 'anointing' of Melech Davidson's body after his murder and, along with the reference to Hans Natonek, a refugee from the Nazis,[46] suggests again the deep connections between the Holocaust and Klein's inspiration in 'Portrait.' Many more or less neurotic images are also of interest here, like Klein's curiously physical economy of poetic indebtedness and his obvious antipathy to the vocation that nevertheless defined him, but the most enervating may be his obvious feeling that he had a duty to reconstruct the world with his praise, not only part by part with particularity, but extensively, comprehensively, as a whole world too. This responsibility is linked, through juxtaposition at least, with an equally surprising impression of having accomplished nothing, as his urgent hope 'yet ... to do something' makes clear. Not only does the outline suggest Klein's (anyway obvious) identification with the emblematic poet of 'Portrait,' but it also helps to explain one at least of the structural curiosities of *The Rocking Chair*: its evident desire for a comprehensive and detailed catalogue – 'things still unpraised ... still unlabelled by my words. My inventory' – of Quebec life.

This aesthetic is obvious if we merely scan some of the titles of the volume: 'The Rocking Chair,' 'Grain Elevator,' 'Bread,' 'The Spinning Wheel,' 'Frigidaire,' 'Commercial Bank,' 'Quebec Liquor Commission Store,' 'Filling Station,' and so on; to these might be added 'Dentist,' 'Les Vespasiennes,' and 'Dominion Square' from the poems of the *Suite Canadienne* that were not included in the volume. Taking such poems for the moment by the project indicated by their titles, it is apparent that Klein felt a valid task to lie in the recording one after another of various objects, buildings, and locations, and that such an aesthetic has as its vanishing point a book of poems as 'complete' as reality itself. The mood of catalogue is reinforced by the representation in each of these poems of a fixed fact, an object in stasis, the essential properties of which are described (as the poems proceed) in ever more detail and nuance, but remain unchanged from beginning to end. In this sense most of *The Rocking Chair* poems constitute an attempt to separate objects from their contextual narratives: very little in them happens in time. The dimension of time occurs in such poems solely as a plane of the poet's imagination: as he seeks metaphors for his objects of description, he will move freely among centuries and civilizations, but he does so in order to describe an object whose fixity is in stark contrast to that creative play. Rarely enough, indeed, does anything happen here in the dimension of space: adopting in effect the 'camera eye' of 'Portrait,' Klein snaps a series of stills, the power of which lies in the special techniques of their development, not in the objects themselves.

Despite the conviction of 'Portrait of the Poet as Landscape' that the contemporary poet suffers extreme isolation for his Adamic relation to the visible world, Klein's 'green inventory' is a typical forties aesthetic, concerned as it is with exhaustiveness, with the relation between the visual image and the consciousness of its perceiver, with its curious willingness to fragment the 'parts' observed in an attempt to gain a picture of the 'whole.' When I identified an 'aesthetic of accumulation' in P.K. Page's poetry, I was remarking there a collection of intra-poetic devices, such as curiosities of syntax, juxtaposition of brief imagist phrases, the '*a* of *b*' formula, and so on; Klein's analogous urge to accumulation is first visible inter-poetically, in the implications of a volume of poems, one of whose obvious purposes is the containment by the aesthetic will of the details of a world. In this preliminary sense, Klein's aesthetic of accumulation lacks the ability to overwhelm of Page's hyper-attentive eye, for the leisurely reader taking his poems one at a time is in a position to break much of the accumulative momentum merely by setting the book down. Klein's accumulative and catalogic urges do pierce to the level of stylistics as well, however, and if he is rarely as visually and syntactically dense as is Page, he is certainly as ready to go on adducing precise observations until the object as a 'whole' is realized.

'Grain Elevator' is a fine first example of this quality of Klein's forties poetics. Its accumulative methods are various, their general effect an illumination of the speaker's imaginative patterns very like the function I argued, from Kenner, for Imagism. They first emerge in the opening stanza, in which a series of possible identifications of the visual object is offered, in a tone of dubiety intended to suggest sublimity:

Leviathan
swamped on our shore? The cliffs of some other river?
The blind ark lost and petrified? A cave
built to look innocent, by pirates? Or
some eastern tomb a travelled patron here makes local?

(*CP*, p. 650)

These lines only function, of course – and again the method is Imagist – because the title of the poem identifies the object being interrogated. They ask the reader to respond to a speaker's juxtaposition of visual analogies befitting the elevator, and thus engage, potentially, our and the speaker's

Imagist abilities. It is not surprising therefore that the second stanza opens with an assertion that 'even when known, it's more than what it is': the whole energy of the poem thus far has been away from the merely 'known' to a higher order of meaning grounded in transhistorical comparisons, offered so far in catalogue.

This aesthetic makes it unsurprising when we encounter passages in which the one fixed object, the elevator, is compared to many possible analogous objects by metaphoric apostrophe: 'O prison of prairies, ship in whose galleys roll / sunshines like so many shaven heads, / waiting the bushel-burst out of the beached bastille!' Note as well the extremely mixed metaphor of the last image. The speaker acknowledges the randomness of his comparisons, a little defensively, in intermittent passages: 'Sometimes, it makes me think Arabian, / ... Sometimes, some other races claim / the twinship of my thought ...' The poem's accumulation of reference is even figured forth self-consciously in the grain itself: these images are like 'the grain picked up, like tic-tacs out of time: / first one; an other; singly; one by one ...' Indeed the grain elevator is perhaps an ideal object of Klein's accumulative aesthetics, symbolic of stark, strong containment of an all-but-infinite detail and possibility. This drive for imagistic comprehensiveness explains the poem's resistance to its own closure:

> It's because it's bread. It's because
> bread is its theme, an absolute. Because
> always this great box flowers over us
> with all the coloured faces of mankind ...

The unasked question to which 'it' must refer is, *why* does the elevator 'make ... a montage / of inconsequent time and uncontiguous space'? The poem closes, then, with a final cryptic defence of its own aesthetics, for it is the mind of the speaker (and the poet) that has been roaming freely in time and space, and applying fragments of both to a 'montage' of the poetic object. But note that the poem answers the question with yet another catalogue: a series of reasons, and perhaps a series whose incompleteness is noteworthy, the ellipsis at the end being Klein's own.

'Grain Elevator' is typical of the accumulative discursive tendencies of many poems in *The Rocking Chair*, in part because it registers some anxiety at the flourishes of the method. Of course the catalogue had long attracted Klein: his early multivocal poem-portraits, 'Portraits of a Minyan' and 'Design for Medieval Tapestry,' for example, show the young poet's confidence that a representation of Jewish communities can be accomplished by gathering portraits of discrete individuals. That having been said, it is equally obvious that Klein's pre-1940 work shows little of the intensity of image accumulation visible in 'Grain Elevator.' The first signs of such a stylistic tendency to catalogue emerge in 1942, a period in which Klein had begun to compose the odd poem detailing local flora and fauna ('Dentist' and 'Girlie Show,' for example) but which also shows a persistent, somewhat fitful concern with Judaica ('Autobiographical,' 'The Golem'). These early catalogues are rather clumsy: 'Pawnshop,' for example – another edifice ideally exemplifying the poetic's desire to contain multiplicity and randomness – not only catalogues the objects contained, but underscores their *quidditas* with letters and semicolons that enforce our prolonged pause over each item:

(a) family plate – hocked for the widow's mite;
(b) birthday gifts; the cups marked *champion* (c);
(d) tools; (e) special, vase picked up in Crete;
en bloc: watch; ring, endowing bride;
camera; medal; crushed accordion ...

(*CP*, p. 576)

Predictably the poem closes, once again, with the speaker's accumulated interpretations of what he has recorded:

This is our era's state-fair parthenon,
the pyramid of a pharaonic time,
our little cathedral, our platonic cave,
our childhood's house that Jack built.

I think we might react in two ways to such passages. Positively we might wish to admire the fertility of the poet's ability to make comparisons, to juxtapose so many vehicles to a single tenor. A more negative readerly experience might depend from an expectation that a poet provide the truest possible metaphor, rather than a range of possible truths. In the latter judgment, given the poem's near-compulsive accumulative method, there is no clear reason for 'Pawnshop' to have stopped – in Gage's words, no 'sense of necessity compelling a conclusion'[47] – nor indeed any appreciable reason for it to continue. Both responses are available to the reader of 'Grain Elevator' as well, surely (although there a consensus over the poem's accomplishment seems to indicate that the accumulative thrust is fairly governed, its *integritas* palpable). In response to such a demur, Klein's technique obviously asserts the poet's duty to emphasize the process, not the results, of comparison: to dramatize the mechanisms of the creative metaphoric sensibility, in keeping with modernist commitment. In order to do so, he lists numerous useful comparisons in hope that their mutuality of reference will tellingly evoke the object, and as that aesthetic idea is very like Page's tendency to pile up disconcerting images in hope 'that the whole may toll' among them, it is not surprising that Klein should happen across it in the first year's run of *Preview.*

Nevertheless this incipient style does not really become dominant in Klein's poetry until the stresses of 1943–4 ended his willingness to deal with Jewish subjects. Once the *Suite Canadienne* was conceptualized in 1944, its inherent principle of catalogue developed rapidly on the level of style. In 'Bread,' for example, with its interesting extrapolation of the last lines of 'Grain Elevator,' the represented loaf is, intermittently, 'Creation's crust and crumb,' 'Seedstaff and wheatwand of all miracles,' 'kneading of knowledge, leaven of happiness,' 'black-bread hemisphere, oblong of rye, / Crescent and circle of the seeded bun' (*CP*, pp. 617–18). Note once again the importance of accumulative apostrophe in the poem's achievement of verbal power: these metaphoric identifications of bread are in effect cries of praise directed to the insentient object, two of them uplifted with the bardic 'O' that was among Klein's signatures at the time. (On this, and on the poem's use of exclamation marks to similar ends, I will have more to say later.) 'Montreal,' noted so commonly for its forceful linguistic play, is less often remarked for its listing habits, divided as it is into stanzas whose very numbering suggests the need for crisp order, and whose primary discursive method is the accumulation of imagistic detail:

Coureur de bois, in posts where pelts were portaged;
Seigneur within his candled manoir; Scot
Ambulant through his bank, pillar'd and vast.
Within your chapels, voyaged mariners ...

But for me also sound your potencies,
Fortissimos of sirens fluvial,
Bruit of manufactory, and thunder
From foundry issuant ...
                    and then
Sanct silence, and your argent belfries
Clamant in orison! ...

The coigns of your boulevards – my signiory –
Your suburbs are my exile's verdure fresh,
Your parks, your fountain'd parks ...

(*CP*, pp. 621–3)

Apparently this accumulative pattern is the actualization of Klein's 'green inventory,' not only in his decision to include a portrait of Montreal in a thorough-going catalogue of Quebec life, but also in its style and parataxis, which intimate that the most accurate portrait of an 'object' is a series of its details rendered each in metaphor or, alternatively, a single detail rendered in a series of metaphors. The effect in either case is of a poet working, to borrow David Canaan's obsessive phrase from Ernest Buckler's *The Mountain and the Valley* of 1952, 'to get it all in,' to leave nothing uncontained by the force of his word-making.[48]

'The Rocking Chair' itself, titular representative of the volume's project, exemplifies these structural tendencies. While the chair is not an object of representation that contains a broad assortment of objects (as were the 'Pawnshop' and 'Grain Elevator'), Klein works to invoke such an assortment *through* the object nevertheless. One way of grasping the effort of the poem is by remarking that its prolonged series of images occur in parallel response to a single unasked question, which might be very simply worded as, 'What *is* the rocking chair?' Once that elided constitutive question is brought to the surface, the poem's cataloguism becomes more apparent. It is 'wooden, – it is no less a national bird,' 'It is also the old man's pet,' 'it is the toddler's game,' 'it is ... sabbatical and clumsy,' it 'is a character,' 'it is alive; individual,' 'it is tradition,' 'It is act // and symbol'– every one of these persistent phrases emphasizing that the poetic's drive is towards identification by accumulation. By the end of this process of intense metaphorizing, Klein has succeeded in identifying the simple furnishing with the whole province of which he writes, the very accomplishment that makes the poem contentious as well, for its implicitly political judgments of the Québécois.

These same structural leanings are arguable in 'The Provinces,' 'Frigidaire,' 'The Sugaring,' and many others. But the urge of accumulation was so powerful at the time that, even in those poems in which it is not a constitutive structural device, Klein shows a tendency to fall back on catalogue at pivotal moments in the description. 'Indian Reservation: Caughnawaga' (*CP*, pp. 641–2), for example, has a structure of comment that is comparatively complex, with its interplay of idealized Indians and actual Native people. Although the poetic 'object' is once again a fixed fact described by the free play of signifiers in the poet's mind – there is no 'story' *per se* – the poem's temporal irony nudges its aesthetics out of the realm of catalogue: we are at first invited to see each 'item' dually through a poet's subjective retrospection, making it difficult to subsume the detail into a neutral or objective list. Nevertheless, once the 'ideal' attitudes of childhood are surrendered, and the temporal complexity with them, a need to catalogue emerges in the third stanza, with its successive images of 'the men,' 'their squaws,' and 'the ragged papooses.' As was his habit in the representation of cruelly used minorities (compare the museum's 'Last Jew'), Klein next launches an archival metaphor that will invite further catalogue: he turns aside to describe the reservation's tourist store, stocked with 'the beaded shoes, / the sweetgrass basket, the curio Indian, / burnt wood and gaudy cloth and inch-canoes,' all that remains of the Native past. It is not, therefore, a surprising resonance when he concludes, in the final stanza, 'these are fauna in a museum kept.' The 'inventory' here has hardly been a green one, nor has the accumulation of 'items' occasioned much real 'praise.'

Rather than invoke further evidence of this general rhetorical pattern in *The Rocking Chair,* I want briefly to consider its implications. Klein's impulse to catalogue is a materialist and positivist response to the poet's Adamic responsibilities: taking the duty to 'name' and to 'praise' 'item by exciting item' from 'Portrait' literally, he proceeds through his actual world, and a number of items, most of them highly mundane, catch his poetic eye. He chooses to represent these, in the apparent conviction that a portrait of Quebec will be effected by the poetic transfiguration of their mundaneness, and subsequent collocation in a volume. Many of the resulting poems are structured as inventories, catalogues, themselves; most of the rest show the persistent urge to list things that is fundamental to the project. On the most local level, he tends to provide not one metaphor for a detail, but two or three, to list not one detail, but a handful. He tries, with an ironic awareness of limits that David Canaan does not have, 'to get it all in.' But such a rendition of *The Rocking Chair* project should be complicated somewhat, first by remarking its consonance with a number of general concerns of the forties, and second by considering its relation to Klein's sudden abandonment of the Jewish subject in verse *circa* 1944.

Klein's aesthetics are not peculiarly his, even if his techniques remain idiosyncratic. Just as with Page the tendency to accumulate startling metaphors raised a degree of stylistic and structural tension in her poems, so Klein's evident thrust towards comprehensiveness brings with it challenges to *integritas* that are latent in the poems of *The Rocking Chair.* The evident desire to inventory the world is a sign in Klein of both a remarkable imaginative capacity for metaphorical praise *and* a degree of anxiety as to the sufficiency of that capacity for the presentation of the world's wholeness and richness. These twinned impulses are figured in 'Portrait' as the dual need to praise 'item by exciting item' and still to 'look with single camera view upon this earth.' In the individual poem, then, each item in the catalogue is another step towards wholeness *and* another reminder of incompleteness and of the enormity of the accepted vocation. Like Page, who felt the similar paradox that the power of her 'eye' and her ability to render its glimpses in striking imagery were threatening to her poetry's embodiment of sympathy and wholeness, Klein sought balance between a poetic particularism he could not renounce and a desire for unity he could not shake. But whereas Page's challenges emerge largely on the level of style, Klein's aesthetics of accumulation function structurally as well, to organize poems as units, but also to cluster them in search of a larger 'camera view.'

Klein's affinities with and distinction from Page's techniques can be clarified, ironically, if we remember that he shared little or none of her enthusiasm for Imagist possibilities. As a young Canadian poet of the 1920s, he was ideally situated to receive the Imagist example with enthusiasm; instead, his sneering dismissal of it betrays the fundamental conservatism of his poetic ideas during the days of the so-called McGill Movement: 'What today is heralded as imagist is no more than a reactionary reversal to the rebus intelligence, a degeneration into the concrete, an acceptance of the nous of the noun – it is an attempt to say nothings with things' ('Worse Verse,' *LER*, p. 152). The broader attack on 'free verse' of which this passage forms a part is a useful document in the history of Klein's determined maintenance of close ties to the English poetic tradition. Nevertheless, his progress from the twenties to the forties suggests that his original disdain for the 'concrete' and its embodiment of 'the nous' would be replaced by a hope that there was indeed in the description of 'things' a chance to see through them to the noumenal. It is after all something like a 'rebus intelligence' that would ask us to conjoin 'Leviathan,' 'The blind ark,' and 'some eastern tomb,' and arrive thereby at a heightened representation of a grain elevator.

Klein's early disdain for this fundamental concept of modernist achievement denies us the explanation for *his* accumulative aesthetics that was illuminating for Page. There is no evidence that he ever reconsidered. His very indifference to Imagism itself makes a strong case, however, for the influence of Page and *Preview* on his poetry, removing as it does the possibility of his having arrived at her manner by a similar trajectory. I would in fact argue that Page's influence is general in the poems just discussed, but it is more immediately palpable in, for example, 'Lone Bather':

Upon the ecstatic diving board the diver,
poised for parabolas, lets go
lets go his manshape to become a bird.
Is bird, and topsy-turvy
the pool floats overhead, and the white tiles snow

their crazy hexagons. Is dolphin. Then
is plant with lilies bursting from his heels.

(*CP*, p. 685)

The poem's opening is notable for its parallel relation of a series of clauses related by anaphora to a singly deployed subject: 'the diver' as noun phrase has in this stanza alone four predicates, three of them copular (note the urgency of identification again) and the first doubled around an enjambment, to suggest the hesitation of the diver before plunging. We saw similar anaphora and suppression of pronomial subjectivity in Page's 'The Permanent Tourists,' for example; such striking predication continues throughout Klein's poem. 'Lone Bather' also shows Page's tendency to neologism, as when 'snow' is made transitive in the fifth line. Later her '*a* of *b*' formula becomes dominant: 'melonrinds of water,' 'rung of water,' 'gloves of greeting,' 'the eight reins of his ponies.' Indeed, the entire portrait is in a genre Page perfected, the brief objectifying glimpse of an eccentrically rendered character. So strong are these stylistic echoes that I would contend that 'Lone Bather' could be slipped into a Page volume and we would have no suspicion of a forgery. The same might be said of Klein's 'Frigidaire': the anaphora re-emerges, the '*a* of *b*' formula is reasserted. In 'Frigidaire,' however, one might equally argue for Anderson's contribution to Klein's formation, despite his disdain for the *Preview* editor's political callowness; the poem's diction of winter landscapes is strongly evocative of some of Anderson's most successful Canadian scenes.[49]

There is nothing exhaustive in such suggestions; a more complete rendering of the stylistics of 'Lone Bather' would also have to consider the likely impact of Irving Layton's 'The Swimmer' of 1944 on Klein's choice of subject and imagery three years later. (Indeed, the possibility of Page's and Layton's having a simultaneous influence on a fellow poet points up some of the fundamental affinities between them that will emerge in the next chapter.) From such literary-historical claims I also want to return to the evident anxiety registered in Klein's fragmentary outline for 'Portrait of the Poet as Landscape': that jotting's keen sense of failure-to-date and of passing time ('I have yet in me to do something') suggests that the urge to itemize is closely bound up with his sense of his own poetic worth. I think this is why he remarks in the fragment, '*My* inventory has not been taken' (emphasis added): the ambiguous possessive pronoun collapses the distinction between 'Klein's inventory of the world' and 'an inventory of Klein,' revealing once again that permeable boundary between the self and its surroundings that can be both threatening and enabling in Klein's poetry. If we consider that patterns of accumulation and catalogue come into sharp focus in Klein's career coincident with his full experience of the Holocaust, and assuming as I have that such historic trauma had a quick shattering effect on all aspects of his self-identification and sense of a world, it is not surprising that he should begin a new poetry whose emphasis is on the gradual, step-by-step identification and containment of things. The Adamic metaphor underscores not only his power-to-name but also the intense strangeness of the world in which he moves; the 'nth Adam' must put his feet down gingerly in a world to which he can have no confident verbal relation.

The conjunction of Klein's affinity with Page and need for a stable relation to a new world draws into focus another striking feature of catalogue in *The Rocking Chair*, that is, Klein's marked tendency to the verse portrait. Once again a survey of the titles is instructive: 'M. Bertrand,' 'The Notary,' 'Monsieur Gaston,' 'Sire Alexandre Grandmaison,' 'Hormisdas Arcand' are a cluster of poems in the second half of the volume, their juxtaposition with one another suggesting Klein's awareness that they, too, composed a useful sub-catalogue of Quebec culture. To these must be added the far better-known 'Political Meeting,' itself a more or less explicit portrait of Camillien Houde,[50] Montreal's anti-conscription and Fascist-sympathetic mayor of the period; of course all these poems are governed somewhat by their proximity to the aptly titled 'Portrait of the Poet as Landscape.' Other uncollected pieces suggest the persistence of the genre from 1944 to 1947, poems like 'The Library,' 'Doctor Drummond,' 'Portrait, and Commentary [Version 2 of 'Lowell Levi'],' and 'Les Filles Majeures.' It is easy to recognize the *generic* affinity between such poems and Page's many verse-portraits; the poems of *As Ten As Twenty* had appeared throughout the early 1940s, and among them Klein would have encountered group-portraits like 'The Stenographers' and individual treatments like 'Landlady' and 'Only Child.' This time the comparison with Page is instructive not only of Klein's affinity with his contemporaries but also of his difference from them: for Klein's verse-portraits tend, to speak generally, to have a sociopolitical and satiric context, and to represent named historical *and* semi-fictional men and women; whereas Page's, as we have seen, take a psychological approach to the portrayed individuals, most of whom remain anonymous, and jettison all concern with public verisimilitude, preferring to explore consciousnesses otherwise concealed from our scrutiny.

Klein's Québécois portraits show a distinct conviction that people are not what they seem, that protestations of sincerity in their self-representations tend to dissemble more dangerous and divisive impulses. Such ironies are played out in a context of race (note that portraits of non-francophone

Québécois were excluded from the volume), a matter that becomes thematic, of course, in 'Political Meeting.' That poem and 'Hormisdas Arcand' are evidence that Klein's scrutiny of the Québécois is in part an anxious examination of the potential for anti-Semitic violence in his own world, and they contribute to these portraits – a few of which are merely amusing – a disturbing context in which ancestral rhetoric may be overturned by racism at any moment. 'The Library,' despite its refusal to specify the race of the observed interlocutor and its consequent exclusion from *The Rocking Chair,* typifies the irony: in this poem of 1944, the speaker 'sat and talked only of *amor intellectualis*' with an aristocratic companion, little imagining the violent architecture of his refinement, until

> suddenly, and for no reason at all,
> his temper changed, and all his breeding sloughed ...
> ... As if the books were boards,
> and, at a button, had slid away, revealing
> bars, and behind, cement – his secret – where wild beasts
> yawned, and waved paw, circled, ran forward, roared
> for the week's meat.
>
> (*CP,* p. 620)

The suddenness with which the speaker's companion has changed is reflected, significantly, in an unstable physical world in which the very institutions of learning can in a moment become halls of imprisonment and torture. It also enforces a disconcerting randomness in the poem's syntax, emblematic of the rupture of Klein's own poetic language at the period of its composition.

The pattern of ironic revelation in 'The Library' is general to Klein's portraiture in *The Rocking Chair,* from the concealed plebeian background of 'Monsieur Gaston' to the corroboration of 'Sire Alexandre Grandmaison's' aristocratic pretensions by his ownership of 'Quebec Paper Products, Ltd. / Champlain Industries, Inc.' and so on (*CP,* p. 696). 'Hormisdas Arcand' is an exception only in that its portrait of Adrien Arcand, leader of Quebec's Nazi party, involves little dissimulation on the subject's part: the first line of his 'historic manifesto' and the last of Klein's poem converge on the '*A bas les maudits juifs!,*' beyond which Arcand's thinking never ventured (*CP,* p. 681). Unquestionably the most representative of these portraits and their ironic venom is 'Political Meeting,' in which Houde's brilliant tactical oratory binds his francophone audience not politically, but racially, in an incipient fascist darkness:

He is tearful, choking tears; but not he
would blame the clever English; in their place
he'd do the same; maybe.

Where *are* your sons?
The whole street wears one face
shadowed and grim; and in the darkness rises
the body-odour of race.

(*CP*, p. 658)

The frightening collectivity demanded by Houde – among whose historic 'rhetorical' gestures in his speech to the YMCA was the remark that 'French Canadians are Fascists, not by name, but by blood' (Caplan, p. 82) – offers a subsidiary explanation for Klein's portraits. They may be seen to refuse the latent violence of racial collectivity by returning 'the people' to their more ironic and demonstrably fraudulent status as individuals: when the 'whole street wears one face,' it is harder to see, and harder to combat, the spurious motives of their behaviour.

Klein had no wish to demonize the Québécois. His various portraits of individuals do have mild collective force and thus underscore – in the light of his earlier portraiture – his broad sympathy with their marginality in the Canadian polity. He was nevertheless clearly disturbed by any expression of Quebec's aspiration in appeals to race consciousness, and anxious about a culture torn between a hierarchically applied law ('The Notary,' 'M. le juge Dupré') and a disturbing appetite for social and political change ('M. Bertrand,' 'Monsieur Gaston'). It is hardly surprising, then, that he should return to portraiture for their thematization as a marginal people akin to his own, but do so with the emphasis on ironically rendered individuals kept separate from one another in a catalogue of clearly demarcated, Christian-named or surnamed poems. By 1944, we might hypothesize, individuals were more explicable to Klein's poetic imagination than collectives, the motives of which were obscure and could easily be perverted.

From imagery to structure to theme and irony, then, catalogue is a fundamental element of Klein's aesthetics in the years following the Holocaust revelations. In my view it should be interpreted dually, as a sign of the capacious Adamism towards which he aspired in the period and as a marker of a certain anxiety about the precise character of the ground on which he stood, literally in his own physical environment and figuratively in his ambiguous relations with others and in questions of race consciousness that were horribly vivid to his mind at the time. As a poetic task, catalogue raises the stakes of poetic accomplishment, as its theorization in 'Portrait of the Poet as Landscape' implied, for the poet's duty to comprehensiveness – so keenly felt in the forties – is powerfully challenged by his successful rendition of the fragmentary details of a life. Catalogue risks, as I believe Klein knew full well, the appearance of mere fragmentation, inchoate randomness of precisely the kind he was wanting to resist in his reading of history. Any given reader of a poem will have to decide – we can think back to '$x^2 + 2xy + y^2$' – whether its catalogues are of a nature powerful enough to leave him or her impressed with poetic accomplishment rather than the poet's helplessness before infinity. That evaluation will remain, as I have worded it, individual, although it seems clear enough that the poems of *The Rocking Chair* are judged by most readers to be of an order of accomplishment that easily subsumes their occasional – and occasionally crucial – reliance on aesthetic cataloguing.

Klein was himself, I believe, less confident about the project than are his later readers. If my reading of 'Portrait's' climactic ambiguities is accurate, this is hardly surprising; nor is it odd to think, if a connection between Klein's shock at the Holocaust and his turn to quotidian catalogue of a Christian society is now accepted, that he should view the project with deep-seated uncertainty, as to its aesthetic value and its intelligence as a response to the trauma of European Jewry. That a 'green inventory' was more or less licensed by contemporary English poetics of the forties would not have gone far, probably, in reassuring him, and the fact of catalogue's roots in his earlier celebrations of Jewish communities ('Portraits of a Minyan') could have done little to comfort a poet looking for new methods in the face of that community's annihilation. A second examination of the poems reveals instead that Klein was aware of the aesthetic's potential replication of the chaos it was meant to counter, for it is in response to such concern that he begins to emphasize, and to exaggerate, a series of stylistic gestures clearly intended to underscore for the reader the poems' achievement of force.

Klein certainly disdained the more simplistic modernist methods for the representation of cultural disorder. One of the 'Marginalia' fragments, 'A Conversation,' pits a modern poet (butt of irony) against a Socratic interlocutor with whom Klein is clearly in agreement. The modernist poet contends that a poem he has written 'has no form' because it 'was meant to mirror contemporary life' (*LER*, p. 189). The ironic interlocutor points out that as any part of chaos must be indistinguishable from all other parts of chaos, there can be no better or worse poems 'mirroring' chaos. The chastened poet is forced to end the dialogue with petulance: 'I *know* I'm right' (p. 190). Meanwhile our representative thinker has demonstrated that the poet choosing images from chaos will have to retain a principle of selection and a principle of aesthetic power, both of which are contradictory to the spirit of submission to chaos in which he began. Thus rendered, the dialogue is exemplary of the forties poets' search for an *integritas* that would sustain without over-determining their fragmented metaphoric visions, but it has no time to establish the bases of these principles, nor their appropriate manifestation in poems. Klein, however, has made it clear enough that he has no truck with a modernist aesthetic that accounts for formal incoherence by a pseudo-mimetic appeal to *Weltschmerz*, and although the fragment was penned after *The Rocking Chair* had appeared, its urbane convictions seem to hold good retroactively.

The exclamatory mood of much of Klein's forties work is one sign of his uneasiness about his own poems' force of expression. It emerges in the early 1940s and quickly becomes one of his weakest poetic habits, taking on compulsive form in 'Ballad of the Werewolves,' for example, a poem in which twelve of twenty lines end with an exclamation mark. The roughly contemporary 'Yehuda Halevi, His Pilgrimage' is vitiated by the emphasis:

Quoth now the Berber captain, wrathfully:
'There is in our midst an unbelieving cur,
Faring to Egypt with his heathenry!
Into the sea with him, young mariner!
In fish's belly, let him reach Iskandahar!'

Answered Halevi: 'Pray unto your God!'
'Aye, that we have!' 'Then let me pray to mine!'

(*CP* p. 551, ll. 230–6)

But in such poems, with their unworldly materials, the exclamatory mode is appropriate enough: Klein is drawing on the realm of legend, in which grand sentiment is the basis of grander action, and if 'Yehuda Halevi' blurs into Douglas Fairbanks at times as a result, the slippage in the poem's apparent purposes is minimal. It is in a poem like 'Dentist,' an early sign of the turn to the mundane that would become prescriptive by 1944, that the exclamatory urgency seems wishful rather than decorous:

May thirty-two curses blight that torturer!
May his gums soften! May he lose his friends
Turning in silence from his exhalations!
            His tinsel wreath
Fall from his mouth, abscessed, with clotted gore

At its forked ends!
Thirty-two curses on his thirty-two teeth!

(*CP*, p. 568)

I will be accused perhaps of missing the poem's light heart if I remark that the chief effect of this punctuation on my ear is that of a poet trying to whip himself up into a frenzy over a subject that is beneath him. But Klein let 'Dentist' pass after its *Preview* appearance, and so can we.

When the same technique dominates *The Rocking Chair*, however, the questions attendant upon it may seem more worthy of examination. Why should a loaf of 'Bread'– if it is a subject worthy of elaboration, as Klein's poem insists – require such a response-enforcing technique as the exclamation mark to convince us that 'By [its] white fiat' the 'World moves' (*CP*, p. 617)? If we are likely to accept the idea that 'History yearns upon [bread's] yearning yeast,' are we likely to want the idea insisted upon in punctuation? The gap between the loaf of bread and its world significance is perhaps great enough without the poet's widening it by heightening the degree of significance he claims with the poem's style. Indeed, it is a possible and reasonable readerly reaction to feel that a needless exclamation mark has slighted one's ability to take the poet's point; I seem to require knocking on the head. And this difficulty emerges in reverse when the poetic object is more obviously, perhaps inarguably significant, as in 'Montreal.' In this stunning poem of sixty-four lines, fourteen of which end in exclamation (and all eight stanzas of which do so), Klein may be gilding the lily with a punctuation that seems, if anything, to demand the last drop of our admiration by way of stanzaic closure even when we have been breathless with admiration throughout. Does such an emphatic assertion of one's own power indeed add to that power – or render us, its interpreters, cautious, even ironic? (It's a fact worth remarking that the most-anthologized poems from *The Rocking Chair* are the least exclamatory: 'Political Meeting,' 'Grain Elevator,' 'The Rocking Chair' itself.)

In this light it is interesting that exclamation marks tend to surge forward in 'Portrait of the Poet as Landscape' in those passages in which the emblematic poet is depicted in his relation to his art: as, for instance, in the 'shaped and warm auxiliaries!' and 'dimple and dip of conjugation!' in Section II, in the condemnation of cheap modernists in Section III ('how they do fear the slap of the flat of the platitude!'), and in the Adamic vocation of Section VI – the middle stanzas of which all end in a foregrounded raising of the voice. Klein seems especially eager to assert the *vocation*, the true calling, of the poet in these lines: he wants to leave little doubt that the poet's motivation to literary art is genuine and passionate, even if the last section's punctuation functions ironically as well, to suggest the extremism of his aesthetic aspirations. The pattern suggests, if not an anxiety as to the power of his own poetic vocation, then at minimum an anxiety as to how his (let us say confident) vocation will appear to others if his poems take particular forms. The exclamation marks are compensatory, in this sense, to the uncertainty of public purpose that is thematized in 'Portrait.'

To identify the exclamatory mode with the liberality of exclamation marks in Klein's punctuation is insufficient, obviously, and there are many other rhetorical gestures in the poems that function similarly to assert poetic power. One of these is the bardic 'O' that Klein found especially attractive, so much so that Frank Flemington, an assistant editor with Ryerson Press, remarked upon it in a letter of 26 February 1948: 'Has it ever been brought to your attention how many "O's" appear in this MS. I think it appears over fifty times. Often it gives the same impression as Matthew Arnold's "Ah's".'[51] My own count renders twenty-seven Os (perhaps Klein excised a few after Flemington's exaggerated remarks), still a striking number for a collection of thirty-seven poems. The habit was so archaic that Klein's contemporaries might be forgiven for assuming his bardic instances were ironic: they are rarely so. They function in the poems' effort of 'praise' (to persist in the critical language of 'Portrait'), and are related as well to Klein's long-familiar imitation of biblical language and rhythms. But they also serve the more utilitarian purpose of assuring us of the poet's afflatus – should we have been questioning it – and their frequency suggests that Klein wished often to provide such assurances.

A last feature of the exclamatory mood in these poems is the poet's tendency to superlatives and hyperbole in his claims for an object's meaning. Often related to the volume's interest in apostrophe, this insistence on superlative conditions suggests once again how far the poet wishes to elevate his materials. Klein's is no simple task of re-presentation, but rather a transfiguration into a condition of such significance that no comparison by degrees is possible. 'Bread' is 'wheatwand of *all* miracles,' and '*No* house is home without [its] wifeliness' (*CP*, p. 617). In the 'Commercial Bank' '*all* fauna meet,' even though its 'flora *none* can seek' (p. 618). Montreal's historic personages are '*All* present from your past!' (p. 621); the poet is the '*chiefest* ... / Auditor' of that city's 'music' (p. 622). The ice of the St Lawrence is first rendered in 'The Break-up' by its absolute infrangibility: 'There are *no* hammers will break that granite lid' (p. 647). Bread is an '*absolute*' in 'Grain Elevator': '*always* this great box flowers over us / with *all* the coloured faces of mankind ...' (p. 651).[52] And so on. Few of these claims are overturned by later ironies, and the poet's easy drift into the superlative mood suggests once again how much he wanted to reassure us, and perhaps himself, of the significance of his catalogued objects.

The insistence audible in such inflationary rhetorical techniques seems to me to have to do with the distaste for modernist chaos recorded in the fragmentary 'Conversation.' Because nothing inherent in the accumulative aesthetic of *The Rocking Chair* guarantees the significance of its accomplishment – and this should I think be compared to Klein's Judaica, which are explicable and justifiable at the very least, no matter what the poet's skill, by God's having himself 'chosen' the Jews as *His* favourite subjects – there is a risk that the deliberate mundaneness of the poetic object will be primary in the reader's experience of the poems. Klein's ability to 'write up' the discrete particulars of the world in high style is the most obvious counter to this fear: its clear purpose is the elevation of his quotidian catalogue to the level of Adamic praise. But even the most accomplished style leaves him with a volume made up of randomly sighted and gathered objects, the mere juxtaposition of which does little to assure us of the poet's comprehensive visionary ability – the 'single camera eye' that is desirable in 'Portrait of the Poet as Landscape.' Klein clearly wanted a complete and vivid world view to resonate among the poems as well: wanted *The Rocking Chair* to be not only about Quebec, but about 'all mankind,' as 'Grain Elevator' has it. That is the aesthetic challenge I suggest he feared he had failed to achieve with the volume, and it has its rhetorical corollary in the constant gestures of exclamatory reassurance I have cited.

Klein's decision to turn away from a lifelong subject whose significance was assured to a modernist aesthetic of local accumulation was fraught, then, with uncertainty that is registered stylistically in the poems. The structure of my argument has suggested that this anxiety cannot be separated from the psychic and spiritual burdens of the Holocaust stories emergent at the same time: that the urge to bardic exclamation is a vestigial gesticulation in the direction of prophecy in the time of his people's greatest need. This decision was attended by a destabilization of his own sense of personal affiliation and privacy: to turn away poetically from the suffering of his people was not necessarily to turn fully towards the interests of another. Given Klein's already routine figuration of bodily and domestic boundaries against external forces of rupture and change, it is not surprising that another motif of *The Rocking Chair* is the speaker's concern to establish his psychic and corporeal relation to his surroundings. He is especially concerned to centralize himself in his narration of Quebec, to show himself essential in his 'new' poetic home, even as he fears that desired centrality – a typical Klein ambivalence – as an erasure of his special identity. This paradoxical pull of desire for centrality and fear of erasure has much to do with Klein's urge to catalogue: his wish to 'get it all in' is partly a wish to control 'it all' within the 'body' of his own imagination, to incorporate and thus limit the otherness of the world,[53] but (like the 'prowler in the mansion') the world so embodied will change him profoundly, will remove one powerful identity and replace it with another, at a time when the Jewish 'identity' is threatened not with assimilation, but with elimination.

Such anxieties register Klein's judgment, particular, as I have suggested, to the middle of the forties, of an enervating opposition between the self-effacement of anonymity and the self-affirmation of subjective speech. The poet who earlier trusted that true anonymity rested only with God and that all human poetry was inevitably self-affirmative seems in *The Rocking Chair* poems to feel that he has come too close to an ideal impersonality and necessarily been rendered insignificant in the process. There is no other explanation for the more urgent rhetorical gestures of the volume: the suppression of his selfhood and of his race's consciousness had to be countered by subliminal self-assertions precisely because the facelessness of impersonality was not conceptually benign to him at the end of the war. He adopted the impersonal manner in part because it justified the suppression of his particular historical consciousness at a time when that consciousness was unbearable; but the consequent erasure of his distinct identity could hardly have been reassuring of his people's endurance. This is why anonymity takes on such ambiguous resonances in 'Portrait of the Poet as Landscape,' and why Adamic cataloguing – with its cancellation of the particulars of our n^{th} Adam – cannot really restore the poet to his original social function. He can only hope that the items of his 'green inventory' will suggest in their juxtapositions a force of consciousness and poetic giftedness that will not only make the world coherent but make his own being a ground of that coherence despite its absence from the poetic range. He must seek, in effect, to stand in for the *integritas* of each poem – the anonymous principle of wholeness to which its details may be referred.

The full complexity of these forces is visible in 'Montreal,' which may now be remarked not only for its exclamatory urgency, but for its near-complete erasure of the Jews of the city as well. That a poem so concerned with his city's multicultural texture should stringently avoid all explicit reference to his own 'third solitude' so pivotal in its development is, to say the least, curious and, in the context of international genocide, starkly disturbing. It suggests a depth of unease in Klein's creativity at the time comparable to that which I have argued from his biography. But there are countering forces at work in 'Montreal' as well, which serve to reinstate the centrality of Jewish culture in the city by figuring the poem's speaker as its metaphoric body. This is why so many of the poem's exclamations pertain to the physical and psychic incorporation of Montreal *into* the speaker's selfhood:

O city metropole, isle riverain!
Your ancient pavages and sainted routs
Traverse my spirit's conjured avenues!
Splendor erablic of your promenades
Foliates there ...

(*CP*, p. 621)

The force of such proclamations is at first only to emphasize the retrospective poet's loving memories of his city, but the pattern continues and becomes increasingly bodily: 'You populate the pupils of my eyes,' for example, is a literalization that allows his vision to surround the loved objects and to contain them as insight. The motif becomes dominant for the poem's closure:

You are a part of me, O all your quartiers ...
You are locale of infancy, milieu
Vital of institutes that formed my fate;
And you above the city, scintillant,
Mount Royal, are my spirit's mother,
Almative, poitrinate!

(*CP*, p. 622)

Although some of the language here remains spiritual ('almative'), when Montreal's central mountain is rendered 'chest-like' it is also likened forcibly to a part of the physical speaker: as he incorporates the 'quartiers' he is also blurring the distinction between himself and his surroundings that most enervates his consciousness. It is not surprising that the completion of this pattern is invoked for a triumphant peroration:

Mental, you rest forever edified
With tower and dome; and in these beating valves,
Here in these beating valves, you will
For all my mortal time reside!

(*CP*, p. 623)

The emphasis of metaphor in the poem makes plain a driving urge in the speaker to prove his spiritual and bodily oneness with the city. Despite the absence of Montreal Jewish history in the poem, a Jewish poet demonstrates through metaphor not only that he is able to encompass the whole of the city's multiple vitalities – he is its outward border, then – but that he is also its spiritual centre, its heart whose 'beating valves' give Montreal its special pulsation. Indeed, we can watch the progress of the metaphor from impression, as it enters at his eyes, through inspiration (as it fills his 'poitrine') to identification – as he and the city 'rest forever edified' in a single structure. By poem's end, the city is resident in the poet, rather than the reverse.

Pollock helps us to see that these affinities of bodily and civic space in 'Montreal' parallel a continuous metaphorical yoking of the body and the creative vocation in Klein's writing (pp. 119–21 and *passim*). He also exposes a second point of entrance for the poet's Judaism in the final stanza of 'Montreal.' There Klein proceeds with a 'visioning' of Montreal in language that is, for him at least, clearly sacred by implication:

City, O city, you are vision'd as
A parchemin roll of saecular exploit
Inked with the script of eterne souvenir!

Despite the echoes of the Anglo-Catholic T.S. Eliot in the passage, the imagery functions to inscribe Montreal as a new-world Torah, especially by its insistence that the secular and the eternal are one and the same narrative for a chosen people. Few passages in *The Rocking Chair* offer a clearer connection between Klein's people and the people of interest to the volume. Once the echo is established, some of Klein's other diction becomes notable: his reference to his 'exile' in line 54, for instance, cannot have been made without a consciousness of its Jewish resonance, and perhaps its evocation of the destruction of the Temple does a little to explain the later hope that Montreal 'rest forever edified / With tower and dome.'

What we witness in 'Montreal,' then, is a Jewish poet portraying his multicultural city without explicit reference to the major contribution of his own people to that richness, but building into the poem a subtextual affirmation of his people's essential presence, in small part by metaphoric language particular to their faith, but more prominently by insisting on his own bodily and psychic identification with the limits of the city. Small wonder that line 27's superlative is placed so as to create an egoistic enjambment forcing us to honour the poet as the 'chiefest, I' in the city. He is so not only for his ability to take it all within him, but for his paramount 'eye' as well, a pun so common to the forties that it must surely register a key component of their aesthetic aspirations. Note, moreover, how much of Klein's 'Montreal' technique is forecast in 'Portrait of the Poet as Landscape': there, too, the poet is one 'who unrolled our culture from his scroll' (*CP*, p. 635); there, too, the boundary between the poet and the landscape is erased, albeit with cost; and there, too, the poet's ability to incorporate the world is critical to his self-estimation:

> Item by exciting item –
> air to his lungs, and pressured blood to his heart. –
> they are pulsated, and breathed, until they map
> not the world's, but his own body's chart!
>
> (*CP*, p. 639)

The lines assert plainly that the successful poet's 'itemization' of the world will bring about a subject–object fusion in which his own selfhood will become one with the world's. Something of this kind is clearly attempted subtextually in 'Montreal.' But 'Portrait' also warns us of the extremism of such aesthetic goals, when six lines later the ironic narrator remarks, 'and this, / this he would like to write down in a book!' Total identification with the other is, of course, unavailable even to great poets, and Klein had no such inflated self-opinion. Whatever the degree of psychic and physical reciprocity attained in 'Montreal,' the fact remains that it is attained on the subterranean level of the city: there can be, it seems, no *public* narrative of the same celebratory identification of Jewish artist and Anglo-French metropolis.

'Portrait's' generalization of the techniques of 'Montreal' suggests that Klein was thinking consistently in such terms in 1944, the year of mid-decade struggle and transformation. Indeed, the speaker's desire for identification with the Catholic city is rendered to a positive degree that an earlier Klein would have viewed with greater ambivalence. The perimeters separating 'identification' from 'assimilation' and 'elimination' are not always clear, and the urgency of belonging may blind us to their differences. This at least was the bitter warning of the poet in 'Now We Will Suffer Loss of Memory,' one of the 'Gestures Hebraic' of the late twenties:

> We will munch ham, and guzzle milk thereto,
> And this on hallowed fast-days, purposely ...
> Abe will elude his base nativity ...
> To gentile parties we will proudly go;
> And Christians, anecdoting us, will say:
> 'Mr. and Mrs. Klein – the Jews, you know ...'
>
> (*CP*, p. 169)

The personal bluntness of this poem gives its bitter awareness a special thrust. Recognizing that he could never cease to be 'the Jew' to his most liberal Gentile friends, Klein speaks at first as a *naif* who thinks that a change of habit will give him and his wife access to the central culture. The poem's *anagnorisis* is dual: that the desired assimilation will mean self-extinction, and that it can never be complete enough for a real acceptance by the centre anyway. At poem's end the *naif* is neither Jew nor Gentile, a stark warning of the costs of a straightforward identification with a longed-for mainstream.

'Montreal' seems to affirm, however, that a more impersonal manner would permit mainstream cultural identification with less obvious cost to the Jewish poet, its bases not now in social behaviour, but in the juxtapositive dualism of his metaphors. The poet's immersion into the landscape here does not – superficially at least – involve a surrender of distinctiveness, for the poles of this negotiation were never Jew/Gentile, but rather poet/city and body/space. The poem's language is highly insistent that the achieved blurring is a matter of celebration, 'Montreal' being among the volume's most exclamatory and bardic poems. The 'impersonality' of the poem does not require a simplistic avoidance of the first person; it is registered instead in the demonstration that first-person identity is articulable only in relation to a preordained tradition (in this case, a city) in whose terms one functions. In this sense Klein's techniques mirror ideally the model of Eliot's 'Tradition and the Individual Talent': here, too, we have a poet asserting his uniqueness precisely by proving his undifferentiation from the past – and 'the past is changed thereby.'[54]

Such at least is the poem's claim. In order to accept it we must know that our speaker is Jewish, and we must be alert to verbal cues that refer the portrayed city to Judaic symbols. But the fact remains that 'Montreal' has required 'impersonality' of a second, more literal, and more dangerous kind: the longed-for identification of the Jew with the Catholic city is achieved only on an implicit level, requiring subtle reading. On the surface, at least, the warning of 'Now We Will Suffer Loss of Memory' has proven accurate: there can be for the Jew no assimilation into the mainstream that is not also a self-erasure, no identification with the central body that is not also a dismemberment of one's own.[55] 'Montreal's' insistent mood of celebration partakes of *tour de force* because it seeks a degree of belonging that Klein knew full well to be illusory: style and exclamation are called up in the service of a wishful idea, to struggle against the poet's deep recognition of alienation.

Other tropes of *The Rocking Chair* that serve to render the poet central to the Quebec social-historical landscape are less self-consciously successful than the gestures of 'Montreal.' 'The Provinces,' for example, a forced effort of patriotic allegory, is predicated on a similar but much less fluid identification of body and physical environment, in which the prairies are 'the three flat-faced blond-haired husky ones,' the Maritimes are 'Great fishermen,' and so on. The poet's gifts of juxtaposition and *integritas* become pivotal in the subsequent attempt to register a 'Canadian unity' among the predictably incarnated provinces, presumably because his 'heart seeks one, the heart, and also the mind / seeks single the thing that makes them one, if one' (*CP*, p. 643), an abstract and somewhat tentative remark that might be taken as a motto for the whole volume's aesthetic project. Other poems pick up 'Montreal's' themes to similar effect. The three Mount Royal poems, for example, again exemplify Klein's desire for centrality and significance in Montreal, as in the remembered small boy atop the 'Lookout: Mount Royal' who briefly shares the 'camera eye' of 'Portrait' – 'to click the eye on motion forever stopped' – and uses it chiefly to locate 'the sought point, his home. // home recognized: there: to be returned to' (*CP*, p. 687). He is more confident of place than the retrospective adult of 'The Mountain,' who 'daily in a streetcar ... surround[s]' Mount Royal and insists somewhat nervously on its continuity with his own waning life: 'O all the amber afternoons / are still to be found // ... And Cartier's monument ... / still stands ... // The birchtree stripped by the golden zigzag still / stands ...' (*CP*, pp. 689–90).[56] Such poems register in their tone of wish-fulfilment the ambiguity of Klein's *Rocking Chair* project.

'Montreal's' implicit location of the Jew at the heart of the city persists largely as a matter of diction in other poems of the period. 'Grain Elevator's' references depend for part of their suggestiveness upon our ability to recognize the speaker as a Jew, for instance, for whom the evocation of words like 'babylonian,' 'Leviathan,' 'blind ark,' 'eastern tomb,' and 'Arabian' would be vaguely threatening, as indeed must have been the conjunction of 'prison' with 'shaven heads' in lines 14 and 15. As we have seen, a structural subtext is the poet's awareness of his own image-making upon the elevator, and the last stanza offers an unasked-for justification of his prolonged attention to such an object. These features underscore a degree of self-consciousness in the poem's aesthetics: its impersonality is offset by a personative voice seeking authorization and validation for its special insights. In the related poem 'Bread,' from whose images 'Grain Elevator' borrows closure, the speaker desires that the bread '[b]ind me forever in your ritual, your / Worship and prayer, me, and all mankind!' (*CP*, p. 618). The figure suggests the speaker's need for re-enclosure in the 'ritual' of his people: the bread's makers are 'most priestly,' 'White Levites at ... altar'd ovens' who he hopes will have the power to restore him to the faith he has lost, as he tells us in 'The Cripples.'

The latter poem is noted as among Klein's clearest statements of his loss of Jewish faith, but it might now be remarked for its essentializing turn towards Jewish selfhood at the end. Whatever the metaphoric power of the faithful at the Oratory (or for that matter in the 'Sisters of the Hotel-Dieu' [*CP*, pp. 648–9]), it is the self-divided poet-speaker whose consciousness of his own separate faith gives the worshipping Christians their *poetic* significance.

A final indication of Klein's need for self-affirmation in the impersonal catalogic method he had adopted for *The Rocking Chair* is the tendency of the poems to a greater self-reflexivity than he had permitted himself before. There is a concern in the volume that poetry be taken as the measure of other things, and that poets – among them Klein – be recognized as the principle of creation in the world. This was certainly the argument of 'Portrait of the Poet as Landscape,' and that poem's prominence, in its length and its appearance at the end of the volume, gives it a thematic governance over the whole. 'Grain Elevator,' as we have seen, is anxious about the reasons for the poet's prolonged metaphor-making. It is perhaps in 'Krieghoff: Calligrammes' that the breadth of the claim is most visible: in this sardonic treatment of a fellow portraitist of Quebec, the whole force of metaphoric achievement drives towards the transformation of the painter's canvas into the poet's 'paysage page.' All objects and characters in the painting can be rendered, the poem implies, by a fitting deployment of the alphabet, and whereas the painter is confined to two colours, the poet can render each of them multiply: the blunt 'red' of Krieghoff is to the poet the full palette of 'red rufous roseate crimson russet red' (*CP*, p. 682). The poem's claims collapse poetry with painting, and then all the arts with landscape itself, suggesting the ability of words to incorporate the whole of human life: as, indeed, the divine 'fiat' of the opening does, when the empowered poet echoes his God's first words: 'Let the blank whiteness of this page be snow.'

This note of self-reflexivity in the volume is not surprising, since, as I have argued, *The Rocking Chair*'s project can be understood only in relation to the perceiving eye and transfiguring imagination of a gifted poetic speaker. His purpose must be understood in the terms already borrowed from 'Portrait of the Poet as Landscape': he seeks an aesthetic that will find significance in each item of the visible world even as it seeks to subsume each item in a perspective that can only be called cosmic. His goals require an alert and sensitive physical eye and a gift for verbal style, and when these are engaged we are able to see with him into the significance of the mundane, and perhaps beyond that into some larger significance for the wholeness of our reality. One effect of this exchange is the poet's disappearance into the landscape he actualizes: it is his impersonality that allows him to mediate the significance of externals. Another effect is his deification: his heightened eye and capacious selfhood permit him to subsume the otherness of the world within his own consciousness. The purposes thus enabled accord poetry a central role in our lives, and naturally the poet is rendered essential as well.

Countering this rendition of the inspiration of *The Rocking Chair*, however, is an uncertainty as to the validity of his poetic project and/or his ability to fulfil its above-human purposes. The poems show a degree of exclamation and an urge for bardic elevation that is suggestive not of their degree of power, but of their anxiety regarding it. They register as well the poet-speaker's persistent need to affirm his centrality to the culture in which he finds himself, as well as – in the darkest moments of 'Portrait' – a certainty that he has been wilfully eliminated from that culture. Nor can he feel sure of his own wishes in the matter: it is persistently important to him to affirm his difference from the culture he represents, and a central position within it might be tantamount to an acceptance of erasure. When he tries to reassure himself of his typicality by portraying specific individuals from the mainstream, he finds everywhere figures who are deceptive or inscrutable: people whose behaviour and ethics are clearly not to be trusted when it comes to a sensitive discrimination of race difference. This attraction to and fear of the mainstream is reflected on the level of Klein's poetic style, as he drifts towards the mannerisms of Page and Anderson while maintaining some of the residue of prophetic language more typical of his earlier poetry.

'Portrait of the Poet as Landscape' is Klein's greatest poem because it so brilliantly accommodates both these thrusts of his forties poetics. That long poem's ambiguous enactment of poetic aspiration and anxiety was never again achieved. After the poems of *The Rocking Chair* were completed in 1947, his interest in or ability for poetry waned drastically, and it is hard to imagine that the volume's thrust towards celebration and self-affirmation was felt unambiguously by the poet. We must remember that Klein proceeded through such aesthetic uncertainties during the period in which the full scale of Holocaust atrocity was made apparent to him: that *The Rocking Chair* is a form of testimony that bears only silent witness to the devastation of his cultural roots. Even when in 1947 he would briefly return to the subject of the Holocaust in verse, in the bleak horror and anathema of 'Elegy' and in the bitter assault on Christian hypocrisy of 'Song of Innocence,' Klein also carried on penning contributions to the Quebec catalogue, the uneasy portraiture becoming especially frequent in that calendar year.

In 1944, then, Klein turned away from Jewish subjects for his poetry and turned towards a more complex impersonality and modernist aesthetic of accumulation: the two decisions are profoundly related. A shattering assault on his people finds little expression in his poetry for three years, but mannerisms serving to reaffirm the centrality of his own selfhood in the world he knew become prominent: and those two themes are related. Even as the known world slipped out of his grasp as a North American Jew of 1944, he adopted a poetic that would allow him to put his feet down, step by step, once again, in that world's details. And as the poetry yearns towards a God-like transcendence of the world's conflicts, its rhetorical gestures register more and more *desire* for transcendence, more and more awareness that it was unavailable. He would write, before his mental collapse put an end to his creativity, only a handful more poems; whatever confidence of voice remained to him in prose, it was unalterably separate from his sense of his poetry's value. The period of *The Rocking Chair* was one of many powerful and conflicting needs. The reconciliations he found for them in the years from 1944 to 1947 were vigorous, gifted, insights of genius: but they could not be sustained. Whatever he was suffering as an individual, it needed a different expression; and, thereafter, none at all.

Klein and the Forties

Pollock's contention that the great variety of Klein's creative aspiration and accomplishment can be read in relation to a sustaining central 'vision of the One in the Many' (p. 3) has found many echoes in the lines above. On the one hand, I have emphasized Klein's tendency to catalogue and accumulate the intense detail of a world passing into historical incoherence; on the other, I have sought to articulate the kinds of centrality and *integritas* that allowed Klein to sustain that fragmentation at high pitch in the poems of the *Rocking Chair* period. I have not sought to supersede the explanatory force of Pollock's master narrative of Klein, although I have tended to read Klein's poetry more for its indications of conceptual and stylistic stress – its anxiety at Many-ness – than he, for whom the power of Klein's adumbration of the One is finally more convincing. At minimum I hope to have shown that one cannot separate questions of poetic unity, of mental coherence, of impersonality, of suppression and repression, of world-praise and alienation from the world, in the case of Klein – nor, implicitly, in study of the Montreal forties. I have tried to avoid pulling the threads that bind all these issues too taut, in part because their precise entanglement will always be mysterious to me, in part because my attempt at their unravelling will have to be corrected and refined later. For now at least, I find a concept of *integritas* necessary to my thoughts of Klein, and my grasp of forties literary culture is changed by his situation within it.

In P.K. Page's early poetry, the idea of *integritas* alerted us to her deployment of complex clusters of difficult images and to the poetry's search for suggestive means of coherence and delimitation other than that which would direct us outward to a lyric personality. We watched as the complexity of her poetic language became rigidified prior to her middle silence and concluded that her strenuous adherence to modernist impersonality denied her a satisfactory poetic ground for the integration of her local verbal richness. While her poetic stifling may be analysed from a feminist perspective that reads the modernist injunction of impersonality as an enforced silencing of a female voice, there is no evidence at all that her stylistic and structural difficulties on paper were carried over into or reflective of a parallel sense of psychic, or even psychosocial, challenge.

Klein's poetry takes in Page's effects, most obviously in a few poems directly imitative of her work, but more tellingly in *The Rocking Chair*, whose aesthetic of accumulation relies, like hers, on the conviction that striking representations in juxtaposition without useful explicit reference to a perceiver may nevertheless evoke a wholeness and complexity comparable to that of a lyric personality *in absentia*. The poems of *The Rocking Chair* speak to us of a poetic mind in search of forceful stylized representations of its daily reality; that mind wants the patina of objectivity to surround and endorse its representations, to give their particularity, as it were, a universality unavailable in the impressions of the lyric observer. The reception of the volume suggests that the project was valuable and successful, but the poems also register Klein's anxiety over their theoretical objectivity by giving us frequent and occasionally forced assurance of their own significance, of the poet's exclamatory mood, of his centrality to the world he records. The demands of subjective testimony were such, for a Jewish poet of the mid-1940s, that a purely objective witnessing could not be sustained without compensatory gestures serving to affirm one's own creative significance and comprehensive vision. The only difference from Page here is that she was more confident, for a while, of impersonality's value: she soldiered on without such compensations in an ever-increasing stylization, until the critical conflict with a felt need for sympathy and humanism put an end to her imitation of first-wave modernism.

The key questions of forties *integritas* that I articulated in regard to Page are obviously useful in an approach to Klein: by what means may I unify my experience of a fragmented and incoherent world in poetry, without merely restoring cashiered traditional unities that would resolve that complexity into a series of absolutes? How may I persist in my conviction of poetry's impersonality and objectivity at a time when I feel called upon to bear witness to my age? By what means can my private experience enter my poetry without festering into the sheer subjectivity I have been taught to shun – or to fear? Such questions are especially pertinent to Klein's development after his first exposure to the atrocities of the European Holocaust, but they are not without value to his earlier career as well. After all, Klein has been remarked upon, at least since Earle Birney's early review,[57] for the intense and obscure allusiveness of his Judaica, for the range of learned reference to Jewish tradition that his pre-Holocaust poetry displays. A stark modernist reading might compare this elaborate reference to Eliot's attempt in *The Waste Land* to reinvigorate the European cultural tradition by forcing his readers back into their own cultural past in order to make sense of his poem of modern life: Klein would thus serve as a conduit of Jewish consciousness, and perhaps of Gentile sympathy and understanding as well. A more sceptical and contemporary treatment would underline, though, the self-celebration involved in Klein's earlier erudite gestures: one powerful effect of his Judaica, surely, is our recognition of his capacious learning, of the superiority of his cultural literacy to our own. In other words, we read the early Klein, even in the most objective and impersonal poems, as the bearer of multitudinous cultural fragments; as the sole mind, like Felix Prosper in Sheila Watson's *The Double Hook*, capable of aligning the lost remnants of a great cultural past in order to recapture the depth and vividness we have surrendered to modernity. To make sense of the encyclopedic quality of Klein's poetry, we must refer, however obliquely, to the scope and comprehensiveness of his genius: not in some abstract sense demanding idealization, but in a practical acceptance that a single Montreal mind and brain could focus and make whole again so much of the fragmented Jewish past. Heretical as the borrowing may be, it seems to me that his own epigraph to *The Second Scroll*, addressed to God, might be as well addressed to Klein, as we read his poems:

> And where art Thou not to be found?
> Wherever I fare – Thou!
> Or here, or there – Thou!
> Only Thou! None but Thou!
> Again, Thou! And still, Thou!

Klein, no doubt, would have shunned such a claim for the profound and ambivalently subjective *integritas* of his poetry.

There seems no way to keep these ideas from spilling over into our responses to Klein's mental crisis and creative silencing. Mental illness is always spoken of through metaphors (except, perhaps, those kinds treatable chemically), and the metaphor of poetic *integritas* seems ideally suited to Klein's personal well-being and balance through most of his life. He had always played on the boundary between self-affirmation and self-concealment in his poetry, and Caplan's portrait suggests that such a dichotomy was structural in his private life as well. Taking that tension as the perimeter within which his astonishingly rich mental life played itself out, we are enabled to remark both Klein's powerful sense of his own identity and purpose, *and* his persistent tendency to self-effacement, in sharply focused relation to the complex persons and worlds he could assimilate into his own experience. All forms of containment, however, require both stability and tension, and all have their breaking point. The Holocaust would seem the inescapable historic fact to the incorporation of which Klein's fruitful mental tension was not sufficient; and many of the best poems of his truncated career were written in response to a perception, subliminal or conscious, of the new incoherence of his physical and psychic world, and of his own sudden sense of himself as a poet whose desire simply to 'praise' had been hopelessly contaminated by a desperate need for visible order and – despite his people's near-erasure – ongoing cultural significance. In facing these challenges Klein is powerfully typical of Montreal poets of the forties; only in the shattering acuteness of their specific impact on his Jewish mind was he alone.

3

Image and Ego: Layton's Lyric Progress

Irving Layton, 1943–1953

Only in retrospect does A.M. Klein's dispersal into silence in 1953 seem exemplary of a significant end to the Canadian forties. Several years passed before the permanence of his reclusion became apparent to many beyond his intimate circle, and few who knew of the conflict within the forty-four-year-old can have imagined how complete and final his severance from the written word was to be. Little has been documented of the immediate reaction of his friend and earlier acolyte Irving Layton, no doubt in part because the collapse was not public enough to warrant much comment in the latter's correspondence: nevertheless, Elspeth Cameron notes that, coincident with the outbreak of Klein's distress, in 1953, Layton made a remark somewhat disparaging of his friend's public persona ('too smug, too petit-bourgeois') and concluded, 'I don't think he'll ever write another poem.'[1] The latter comment may have been no more than a lucky guess at Klein's lapsed creativity – it *had* been five years since *The Rocking Chair* appeared – but even if Layton had intuited the full extent of damage to Klein's consciousness, he appears to have seen no broader significance in the tragedy.

Klein's breakdown can hardly have been functional, then, in Layton's own abrupt attainment of a sophisticated and ironic subjectivism in the spate of great poems he began to compose at the time of Klein's exhaustion and first severe depressions, in 1953. I have read Klein's breakdown in relation not only to its historical circumstances, but to its aesthetic contexts and implications as well: thus as an event not easily separable from the wavering commitment to modernist impersonality that marked his forties writings. It is easy to fancy that such connections might precipitate in a younger friend's creative mind as the 'lesson' of Klein's collapse and inaugurate his swift rejection of said impersonality, but that tantalizing argument makes an actual and linear past out of what can only be a useful way of imagining a particular juncture of literary history. Still, my situation of Klein's writings and his mental life in a single manifold narrative presumes that for poets of the forties crises of poetic structure and modernity's pressures on personal identity were analogous to, and indeed inseparable from, one another. That constitutive forties intuition was in fact to determine the lines of forward movement for poets whose significance was not to be proven until the 1950s. All this is certainly true of Layton, whose most impressive period of poetic growth occurred when he recovered the analogy's obverse opportunity: that the dynamism of mental structures, the robustness of psychic life, could subtend a substantial and self-distinguishing renewal of modern poetics.

Layton's celebratory subjectivism in the 1950s could not be released unscathed, however, from the limbo of early modernist impersonality, nor could he – and here again the metaphor of Klein's suffering is functional – simply ignore the historical assault that had taken place on the individual, especially on the Jewish individual, under the century's flirtations with totalitarianism. The new speaking subject of modern poetry would have to stand proof against the complexes of experience that had shattered individuals like Klein, and this need brought about two seemingly contending responses in Layton's poetry: first, and best-known, the compensatory egoism and self-celebration of the superior man, and, second, and little-remarked, the ironizing of that superiorism by the persona's permeability in a universe where murder is continuous and meanings are, if immanent, inaudible. If Klein's withdrawal into silence had any message for Layton at the time, it must surely have been that even the most robust and energetic personae will undergo centripetal social and historical pressures whose force is a continual challenge to identity and rectitude. A postwar poetics that simply returned to lyric affirmation in defiance of such forces could have no real ground. No poet schooled in the forties – and I shall insist on Layton's prolonged education in the poetics that nurtured Page, Anderson, and Klein – could advocate a subjectivism half so naïve as that condemned in Layton by his detractors.

These comments renew our attention to the surge of creativity *circa* 1953 that so distinguishes the mature and successful Layton from the relatively unprolific poet of the forties. Of the later poet we have a good, though not sufficient, etiological criticism: his dynamic rejuvenation has been chiefly referred to Friedrich Nietzsche's impact on such masterpieces of the 1950s as 'The Birth of Tragedy' and 'For Mao Tse-Tung: A Meditation on Flies and Kings.'[2] There has been some difficulty in dating and qualifying Nietzsche's influence, but most commentators take it that Layton and other *First State-*

ment partisans were reading him from the earliest days of the little magazine.[3] Such studies had little visible influence on Layton's 'two slim volumes'[4] of the forties, however, and although Nietzsche obviously illuminates the achievements of the 1950s, he can shed much less light on Layton's first decade in print, or help us with what precisely changed at the time of Klein's collapse. In fact, critical reference to the poetry of the first two books is rare; we have all heard of 'The Swimmer,' and Layton himself points to that poem and one or two others as having promised his greatness to come,[5] but the other poems from the *First Statement* days, and Layton's apprenticeship in the poetics of the forties, are largely elided by a criticism that has been kept busy, naturally enough, with the enormous output of the later, more assured, poet.

Thus Layton's status as a major Canadian poet (for those who still accord it) is based almost entirely on poems he wrote after the collapse of the forties literary culture that culminated symbolically in the silence of Klein. His work during that transitional decade was strikingly limited in quantity and – in the contention of this chapter – uncertain of direction. To be sure, he published in *First Statement* regularly after the ninth issue, sometimes reprinting material there that other journals had run previously, and the best of those poems were gathered in *Here and Now* of 1945 and *Now Is the Place* of 1948, both appearing with First Statement Press. A full sixteen of the twenty-seven poems in the second book, however, were reprinted from the first, and little revised; so the two Layton publications from the forties sport a total of forty-three poems. If we add to this the seventeen forgettable poems from the decade that David John includes in *The Uncollected Poems of Irving Layton* and that do not appear in either volume, we have a total Layton output of sixty poems in the 1940s. Compare this cursorily with the unsilenceable Layton of the 1950s, who produced sixteen books, ten of them collections of new verse and two major selected volumes. Clearly some profound aspect of Layton's creativity, or at least his understanding and enforcement of it, changed in the early 1950s, in keeping with so many other crucial features of modern Canadian poetry. This change has appeared so profound in his own estimation that only a single poem of the 1940s justifies the title-range of his *Selected Poems, 1945–1989: A Wild Peculiar Joy* – again, the standing favourite 'Swimmer.'

The forties were not, then, Layton's decade. And yet the narrative of his self-transformation *circa* 1953 is curiously in keeping with the less happy changes visited upon his colleagues of the little-magazine years, and not only Klein. Page's departure for Australia in 1953 was anticipated, as we have seen, by remarks as early as 1952 about her estrangement from the contemporary poetic idiom. Patrick Anderson, finally back in England *via* Malaya, had written little poetry since coming to terms with his homosexuality: by 1953 he was refashioning himself as travel writer, with *Snake Wine: A Singapore Episode* to appear in 1955. On an offbeat but no less telling note, John Sutherland converted to Roman Catholicism in 1954 – in part because, in Miriam Waddington's interpretation, his faith in Canadian literature had failed him[6] – and left Montreal for Toronto in early 1955, taking his lonely editorship of *Northern Review* with him for the last year of their mutual life. Of course, as with Klein, the degree of Layton's alertness to these coincidental disappearances is debatable. The abandonment of the field by his former confrères may well have encouraged his sense of election and durability, but it was probably only the shocking experience of his friend that he registered with immediate personal force.

Such a shift in *Zeitgeist* helps to account for the current lack of interest in Layton's poetry of the forties. The poems generated real critical controversy at one time, though, in a well-noted exchange between A.J.M. Smith and Louis Dudek.[7] In a 1956 retrospect Smith justified his early dismissal of Layton by saying that only his work of the 1950s showed a real poetic gift.[8] Dudek retorted that all the qualities Smith praised in the 1950s had been visible – to a sympathetic or merely objective eye – in the forties material.[9] Dudek would go on, as his own ruptures with his friend supervened, to suggest that the forties poetry was indeed the *only* valuable Layton, the later work having devolved into a 'well-nigh demented'[10] celebration of what Dudek saw as principles of barbarism. Layton, it would appear, came to agree retroactively with Smith – perhaps by way of fending off Dudek – if his later-day suppression of his own early poems is any indication. After their final break in 1958, Dudek was persistent in remarking 1953 as the pivotal and detrimental year of change for Layton's poetry. Its vitiation began, says Dudek, when Layton 'decided that he was a "major poet" – about 1953 as I recall ...'[11] 'He has done some very good things, especially in the decade before 1953';[12] 'his poetry until about 1953 ... was also his most authentic and convincing work.'[13] Details both bibliographical and biographical indeed suggest that the period from 1952 to 1954 saw the emergence in Layton of a substantially reconceived public poet and persona[14] whose exploitation of local and international literary milieux was to rival the brilliance of his poetry as the decade progressed. I have suggested that the incremental changes in Layton's persona are one of the richest lodes, for example, in the Layton–Creeley correspondence,[15] which was intense from 1953 to 1955. In perhaps fortuitous keeping with Layton's own concept of his 'murdered selves,' a phrase he first penned in the summer of 1954,[16] the 'new' figure of

Layton bore little resemblance to the less assured, impecunious late bloomer of the forties. More than any other poet of the forties, Layton appears to have intuited the shift in literary consciousness of the early 1950s and turned it to his advantage; equally accurate would be the claim that he turned himself to the decade's advantage, forging with burgeoning confidence the different audience his new poetics and apparently new self-image required.

Poetics and self-image are more closely linked in Layton than in any other modern poet I can think of; that they also form the negative binary of Klein's self-erasure makes Layton's reconstitution *circa* 1953 especially fruitful critical terrain. I do not share Dudek's early disparagement of the mature work, nor, consequently, his elevation of the Layton poetry of the forties (and he has not repeated the judgment in many years); but I do share his intuition of an essential change in Layton's creativity at that time, a change I think to be representative of Canadian poetry's broad rewriting as the terms and prescriptive force of forties aesthetic contestation changed. Thus I am intrigued by a set of questions deriving from the conviction I share with Dudek, that Irving Layton was not much the poet we know for the first ten years (his *thirties,* by the way) of his extended publishing career. Among these are: What were the inadequacies of his early poetry that led him to such a major revision? How did the early poetry accord with the prevailing tastes and poetics of the forties? What light is cast by his rejection of his early manner on the *Preview–First Statement* controversies, of the period and surviving in the present day? And what gestures can we see in the early work towards the distinctive qualities – and quantity – of the poetry of the 1950s? The answers to these questions encourage a substantial redrafting of the lines of debate about Canadian forties poetry, and particularly about Layton's role in the Montreal *cénacles;* for Layton entered the *First Statement* camp very much in the supposed *Preview* tradition, as an impersonalist social and political observer whose respect for Imagist objectivism will be patent. That early modernist training, so critical to Page's development and frustration, was also binding on Layton for several years, until its fundamental dissonance with his inherent gifts of self-affirmation, celebration, and rhetoric forced him forward into a new manner. Observation of his gradual release from those constraints can tell us much about the pressures of conformity and individuation that characterized the writing of poetry in the forties in Canada and give us a better grasp of the historical similarities between Layton's dramatic inward turn in 1953, and Klein's.

Their shared intuition of the analogies of poetic and mental structure certainly resonated in a good deal of contemporary prose opinion. In trying to detail the survival of Imagist principles into the Canadian forties for my remarks on Page, I have already referred to Layton's 'Politics and Poetry,' in which his deprecation of the poetry of the 1930s is balanced by an enthusiastic response to poets of the New Apocalypse in England. I want to return to that essay now in a different vein, in part to refresh our sense of the overlap between long-standing 'little mag' criticism and the polemics of Layton, Dudek, and Sutherland in *First Statement*, but chiefly to draw from it a grounding of the 'wholeness' of the poem in the 'wholeness' of self that will help to illuminate Layton's opportunities and frustrations in the forties. 'Politics and Poetry' appeared in *First Statement* in August 1943; the gist of the article is Layton's assertion that the poetry of 'Auden and Co.' is passing out of fashion and relevance, to be replaced by a poetry that is more immediate, personal, lyrical, and engaged with the visible world. The poetry of the thirties is referred to with rough justice, but with occasional disparagement which reveals the author's bias: it was 'a poetry of social criticism and frustration,' the poets 'were expressing their own maladjustments,' they were 'hostile to their society and rejected it' by fleeing into 'desiccated coteries.' Their poems were 'dry, puritanical exercises' in a 'clipped, tortuous style,' rising from a 'set political programme and ideology.' Their impersonal manner, derived from the dicta of Eliot, led to 'poetic rigidities'; fortunately, says Layton, 'the note of individualism which T.E. Hulme and Eliot thought they had banished forever has crept back into English poetry.'

The new British poets who had emerged to sweep all this stuffy verse under the carpet reveal a 'personal, free-flowing and ... more elastic and colourful' manner which is 'full of promise':

> For the doctrinaire Marxism of the thirties, they have substituted a willingness to observe and experiment; for metaphysics, science; for rationalism, empiricism, and for a narrow dogmatism, an active skepticism. The search is still for a formula, a synthesis, but the formula and synthesis must be broad enough to include the many facets of the human personality.

Largely because of the new 'emphasis upon personality,' '[c]learness and intelligibility have been restored to English poetry.' Poets no longer seek to cut themselves away from society; instead they derive their 'main vigour from an identification with it.' They appeal to 'the common fund of reasonableness and goodwill in any community.' The result of all this exuberance is 'a new romanticism,' 'individualism and naturalism.'

Erwin Wiens, in an excellent and too-little-remarked article on Layton's early criticism, has noticed that 'Politics and Poetry' reads 'like a sharp polemic against the *Preview* poets. Layton's immediate point is that while the anglophile *Preview* poets were still self-consciously cultivating the attitudes and mannerisms of Eliot and Auden, in England itself these were already dated.'[17] Layton's polemic has worn all too well, though, under the scrutiny of the decade's critics. As I have shown,[18] the *Preview* group was also attacked for being a 'coterie,' for being out of touch with the prevailing societal mood, for elaborating style over subject matter, for playing at intellectual exercises instead of poetry, for espousing too doctrinaire a socialism, for writing a detached and impersonal poetry lacking conviction and expression – for anything 'Auden and Co.' are attacked for by Layton. One can't fault Layton or *First Statement* for this; in a little-mag rivalry his was a fine tactical move, an implicit alignment of *Preview* with the *passé*, and of *First Statement* with the new and immediate. But Wiens, his attention elsewhere, fails to draw the pendant conclusion: for over fifty years Canadian criticism has been unable to distance itself substantially from the rhetoric and polemic of a tactical article published in one of the two rival journals, a fact witnessed by Wiens's reliance on Wynne Francis's forties narrative for his summary of the decade's currents. Layton's article of 1943, Francis's of 1962, and Wiens's of 1985 are in startling agreement in their overview of the Montreal forties; they share an attitude to *First Statement* and *Preview* that begins in polemic and ends in distorted generalization.

But just as Francis's 'Montreal Poets of the Forties' contains useful biographical snippets despite its effusive misreadings, Wiens charts a clear direction for critics who want to get beyond fifty-year-old approaches to the poetry of Layton and his contemporaries. He is the only critic who read 'Politics and Poetry' with more than passing interest, who followed up Layton's references to a handful of British poets of the forties and attempted to explicate his interest in them. He was the first to note that Alan Rook, Henry Treece, and M.J. Tambimuttu – three of the four British poets mentioned by Layton – bear a concidental relation to that little-known coalescence in British 1940s poetry, the New Apocalypse. With careful reference to a number of documents of the British poets, Wiens claims that Layton's knowledge of them appears to have been quite limited and that he somewhat distorted the British situation in order (as Wiens puts it) to 'declare his own colours.'[19] Wiens's summation of the Apocalyptic 'program' is excellent, but I must admit some disappointment with its self-defensive conclusion, that 'it would be very easy to overstate their lasting influence upon [Layton's] work.'[20]

Layton's Apocalyptic reading is in fact exciting for many reasons. We can immediately conclude, for instance, despite the dichotomy that would have *Preview* nourished by the English and *First Statement* by the American poetic traditions, that at least one major figure of the latter magazine found inspiration across the Atlantic. More important, we must accept that Layton's early poetry can be elucidated in relation to contexts broader than the *Preview–First Statement* rivalry, more immediate even than his own later poetry, more international indeed than the context of Canadian modernism itself. Wiens's illumination of the New Apocalypse is fresh and suggestive. I will distance myself from his conclusions only by quoting from a few documents which he does not treat, because they suggest that the relation between Apocalypse and Layton cannot readily be closed off, and show how steeped in the *forties* creative ethos was the poet who found his voice and fame well after the Apocalyptic decade had closed.

Henry Treece did much of the Apocalyptic theorizing; in his *How I See Apocalypse* of 1946 he elucidates a vision of the poet and poetry which any Layton critic will I think find fascinating:

> Apocalyptic writing ... is the art form of the man who can recognize, without fear, the variety and the multiplicity of life; of the man who acknowledges his dreams and his laughter, and the tiny and almost unmentionable things of life, as being real and desirable for sanity's sake. And the Apocalyptic attitude will teach poetry to be broad, deep, limitless, like true life. It will teach men to live more, and to exist less; it will be militant against all narrow, shallow, half-thoughts and back-door sniggerings. Such poetry will burn with a great fire, intensely, and out of that fire will spring a remoulded life, strong, happy, prophetic, scorched free of dross and cruelty.[21]

Such prophetic and redemptive language is everywhere in Layton, of course; the latter image is ideally endorsed, for example, by his 'Esthetique': 'Out of rubbish burning and burning comes / Mozartian ecstasy leaping with the flames.'[22] Treece's description of the Apocalyptic vision strikes so many chords of the later Layton poet-persona that Layton's praise for the poets of the New Apocalypse in the *First Statement* article becomes intensely suggestive. He might easily have penned Treece's cadences himself in one of his many prefaces. We associate the mature Layton exuberance, anarchic laughter, and prophetic egoism so readily with the Nietzschean philosophy we know he emulated, but we may find ourselves invited by an examination of the New Apocalypse and his other forties readings to revise that estimate, or at least to suspect that he was primed for the Nietzschean influence by an early sympathy with the British minor school.

Treece's remarks indicate once again how important it was in the forties to articulate an aesthetics that was as applicable to consciousness as to works of art. A persistent, typically forties strain in Treece's 'How I See Apocalypse' is this effort to coordinate the state of the individual with the state of the art and to insist that the healing of poetry will occur only with the rejuvenation of the 'whole man':

Apocalyptic writing is opposed to all footling defeatism, to the exquisite, the flaccidly nostalgic, the bonily classical, and the sloppily Romantic. It insists on the fusion of all elements of life and thought, at the highest pitch of intensity. It will teach man to aspire towards wholeness: it will inspire in him faith and enthusiasm for living. It believes that failure is impossible where man has come to know fullness.[23]

Such theoretical gestures suggest the forties poets' sense of entrapment in an outdated oppositional modernism, wherein apparent choices between 'classical' and 'Romantic' stymied forward progress in the arts. Contemporary poetry, faced in Treece's view with a series of such false choices, must carry a principle of 'fusion,' of 'wholeness'– here also 'fullness,' though Treece is usually willing to stay with the earlier terms – into all domains of human life and endeavour. Failure to do so merely ratifies the 'split' that modern life has foisted on the individual. Treece quotes G.S. Fraser's summation of J.F. Hendry (all of them Apocalyptic affiliates):

Hendry's Apocalyptic theory does not stop there, however, for he goes on to explain how such a philosophy might be employed in what he calls 'the reintegration of the personality.' He believes that the unnatural economic life of the present time has produced a split in man's mind, has made of him a half-conscious, half-living machine. For Hendry the first object of any art is therefore to restore the wholeness of man, to make him conscious once more of all his faculties, of the variety of worlds in which he moves.[24]

The Apocalyptic insistence that a renewal of aesthetics must be grounded in a renewal of artistic selfhood will have its powerful fruition in Layton's reconstitutions of the early 1950s. Here, too, is secondary authorization for my earlier contention that Klein's psychic disintegration must be interpreted in the context of a decade centrally preoccupied with the kinds of *integritas* available to the poet who remains committed to modernist fragmentation, multiplicity, and objectivity. In the Apocalyptic mood there is no separating the crisis of the modern poem and of the modern poet: both are to be seen as in a condition of disturbance, even disease, and both must be treated by a holistic ethics-aesthetics whose metaphors lie in the idiom of self-assertion and personal growth. It is impossible to know whether Layton remembered these Apocalyptic gestures in the early 1950s, when his own movement towards a new 'fusion' in ego and art coincided with the collapse of Klein's mental life; indeed, it is impossible to know whether his eyes ever fell on these ideas of Hendry, Fraser, or Treece. Nevertheless, it would be imprudent to disregard the collocation of aesthetics and psychologies in Apocalyptic theory when it anticipates so suggestively a range of events both happy and tragic for the Canadian poets.

The fruition of Apocalyptic selfhood in a theory of the Image has already been noted (above, pp. 64–5) and needs little further explication. Treece's 'More Notes on the Image' cited the image-obsessiveness of much thirties poetry, located its wellspring, as would Layton, in Eliot's idea of the 'objective correlative,' and derided the 'image mania' that had persisted well into the 1940s. The reaction against such image-mongering was also, curiously, initiated by Eliot, when in the *Four Quartets* he began to use the individual image 'as a maturely evocative and dynamic mechanism'; with the 'subdued philosophic statement' of 'East Coker,' 'dependent less than ever before on the emotive image ... the curtain comes down on a decade of picture-makers.'[25] Anticipating what may eventuate from this change for the better, Treece points out that poets now had two choices of image-manner when they wished to express dissatisfaction with their times: they could change their image of the world 'by a casual, arbitrary selection,' which would lead to 'Surrealism in the Bad Old Manner,'

> [b]ut where the change is consciously willed and motivated by a sincere and consistent philosophy, the result, though possibly startling, as are so many things when seen clearly for the first time, or seen set against a new background, must be artistically rejuvenating, and at the lowest level, psychologically useful ... The image must be reborn then, to heart as well as to head, to sense as well as sound, to health as well as sickness, to the world invisible no less than to the world of objects. In short, to a new WHOLENESS.[26]

Treece's anti-formalist point is that no image, however brilliant, should be allowed to have entirely autonomous aesthetic force within the whole poem. Like the stricken modern individual, the poem must find a 'sincere and consistent philosophy' which casts each vibrant sensation into healthy subordination. Treece's attacks on the imagery of earlier poets are, as remarked, clearly echoed in Canada in *First Statement*'s repeated attacks upon Anderson and Page of *Preview*, for their decried tendency to let the single impressive image stand as a sufficient aesthetic achievement, and to neglect the integrity or 'wholeness' of the poem in consequence – and note that such *aesthetic* attacks bore fruit repeatedly in disparagements of *Preview personalities* as well. The consonance of British and Canadian opinion here suggests that Layton had not misrepresented the Apocalyptic idea as interestedly as Wiens suggested. It would seem instead broadly characteristic of English-language poets of the 1940s to seek new means of integration both psychological and aesthetic, on the assumption that an intense splitting apart of perception, experience, and intellection was vitiating of 'wholeness' in both realms. Here we have a well-marked route into Layton's development during the decade.

But before exploring these resonances, I need a more influential, less casually intertextual, consideration of how well Layton knew the New Apocalypse. The familiarity with the British poets in Layton's essay 'Politics and Poetry' is not entirely isolated in *First Statement*; a month later one Paul Halley (of Vancouver) published a quasi-sonnet entitled 'Apocalypse' that manifested many of the ideas and techniques of the school:

The night exposes corners in the view
And sets the heart to crooked hoping.
Always the morning shows the dreaded true –
Atlas quite tired and his shoulders sloping.

Under the sun I am a skull
And rasp my boniness to work at time;
In night I seem a man, and nearly whole,
Who dares to watch at windows, hopes to climb
Any pest-house with fingers snooked.

Halley's interest in a persona who is 'nearly whole' coincides nicely with Treece's emphases. So does Layton's observation in 'Politics and Poetry' of the Apocalyptics' search for a 'synthesis' of understandings that would 'be broad enough to include the many facets of the human personality': indeed, as we shall see, his own poetry begins to pursue such a synthesis in the later forties. I think we can take it that some discussion of the British school was current among *First Statement* poets, and that in 1943 at least one of them had indeed read the poetry – and very likely the theory – of the Apocalypse; in fact, as late as 1951 Louis Dudek was recommending a Treece-edited anthology of British poetry of the forties to Alan Crawley.[27] Three anthologies of the New Apocalypse had appeared before Layton and Halley made their allusions: *The New Apocalypse* (1939), *The White Horseman* (1941), and *The Crown and the Sickle* (1943); any of these might have been available to the Canadians. I will also point out, gingerly, that Treece published some of his Apocalyptic writings in the London miscellany *Here and Now*

(1940–9) and that the same title served for Layton's first volume of poetry.[28] (Perhaps, too, Layton's third volume, *The Black Huntsmen* of 1951, echoes faintly *The White Horseman*, the second of the Apocalyptic anthologies.) Since Halley and Layton kept watch, apparently, on poetic developments in England, and since Layton would hear of the Apocalyptic poets by keeping up to date with English periodicals, I incline towards his having encountered the London miscellany in the early forties, and perhaps having found Treece's work therein.

By 1943, at any rate, Layton had some degree of creative contact with an elaborated poetics that insisted the image be restrained within the 'whole' of the poem, that linked such a poetics to a coherent individuality and philosophical expressiveness, and that could have inspired as early as 1943 the exuberant poet-persona that did not emerge fully in his poetry until the early 1950s. Without caring to posit a clear and direct influence that the evidence cannot substantiate, I will nevertheless go on to argue that Layton faced aesthetic challenges to his poetry in the forties that are directly anticipated and in some part explained by these Apocalyptic writings. One goal of my argument will be our final abandonment of another of the conventional categories of Canadian forties criticism: for the young Layton who appreciated but could not yet integrate the Apocalyptic program was a student, along with Page, Anderson, and Klein, of the very 'Auden and Co.' the New Apocalypse was trying to force into history. During the forties, at least, he was little prepared to sacrifice objectivist social comment for Apocalyptic or Nietzschean self-transformations. Presumably the Apocalyptic articulation of a nexus of selfhood, image, and *integritas* was as yet too theoretical to contend much against the powerful duties of Imagist difficulty and impersonalist catalogue that were binding, and fruitful for a time, for his mentor Klein. Only when Klein's experience came to exemplify the negative pole of Apocalyptic rhetoric – the modern individual 'half-conscious, half-living,' with 'a split in [his] mind' – would Layton lay claim to its positive image, of a man 'conscious once more of all his faculties, of the variety of worlds in which he moves.'[29]

Layton in the Forties Manner

Here and Now appeared with its impact-claiming title in 1945, first product of the new First Statement Press. It gathers Layton's work from the early forties to the last issues of *First Statement* and, like P.K. Page's *As Ten As Twenty* of a year later, naturally demonstrates the eclectic range of a young poet looking for the voice and manner that would sustain his creativity into a mature period.[30] In the case of Page's first volume, such eclecticism indicated a fluidity of experiment and expansion that was to run dry in the years leading up to *The Metal and the Flower* of 1954. Arguably the reverse is true of Layton's early formal uncertainty. Unlike Page's sure-handed apprenticeship to a variety of formal and stylistic possibilities, Layton's casting about for a voice, mood, and theme signals a lack of sympathy with the available poetics of the day. Until the consolidations of his poetic training and less articulable personal growth coincided in the sudden fruitions of the early 1950s, Layton was largely an imitator of poetic ideas and gestures the authenticity of which his personal creativity and experience did not fully corroborate. My rendering their two first volumes antithetical by these means must be superseded, however, by a deeper likeness in their careers, that is, by their mutual rejection *circa* 1953 of their apprenticeship poetics in favour, in the one case, of unwilling silence and, in the other, of a burgeoning subjectivism. Furthermore, my work with Layton will suggest that (despite the antithesis of their responses) his and Page's implicit judgments of their early poetry's weaknesses were remarkably similar and pertained to the issues of poetic coherence and testimony that marked the 1940s as a decade of literary change.

A point of view that allows us to align the self-critiques of Page and of Layton in the early 1950s would seem almost inherently useful, so rigorous has been their contrasting. But because these new perspectives force me to a partial disparagement of Layton's poetics in the forties, particularly of the poetry's general lack of *integritas* and typically uneven exploitation of isolated and histrionic images, and because I would not wish to dwell only on weaker poems in order to elaborate my point, I want first to discuss the superb 'The Swimmer' in a manner which will counterpoint my readings of other, less successful poems, and contextualize their shortcomings. The poem opens with beautifully confident rhythms:

> The afternoon foreclosing, see
> The swimmer plunges from his raft,
> Opening the spray corollas by his act of war –
> The snake-heads strike
> Quickly and are silent.[31]

The extension of the third line to thirteen syllables after the relative regularity of the first two tetrameters aptly parallels the abrupt energy of the swimmer, which peaks at his point of entry into the water. The suddenly truncated fourth line breaks that crescendo of energy with a crowding of stresses; the fifth swallows him up in a vacuum of weak syllables. The swimmer has disappeared from the original visual plane, in a gesture of self-baptism that will be drawn upon later in this retrospectively self-reflexive poem of initiation.

The diction, however, is initially confusing: 'foreclosing' seems as yet an unnecessary pun (what financial-economic point justifies it?), and the rapid comparison of the splashing water first to a 'corolla' and immediately after to 'snake-heads' forces the reader into his or her own quick plunge into the meteoric workings of the poet's language. If one reads sceptically, the confusion lingers as images accumulate: the swimmer becomes 'a brown weed' that 'lies imminent upon the water'; then the water is a 'gonad sea'; when he dives under again, 'his blood sings,' he is 'a male salmon' but passes through 'underwater slums'– and so on. But if one accepts the casualness of structure Layton is working out in the poem – a seemingly indifferent, but in fact stringent, deployment of images that coalesce and accrue suggestive meaning, rather than 'correlating' a determined object – the confusing imagery hangs together better. Observe how the economic grounding of 'foreclosing' is relied on, for instance, to load the images of 'thief' and 'slums' in the third stanza; how the 'snake-heads' echo in other animal references, 'cockle-shells,' 'tiger,' 'salmon'; how words like 'imminent' in the second and 'instigated' in the final stanza resonate phonetically and connotatively; how the visual focus passes from 'raft' to 'beach,' so from water to land, from fluidity to fixity; and how – this much is obvious – sexual language governs the entire experience: the male is 'imminent,' the experience is 'passion,' he lies in a 'gonad sea,' he is a 'male salmon' passing through 'fretted stairways,' presumably to breed, and the result is a passing of 'boyhood.'

In effect, our immediate sense of the poem's impact is granted at least in part by its brilliant integration of two creative forces: the poet's image-generating power, at a high pitch here, and his power of verbal and visual association. However I might care to proceed from such an initial impression of the poem's coherence and force to articulate the themes of 'The Swimmer'– say, 'a fall from spontaneity, energy and fluidity to self-absorption and fixity is a part of growth from sexualized pubescent to mature adult'– these tensions of imagery will be central. They grant the poem dense aural and visual coherence, and suggest meaningfulness even when the poet deliberately refuses to lay explicit meanings in front of me. 'The Swimmer' does not clarify itself by abstract statement; it refuses to elaborate emotion or sentiment. The imagery of the dive which opens the poem so resoundingly is soon recognizable as merely one bold image among the poem's many. 'Diving' is not here, as it was for W.W.E. Ross and would be for F.R. Scott, a conceit structuring the whole poem. On the contrary, the poet has raised the stakes on his poem's achievement of *integritas* by deliberately incorporating a multiplicity of image categories and a daunting breadth of reference: that is critical to the poem's confidence of accomplishment. We have in 'The Swimmer' an intimation of the non-rational and alinear *integritas* that characterizes the mature Layton, and it is, on that basis, indeed the most successful poem in *Here and Now*.

To return to Treece's terms, terms I think Layton would accept in late 1944, when 'The Swimmer' was published, the images of the poem are powerful and resonant, at times with the flair of the virtuoso, but no single image is so dominant or so clever that the wholeness of the poem suffers. There is *integritas* generated here that is obviously not like the unity of reason, but it is as aesthetically convincing – here my argument becomes particularly relative to my own perceptions – as a rational and entirely explicable unity would be. I emphasize this point because, for these very reasons, 'The Swimmer' is a rarity in *Here and Now*, and I must proceed to criticize many of the volume's other poems for a lack of exactly this force of *integritas*; but, as in my treatment of Page and A.M. Klein, I don't want to demand of Layton a linear and rational aesthetics of unity that was entirely inappropriate to his attempt. What I do want from Layton, as his 'Politics and Poetry' and his later self-assessments would suggest he wanted from himself, is the kind of emotive structural integrity that so distinguishes 'The Swimmer,' its taut dialectic of image and *integritas*, and I seek it first in poems contemporary with that first accomplishment.

Layton has frequently described the ecstatic process that generated 'The Swimmer' in five minutes on a restaurant napkin in mid-1944, and he asserts that the result, which required no revision, gave him the vocation and sense of election of a poet.[32] It is not surprising, given such retrospective appraisal, that 'The Swimmer' emerges as a triumph in its volume, especially since four-fifths of the datable poems in *Here and Now* were written before this moment of vocation.[33] 'Newsboy,' for example, was published a year and a half before 'The Swimmer,' in Raymond Souster's little magazine *Direction*;[34] although Layton at one point compared its success with that of 'The Swimmer' and claimed for it a comparable accomplishment, 'Newsboy' suffers in the absence of the later poem's *integritas*. The opening stanza is representative:

> Neither tribal nor trivial he shouts
> From the city's center where tramcars move
> Like stained bacilli across the eyeballs;
> Where people spore in composite buildings
> From their protective gelatine of doubts,

Old ills, and incapacity to love
While he, a Joshua before their walls,
Sells newspapers to the gods and geldings.

There is clearly a different kind of energy here. The rhythms alternate between iambic pentameters and looser four-beat lines; while not particularly weak, they are not particularly striking. The rhyme and half-rhyme pattern established is briefly interesting, but dropped in later stanzas. The power of enjambment is noteworthy: but the real force of 'Newsboy,' for good or ill, lies in its image-manner. The immediately flaunted pun on 'tribal' and 'trivial' asserts much cleverness with language, and the comparison in the third line of 'tramcars' with 'stained bacilli' is shocking, 'metaphysical,' and Eliotesque – one thinks readily of the etherized patient who bursts into the third line of 'Prufrock.' The ironic imagery of procreation in the succeeding lines is deliberately complicated by extensive subordination: 'spore ... / From their protective gelatine' is the syntactic ground of the lines, the basic meaning on which the subordinate metaphors must depend. But the curious idiom that allows 'spore from' in the sense of 'procreate thanks to [their protective gelatine]' creates some immediate obscurity. 'In composite buildings' intrudes right in the middle of this preliminary difficulty, suggesting universality of locale (which must then be related to 'sporing'), and 'gelatine of doubts' concludes the procreative diction with a final metaphorical complexity in the *a of b* formula of Page. Should we now conclude that the idea of 'doubt' is the whole point, and 'sporing' merely an ironic and elaborate way of talking about the interbreeding of human anxiety in a commercial society? If so, is the poet justified in articulating so many subordinate images before resting so much weight on the abstraction of 'doubt'? And incidentally, if 'doubt' is 'protective,' how does it permit 'sporing' with others? (It might be worth pausing to remember that a common claim of *First Statement*'s partisans is that the journal brought a more natural idiom to Canadian poetry, the 'clearness and intelligibility' Layton had found attractive in the new British poets; in Layton's case, as we will continue to see, the forties idiom was more often idiosyncratic and difficult.) Possibly my remarks are carping. However one might wish to defend Layton from my subjective complaints, though, I think all can agree at least that his manner is purposively difficult, and the difficulty has to do with the complexity and proportion of imagery he offers in relation to the complexity (or rather simplicity, unidimensionality) of the represented object.

'Newsboy' continues with such crowding of imagery: the newsboy is '[i]ntrusive as a collision,' then he is '[t]he Zeitgeist's too public interpreter,' then 'a voice multiplex and democratic,' then he is like 'Clotho' a spinner of human fates, and so on. In fact, by the end of the poem the newsboy has been embodied in fourteen distinct metaphors (by my count, but if anything there are more), and the only ones that anticipate and echo one another, as would those in 'The Swimmer,' are, at a stretch, 'Joshua,' a Judaeo-Christian allusion, and the later reference to 'mitred cardinals ... in / Conclaves' in the third stanza. The structure and method are very like those I discovered in Klein's 'Grain Elevator'; in fact, the aesthetic here is one of similar catalogue and accumulation. The poem proceeds and unifies itself only in the relation between one boy, tenor, and the consecutive vehicle-making power of the poet. He thinks of as many energetic metaphors for the newsboy as he can, he submits them to a loosely governing rhythm, he threads through a sustained contempt for those who buy the newspapers, and he has completed a poem. I do not dismiss the poeticality of 'Newsboy,' but I feel a need to resist its desire to impress me with the power of images that do not cohere except in so far as the represented object is itself coherent. By the third stanza, the effect is exhausting:

> For him the mitred cardinals sweat in
> Conclaves domed; the spy is shot. Empiric;
> And obstreperous confidant of kings,
> Rude despiser of the anonymous,
> Danubes of blood wash up his bulletins
> While he domesticates disaster like
> A wheat in pampas of prescriptive things
> With cries animal and ambiguous.

Layton's syntax, moreover, which might well have been simplified in keeping with *First Statement* dogma in order to relieve the pressure of the image-making somewhat, is instead full of inversions, elaborate parallelisms and accumulated adverbial clauses. The assault on the presumably complacent reader is thorough and continuous, but it is an assault that never seems prepared to admit its own victory.

The difficulties of 'Newsboy' and the successes of 'The Swimmer' can be attributed in part to the year and a half of Layton's creative development that separated them. The cluttered 'Newsboy' manner is in fact typical of Layton in 1943. The contemporary – and aptly named – '1943' reveals the same mannerisms, the tendency to propose and accumulate difficult images and weave abstraction through them in attempted integration:

Now turn we from the tramcar's logic
The symmetric hopes snug
As a commodity on a grocer's shelf;
We stumble over tombstones in tall grasses;
Our shod, firm feet obliterate
The epitaphs to our rescinded selves,
And like flies thickening, dying
On cold, autumnal window-sills
So flutter out finally our fears and irresolutions.

Certainly this passage is more obedient to prose syntax than 'Newsboy' and earns from it a greater legibility. But '1943' was nevertheless excluded from *Here and Now* and *Now Is the Place*, and when it did finally resurface in *The Black Huntsmen* of 1951, the moderately elaborate central stanza just quoted was dropped. What 'The Swimmer' achieved, clearly, had helped to cast a degree of ironic light on the rest of Layton's work to that point.

Not to say, of course, that the poet's auto-*anagnorisis* in 'The Swimmer' changed him overnight: his tendency to structure poems, or extended passages, in the earlier manner persisted. 'Words Without Music' appeared simultaneously with 'The Swimmer' in *First Statement*; granted, its complicated mannerisms and its military imagery, since Layton was discharged in June 1943, suggest earlier composition. The poem opens in matter-of-fact clauses: 'Their dufflebags sprawl like a murder / Between the seats. Themselves are bored / Or boisterous.' Despite the affectation of 'Themselves are bored' – the reflexive pronoun meant to highlight the soldiers' objectification, their similarity to their dufflebags – and the awkward substitution of action for effect ('like a murder' instead of a 'corpse'), a relatively straightforward syntax keeps the steadily accumulating images in better control for the first half of the poem. By the end, though, the suffocation of 'Newsboy' is creeping back in:

        Air is thin slightly neurasthenic
Over the distant indiscriminate trees
That posture on hillsides gross and secretive
As women staling. Pins withdrawn suddenly
Barns collapse like real estate models. The senses
Run like swift hares along the fences;
These are the fire lands and this a sealed train
Of cold excursionists throats buttoned up

With yellow timetables. On folded hands
The minutes drop like dandruff, the
Jetted column survives in a black foetus
And the goats leap into our faces shrieking.[35]

Even accepting that all of this visual material is an objective correlative of the emotion the poet wishes to evoke, the reader is asked to do a great deal of consecutive correlating in this poem in proportion to the central emotion it seeks to objectify, a problem I remarked in much of Page's poetry leading up to *The Metal and the Flower.* There's a curious inconsistency in most of Layton's images, to my mind, a tendency to allow the vehicles of metaphors to run on or collide needlessly until their coherence is in danger. At the risk of another indictment for pedantry, I feel constrained to ask: can one 'posture indiscriminate[ly],' or does posturing take precision? Do hares 'run along ... fences'? Does dandruff often fall on hands? Curious as the final image is, there seems more poetic truth in the 'goats leaping' and 'shrieking' – as a hellish climax of bestiality awaiting the soldiers – than in these Surrealist images that try to evoke an emotion through improbable juxtapositions. The poet appears to have felt a cultural pressure at the moment of composition to reveal his dramatic image-making power, but the strenuousness of the process is visible.

Some of these effects are attributable, first of all, to Layton's youthful schooling in the thirties poetics of 'Auden and Co.,' the dominant poets whose hegemony he had claimed to sense faltering in 'Politics and Poetry.' As subsequent quotations will show, Layton's commonplaces of the forties include his favouring of the first-person plural in poems assertive of broad collective truths, and his reliance on 'history' both as governing context and as windy abstraction for the organization of his attempts at social comment. Both derive very apparently from readings in Auden and his imitators, notwithstanding the usual assurances from commentators on the forties that Auden's influence is pertinent only to *Preview.* Layton's 'Forecast' pays the most explicit tribute to Auden's style:

To the seer alone
Permit the savage, disastrous rumour
Since touching the bone
Of each man's humour
For men astigmatic, prone
He bares an epoch's tumour;
Illusionless, plain,
Stark, individual as pain.

Nor should we assume that Auden was influential only on Layton's juvenilia: 'Forecast' was published in *First Statement* in the summer of 1943, in his thirties, after a year of his contributing to the little magazine, and he was to continue to write lines in this vein well after 'The Swimmer' indicated a redirection of his talents.

We obviously cannot continue to speak of the 'totally English influence' on *Preview* (Norris's term)[36] or of *First Statement*'s distinct Americanism.[37] Instead Layton's case confirms a view of each Canadian poet searching between those two idioms for authentic expression. From that conclusion practical criticism could proceed to analyse the patterns of stylistic growth and exchange in each, in relation to a more complex understanding of the cross-fertilization of American and English poetics. Auden's influence was perhaps too general to the period, though, to be helpful in our attempt to sort out further the contexts of Layton's development: that is, if most poets of the 1940s responded willy-nilly to Auden, we can learn little that is particular to the Canadian individual in isolating his influence. In company, however, with Layton's citation of the New Apocalypse, another of his English sources, as well as with his eventual welcome of Surrealist landscapes in the masterpieces of the early 1950s, Auden's apparent impact returns us to the Imagist trajectory I had occasion to trace in relation to the growth of Page.

In this book's ongoing hypothesis – and in Treece's, and in Layton's in 'Politics and Poetry' – Imagist prescriptions remained powerful enough in the 1940s to have encouraged both persistent imitation and frustrated critique, and those terms certainly played a role in Layton's conceptualizing his own poetry's growth. Indeed the first poem he published, 'Vigil,' which appeared under the name 'Irving Lazarre' in *The McGilliad* for April 1931 (with the help of A.M. Klein), reveals how quickly Imagist fragments had devolved into simplistic accumulations with little poetic tension:

> Evening ... the feathery grass ... boughs
> That coldly lift a silent offering.
> The shadowy swaying of trees
> Like hooded nuns in a forbidden dance,
> The yearning stillness of an ended night
> And clouds the colour of oyster shells
> Clustered about a comfortless moon.
> Dawn.

In the six lines that follow, no syntactic energy breaks the smooth surface of these catalogued noun-phrases, the last of which is 'suns that turn the wayside streams / To moving panes of light.' The poem is good enough, perhaps, from a nineteen-year-old hand, but Layton interestingly chose to reprint 'Vigil' in *First Statement,* in a selection of four poems intended to represent the 'new' poets to the magazine's readers. This was in February 1943, a winter and spring in which his publications briefly took on a distinct Imagist complexion. A poem like 'Mortuary,' also from February 1943, with its careful articulation of a brief conceit likening trees losing their leaves to bones losing their flesh, reveals Layton's ability to obey fairly humbly the binary prescriptions of the Pound image:

Flesh has fallen away. Trees
And buildings are summer's skeleton,
Wind has loosened, disarrayed
The separate ribs, the evidence of bone.
Dead, deposited relics
Shored up clean against a stiffened sky,
Fixed by the mortician cold
Moving his fingers over them ceaselessly.[38]

The stiffness of 'Mortuary's' comparisons, however, its consciousness of its own metaphoricality, suggests in germinal form Layton's irritation with the codes of Imagist objectivism, which in Pound's reading at least demanded a less structured and more sheerly juxtapositive basis for visual conceit than this. I set aside the secondary issue here (to which I have given time elsewhere)[39] of such poetry's approximation of a genuine radical Imagism. None of the poems of 1943 should simply be tagged 'Imagist,' but many of them indicate equally clearly Layton's awareness of a general post-Imagist licence in the forties for brief, impersonal, visual poems. Granted there is something half-hearted about the exercises. Although in his later career Layton would return to quasi-Imagist poetry, especially to record periods of travel, there is little of the later poet to be recognized here.

Between these exercises and the subterranean imagistic premises of the more complex 'Newsboy,' however, there is less distance than may at first appear. Clearly Layton's was not a poetic personality that could easily accept the anonymity (Klein's term) and apparently passive representationalism of originary Imagism. Among his first attempts to affirm and extrapolate upon the shock of recognition fundamental to Imagist poetics – very like P.K. Page's – was his insistence in longer forms that each cadence offer a startling Image (and here I think the Auden style to have been briefly exemplary). Taken to an extreme, as it is in 'Newsboy' and 'Words Without Music,' such a decision tends to an accumulative aesthetics, in which image-making occurs in arithmetic relation to the number of lines written and in geometric relation to the breadth and deep interest of the thing portrayed. The attempt is natural enough, and for Page it led to a decade's worth of creative momentum and acclaim; Layton, on the other hand, spent most of the 1940s looking for alternative methods of organization and verbal power.

One can establish a hypothetical model of Layton's subsequent negotiations with the Imagist example by watching the chronological appearance of urban, quasi–imagistic poems like 'Upper Water Street' (June 1943), 'DeBullion Street' (March 1944), and 'Jewish Main Street' (June 1944). Layton initiates each in the late Imagist manner, but each attempt raised questions of post-Imagist address and structure which he was as yet unable to answer. 'Upper Water Street,' the earliest, begins with images of urban fog extremely evocative, as others have noticed,[40] of Eliot and Carl Sandburg:

> The fog spreads her grey belly
> over the yellow tramcars,
> brushes past, on silent feet,
> shabby Paint and Hardware stores,
> or flattens her wan face
> against the illuminated shop windows
> of department stores.[41]

After this first stanza, however, the poem finds no conceptual room to develop; each ensuing stanza echoes the phrase 'the fog' to get going, but the comparisons become increasingly clumsy, especially as they abandon Imagist neutrality for more explicit emotionalizing. The animalized and pathetic fog above becomes 'comradely' in the second stanza, in the third it 'bandages' the 'failures' of men, in the fourth it 'tickles' itself and is 'chlorotic,' and (a profoundly pathetic fallacy) 'laughs / inaudibly.' As the fog-lore accumulates, the poem risks structural incoherence: a prophetic vision of 'pitiful' mankind threatens to break the surface of visual objectification and cunning.

'DeBullion Street,' easily the best of the three street poems, appeared nine months later, in 1944, a calendar year of consolidation and excitement for Layton's poetic confidence, as for Klein's. The first two stanzas contain remarkable descriptive power, some of it earned by typical Imagist juxtapositions:

> Under the night's carapace, the soft lanes
> Are listening ears where sudden footfall

Starts a choir of echoes. A red light winks
Viciously; and the wind's occasional
Sigh lifts from the garbage pails their stinks.[42]

By the third stanza, however, the poet feels a need for sociopolitical comment: 'Here private lust is public gain and shame.' As if to compensate for the unPoundian abstraction, he concludes the stanza with a brutal image: the local mission and church are 'hemorrhoids on the city's anus.' In the fourth stanza, perhaps now feeling the unity of the poem slipping, the poet must raise his voice: 'O reptilian street whose scaly limbs ...' The bardic 'O' responds to a similar structural urgency in seven other poems in *Here and Now* (compare Klein's excessive use of the interjection in *The Rocking Chair*), but they are usually minor pieces. 'DeBullion Street,' on the other hand, is a major work of the 1944 manner (note the greater interpenetration of images, the more assertive syntax, the taut rhythm), but it betrays nonetheless the predicament in which the young poet found himself, along with his forties colleagues: at what point can a dedication to perceptual objectivity and the duty of personal social intervention merge in the language of poetry?

'Jewish Main Street' of three months later begins with a similar effect of precise and neutral Imagism but is curiously self-conscious in doing so:

And first, the lamp-posts whose burning match-heads
Scatter the bog fires on the wet streets,
Then the lights from auto and store window
That flake cool and frothy in the mist ...[43]

The 'And first' and 'then' structure of the poem betrays the poet's consciousness of his image-power but may also suggest a felt need for a coherent structural principle: compare Page's 'Stories of Snow,' with its similar organizational formulae, 'And there the story shifts,' 'And on the story runs,' and so on. Such structural self-consciousness in Layton's poem forecasts the later *volta* in which he abandons neutral description, once again, for displaced political comment:

O here each anonymous Jew clutches
His ration book for the minimum
Items of survival
Which honoured today – who knows? –
Tomorrow some angry potentate
Shall declare null and void.

Layton's poem could perhaps have embraced both Imagistic precision and political comment; but when he performs the former primarily in the first stanza and supplies the latter primarily in the third he creates indirection and uncertainty, to be accounted for, to my mind, by the inherent restriction placed upon a neutrally perceiving and reporting image-maker. He needed a poetics that could comprehend personative self-assertion and sociopolitical comment as well as the exacting objectivist image, and the phenomenological-urban manner of these three 'Street' poems more or less resisted his needs.

This process, despite my necessary arrangement of it, was obviously not linear. As late as February 1945 (near the end of *First Statement per se*) Layton would publish poems which merely accumulated urban images, like the brief 'Waterfront':

Where second mates and plain hands
Spend crisis-made dividends;
Where sun peels off the fish smells
From the confusing, black walls,
And market filth is gathered
Into round piles at corners
Of acrostic streets that seem
Like the river's muscles, green:
Lean-to homes, arthritic, dank,
Have mustered at the land's brink
To spy atlantic liners
Stand idle like cows tethered.[44]

We are almost back at the simple catalogic Imagism of 'Vigil' from fifteen years before. 'Waterfront,' in effect, offers brief images at the rate of one per couplet. They are not ineffective, and they are certainly more transparent than the images of, say, 'Words Without Music'; but the problem ahead for the poet is that one can pretty quickly perfect the manner, and can then advance poetically only by letting one's eyes fall on some other scene and describing it: and then the next scene, and so on *ad infinitum* and *ad libitum*. The world provides the poem with its own coherence and order. The poet has contributed nothing but his ability to describe the separable components of that order with some effectiveness. It's not difficult to see that Layton's aesthetic personality could not long be satisfied with such epistemological passivity.

The structural difficulties of 'Newsboy' and 'Words Without Music' can now be more exactly articulated. Whatever brevity and unconventionality had been made available to poetic imagery after the Anglo-American modernist revolution, there was a concomitant pressure to create startling, shocking, or unnatural imagery in every poem, often at the expense, at least in lesser or green poets, of coherence, reflection, and subordination. This pressure would have been exacerbated, if anything, by the dedicated antinomianism of the *First Statement* poets. The only substantive structural difference between poems like 'DeBullion Street' and 'Newsboy' is that the former represents a particular urban setting, and the relatively straightforward images are evoked and circumscribed by that setting. Abstract and theoretical matter that the poet forces into the poem will be in distinct contrast to, and in danger of undermining, the integrity of that perceptual imagery. The latter poem, on the other hand, bases itself not upon a setting, but upon a single exemplar of modern life, hoping thereby to evoke ironic attitudes to all that his commerce signifies. 'Newsboy' comments upon that central figure by worrying at him imagistically, by accumulating a variety of complex individual images through which the central object of observation may be articulated. That variety makes more room for social and political matter, to be sure, but the efficacy of such abstract comment will still be swallowed up in the relentlessness of the poem's image accumulations. In 'DeBullion Street,' then, the danger of the Imagist burden is too great a phenomenological restriction, an exclusion of all that is not 'setting'; in 'Newsboy' the danger is suffocation, the overwhelming of theme, sense, and 'wholeness' (to use Treece's term) by the image mastery of the virtuoso. Whatever their comparative success, both poems are efforts on Layton's part to find the longer vehicle in which to profit from the Imagist legacy without being limited by its impersonal thrust, and both reveal the difficulty of that forties task.

Certainly these few poems do not typify every dialectic of image and *integritas* Layton cast up during the 1940s. Many of the poems appearing up to the publication of *Here and Now* are (for instance) simple satires, traditional in form, image, argument. I have nevertheless isolated from these insignificant pieces a cluster of poems that register Layton's real growth during the forties, and one of the two major challenges to that growth was precisely this question of what kind of image to generate, and what to do with it afterward. The various answers he offered are visible in the preceding discussions, but their relation to his other great challenge during the same period – the establishment of a personative poetry that would permit him at last to range freely from subjective emotion through objective phenomena to sociopolitical comment – cannot be articulated until the first-person work in *Here and Now* and *Now Is the Place* is to hand. In those poems he tried to forge an individualist voice that could encompass and give coherence to his increasingly random images of the world, but he revealed just as clearly the pressures against subjectivist experiments in the literary milieu in which he was training.

The Apprenticeship of the Layton Persona

I have left implicit one obvious thrust of the above considerations: the issues of imagery and *integritas* raised by Layton's early poetry, though inflected differently, are notably like those faced by P.K. Page and A.M. Klein. The consequence of such parallels for this book's larger argument is by now obvious, and I will not nuance them for the moment, except to underscore Layton's distance in the forties from the Nietzschean *Übermensch* persona he would later adopt. The strict impersonality of the several poems treated thus far – poems covering the entire run of *First Statement* as a little magazine prior to amalgamation with *Preview* – is in striking counterpoint to the reputations both of Layton and of *First Statement*. In none of these poems is the 'persona' at issue in his relations with the author; in none must we work through the familiar Layton egoism to a more comprehensive vision (a critical *sine qua non*, I shall hope to establish, of his post-1953 poetry). The closest any of the poems comes to personation is the rhetorical first-person plural of the last line of 'Words Without Music': 'the goats leap into *our* faces shrieking.' But this is the only such pronoun in the poem, which is otherwise strictly impersonal; compare, for instance, the single first-person pronoun used for closure in P.K. Page's 'The Stenographers,' a poem whose impersonality has been taken to be exemplary of the distanced gaze of *Preview*. Considering that many of the poems I have surveyed are also among the most often-reprinted and best-liked poems in *Here and Now*, this anomaly is worth pursuing.

In fact another quick survey of *Here and Now* is revealing: of the thirty-two poems in the book, seventeen are entirely impersonal or assert a speaking subject only with incidental use of the first-person plural so familiar to the thirties poets – 'Auden and Co.' – from whom Layton had wished to distance himself. Four of the remaining fifteen are personative only because they are first-person 'epitaphs' spoken by a 'wit,' a 'philosopher,' a 'Communist,' and a 'Christian,' very much in the manner of Klein (and, for that matter, of Kennedy and Smith). Four of the remaining eleven acknowledge a speaker with a single, incidental pronoun; the 'speaking mask' is a negligible force in interpretation. The seven remaining poems, all spoken by an 'I' or otherwise establishing a persona, would appear to offer the more typically *First Statement* poetic: expression of personality, subjective vision, phenomenological descriptions of the urban world, and so on. They will nevertheless prove remarkable for the same elaborate image patterns and excessively rhetorical manner that characterized the more rigorously impersonal material now considered.

Lest those statistics sound too quick to lay aside 'minor' poems, I want first to show cause to dismiss a handful of mawkishly unsuccessful poems in the first person scattered throughout *Here and Now.* Typical of these are 'Jeremiad'[45] and 'Returning With an Annual Passion.' In the former the first-person is asserted solely through an 'I' in the first line, and then the conventional imagistic cataloguing begins; in the latter the cataloguing, vigorous for twenty-five lines, is capped with a 'my' in the last line. No 'persona' in any meaningful or functional sense can be said to exist. 'Jeremiad's' speaker provides little but vituperative spluttering for closure: 'The rest, / the remaining rubble, the goddamned nowhere nothing / shall time sandpaper into a venomous joke.' The speaker of 'Returning' enters as late as he does in what appears to be an effort to make the poem coherent within a single soldier's experience:

> Returning with an annual passion
> April winds suck buds, and Christ,
> Christ in a fox-hole
> Cannot save my soul.[46]

Not long after, Layton judged this ending unsuccessful, and replaced it for the poem's reappearance in *Now Is the Place* with a last, impersonal image, thus excising all the poem's efforts of subjective voice: 'Against the curbstones like thick nostrils / The sunlight begins to dry / This snotflecked world.' The effort to *épater le bourgeois* is palpable; it is interesting that it required the elimination of the personative gesture.

In my view such efforts merit the disappearance into statistics I accorded them above; they could only clutter needlessly a discussion of the emerging Layton persona in poems of greater value and complexity. Layton's more telling personative experiments in the forties indicate his quick intuition that the taboo speaking subject offered a basis for modernism's poetic renewal, but they show simultaneously that the decade prior to his mastery was not truly conducive to the emancipation of the individual voice, constraints of impersonality and post-Imagist accumulation maintaining their force, for him as for others. 'Gents' Furnishings,' one of seven truly subjective poems in *Here and Now,* offers a minor sketch of the persona's emergence and initial weakness in Layton's egoist apprenticeship. The poem's individual images are less tortured and esoteric than those, for instance, in 'Newsboy,' with which it is roughly contemporary (1943); there is a greater sense of phenomenal reality in the poem. Its problem, as we might by now expect, pertains to structure: how does one establish the structural relation between a persona, recording subjective experience and perceptions, and an objective cataloguing of images that gives ironic counterpoint to that persona?

The poem opens with the early Layton's usual accumulative metaphoricality:

After the casual fret of tramcars,
The flowing of time against the traffic lights,
The engine's re-assertive snort,
And people, vindictive, elate
Spawning by contact ambition
Of affluence and the magic arc of influence:
I, rooted to carpet, note
The fabulous street of St. Catherine ...[47]

Note the Page-like syntax, which delays the subject pronoun of the first sentence for six lines; this contributes to an initial feeling that the image-power of the poet is as yet more developed than the cohering and unifying power of the personative voice. Indeed, immediately after this pronomial establishment of persona, a comparison of the street with a 'river's bed' drags the poem forward for another four lines before the persona's experience comes remotely into play. When 'Gents' Furnishings' does emerge as a fully personative poem, an encompassing irony also sounds:

[I] Am reassuring, friendly, know all the answers –
Last night, passing the Roxy Theatre,
Watched the chorus girls kick their neon feet,
Was tempted, bought ticket –
Now an obscure Churchill–Mussolini,
Conceive the effective lies
That sell Grover's marked-down ties
And plan a strategy
That would fool a prodigy.
Or, while love fingers a bargain shirt,
I perforate the skirt
With eyes
That ask deception of the marriage bed.

Note the tendency, familiar now from Page and Klein, to allow a single pronoun to be carried forward by anaphora to a long string of predicates (in this passage eight predicates to a single pronomial subject). Perhaps one now accepts the initially impersonal catalogue as a personative poem in which the surroundings of the young salesman speaking and his private fantasies will be interwoven in rich contrapuntal images: out of such a reading, presumably, would come the questionable critical view that links the 'proprioception' of the *Tish* poets back to *First Statement* phenomenalism.[48] The germ of personation withers for the second half of the poem, however, and an extended series of abstract references initiates a third and more dubious manner for 'Gents' Furnishings':

> O the dire question dropped from dying mouths
> Rolls down the Caucasus, through disputed lanes
> Of water, the passage people make
> For their escorted hero, deposits
> As a sick vapour on my show-case:
> Does truth unite or divide?
> History walks in like a customer.

The manner has changed dramatically, and although I am inclined to believe that Layton is using thirties-ish abstractions like 'History' parodically – he makes similar ironic references in three other poems – they nevertheless alter the tone of the poem and shake its integrity. The persona struggles to the surface of the poem at the conclusion, but just barely: after references to 'change' as 'circular and illusory,' to 'some Bulgarian street' and the 'creative winds [that] blow equally / Through pyjamas sleeves,' the speaker murmurs, 'And surely today or tomorrow / A stranger will tell me the news, / The morning greet me like a handshake.' The urges towards larger historical perspectives and bitter prophecy do battle here with the narrow viewpoint of a very tentatively established persona, whose gestures of lust and condemnation, familiar enough Layton themes, are too sparse to convey his reality or give his enunciations organizing force.

'Proof Reader' was published a year and a half later, and naturally shows a greater sophistication and control than 'Gents' Furnishings'; the triumph of 'The Swimmer' had intervened, perhaps importantly. But 'Proof Reader' (Layton's claims to the contrary)[49] offers little of the dynamic profundity of 'The Swimmer'; instead it reveals that, in his struggle to establish a personative poetic, Layton was to find his early image-manner returning, and at some cost. The 'Proof Reader' is quickly sketched as a worn-out but poetical member of the proletariat:

But I whose eyes are a transmission belt,
The words depositing like strips of steel,
Think Cyclops luckier in his wounded cave:
Death comes for brothers like Bela Lugosi,
My brothers dying in a Roman hedge,
Their ache is frozen into proper type ...[50]

The metaphoricality of the piece is as aggressive as we have come to expect. One can certainly feel the poet's need to make each line count, to do something imagistically impressive before the pen returns to the left-hand margin. There is a certain histrionic strain in the proof-reader's claim of brotherhood with those 'dying in a Roman hedge' – this presumable reference to the battle for Italy smacks, of all things, of E.J. Pratt's rhetorical manner in poems like 'Brébeuf and His Brethren,' with its 'two slabs of board, right-angled, hammered / By Roman nails and hung on a Jewish hill.' The assertion of a persona does nothing here to impose a more colloquial manner. On the contrary, as if he found personation difficult to maintain, by the end of the poem Layton has practically abandoned his speaker to the welter of obscure imagery:

Till I, cold egret in a mere of ink,
Idly surface the black frogs thick with speech
When History having eyes but no ears
Morsels now sauerkraut now caviar
Seeking the winged serpent in the tree.

Note once again the ironic 'History.' We could, as before, work to untangle these completely baffling lines to arrive at some approximate meaning for them, but I wish primarily to emphasize the disappearance of the persona into the maelstrom of image-making that is more important, voluntarily or otherwise, to the poet's aesthetics.

Layton obviously struggled in both these poems to use the persona as a means of focusing wide historical and phenomenological perspectives. Visible in them is some of the self-fascination and -aggrandizement that will characterize the personae of later and better poems, certainly; but I would still say he is struggling. Although there is in 'Gents' Furnishings' a certain interest in the echoing of the 'river-bed' image by later lines like 'disputed lanes / Of water,' and in the later poem an intriguing conceit linking printer's and soldier's implements, neither poem manages the more complex and spontaneous *integritas* of 'The Swimmer,' largely because both exhibit an uncontrollable urge to make as many striking images and profound allusions as possible before the end. This leads to a crowding of imagery in relation to matter, and an overwhelming of the personative presence by the poet's metaphoric exuberance.

These two poems were composed on either chronological side of 'The Swimmer,' which we might now think to have earned part of its control by Layton's transliteration of subjective speech into the aesthetic distancing of the third person. Since 'Gents' Furnishings' is nearly contemporary with his most obviously Imagist exercises, there was clearly no sudden shift into subjective verse: even as he wrote in and through the impersonal modernist voice, he had apparently some interest in a more immediate and subjective poetry, though the compulsions of Imagist objectivism and modernist difficulty remained strong. We should be careful therefore not to resolve this narrative into a simple choice between modernist impersonality (here largely indicated by the suppression of the 'I') and mid-century subjectivism. Wells's contemporary claim that the most 'impersonalist' poetry will be the most accessible, and often therefore the most lyrical, subjective, and immediate, refutes such polarities,[51] as does Klein's delicate reading and rereading of the interface between anonymity and self-expression. For the moment, Layton appears to have sought an accommodation between these two impulses of voice and *integritas,* although the extremes of his early-modernist inheritance deferred the accommodation well into the 1950s.

The direction Layton would pursue was adumbrated in a third personative piece from *Here and Now,* to my mind the first successful embodiment of the principles towards which he was reaching. 'Spinoza' is also the earliest sign that Layton's readings in philosophy could provide imagistic and personative grounding in a poem, much as some of Nietzsche's ideas would later do. In its suggestive alternation of phenomenal images, personative introspection, and abstract conceptualization, the poem promises the subtle and stringent *integritas* of later work:

Outside a leaf, wind-detached,
Falls through my father-image,
Falls ... falls ghostily to cover
The stones in my gall-bladder.
See how objects run toward me

Along the transom of this page,
Irresistibly make me over
Into four walls and a mirror.
Now there is no room for error ...[52]

The poem remains dense: in a few lines there are many unusual images, startling juxtapositions, even an *a of b* locution. If I am right that 'Spinoza' incorporates these forties mannerisms with a greater *integritas*, it is evidently not because all challenges to structural coherence were dropped from the style. On the contrary, Layton appears to have found, in the energy of personation or the contextual force of Spinozan imagery, a means of focusing the fragmentation of modernist form without reducing its instability to a dogmatic or reductive unity.

The images of room, window, leaf, and mirror blend with the speaker's governing introspection, reflecting the newly fluid boundaries of his self-conception. Layton toys with the rationalism and pantheism of Spinoza in a manner that makes the interiority of his persona at once part of and detached from external phenomena; he evokes his isolation within his 'room' even as he puns on the word, an isolation that blossoms in the last part of the poem without self-pity; and he bases on it a self-celebratory vocation that anticipates the poet to come:

... I am better and gladder;
And I am weaned from singularity,
Or moving myself through spaces:
Mine is the bare, continuous world
Behind that of outraged faces,
Where thoughts like separate twigs
Fall lightly across my marrow,
Distilling from bones a pity
For each bewildered Pharaoh.

Despite his permeability, his unboundedness, the quiet rhythm advances the persona's wholeness, as image-rhymes steadily complete themselves: the 'separate twigs' evoke the 'wind-detached' leaves of the opening line, the 'outraged faces' echo the 'father-image' reflected in the window, and so on. Perhaps only in the ultimate allusion, rhyme-forced, does the persona let slip his tight control on the poem's body of reference – which overlaps, ironically, with his own body's stability as well, a technique we will see Layton develop forcefully in the early 1950s.

'Spinoza' also serves as a first substantive point of divergence between the poetics of Layton and of Page, if we compare it with Page's later 'Reflection in a Train Window' (see above, pp. 101–3). In both poems a central figure observes the 'real' world through a window, and both use that basic image to play on the boundary between penetrating vision and frustrated self-reflection. The aptness of such imagery to the crucial question of personation in Page's and Layton's poetics is beautifully figured in a remark of Daniel Albright's: 'Every persona is to some extent in the position of the young Wordsworth in book 4 of *The Prelude*, staring down from his row-boat at a water surface that is half mirror and half pane of glass: his own face impedes his sight of the pebbles and grasses on the lake bottom. The degree of self-consciousness may be measured by the degree of interference from the facial image.'[53] There is just such a suggestive interplay in the Canadian poems, not only as here between reflection and insight, but also between the interiority and exteriority of the central figures: objects from the outside world seem able to penetrate the 'body' of both observers. And in both poems the pane of glass that separates the observer from the world observed is linked metaphorically to the blank page on which the poet records his or her visions. Both figures, by the way, are surrounded by audiences: in Page, represented by 'the reading lamps of strangers' around her, and in Layton, by the 'outraged faces' that hide a truer, 'continuous world.' And yet in Layton these imagistic collocations point towards dynamic new growth: his speaker is 'better and gladder; / And ... weaned from singularity,' whereas Page's exemplar is left amid 'soft soundless grieving' as 'her trembling image falls, rises and falls.' Where Layton finds a basis for a claim of regeneration, Page finds an ironic martyrdom and a failing self-image. Layton would take full advantage of his poem's findings by the time of composition of Page's poem, in 1954, as his *Preview* rival – and apparent fellow traveller – fell silent.

'The Swimmer' and 'Spinoza' were published ten years before these events, though, in the second half of 1944, and it is difficult not to see in that period a first tentative expansion of Layton's abilities. 'DeBullion Street' and 'Words Without Music' echo in their better passages the abilities of these two strong pieces and also appeared in 1944. It would be incautious to treat the last winter of the war as a Layton watershed, however: impersonal post-Imagist work like 'Waterfront' and weaker personative pieces like 'Proof Reader' had yet to be published. Nonetheless, several of the 1944 poems in *Here and Now* indicate the future achievement of the young poet and imply a course for his development, along two chief lines. The first of these is the relation of the individual image to the *integritas* of the poem, the ability to be locally powerful without losing general structural soundness. The second is the gradual transition from a rigorous impersonality to a cautious and often awkward personation that seeks to subordinate fragmentary observations and opinions to the ironies of a single speaking voice. That much observed, the two challenges are subsumed in their common answer, the 'answer' Layton was to find in the early fifties: for the establishment of an ironic persona replete with philosophical detachment and passionate vision serves to make coherent the constituent images of the poem and to subordinate them to something larger than their status as mere phenomena. His first intuition of this resolution appears, arguably, in poetry written in 1944, shortly after his references in a fugitive *First Statement* essay to the New Apocalypse and its doctrines of wholeness in mind and poem.

Layton's second volume, *Now Is the Place* of 1948, added as remarked only eleven new poems to his canon, and only a few of those demonstrate clear advances upon the work prior to 1945. Noteworthy in the period leading up to the second volume, however, is the increasing proportion of personative poems. From the beginning of the 1940s to the publication in 1945 of *Here and Now,* fewer than a quarter of Layton's poems had sketched a persona; from the publication of *Here and Now* to that of *Now Is the Place* (1945 to 1948), about two-thirds of the few poems attempt the subjective mode. Indeed, the very first poem in the second volume, 'The Eagle,' later renamed 'Lenin' in *The Black Huntsmen* of 1951, appears to address on one of its levels the interrelations of persona, phenomena, and image that were central to Layton's forties development. I will read it on that level, not to ignore the political interpretation demanded by the later title, but to contend that Layton's sociopolitical themes are here, arguably for the first time, unified and made profound by their aesthetic implications.

'The Eagle' begins simply, with a precise two-line image: 'Above the polished snow / The icicles spoil like fruit.' The first stanza ends there, highlighting the pure Imagist manner of the lines. The second stanza then elaborates the 'decadent pastoral'[54] setting into a full-blown personalism and urbanism and thereby ironizes the Imagist method of its representation:

> This is not any kingdom
> But an overripe slum
> Where by narrow runnelled streets I come
> Hoping crazily to find
> A rockbound province of the mind.[55]

The imagery of constriction ('narrow' and 'rockbound') and the obscure antecedence of the initial pronoun suggest that the persona here reflects ironically on the self-containment and aesthetic autonomy of the Image with which he opened his pronouncement: that is to say, Imagism may abstract the slum into 'a rockbound province of the mind' but because of its objectivism can offer the poet no real election, no kingdom. The speaker of 'The Eagle' then, and arguably its poet, has confused Imagist slum for potential kingdom, has tried to establish aesthetic dominion in a setting that resists his rule. He also seeks a 'mind' that could be nourished by that setting, but the slum is hostile to his approach: in the second stanza 'the evil lamps stab [him] – once, twice!' as he moves forward into the scene. In past attempts to establish such a kingdom, he has 'met many princes returning, taller than I. / Their eyes are disenchanted and sorrowful.' Many others, even betters it would seem, have claimed the same kingdom and been repulsed, and the speaker, moved and frightened by their failure, turns back.

> But at each retreat I have heard
> The eagle – kingly bird –
> Blooded by an icicle,
> Heard his inescapable cry and seen it bed
> In snow like a blot of blood and far more red.

The action of the poem thus defers the decision of a further penetration of the slum. When the speaker pushes forward, he is 'stabbed' and sees ghostly omens of his failure. When he retreats, he is reminded by the symbol of the eagle of the sacrificial and regal nature of the kingship he has undertaken.

Had Layton resolved 'The Eagle' in either direction, towards final retreat or accession to a slummer's crown, he would have weakened it. The objectivity of the conclusion, however obscure, shows increasing sophistication. So, I would argue, does the last line's vivid and violent image of blood on the snow: in comparison with the self-conscious artifice and cool autonomy of the poem's opening image, this is a thoroughly naturalized visualization, less dependent on a startling juxtaposition and more coherent within the poem's thematic layers. Indeed the fact that the poem makes prompt and explicit reference to the persona's misrepresentation of a slum after beginning with such a frank piece of Imagism suggests that 'The Eagle' hints, on the one hand, at the impossibility of a whole-hearted devotion to the poetic depiction of the slum world (as in the various 'Street' poems of *Here and Now*), and, on the other, at the necessity of *some* participation in and sacrifice for that world, like the kingly eagle, stabbed as the poet will be if he proceeds. The creative decisions of the persona are thus at issue in 'The Eagle.' Because they have to do with the place of the phenomenal world in his self-delineation, and because rivals 'taller than [he]' have failed the task, and because the initial Image seems asked to embody some essential dilemma of the 'overripe slum,' I read the poem on this level as a symbolic articulation of the creative predicament I have delineated in *Here and Now* and feel that Layton's ability to dramatize it successfully in a strong poem forecasts his eventual triumphs.[56]

Once again I have opened a volume's discussion with its strongest poem in order to mute reservations I must later express with the bulk of its work. 'Afternoon of a Coupon Clipper,' for instance, in which the persona watches his sister cut coupons from magazines and/or have roaring sex with her fantasized 'Toreador' (the difficult interpretative choice is moot), is in a jocular everyday English that would soon be beneath the poet:

'Course she won't say where she got them [her scissors];
I fancy it was Rotterdam
Though, where she went for last year's trip.
Me? I've often seen her go clip
Clip, same as you might with a pair ...[57]

Layton had attempted this folksy tone earlier, in 'Say it Again, Brother,' a poem that thankfully never appeared in a Layton volume:

And when the know-alls were explainin' it,
and fools were shoutin', 'Peace at last,'
you winked an eye: 'Just watch the cannons spit.'

Now what about that special piece of heart
I'm askin' for, – no foolin', Joe.
How shall I put it to you? Where'll I start?

The poem's chatty references to 'Joe' and 'Karl' contrast facetiously with the later allusion to 'Lenin,' but chiefly vitiating such a tone is its too obvious distance from Layton's own delight in articulate, sonorous expression. Developing personae who spoke in this manner would have limited his style to a vague leftist Kiplingism (!) that could not have satisfied him for long. The true Layton 'persona' would come to sound very much like the man Layton in rapid thought: indeed so convincingly so that few have kept the distinction sufficiently intact.

Other efforts of personative innovation in *Now Is the Place* have the tangible virtue of forging crucial qualities of the true Layton voice. 'To the Lawyer Handling My Divorce Case' will be familiar in manner to those who have read Layton's prolific autobiographical poetry. Here the distance between poet and persona is negligible, for the poem obviously retails Layton's life at the time; and yet the poem is of interest for its articulation of a new sense of his ego's multiplicity, vulnerability, and intensity:

In that instant I have plummeted the infinite distance
Between I and Me –
Me is always question-begging, diffident, undersized;
I am Me
When my lawyer addresses me.
We smell each other's absurdity ...[58]

In 'Spinoza' the speaker had been 'weaned from singularity,' but it was probably not this kind of simple self-multiplying that Layton had anticipated in the earlier poem. It is telling that the weakling 'me' is much more completely articulated here than the better 'I,' of whom we know only that he has 'heard of Nagasaki / [And] debated the soul's immortality.' Layton is gesturing towards the superiority of the *Übermensch* but seems as yet unsure of his attributes, or of his own appropriateness for the role.

Other particulars of that exuberant later persona are contributed by 'Ice Follies'[59] and 'A Poor Poet Is Grateful for a Sudden Thaw,' however: his deliberate scandalousness from 'Ice Follies,' with its sneer that 'in canada [*sic*] / you can not say shit too often,' and from 'A Poor Poet' the imagery of dismemberment that would eventually enrich the concept of the poet's 'murdered selves' in 'The Cold Green Element' (a motif we now see as continuous with Klein's nightmare imagery of dismemberment in 'Desideratum' and 'Meditation Upon Survival'). In an interesting echo of 'The Eagle,' 'A Poor Poet' opens with a little winter-urban Imagism:

Icicles zigzagged across the page,
A ready graph for the winter's rage;
And sidestreets mock-heroically
Burned white like tusks of ivory.
The wind crowed through a million cocks –

And thieves were picking at my locks.

A surreal catalogue of apocalyptic images follows, in which glimpses of 'a tyrant' and 'Charles V' are greeted with mutually supportive metaphors of spring and of revolution. The catalogue is climaxed when 'The thieves ran off with the wig of a clown.' Thus anticipating the collocation of clown and king in 'Whatever Else Poetry Is Freedom' of 1958, the Poor Poet persona allows Layton, ironically, to establish some key articles of his later *Übermensch* incarnation, despite the slack randomness of the poem's structure. It is telling that references to the persona are offset in single-line stanzas that are clearly asked to bound the poem's inchoate visions.

By 1948, then, if 'The Eagle' and these fugitive efforts are an indication, Layton had grown much more conscious of his development as a poet, more aware of its challenges and alert to possibilities of invigoration. But there is little as yet in the poems themselves to suggest that his new and better vision had been fully fledged. It is not really surprising that his ideas of poetic growth should precede his ability to embody them, but the poetry's retardation does suggest the persistent hold of the forties manner on his compulsion towards distinctiveness. Of all the new poems in *Now Is the Place,* only 'English For Immigrants,' though it was first published a year before 'The Eagle,' reveals the manner in which Layton was soon to resolve the issues rendered above. Here the effusive and self-aggrandizing persona is more familiar, as should be the controlling irony which governs his treatment. By no means do these achievements mean, as yet, a flight from forties styles. The initial stanza is still image-crowded, but its containing persona governs that richness successfully:

Each Wednesday evening their knees
Pressed together like a pair of saints
They pivot on pencils and with eyes for aprons
Gather the lessonwords 'books' and alien 'hills'
While from the curve of their backs I take my flight –
A hawk, I exhibit the white grubs under my hand.[60]

The poet has aligned himself with yet another bird of prey, and in contrast to his sexually inhibited and frustrated pupils he is in flight: familiar Layton theme. Although his image-consciousness is highly active, the power of the persona's self-rendering integrates the elaborate metaphors of the pupils comfortably: it is clear here, as it is not, for instance, in 'Newsboy,' that a speaking observer is among the poem's representations, and that it is as products of *his* specific consciousness that the metaphors are to be grasped. This would not be the effect, though, if the egoistic persona were not himself subject to some larger field of containment: the force of ego is balanced here by the ironic truth that the 'white grubs' gripped by *this* bird of prey are merely 'lumps of chalk,' as the next stanza reveals. In the midst of his self-aggrandizing fantasy the bored speaker cries out, 'I am Caesar ... I am Saint Francis, / I am this misty slate and lump of chalk,' announcing his exemplary greatness and in fact claiming identity with the tools of the language the pupils struggle to master. Their reaction is merely to 'climb from their steep silence and stare.'

Despite the students' ironic bafflement at the adopted grandeur of the poet's persona, he remains their point of reference in their struggle with English and their sense of what it means to be an articulate member, even on the pedagogical fringe, of North American society: 'Yet from me, a hawk,' the persona continues, 'they take whatever feather / Can start their heavy wishes under a stone.' (The lines anticipate a much later poem, 'Still Life,' in which a vicious stranger throws a large flat stone onto a helpless linnet: 'Only a fluttering wing was visible, / and it looked / as if the ridiculous stone / was attempting to fly.')[61] The persona remains, egoistically, the affirmative centre of the poem, dominant enough to render coherent the whirl of images that begins it but ironized so that we ought not to be detoured into disdain for the pomposity of his tone: he is, after all, aware of its excesses before we are. Egoist or not, he is tied down and sacrificed to the phenomenal reality of individual circumstance – in 'The Eagle's' terms he has retained to his own cost the kingdom of the slum – but he is himself regal and isolated, a figure of striving and energy.

The first attempts at this passionate and self-focused persona are the most significant achievement, to my mind, of *Now Is the Place.* As Layton continued to elaborate the 'bird of prey' into a consistent persona and vehicle for his later, better poetry, he drew away from the histrionic post-Imagism that had dominated his work of the forties. He restrained the merely local impressiveness of the poem's parts and insisted that they flow together under the aegis of the speaker's intense selfhood. He accepted his duty as a poet to establish in the phenomenal world a 'province of the mind' ('The Eagle') from which he could continue to take his raw material, but he also determined to soar above that world, never to be reduced again to the reportage of passive Imagist perception. By no means are all the poems in *Now Is the Place* successfully reflective of this new spirit, but one feels a possibility of real fresh air in the forties mannerism; one or two poems open up the aesthetic question, instead of being penned within it; and when one absorbs the mature Layton and returns to these early volumes, it is in *Now Is the Place* that one sees the first faint outline of later work.

Layton's place in the context of the Canadian forties requires no further raw material. The struggle he visibly undergoes to establish a more personative and less haplessly post-Imagist manner – a struggle he had scarcely begun at the end of the decade – proves finally that the common distinctions between *Preview* and *First Statement* aesthetics have little relevance to the poetic practice *of the forties*. Any critic of the period called upon to identify the journal that endorsed a poetics in which powerful and complicated local images tended to swamp the integrity of the poem, and that adhered to an impersonal method that would elaborate those images without the intrusion of a mistrusted subjectivism, would point the finger readily at *Preview*. Layton's affiliation with *First Statement* while he obeyed such poetics – including his implicit attacks on *Preview*, which we might now think a kind of scapegoating for tendencies he disliked in his own poetry – reveal that we present the decade more accurately and richly if we acknowledge that the supposed *Preview* aesthetic had a powerful attractive force which Layton did not entirely overcome in his poetry until after the forties had ended. (His first attempt, after all, had been to join *Preview*.) The full and final break with the forties styles would come, for him as for Page, Anderson, and Klein, some two or three years into the next decade, in a period of achievement hardly predictable even from his best poems of the forties. He had found in those ('The Swimmer,' 'The Eagle') a means of raising his own voice, but he had yet to incorporate the full-blown ironic egoism, the doubled sense of selfhood's limitlessness and mistakenness, that responded and arguably made him impregnable to the kinds of historical trauma whose worst damage was emblazoned by Klein.

Image, *Integritas*, and Ego in Layton of the 1950s

It appears we do not lack influential explanations of Layton's self-re-creation in the early 1950s. I have remarked the usual Nietzschean contextualizations as well as the biographical incidents that seem suggestive of major personal change. Other 'causes' can be adduced: Al Purdy's remark that Horace Gregory's translations of Catullus had a major impact on Layton's verse forms in the 1950s[62] is in accord with Layton's occasional adaptation of classical techniques of satiric address and a Martialesque epigrammatism in voice and theme.[63] One good business of future Layton criticism could be the recovery and complication of such influences: I have suggested, for example, an Apocalyptic preparation in the forties for his assumption of the Dionysian poet-persona later on, and similar contexts can continue to be debated. What we lack, then, is not a good sense of the 'new' poet's possible literary causes, but a good model of his effects, a way of describing the new Layton poetics of the 1950s that will shed light, not only on its substantial *difference* from his style of the forties, but also on its *derivation* from his early training in the forties manner of imagery, voice, and structure I have thus far tried to draw to the surface.

When Henry Treece suggested how the New Apocalyptic poets were to move on from the rigidities of late Imagism and 'a decade of picture-makers' (above, p. 183), he offered a clear choice between two aesthetics of cultural transformation, a choice that Layton's poems of the 1950s demonstrate, however, to have been falsely articulated. Treece suggested that a world in Apocalypse could be rendered misguidedly, 'by a casual, arbitrary selection' of images evocative of 'Surrealism in the Bad Old Manner,' but that a better representation would occur 'where the change is consciously willed and motivated by a sincere and constant philosophy.' In the latter dispensation the results will include 'artistic ... rejuvenat[ion],' the 'rebirth' of the image, and 'a new WHOLENESS' in both psyche and poem. What Treece could not foresee, despite the many consonances of his visionary 'criticism' with Layton's self-refashioning, is that real forward progress would be made by a poet who insisted on maintaining the 'casual, arbitrary selection' of Imagism *while simultaneously* working through his poems a sustained philosophical legacy from Nietzsche and others that would make such arbitrariness not counter, but fundamental to poetic dynamism and expansion. I will contend as well, incidentally, in the readings that follow, for a Surrealist associationism subtending the best Layton work of the early 1950s, a sign that Treece's early-forties antipathy to Surrealism was of little force in Layton's eclectic discrimination of the influences and contexts of his apprenticeship years. His renewal of the Surrealist effect is hardly surprising, after all, given the common critical perception that in Surrealist poems 'images stand in what seems a grammatical structure, but they make no statement, and express only the emotional effect of their own co-existence' (to borrow the words of Samuel Hynes).[64] The terms are broad, but the Surrealist structure Hynes describes is obviously like the complex image accumulation associated with *Preview*, in whose sources Layton, too, had obviously been schooled; though a more epistemological and less stylistic Surrealism would interest the poet of the 1950s.

Layton's growth from 1940s to 1950s poet should not be construed, however, as a quick rejection of the poetic structures and styles that had thus far held him. He did not simply cut through the Gordian knot that was beginning to constrict Page's freedom of creative movement. On the contrary, I believe he moved forward by making quite gradual though precise responses to the questions begged by his early poems. I do not claim that (and I do not care whether) he made these responses with any conscious or strategic awareness. I simply assert a degree of continuity in the broad project, or, to put it another way, contend that the poet emergent in the 1950s *necessarily* pursued his creative impulses in directions and terms that he had encountered in the forties. Witness as a pithy example his introduction of 'Composition in Late Spring,' in a letter to Robert Creeley of 17 April 1953, as 'a well-integrated constellation of images.'[65] The poem's quite radical departure from his work of the forties did not, evidently, make him feel a need for new terms descriptive of its accomplishment.

In fact it will prove more accurate to say that Layton increased rather than deflated the pressure of Imagist radicalism in his new manner. The great poems of the 1950s are not typically less complex, dense, or difficult than those of the 1940s: on the contrary, they are often more accumulative and their images more anarchically random (and broader in referential range) than most we have seen thus far. This greater complexity is earned and accounted for, though, by a new mastery in his development and handling of personae. The poet who sought in items like 'Proof Reader' and 'Jewish Main Street' to move freely from abstract social and political comment to interior sensation and feeling to the external world's particulars found in the 1950s that a more forceful and definitive persona, valued explicitly for his multiplicity of experience, quick ethical temper, and sensual responsiveness, could subsume without collapsing such disparate categories of poetic experience in the *integritas* of that speaker's vigorously proclaimed consciousness. At the same time Layton intuited (and the readings below will contend) that the expansive self-assertiveness of such a persona would in turn need its own principle of containment in order to function poetically as an organizing and coherent centre for the vortex of image and idea that Layton wanted his poetics to incorporate. Shunning a self-aggrandizing persona subject to no larger principle than his own complacent selfhood, Layton sustains in poem after poem of the 1950s a containing principle of irony, a second perspective from which we view the most arrogant of his speakers as half-mistaken self-celebrants whose inescapable involvement in the world and humankind they think to have transcended is among the most profound of his ethical observations.

Agreement upon this containing irony will obviously be crucial to our criticism as to our appreciation of Layton's poetry. Its structural force shifts the register of arrogance in Layton's personae from incurious egotism to redemptive egoism. (The near-disappearance of the latter word in the late twentieth century suggests that our timid and sensitive political culture is stifling our ability to distinguish egotism from egoism; small wonder that Layton criticism is itself in eclipse as these words are written.) The dangers of a New Critical emphasis on *persona* at the expense of authorial responsibility are vivid these days: we are not inclined to forgive poets their uglier first-person sentiments (lines like 'And I who gave my Kate a blackened eye')[66] simply by granting them the arm's-length defence of personation. On the other hand (as Herbert F. Tucker adroitly notes),[67] a complete surrender of our notion of persona would lead to palpable misreadings of a number of lyric poets, Layton not least.

His 'Cain' of 1957 closes with a representative thematic underscoring of the principle of containing irony that will help henceforth to govern our responses to his speakers' expressions. The persona who in the opening verse paragraph heedlessly lodges an iron pellet in the head of a frog and watches its pathetic death first feels remorse in a fairly obvious and shallow language suggesting little real awareness:

But Death makes us all look ridiculous.
Consider this frog (dog, hog, what you will)
Sprawling, his absurd corpse rocked by the tides
That his last vain spring had set in movement.
Like a retired oldster, I couldn't help sneer ...

O Egypt, marbled Greece, resplendent Rome,
Did you also finally perish from a small bore
In your back you could not scratch?

(*WPJ*, pp. 69–70)

The inflation of language in these middle lines may sound to some typical of Layton's rhetorical self-buttressing, but this is not the final remark of 'Cain's' speaker. A more encompassing irony will emerge 'the next morning,' when the speaker again passes the dead animal:

The frog was on his back, one delicate
Hand on his belly, and his white shirt front
Spotless. He looked as if he might have been
A comic, tapdancer apologizing
For a fall, or an emcee, his wide grin
Coaxing a laugh from us for an aside
Or perhaps for a joke we didn't quite hear.

The delicacy of realization in these lines is nowhere anticipated in the poem's other images of the frog. Their sensitivity is not of an obvious kind: the speaker retains the sardonic attitude and habit of objectification that allowed him to kill the animal in the first place, and no better ethics shows up to 'redeem' him for his action. But he *is* now far more aware of his likeness to the life he has ended: he is, after all, 'Cain' to the frog's Abel, keeper turned murderer. Like the other shabby performers listed in ungenerous metaphor, he and the frog suddenly share the kinship of ridiculousness; and in the final line he is no longer the all-knowing, deeply visionary student of Egypt, Greece, and Rome, but the butt of an unheard joke, the significance of which he will never recover. The irony in the lines doesn't *excuse* him his violence, but it does resituate it in a broader ethics, in which the next random bullet may be for him.

These themes are not fortuitous in 'Cain.' Layton had been articulating them since *First Statement* days, but their most deliberate expression (and most evocative of the language of 'Cain') occurs in another letter to Creeley, this one of 26 May 1953:

> The quality of irony which you rightly detect in the poem ['Vexata Quaestio'] is the self-ironic smile of a man who sees the drift of the joke – and sees that the joke is on him. But all irony in poetry, I believe, is the consequence of the two antithetical roles the poet embraces, that of passionate participant and detached observer. It springs from his ability to keep a number – the more the better – of contradictory thoughts and emotions in suspension.[68]

A teacher of literature for several years, Layton may well have recognized the New Critical emphases of his interpretation. Note as well the typically Apocalyptic (not Nietzschean) insistence on synthesis as a principle of poetic complexity, the synthesis of participant and observer, of 'contradictory thoughts and emotions': the language of fusion and wholeness from Treece's writings is not far away from Layton's expressions here.[69] Until Layton developed the self-celebratory Dionysian persona of his work in the 1950s, the irony available to the personative mode would not be crucial to his achievement: and once he had the Dionysian habit, no poem could do well without that irony, for the tension between effusion and self-containment is a major source of the energy of *integritas* in his best poems.

'The Cold Green Element' is one of those best, by a critical consensus as total as need be. As soon as Layton wrote it, in the summer of 1954, he thought it 'perhaps [his] best to date.'[70] The poem achieves its power in part from its significant working through and dramatic supersession of the aesthetic difficulties and potential of his earlier manner. Although it is only partially a statement of aesthetic, a good deal of the poem's resonance is earned after the fact by our retrospective ability to situate it in the narrative of his development and illuminate it *vis-à-vis* the conventions and crises of his forties poems. For one thing, the poem's associative organization of imagery reveals a rich variety of responses to his training in a late Imagist tradition, despite its insistent subjectivism:

> At the end of the garden walk
> the wind and its satellite wait for me;
> their meaning I will not know
>   until I go there,
> but the black-hatted undertaker
>
> who, passing, saw my heart beating in the grass,
> is also going there. Hi, I tell him,
> a great squall in the Pacific blew a dead poet
>   out of the water,
> who now hangs from the city's gates.
>
> (*WPJ*, pp. 45–6)

We need first to speak with precision of what has changed in the Layton style. Autonomous images of inordinate abruptness and difficulty ('Morsels now sauerkraut now caviar / Seeking the winged serpent in the tree' – 'Proof Reader') are no longer needed: poetic language is deployed here not to shatter, but rather to exploit, referentiality by assuming a degree of connotative community among and with the poet's readers. None of the difficulty of the above passage is achieved through obscure usages or startling juxtapositions of dissonant terms: even if we cannot know what the wind's 'satellite' is (I am never satisfied by my *ad hoc* pre-lecture guesses), the brief problem is one of reference, not of a slippage in denotation or connotation. The poem's gifts of surprise, dissonance, indeed the 'feeling of sudden light' that Pound demanded of Imagism, arise instead from the speed with which the persona's mind whirls forth its highly accessible images, as well as from the difficulty we will undergo if we ask of them an obvious unity or theme.

It is in this sense that Layton has raised the stakes of his apprenticeship post-Imagist aesthetics. Principles of poetic structure dear to the Imagist are retained and arguably heightened here. Whereas in the forties the force of juxtaposition and dissonance in his poems was occurring on a minor and local level only (producing a degree of bafflement in some poems that could easily derail vision into brinksmanship), in 'The Cold Green Element' our potential confusion will probably pertain to the wholeness, integrity, and articulability of the speaker's consciousness: to the interpenetrative stability of his subject and object worlds, as it were, rather than to his 'verbal legerdemain.'[71] Yet we will also have to submit to the happy anarchy of his psyche: the principle of forward movement in the poem's imagery is analogous to that of free association, in which each image gives rise to an associated image, until we have moved far from the original phenomenon that launched the speaker's observation. The poem's rich associationism motivates some breathtakingly arbitrary, beautifully integral gatherings of imagery:

> The ailments escaped from the labels
> of medicine bottles are all fled to the wind;
> I've seen myself lately in the eyes
>   of old women,
> spent streams mourning my manhood,
>
> in whose old pupils the sun became
> a bloodsmear on broad catalpa leaves
> and, hanging from ancient twigs,
>   my murdered selves
> sparked the air like the muted collisions
>
> of fruit. A black dog howls down my blood,
> a black dog with yellow eyes;
> he too by someone's inadvertence
>   saw the bloodsmear
> on the broad catalpa leaves.

The alertness to 'ailments' was called up by the prior image of a 'dead poet,' and his confrere the crowned 'hunchback' who emerged just before these lines. The ailments in turn call up consequent ideas of age (the *double entendre* of 'spent streams') which themselves anticipate the pun on 'pupils': those pupils in the eyes of old women and those students of the exemplary poet, the 'young boys' who will re-emerge for later closure. From there to the 'blood-smear' is no easy leap (though the loosely sexual paradigm of these images suggests themes both of deflowering and of menstruation), but that very elusiveness is part of the poem's breathtaking freedom of association: the broad themes of drowning and murder in the poem here coalesce into a free-floating signifier of sacrifice, and from there it is not far to the image of the sacrificed poet, his 'murdered selves' at the very core of the poem's enactment of transformation and growth. Of course, as the persona is 'hanging from ancient twigs' he is reincarnating the earlier 'dead poet' 'hang[ing] from the city's gates.' And as a sense of his own processive selfhood is impressed upon him, the images become at once nightmarish and releasing, for the only way to deal with the 'black dog' swimming in his 'blood' is to keep 'breathless[ly]' swimming himself 'in that cold green element,' as in the vernal grass in which his 'heart [was] beating' as the poem opened.

The breathlessness with which new visualizations accrue in this poem has surely been enjoined upon Layton's readers as well, as we struggle to read through these seemingly infinite associations, to their coherent core. But (as is perhaps woefully obvious) the remarks above do not establish a thin 'unity' or narrow a theme for 'The Cold Green Element.' Indeed, Layton mocks any urge we may have to unify all this visual richness on too-easy terms, when he defiantly recycles – and thus falsely centres – the vivid image of the 'bloodsmear on broad catalpa leaves' for a later stanza: as if daring us to find peculiar or essential meaning in the doubled line, rather than in the freer associative rhythms of the whole poem. His triumph in 'The Cold Green Element' returns us to the perceptive notebook aesthetics of A.M. Klein, who advocated with mild irony just such a principle of free association as a means of moving forward with poetry: 'and you will be surprised,' he remarked, 'to what a point you will come' (above, pp. 112–13). Klein knew, of course, that a principle of pure association and his standards of poetic value were incompatible, and certainly he never came close to endorsing his intuition in actual poems. The critical analogy with free association could be vitiating of poetic coherence, for the chain of free association has no principle of closure (even if it has, for the Freudian, an absent yet meaningful core);[72] but Layton's poem takes its force of closure and its justness of inclusion from its outer sphere of reference: the phenomenological register that is the persona's consciousness.

Perhaps more important, Layton seems determined to establish a consciousness whose very elasticity and multiplicity – of ego, now, not of perception – and freedom to move in time and space keep him psychically intact even when the forces of ocean, 'wind,' 'lightning,' and 'old women' threaten to pull apart his bodily frame. He may endure all those 'murdered selves,' he may 'hang from the city's gates' one day too, but he will always be able to cry 'I *am* again' (emphasis added to the poem's short penultimate line) soon after the murderers leave his 'heart beating in the grass.' In fact, Layton posits a transformational aesthetics of the self as much as he forges one in the poem's associationist image clusters. The twin forces of expression are fundamentally one tensile structure now, selfhood finding its coherence and survival in the juxtapositive energy of the poem's images, the poem in turn finding its stability and power in the shifting perimeters of the speaker's mind. One doubts that the vision could have helped Klein; but that it was dialectically inspired by his articulation of mental cost in the fallen postwar world remains a possibility.

Treece's Apocalyptic theory prepared us for such a swerve in Layton's poetic education, of course, with his early-forties insistence that the recovery of structural integrity in poetry would have to coincide with the restoration of wholeness in the individual: the reverse being equally true, at least for the poet. One way of demonstrating just such a congruence of personative and poetic structure in 'Element' is by noting that their *integritas* is mutual. If we seek some means of rendering coherent the vortex of the poem's imagery – whether that means seeking a governing unity of theme or some less deterministic critical practice – we *must* do so by inquiring into the emotional or intellectual state of the imagery's projector. We are not here enjoined, I would argue, to read the 'world' of the poem for the poem's deeper *integritas* – as we are with the earlier 'Waterfront' and 'DeBullion Street,' for instance – for 'Element' too clearly transforms that world for purposes of the persona's own visionary reconstitution. The principle of inclusion in the poem, for instance, is determined entirely by the vagaries of the persona's consciousness. The principle of accumulation is governed, I have argued, by the 'associational promptings' (Klein's term) of the persona's psyche. And yet there is no sense in which the poem is made simple by its subjectivism. Layton has clearly sought a modernist poetics in which a return to lyric would not run counter to, but would rather augment the juxtaposition and intensity of his imagery, and he found one by breaking through the conventional boundaries of selfhood, especially that boundary that divides our conscious experience into 'subjective' and 'objective' records.

Indeed, the interplay of subjective and objective modes is central to the transformational aesthetics (of the self, of the poem) that are underscored by the imagery's associative movement. Clearly, Layton's poetic instincts still endorsed the goals, if not the methods, of an Imagist objectivism: it is patently false to suggest that 'The Cold Green Element' is a unidimensionally subjective poem, since the persona's lyric experience is mediated to us only by its incarnation in a series of objectively rendered and relatively unsubordinated visual phenomena. In fact I want to contend strongly for a competing objectivist strain in the poem's construction, and this despite my argument that the persona's boundaries as a self are in effect the boundaries permitting poetic coherence in the poem. The outside forces that govern the boundaries of selfhood, after all, are necessarily forces of objectification, external subjects through which we see ourselves as objects, with a history and a trajectory of which we have only limited control and awareness. Surely that is a theme in 'The Cold Green Element' as well: whatever the inflation of poetic expression the persona permits himself in the poem, he is at least as significantly a constrained consciousness, subject to a catalogue of external forces any of which might lead to his murder as a traitor or to a 'crown of leaves.' The objectification of the speaking subject is beautifully rendered when he 'see[s him]self in the eyes of old women,' the doubling up of an objectifying gaze suggesting precisely the manner in which we are to 'see' the persona ourselves, as both subject and object of his own consciousness.

These remarks may seem thematic; they are really structural in import. If the establishment of a persona is to have an integrating and cohering effect on a collection of near-random images and is thus to imply a formal boundary between the poem and the world it catalogues – if the poem is to be 'apprehended as selfbounded and selfcontained upon the immeasurable background of space or time which is not it,' as Stephen Dedalus put it in his definition of *integritas*[73] – that persona must himself have a delineated, a bounded existence, cannot be allowed to replicate the world's infinitude. Layton's egoist personae could not supply a sense of boundedness were they not themselves framed by some larger context in which they were merely one of many constituent elements. Layton achieves personative perspectivism largely through the consistent, albeit highly subtle, deployment of irony, so that when we cast about for the field of reference in which the poem's random images make sense, we can arrive at a bounded context – the persona – beyond which we feel no need to move for a greater coherence or comprehensiveness, that broader perspective having already been implied by his ironic characterization. The irony must be subtle lest it stifle the persona's exemplary inclusiveness, just as the force of *integritas* must be subtle lest it stiffen the poem's atomistic looseness into a formalist unity. Such ironic personation is evidenced in 'The Cold Green Element' in the watching eyes of 'old women,' as I remarked; in the poet's vulnerability to murder and dissolution, especially at the hands of his indifferent, orange-peeling audience; in his ignorance and mistakenness ('their meaning I will not know'; 'misled by the cries of young boys'); and in the crucial impermanence of his selfhood, his awareness that he is always 'turning over [to] embrace like a lover' some new version of his own being, soon to be 'murdered' in turn and hung from the twigs in his surreal garden.

The Surrealist and Apocalyptic flavour of the poem's images may be fortuitous; they do ideally illustrate Jacqueline Chénieux-Gendron's description of one key energy of Surrealist aesthetics, which 'consists of negating the meaning of space and of the human body, by the introduction of all possible meanings in a dionysiac investment of space, even at the price of tearing apart and scattering the human body.'[74] As the black-hatted undertaker surfaces and disappears, as the speaking poet observes his own beating heart, as medicine bottles and dead bodies whirl through the air, the visual surface of

'Element's' world is decidedly Surreal. And indeed the 'black dog,' with his evocations of the Hound of the Baskervilles, the Hound of Heaven, and other imprecatory canines, makes tangible an apocalyptic quality in the poem that had first arisen in the images of 'wind,' 'lightning,' and 'a great squall in the Pacific.' It hardly seems surprising that such a mood should emerge at that point in Layton's poetic advancement when he most visibly pursues the prescriptions of the Apocalyptics – eschewing Treece's polarization of the surreal and the 'sincere and constant'– into a new intensity of subjective and objective 'fusion.' Later poems of the 1950s would certainly exploit the apocalyptic mood as a means of centring the persona as observer-in-the-maelstrom: witness 'In the Midst of My Fever,' where the boundary between subjective and objective apocalypse is inarticulable, and 'The Improved Binoculars,' where a conflagration in the object-world seems more tangible: 'Below me the city was in flames. / The firemen were the first to save / themselves. I saw steeples fall on their knees.' Nevertheless the speaker's acute visionary nature is critical to the latter poem's intensely catalogic structure, which culminates bathetically: 'All this I saw through my improved binoculars' (*WPJ*, p. 44). The rendering of apocalypse does not, granted, indicate the influence of Apocalypse. Certainly there was no Apocalyptic program, and at this point of his maturity Layton would not have followed it slavishly anyway; but it seems fair to say that poems like 'The Cold Green Element' respond ideally to the Apocalyptics' calls in the 1940s for a new poetry of rejuvenation and 'wholeness,' after the poet and his world have been 'scorched free of dross and cruelty.'[75]

'The Cold Green Element,' then, might well be the Apocalyptic poem *par excellence*, though in Canada it signalled not the beginning, but the end, of a distinct forties style. Layton's development from the most competent work we saw in the forties – say, 'The Swimmer' and 'The Eagle' – to the real mastery of 'Element' is not easy to chart, in part because his art did indeed grow so rapidly and unpredictably in the early 1950s, in a sudden increase of inspiration and giftedness to which rational critical language cannot be entirely equal, and in part because he wrote relatively few poems in the period prior to his sudden flourishing. One of the poems from the transitional period of 1948 to 1953 that does, however, remain largely faithful to his forties apprenticeship while anticipating the later genius is 'The Black Huntsmen,' the title of which has Apocalyptic resonances I have already remarked. The poem reflects both the early and the mature poetics of Layton, as well as reaching for the crucial epistemology that would resonate in his later egoist personae. The forties desire to represent the slum world of his childhood persists in 'The Black Huntsmen,' certainly, even as the persona, acknowledging his place and history in that neighbourhood, begins to take on the quality, and function, of self-celebration and self-irony needed for later achievement:

The childish heart then
Was ears nose eyes twiceten fingers,
And the torpid slum street, in summer,
A cut vein of the sun
That shed goldmotes by the million
Against a boy's bare toe foot ankle knee.

(*WPJ*, p. 18)

The vestigial Wordsworthian tone here is vaguely reminiscent of Klein's 'Autobiographical,' which had recently reappeared in *The Second Scroll*, but the likeness is ironic and temporary. Nor are we really far in these lines from the slum Imagism of 'DeBullion Street': note the brief gestures of impersonalization, the persona's self-objectification as a 'childish heart' and as 'a boy.'

The next two stanzas, however, will allow the persona a greater imaginative capaciousness, returning him to the first-person while providing an etiology for his mythic imagination. An encounter with Tennyson's *Idylls of the King* teaches him to transform his narrow childhood world into a place of fantasy and danger, the sudden potential of which he renders with an associative visual imagination that would flower in 'The Cold Green Element' two years later. Here the newly visionary adolescent is the forceful centre of the poem's comic-surreal narrative detail:

I discovered Tennyson in a second-hand bookstore;
He put his bugle for me to his bearded mouth,
And down his Aquitaine nose a diminutive King Arthur
Rode out of our grocery shop bowing to left and to right,
Bearing my mother's *sheitel* with him;
And for a whole week after that
I called my cat Launcelot.

The boundary between the world as it is and as it is imagined is obliterated here by the confidently expanding presence of the Layton persona. Here, too, in gestation, is the typical containing irony surrounding the persona's transformative capabilities: his Surrealist's eyes are opened for the first time, but he remains a boy whose pronouncements rename the world for 'a whole week' at best. He is himself changed, though, and apparently for good: Tennyson's verse has given him a powerful figuration of the world's meaningfulness – and the dangers of pursuing its meaning. The poem's opening informs us that after his reading he had come to know that 'men were hunting [him],' that he might have to pay for his sudden transliteration into the romance ethos: 'Now I look out for the evil retinue / Making their sortie out of a forest of gold.' Though he would have 'preferred / A death by water or sky' – note the laying aside of Eliot implied in the image – he will be pursued instead by 'black huntsmen,' suggestive precursors of the 'black dog howl[ing] down his blood' in 'Element,' who frighten him, certainly, but also attract him libidinally: they emerge from a secret place of 'gold,' and after his (inevitable?) murder 'their dames shall weave my *tzitzith* / into a tapestry.' The persona who carries the poetic principle into an imaginative re-creation, and indeed collapsing, of his subject and object worlds will have to accept the consequent vulnerability of his selfhood, but he will in the end be woven into a fabric made up of veneration (the sacred *tzitzith*, or prayer shawl), sexuality, and poetry.

'The Black Huntsmen' implies that the passage from impersonal catalogic renderings of the object world to the masterful, self-celebratory, and transformative garden poet of 'The Cold Green Element' (and of 'The Birth of Tragedy,' to which I shall turn in a moment) occurred for good when Layton decided that his apprenticeship poetics had failed to accord the poet's (that is, his own) transfigurative and reconstitutive imagination sufficient visibility and freedom. The poem also suggests that even his earliest celebrations of his own imaginative capacity were held in artful check by an instinct for irony that was to keep the persona's awareness of his visionary ability from overwhelming the principles of inclusiveness and objectivity that remained, though altered, central to his poetic convictions. 'How to dominate reality?' the persona asks, rhetorically, in 'The Fertile Muck': 'Love is one way; / imagination another'; and certainly 'The Fertile Muck' of 1956 could be taken to thematize a one-way domination, of world by poet, that counters my remarks. Yet the result of the poet's ability to 'dominate' is that he is 'deposit[ed] / ... on the leaves of elms / or fold[ed] ... in the orient dust of summer' – he is carried away, and naturalized, by the very creatures he seems to dominate imaginatively. The fruit of his work of domination is a kind of passivity ('deposit me,' 'fold me,' 'release me') that beautifully anticipates the closing image of himself and his beloved sitting, their 'fingers touching the earth, like two Buddhas' (*WPJ*, p. 56). As in 'The Black Huntsmen,' the poet who joins the imaginative romance desiring to dominate his reality is ironically rendered vulnerable to the intensity of his own transfigurations – made a thing that can be lifted by the 'winged insects' around him, a being without the usual boundaries of selfhood in time and space. Liberating, yes, but disturbing as well: the Dionysian, after all, will have to die repeatedly.

This doubled movement of self-affirmation and self-dissolution, of which we have a telling, albeit crude, glimpse in 'The Black Huntsmen,' was to be extended and complicated in the most memorable poems Layton wrote in the 1950s. Ironic and egoist personation would permit extremes of Imagist juxtaposition going well beyond the associative currents that structure 'The Cold Green Element':

Conscience more flat than cardboard
   Over the gap in a sole,
I avoid the fanatic whose subway
Collapsed in his brain;
There's a sinking, but the madonna
   Who clings to my hairlock
Is saved; on shore the damned ones
Applaud with the vigour of bees.

(*WPJ*, p. 31)

Indeed, 'Composition in Late Spring' is distinctly reminiscent of the clutter of metaphors that partially vitiates the accomplishment of the early 'Newsboy.' Yet their likeness is more seeming than real. To be sure, there is in the poem of 1953 a similar urge to accumulate metaphoric vehicles to evoke a single tenor. But 'Composition in Late Spring' has made that very process of metaphor production one of the explicit and ironically handled qualities of the insistent 'I' and has done so right from the opening lines: 'When love ensnares my mind unbidden / I am lost in the usual way ...' The motions of the poet's mind *constitute* the field of the poem (and here we are returned to Kenner's definition of the Imagist subject). Their interest lies in a gradual adumbration of the outlines of his personality: 'The "plot" of the poem is that mind's activity, fetching some new thing into the field of consciousness.'[76] 'Newsboy' gives us no such personative frame within which to coordinate the poem's references and meaning.

More important, 'Composition' relies on the persona's grandeur for the energy of structural coherence, while simultaneously undercutting that grandeur – preventing its collapse into heedless and formless egotism – with a containing irony of which he is keenly and happily aware:

No one is more happy, none can do more tricks.
   The sun melts like butter
Over my sweetcorn thoughts;

And, at last, both famous and good
I'm a Doge, a dog
    At the end of a terrace
Where poems like angels like flakes of powder
Quaver above my prickling skin.

Note the associative poetics exemplified in the penultimate line, in which an initial likeness between imminent poems and hovering angels serves as a bridge to a less intuitive comparison of poems to 'flakes of powder,' a tongue-in-cheek vision of composition as a soothing talcum for the irritated flesh of the inspired poet. The comprehensive happiness supposedly experienced by a poet who is 'both famous and good' is instead, surely, a sign of his deeper disdain for fame and goodness; and since he is both 'Doge' and 'dog' – both head of state of a great city-republic and obedient servant of many masters – his fame and goodness will be moot in any case.

This was the poem Layton spoke of to Creeley as 'a well-integrated constellation of images,' and he was right to do so. It is not so integrated, I repeat, because he was careful to instil a deep unity among the various and fragmentary images, nor because he had learned to restrict their range and complexity (far from it), but because he found in the patterns of subjective consciousness a predicate for *verbal* freedom and energy. On the other hand, the poem is not integrated *via* a conventional lyricism that makes its metaphors a linear chart of the speaker's unfolding consciousness and organized expression of self: Layton obviously desires a much greater freedom of objectivist structure than such monolithic subjectivism would permit. The poem's *integritas* lies, instead, in its careful and delightful movement in both directions: outward until the subjective consciousness has 'dominated' all objects of its perception, *and* inward until the world observed expresses itself most richly in the selfhood of the persona. Moreover, these two movements meet, in effect, at the skin: at the blurred boundary of subject and object worlds; even as they transgress it. They permit a keen sense of self to emerge even as they work to render artistic selfhood permeable and vulnerable. Such a fusion of subject and object worlds in the media of the poem and of the poet's mind permits a spectacular freedom of imagistic movement and a fine interpenetration of conscious thought and delicate sense in the subjectivist Layton poem of the 1950s.

This model of Layton's sudden achievement explains, perhaps, the compelling quality of imagery that opens 'The Birth of Tragedy,' written in that remarkable summer of 1953:

And me happiest when I compose poems.
  Love, power, the huzza of battle
  are something, are much;
yet a poem includes them like a pool
  water and reflection.
In me, nature's divided things –
  tree, mould on tree –
  have their fruition;
I am their core. Let them swap,
bandy, like a flame swerve.
I am their mouth; as a mouth I serve.

(*WPJ*, p. 15)

It is hardly surprising, after the preceding commentaries, that this perhaps most canonical of Layton's poems opens with an immediate assertion of the 'me' and its practical identity with the spontaneous and continual composition of poetry: Layton's better personae have never thought the poem through before they begin to speak. The stanza proceeds by pointing out the ability of both 'a poem' and 'me' to contain apparently 'divided things'; hardly surprising, since in the sense Layton intends the poem and 'I' are one and the same force. The boy who in 'The Black Huntsmen' 'knew delight as water in a glass in a pool' finds his continuation here, in the intensely beautiful and true image of the 'pool' that is at one and the same time both water (object) and reflection (subject) of the poet's meditation. He is also, as we should by now expect, his own chief celebrant ('I am their core,' 'I am their mouth') and ironic commentator: 'as a mouth I serve.' 'And I *ob*serve' opens the second stanza but completes the thematic pattern of the first: the persona's intense observation of the objective world allows him to blend into it, indeed to become its core, while at the same time his 'compos[ing] poems' is the happy service he performs in return.

'The Birth of Tragedy' gathers up another of the threads spun in 'The Cold Green Element': the poet's welcome submission to the endless round of death and resurrection that infuses the world with which he is one. In the latter poem the idea surfaced in the cycle of the 'murdered selves,' the poet's simultaneous multiplicity of ego rendered as successively transcended incarnations. In 'The Birth of Tragedy' that broader process is figured in a single, brief fusion of life and death forces in the persona's being:

A quiet madman, never far from tears,
  I lie like a slain thing

under the green air the trees
inhabit, or rest upon a chair
towards which the inflammable air
tumbles on many robins' wings;
noting how seasonably
leaf and blossom uncurl
and living things arrange their death,
while someone from afar off
blows birthday candles for the world.

How easily the poet-persona slips from a condition in death to a point of still life, indeed the still centre of a world whose 'bandying' and 'swerving' energy moves perpetually towards *him*. The world is itself in that both/and, either/or[77] moment of life and death: and the poet (in at least one role) is the passive register of the world's life force and death passion. The celebration of the final image is not so much directed at the beauty of the poetic 'garden ... / of flowering stone' he has built, then, as it is at his ideal dissolution into that place's 'green air.' It is in such a self-losing union with the world, in its condition of perpetual birth and death, that the Layton persona's real complexity emerges. Those who imagine that his Nietzscheanism has given him little beyond a false sense of transcendence and *Übermensch* superiorism need to meditate further on this persistent self-ironization as 'madman,' 'slain thing,' and 'murdered selves,' to understand the forces that curtail *and* liberate the expansiveness of his personative egoism.

There seem grounds here for the identification of mid-1953 to mid-1954 as an *annus mirabilis* for Layton, but certainly not because he came in that year to a poetic structure and voice that he was to persist in throughout his maturity. Obviously the very principles I have discussed would militate against any fixed poetic consciousness upon which he was thenceforth to rely. The spontaneous accomplishment of 1953 has to be understood instead as specific to a season in which Layton was withdrawing from early-modernist and late-Imagist strictures, in the direction of a greater and more complex modernist subjectivism than Canadian poetry had so far witnessed. Five years later, at the time of his composition of 'Whatever Else Poetry Is Freedom,' for example, many of the pressing questions of that forties-to-fifties transition were not only answered, but answered so well that they had ceased to press in vitally on his structural imagination. Others could be comfortably theorized in abstract terms, rather than worked out reflexively in the very organization and consciousness of poems. By 1958, partly because of his own achievement to that time, the broad and persistent Imagist and objectivist pressure I have hypothesized for the forties was lifted, and while Layton never surrendered his penchant for startling and at times surreal juxtapositions of an imagined Nietzschean and a stifling objective world, he did turn away for the most part from the Image as fundamental constituent of poetic structure.

The subtlety of this turn is most clearly demonstrable in 'Whatever Else Poetry Is Freedom,' although other masterpieces of the late 1950s might serve as well, 'For Mao Tse-Tung: A Meditation on Flies and Kings,' for example. 'Whatever Else' certainly cannot be said to lack a splendid intensity and freshess of imagery:

And Time flames like a paraffin stove
And what it burns are the minutes I live.
At certain middays I have watched the cars
Bring me from afar their windshield suns;
What lay to my hand were blue fenders,
The suns extinguished, the drivers wearing sunglasses.
And it made me think I had touched a hearse.

(*WPJ*, pp. 65–6)

It is nevertheless true that the poem's images are significantly less fragmentary than those at the root of structure in the work of the early 1950s. Indeed, the poem is organized into stanzas, each of which develops and extends a central image in the direction of a sustained conceit; and although the effect of *stanzaic* juxtaposition is rich and disconcerting, it is clear that Layton is less concerned with the vortex of surrealist visuals now than with the use of images in the furtherance of abstract thought. The poet is much less concerned to represent the random and associative tendencies of his visual imagination, a habit we saw in its 1950s extreme in 'Composition in Late Spring': it is immediately evident, from the opening line, that he has a point to make, and the process of its revelation to his mind is not embodied self-reflexively in the motions of the text.

I have had the opportunity to develop elsewhere my intuition that 'Whatever Else Poetry Is Freedom' relies substantially on the figuration of a destructive audience for its ironic containment of the exuberant Layton persona.[78] In the present context I would want to suggest that the audience's impact is somewhat vitiating of the complex irony with which the speaker was handled in poems like 'The Cold Green Element.' Certainly there are as well the more familiar containing principles of the earlier work, the 'mist,' mortality, and 'paraffin stove' of 'Time' to which he had been subject ever since his personative voice had established itself; but the disdained audience offers a shallower curtailment of his egoism, and it invites a hardened scorn for the crucial limiting forces surrounding and defining that ego. It is perhaps too easy to mock the gapers whose admiration threatens to knock him off his stilts, the courtiers of Canute who set up 'the foolish trial' at the sea's edge. The risk here is a greater dismissiveness of the object-world's limitations on the poet and, in consequence, an egoism that goes less questioned, shades into egotism. If the complexity of subjective and objective exchange hardens into a me–them opposition, much will have been lost to Layton's poetry.

A more stimulating development is the opposition of 'crown' and 'clown' that emerges in the third stanza with the story of Canute and remains functional for the balance of the poem. The Canute legend is called up associatively by the persona's call for 'a crown ... for his buffoon's head,' a lovely evocation of Lear that plays on his distinct incarnations, his separable selves, as 'Lord' and clown. The poem's ability to hold these two identities in suspension throughout and thus predicate them as the inescapable doubled ground on which the poet must stand surely looms large in its sophistication and power. Still, I would want to contrast this very carefully posited and demonstrated 'theme' with what I have taken as a more *structural* principle of ironic containment in earlier poems. Whereas in 'Composition in Late Spring,' for example, the persona passes continually from a condition of revelation to a condition of error and mistakenness, and that vacillation has a containing and structural force in the rhythm and arrangement of the poem's image-cataloguing, in 'Whatever Else' a prior decision has been taken and philosophy sustained in which the alternation of error and vision has been theorized, to be demonstrated (as the validity of a metaphysical conceit might be demonstrated) in the poem's argument. This is at once a sign, I take it, of the earlier method's continued success and efficacy in the intervening years and of its diminishing function – its urgency now controlled, abstracted – in the poetry that lay ahead.

To return exclusively to matters of structure (for in a sense I have been arguing that elements having structural force and effect in the earlier poetry are here thematized into a reduced integrative purpose), the new poetics of 'Whatever Else Poetry Is Freedom' is hardly, the above notwithstanding, given over to a high degree of organization and lucidity. The poem remains baffling, dissonant, obscure to good readers, and I have heard many students' suggestions that there is little to choose for lucidity between this and 'The Cold Green Element.' But differences are clearly visible: in the greater regularity of rhythm and solidity of stanza, in the more restricted syntax. The point of the poems' greatest divergence, however, is also the point of their clearest continuity: in the extrapolation in 'Whatever Else' of 'Element's' celebration of the irrational, a principle that functioned earlier, as I have remarked, in a free-association of imagery replicating the density and vividness of the speaker's mind. We do not have in the 1958 poem a similar effort to reproduce the stream-like motions of consciousness: that modernist principle now seems distinctly in the past. Persistent, however, is the Nietzschean conviction that logical, coordinated argument – Socratism – is antipathetic to human growth and passion. Indeed, 'Whatever Else' flings down the gauntlet of aleatory 'proof' in the deliberate repetition of its declamatory opening line for the flat opening of its final stanza, with the powerful coordinator 'So' to introduce its second appearance. 'So' clearly suggests that something *has* been proved in the six stanzas intervening: it is a slap in the face of a reader who needs visible logic to be convinced of a philosophical truth. If we *are* convinced by the end, it is because a series of random narratives – not, I must repeat, random local images – has been accumulated with a single powerful truth resonant in the interstices among them. This principle of non-rational argument works analogously but not identically to the principle of *integritas* on which Layton had relied for the liberal governance of his earlier image-dense poetics: and there is, indeed, a similar free-associative principle afoot, as we leap from the poet's cry for a 'crown' to his memories of other 'unkingly' kings (Canute, Lear) who were likewise to be found in a condition of brilliant error.

'Whatever Else Poetry Is Freedom,' then, is of a period in Layton's growth distinct from that in which he first accomplished his estrangement from forties poetics. Its dynamism, its intuitions, and its structural freedom were nevertheless conditioned, not only by the brilliant work first truly emergent in 1953, but by his apprenticeship to the forties search for a route out of objectivist representation that would respond more fully to a world in economic, military, and spiritual crisis. No one would deny the claim, I imagine, that Layton's real poetic nature lay in the exploration and expression of the subject and of the ego; but the force of early-modernist prescription in the forties was clearly such that even so ebullient a creative personality would be constrained by it well into the following decade. I would want to argue, moreover, that his release from that objectivist constraint did not require an utter break from the impulses he necessarily inherited from Eliot, from Auden, from Thomas, and perhaps from Anderson and Page, and certainly from Klein, during his apprenticeship. His real forward movement – his real genius – was a response to the debates of poetic structure, of Imagist objectivism and the needed integrity of modern selfhood, that were so enervating and enlivening to the decade in which he first experienced an inescapable sense of vocation.

The Story So Far

Irving Layton's self-refashioning *circa* 1953 was determined in part, then, by his training in a decade particularly alert to problems of *integritas* in modernist poetics and increasingly aware of a fruitful metaphor linking the psychological and poetic organization of the fragments of artistic consciousness. In turn, his abrupt mastery in poems like 'The Cold Green Element' casts a needed rearward light on the little-known poetry he had written until that time. His 1950s turn to a complex subjective poetics with some of its bases in Imagist objectivity and Surrealist free association ought really to highlight for us the relative absence of such resonances in the prior accomplishment and invite our further examination of the principles in which his poetry was first nurtured. I have pursued that case here, to a point at which I hope the similarities between poetry of the *Preview* and of the *First Statement* camps are coming clear. These similarities pertain most powerfully, as is evident, to matters of deep poetic structure, to the Canadian modernist period's gradual transition (broadly speaking) from the fragmentation and surprise of the autonomous Image to the increasingly integrated and coherent lyric whose epistemology retained, nevertheless, some portion of Imagist prescription. In Layton's earliest poetry, furthermore, the similarity is also one of style: not only is his early poetry redolent of the manners of Eliot and Auden, his early diction distinctly mid-Atlantic if not nakedly Anglophile, but his early idea of how an image was to be made is very little distinct from the ideas of Page and of Anderson on the same score. They are, of course, associated with that image-manner, and Layton is not, primarily because he found it insufficient to his creative growth, whereas they found it so essential to their modernism that they held to it long after its stymying effect on their creativity had become apparent. But if we wish to speak of 'the forties,' that decade of Canadian literary advancement to which so many critics were once attracted, we really do have to speak of the three poets' common nurturing in an identifiable, and fairly narrow, poetic context.

For those who still want Layton's later originality to have been immediate and distinct to *First Statement*, the contrast with A.M. Klein rather than Anderson or Page would perhaps be more promising. Because Klein pursued the Page–Anderson image-manner more frankly (though briefly) and turned its catalogic force to a search for a coherent and trustworthy object-world in which his own pained selfhood might be restored through poetry, Layton appears even from the earliest days more self-arrested, more lyric and forward-looking than his friend. Still, their comparison has more fruitful matter to offer than this: their mutual desire, however differently pointed, to bring a needed subjectivist leaven to the early-modernist emphasis on objectivity and reportage. Again – as I have suggested from the outset – the answers arrived at by both men are far less interesting than the commonality of the questions they appear to have asked themselves. I have contended that the possible fusion of impersonality and subjectivity is a significant aesthetic exploration in most of Klein's forties work, from 'The Psalter of Avram Haktani,' through the (apparently) impersonal poems of *The Rocking Chair*, to the complex interplay of autobiography and self-objectification that takes place in *The Second Scroll*. At no point does Klein opt plainly for a subjectivist *integritas* as a means of synthesizing the bewildering whole of his own and his people's experience, for reasons I have hoped to make clear. His goal, instead, was an immediate objectivity that could take a deeper *integritas* from the exuberance of subjective perception, without merely slipping (a key modernist phobia) into the solipsism of lyric expression.

The terms I have used of Klein are not ill-fitting for Layton's apprenticeship decade. His early impersonality and post-Imagist accumulative aesthetics make plain the power of the poetic prescriptions and proscriptions that were functional for Klein, and even his early efforts at personation show a drift towards the histrionic that suggests, ironically, how stringent a taboo he sensed he was breaking. There is indeed little in that early poetry that will alert us to the substantially superior poet of a few years later, and no doubt the suddenness of his emergence speaks to the continued weakening of such aesthetic dogma in the years of upheaval following the end of the war. Klein, of course, was unable to partake of the new atmosphere, the boundaries between subjectivity and objectivity having been sadly rewritten for him by 1953, that same year in which Layton was to find his consistent mastery. It is persistently tempting to imply a greater connection between Klein's mental collapse and the new assertiveness of selfhood in Layton's poetry: to imagine that assertiveness as compensatory, a kind of redoubled energy of constitutive ego in subliminal response to a friend's self-effacement and silencing. But on what sort of evidence might we be convinced of a causal relation between the two coincidentally timed events in the poets' personal histories? Lacking methodological precedent, I keep Klein's story in mind as an obverse metaphor in my attempt to detail the sudden flourishing of ironic egoism in Layton's poetics.

Readers will, I hope, have taken for granted the most patent differences between Layton's style and the manner of these three of his colleagues. He showed from the start a greater delight in the immediate architecture of his ghetto childhood than in the equally true, merely less immediate, landscapes of Page; he was early on much more attracted by a crude bohemian diction, the 'stinks,' 'women staling,' 'stained bacilli,' 'hemorrhoids,' and 'chlorotic gums' of the poems discussed earlier, than by Anderson's far less bawdy slanginess. And a survey of his distance from Klein might begin with the near-absence of Jewish allusion and reference in his early poetry and move on to consider Klein's persistent (albeit often underlying) civility of tone and mood. I would hardly want to suppress the truth of these obvious distinctions, though it is true that I consider such matters of diction and setting more atmospheric than substantive in the present critical consideration. The deeper unity of challenge, struggle, and resolution among these poets, though it is so much a matter of structure and though we have not had much time in recent years to consider the nature of Canadian poetic structure and its relation to epistemology and perception, strikes off to me a more telling narrative of the period in which they were first broadly acclaimed, the period which for Layton alone of those so far considered was a preparatory ground of sustained, of stunning, advancement in the new literary contexts of the 1950s.

4

Forties Continuations: Dudek's Long Poems and the Period Style

Dudek's Generation

At the historical heart of the Canadian 1940s, but in England, Alex Comfort penned these polemic remarks for *Art and Social Responsibility: Lectures on the Ideology of Romanticism* (1946): 'The romantic recognises a perpetual struggle upon two levels, the fight against Death which I have described, and the struggle against those men and institutions who ally themselves with Death against humanity, the struggle against barbarism.'[1] Few of the Canadian poets of that decade would identify so unambiguously as had Comfort with Romantic tradition, although, as we have seen, Irving Layton admitted in 1943 the exemplary force of an emergent neo-Romanticism, the New Apocalypse, in British poetry: 'Men have begun to dream again, but this time with only one eye shut: the other eye is carefully focussed on the doings of their rulers. Romanticism, yes, but within the context of the machine age and power politics.'[2] Layton's *proviso* was typical. An anonymous correspondent to *First Statement* similarly praised the magazine's latent Romanticism but noted that 'our romanticism is the sort over whose eyes nobody is going to pull any wool.'[3] Comfort's prose lacks entirely these Canadian hesitations. For him Romanticism had returned full force in the early 1940s, in the context of a war that made the battle between vitality and 'Death' the whole point of poetic expression.

Louis Dudek would no doubt be the last to endorse this Romantic purchase on forties poetic innovation, despite the naturalism, lyricism, and occasional sentimentalism of his own work in that decade. Raymond Souster, too, we have been taught to see (largely by the fine criticism of Frank Davey on the two) in a tradition of minimalism and self-effacement in clear opposition to the self-authorization that Comfort finds in the British neo-Romantics.

Dudek, Souster, *and* Layton, however, can all be caught in the descriptive force of his polemic. The broad strokes of Comfort's language make it easy to read the life's work of each Canadian as a struggle against mortality: their own deaths, no doubt; but against the worldly troops of Death, particularly against those individuals, or corporations, or states, or artists who work for sterility and anonymity to the cost of humankind. Layton has been taken for a barbarian himself (first of all by Dudek, of course); nevertheless, both he and Dudek have persistently construed themselves as the last sentinels at the barricades, calling out imprecations against the uncouth hordes who come to violate human liberty, imagination, and power. The sense of having been called alone to arms, of a responsibility to live *and write* an exemplary life against a swelling barbarism, is powerful in each – and a typical vocation, Comfort says, of the poet schooled in the forties. Souster has less of the ego needful for these battles: but Davey nevertheless insists that he, too, 'has usually associated poetry with "prolife" forces – with spontaneity, biological process, love and fertility; [while] he classes those who would bind poetry into inherited forms with the "antilife" forces – with war, business, the academies and death.'[4] The language is strikingly akin to Comfort's.

Layton, Dudek, and Souster – the '3 headed beast'[5] of *Cerberus* in 1952 – were spoken of very early on as the significant poets to emerge from the *First Statement* cadre. John Sutherland's 1946 introduction to *Other Canadians* first construed the poets as a trio for their 'more Canadian point of view, a greater interest in themes and problems of a Canadian kind, and a social realism which distinguishes [their work] from the political make-believe of other poets.'[6] We know enough by now to doubt the critical disinterestedness of Sutherland's *First Statement*–centralizing triumvirism. Certainly his emphasis on the poets' Canadianism is undermined by Souster's and Dudek's later break with him on this very point of a nationalist criticism;[7] but the effect of a united three-man front he wanted has been persistent, even in the face of Dudek's open and running conflict with Layton during and after the late 1950s.

Such exaggerated unison was in part their own creation. Davey quotes a letter from Dudek to Souster (18 May 1955) that makes plain the *First Statement* trio's flair for self-promotion (and its inevitable corollary, devaluation of rivals):

> It will have to come to be realized, I don't know when, that what counts in poetry in this country from 1940–1960 or so is yourself, Layton, and I. Smith & Scott are very thin predecessors ... Page & Anderson really don't count ... Klein had failed. All of them are very nice, mind you, and good to have around; but the real trail is the one we blazed ... (qtd. in Davey, p. 23)

The broad dissemination of this self-interested polemic has been insufficiently remarked, though Canadian criticism *is* becoming more reactive to the unfair devaluation of Page and Anderson, stated nakedly here but still functional a dozen years later when Michael Gnarowski joined Dudek in selecting the documents pertinent to the making of Canadian modern poetry.[8] Gnarowski has since cast useful doubt on some components of the trio's self-mythicizing, notably demonstrating that 'by the standards of those days [the 1940s and '50s] Dudek and Souster could not really complain that they had been ignored, and it was only Layton who had a grievance against the established publishers.'[9] Davey remarks of the three that 'as a group they needed not only to establish a mythology in which they appeared as leaders of art and poetry against the forces of materialism and corruption but also to establish themselves as major poets' (p. 22). Note again in Davey's language the neo-Romantic premises of Comfort; of course, such gestures of self-aggrandizement are as common with young poets as wasted ink.

The more immediate limitations of the *Cerberus* myth for my purposes are its real irrelevance to the forties – given Souster's distance from Montreal, Dudek's residence in New York from 1944 to 1951, Layton's time in Petawawa and Nova Scotia, a minimal correspondence to overcome such distances, not to mention Dudek's first rupture with Layton from 1947 to 1952 – and its tendency to cast up critical polarities of the two-against-one kind. This impulse is of course badly contaminated by the severity and publicity of Dudek's breaks with Layton in 1947 and by 1959: it is awkward indeed to imagine at this point a study of *their* affinities, although what follows is intended in part to suggest the need for one. On the contrary, it appears that the *Cerberus* trio breaks down into an abiding distinction between Layton on the one hand and Dudek and Souster on the other. This is partly a consequence of ill-adjudicated fame: surely one motive for Frank Davey's pairing in *Louis Dudek & Raymond Souster* was an acute sense of their neglect by critics who had shown (and at its appearance in 1980 were continuing to show) considerably more attention to Layton, their contemporary and fellow.

In the course of his exemplary study, Davey offers broad grounds for the linkage of Dudek and Souster, and often enough these imply the pair's distance from Layton on comparable issues. Davey finds a profound distaste for the commodification of poetry and the arts to bind Dudek to Souster, and he sees in both poets an attraction to minimalism as a counter to the 'commodity fetishism' of poetry (pp. 137, 129). These remarks contrast Davey's view of Layton, one of a number of poets 'openly inviting a popular response to their work'; Layton's 'bombastic rhetoric and sensational opinions' run harsh counter to the minimalist currents of Dudek's and Souster's development in the 1950s (p. 126). Davey is sure enough of the soundness of his critical couple to give partial attention to the inarguable matters of distinction between Dudek and Souster: for example, Dudek's rationalism as against Souster's intuitionalism, Dudek's 'large historical view of literature' as against Souster's lack of one (pp. 98, 103). These details are usually taken by Davey as signs of deeper affinity, though, as when he reads Souster's 'preference for a colloquial, spontaneous, undecorated poetry' as 'an unsophisticated version of Dudek's "functional poetry" thesis' (p. 103).

The Dudek–Souster pairing is maintained by a tradition of Layton–Dudek polarization that is hard to overcome. Wynne Francis remarks Dudek's growing respect for the academic tradition as a major source of tension and distinction between him and Layton.[10] Elspeth Cameron cites a number of reasons for Layton's envy and the friendship's subsequent breakdown: among them Dudek's gradual rejection of Marxism under the tutelage of Lionel Trilling at Columbia, his wide network of American literary contacts, his academic and professional establishment by 1951, his prominent alignment with Souster thereafter.[11] Such sharp lines of contest, especially once hardened into scurrilous ridicule by Layton in the 'Open Letter to Louis Dudek' of 1962, would seem to make hay out of any attempt to realign Dudek and Layton. Dudek himself, though, has been willing to see the affinities of endeavour between himself and Layton, remarking, for example, that his and Layton's contributions were the most characteristic of *First Statement*.[12] But the Dudek–Layton affinity is all but invisible now, Davey seeming to have established the commonality with Souster once and for all; and little enough work on either poet has followed his binding them.

Layton and Dudek are nonetheless linked at a number of points crucial to their poetic characters: by their mutual elitism, for instance, a quality that will need no substantiation in Layton, and that has received repeated acknowledgment from Dudek: 'Oh, I damn well am an elitist!', he growled at Michael Darling in an interview of 1975, obviously impatient with any interlocutor who thinks the term pejorative.[13] Dudek and Layton share as well a powerful vision of the ateleological and Heraclitean nature of time and human development, though this claim runs counter to Davey's conviction that Dudek believes in 'the linear growth of human culture and civilization' (p. 94). (Comfort is instructive: he posits that for the forties neo-Romantic 'history, in so far as it is the history of power, is not to be regarded as a steady progress in any direction, whether moral or political, e.g., towards civilisation, goodness, socialism, but as an oscillation about a fixed point, a series of self-limiting ecological changes.')[14] Certainly the two are powerfully connected by their common revulsion for 'barbarism,' an instinct Comfort associates with his decade's forced *anagnorisis* of humankind's potential for evil.[15] They do not respond similarly (Layton meeting savagery and ignorance with his own 'barbaric yawp' learned from Whitman,[16] while Dudek seeks an ever-more powerful vocalization of his own cultural convictions), but their common alertness to the negation of grace and compassion in their contemporaries is an inescapable sign of their elitist sympathies, as of their mutual sense of modernity's 'fragile tenure' (in John Glassco's phrase) among civilizations. I will not endeavour to make plain the ambivalent aestheticism of Dudek's cultural responses nor Layton's persistent responsiveness to Decadence, though my remarks on Dudek's long poems will adumbrate a longing for beauty that suggests another current in the flow of cultural ideals between him and Layton.

Conversely, a number of these grounds of affinity between Layton and Dudek work to their joint distinction from Souster, who shares little of their elitism, or admits to little of it, and nothing of their legacy from Aestheticism; although he clearly shares their pessimistic purchase on modernity, he can do little to articulate it within the constraints of his minimalist and anti-intellectualist poetics. Souster's unrelenting persistence with a derivative of social realism and lyricism will also have to be recognized for a point of stark distinction from Dudek and Layton, both of whom had to reject their social-realist aesthetic education in order to move forward as poets. Finally, and the thesis here, Dudek would attain in the course of the 1950s and 1960s a radical new poetics fusing the objectivism of late-Imagist reportage with a subjectivist reliance on the shifting boundaries of selfhood as a basis for poetic order, coherence, and resonance; in doing so, he necessarily joined Layton, whose project was similar whatever the gestural differences of his method, and withdrew tellingly from Souster, whose avoidance of such questions throughout his career has led numerous commentators to observe how little Souster's poetry has changed from its incarnation in the forties to the present day.[17]

In suppressing such nuances, our persistent version of a forties literary history dependent on little-magazine narratives has been at fault. If we are judging cases solely on affiliation with this or that little magazine, Dudek and Souster will inarguably have to stay gratuitously conjoined, not only for their highly mutual work on *Contact* from 1952 to 1954, but for their symptomatic redirections of *First Statement* as well. Norris's claim that Dudek's and Layton's poetry most clearly distinguished that magazine from *Preview*[18] is severely problematized, to say the least, by the affinities now apparent between Layton's apprenticeship poetics and the supposed *Preview* manner. On the contrary, it was largely in the affection for lyric, attempted casualness of diction and tone, and willing traditionalism of Dudek and Souster that *First Statement* made any mark independent of the powerful styles of Page, Anderson, and Klein. Whereas Layton would come to explore their later-Modernist styles only in the early-1950s climax of his artistic maturation, Dudek and Souster were distinctive from their earliest contributions to the magazine.

Suppose we opt, then, *contra* Norris but keeping to his basic tactic, for a reading of *First Statement* characterized not by Layton's and Dudek's, but by Dudek's and Souster's poetry (perhaps desiring to stabilize and eternalize Davey's pairing of the latter two). We might shore up this claim by noting that *First Statement* only really went after *Preview* once Dudek came on board: essays such as 'Geography, Politics and Poetry' and 'Poets of Revolt? Or Reaction?' contain the most inflammatory gestures against the rival magazine, Sutherland's prior polemics having had a distinctly cautious, even bashful, quality. Dudek was a chief exacerbator of *First Statement*'s differences with *Preview,* and when we return to his poetry's eclectic divergence from prevailing forties practice and bring it into focus alongside Souster's even more idiosyncratic and eccentric lyricism, it is highly tempting to make statements about *First Statement* in general based on their individual and particular contributions.

Let's throw off, though, little-magazine *parti-pris,* and consider the three poets of *Cerberus* without these predicates. Souster contributed no prose statement whatsoever to the *Preview–First Statement* squabble: it was a local antagonism, perhaps somewhat unreal to the lonely young poet in the Maritime barracks. Layton, on the other hand, did have a role in the attack on *Preview,* as his 'Politics and Poetry' has already made plain: in that, *he* is Dudek's more obvious confrère. All three would become estranged from Sutherland in time, Dudek so much so that, as Terry Goldie puts it, he 'has always emphasized the limitations of his involvement with [*First Statement*] ...'[19] and indeed remarks his sense of having been neglected by his affiliate magazine and press.[20] Souster, on the other hand, *was* published by First Statement Press, even though his editorial involvement with *First Statement* itself was negligible. And if Layton has just been correctly characterized for his 1940s attraction to the manner thus far associated with *Preview* rather than with *First Statement,* and if Sutherland's own poetry can be shown (as I have tried in the introduction) to reflect none of the neo-Romanticism of later forties styles, does it remain meaningful to speak of Dudek's and Souster's voices as 'characteristic' of *First Statement*? Can two poets, practically alone in their distinct innovations, accurately characterize a little magazine that published dozens of others, albeit with less regularity? Out of all of these entanglements, are there any distinct qualities we would still wish to associate with *First Statement*, in clear opposition to *Preview*, and in special anticipation of the changes that lay ahead in the 1950s? We do best, on the contrary, to conceptualize little magazines not as the bearers of new standards of vision, but as vehicles for understandably self-interested poets whose individual affinities and antagonisms are personally motivated, not inherent in or essential to the periodicals in which they happened to publish themselves.

Dudek's attainment of a sophisticated subjective poetics in the 1950s, with roots in Imagist juxtaposition and maintaining the force of ironic personation as a principle of coherence, has to do, I believe, with his eclectic and responsive formal imagination in the forties. His interest in the possibilities of Page's and Anderson's poetics is visible in numerous poems, from the *First Statement* years to the end of his first major period in 1952, although his concomitant pursuit of lyric in the same period would prevent any complete affiliation with the dominant poetics of the stereotypical *Preview*. Although he pursued these matters of poetic change with relatively little apparent attention to the deeper issues of *integritas* that were increasingly stifling to Page, the dramatic developments in his poetry from 1953 on depended largely on his providing answers to the forties conundra that converged in her silence by 1954 – notwithstanding his *First Statement* affiliation and his work's relative distance from her manner. Souster, by way of clarification and contrast, passed through the forties without once dabbling in the available manner of his contemporaries. His lyric devotion was entire, and he appears to have had no interest in aesthetic debates from whose articulation both he and his poetics were remote. I take his severe distance from dramatic issues of poetic transition in the Canadian forties to be in keeping with his poetry's failure to move forward in any significant formal way in the 1950s or thereafter: he was never to develop the more complex models of personation, nor was he ever to attain the post-Imagist structural complexity, that made of Dudek's 1950s work one of the pivotal accomplishments of Canadian modern poetry.

I will not hope to prove that some negotiation with the poetics that were more clearly dominant in *Preview* than in *First Statement* was *necessary* to a poet's growth and significance in the movement forward from the 1940s. I will continue to claim, though, that the aesthetic challenges faced by Page, Klein, Anderson, and Layton were the deepest issues of poetic change at the time of Dudek's apprenticeship. I take it that no poet of substance can ignore such profound and general matters of contemporary poetic innovation and retain his or her hold on our critical or readerly imaginations for long; which is why, in my view, Dudek's growth into a profound and important poet, to say the least, coincided with an extended consideration of the questions of poetic structure and voice that had been critical to his first decade of publication. This view allows us to place Dudek and Layton as the two most significant poets of *Preview* or of *First Statement* to move steadily beyond the forties, into a period of creative dynamism whose terms were, inevitably, configured by a decade of aesthetic debate they both welcomed.

Dudek's poetic practice was moreover exemplary for later generations of poets, and it is ironically he, who looks at first so little like a forties poet in his poems of the 1940s, who suggests most clearly a trajectory from the troubled poetic generation of Page and Klein to the late modernism and postmodernism of George Bowering, Davey himself, and Robert Kroetsch. While it is true that Layton's example was also powerful for a later, more circumscribed, group of poets in the 1960s and 1970s, only Dudek can help us chart the full formal implications of forties poetic debate, as they filtered along the deltas of his own long poems. For such reasons this final chapter in a descriptive formal history of Canadian poetry in the forties will begin idiosyncratically with a close look at Dudek's long poem of the 1980s, the *Continuations* that respond more fully and with more probity to the difficulties of poetic transition in his apprenticeship decade than any other work in the half-century since. From there I mean to follow Dudek backward to the forties, in a final contention of that decade's durable impact on the fields of later Canadian poetry.

Continuation I: The Sublimated Egoist

> In the case of poetry, there can be no poet's voice, no mimesis of a man thinking, that can be the exact equivalent of a human voice, or an exact replica of someone thinking. We can only give an ever more convincing imitation of that kind of thing. And the poem is only art if it is aware of this distinction.[21]

The critic's task in these primordial days of Dudek scholarship is partly descriptive, few having read his *Continuations* volumes, fewer still having written about them, and most of those the original reviewers. It is suggestive that a poem in which the status of the speaking ego is so much at question should be received with a critical indifference that has made Dudek's formal self-effacement a matter of his reception as well. Davey reassures us that Dudek has taken a courageous high road, whereon the poet affirmed himself indifferent to the fame or ignorance with which he was greeted by others (p. 81). My own reading of Dudek's appetite for popular and favourable response is slightly more cynical and less idealizing than Davey's. *Continua-*

tion I is acutely aware of its implicit audience's lack of interest, and the speaker projects in and among his fragments a mood of resignation, even haplessness, in response to 'the twentieth-century game of fame' (*cf.* Michael Ondaatje's Buddy Bolden) that he also assaults so bitterly. In this context of inattention to Dudek it seems reasonable to begin in a chiefly descriptive mode: what is this long poem attempting, and to what extent do we accord it success in its goals?

'So let's continue,' Dudek[22] remarks by way of brief invocation. This opening *in medias res* invites us to contemplate projects or aesthetics of Dudek's past that are to be carried on here, as well as to consider the work to hand as premised somehow upon the whole idea of 'continuing.' The first suggestion I will pursue later, in remarks on *Europe* and *Atlantis*; it is the second, the idea of a radical new poetics, that subsequent lines engage immediately. The term 'continuation' quickly slips into new meanings as we read on: as 'These vast accumulations / not without reason, that may have a use / or none' (p. 11) suggest, the implication of 'continuity' in *Continuations* is questioned immediately, in an alternate emphasis on a haphazard gathering up of fragments, whose continuity – implication and relevance backward or forward – will not be clear. Dudek's resignation to a poetics of accumulation is particularly resonant in the present context, I imagine, given the aesthetics of accumulation that finds its most formalist expression in Page's poetry and governs both ego *and* poetic form in the poetry of Klein and of Layton from the 1940s and 1950s. The line of inheritance from Page's late-Imagist helplessness in 'After Rain' to Dudek's accumulative resignations is not clear, but may become so as we work backward through the latter's career.

The accumulative premises of *Continuations* are also one of the poem's more persistent themes. They are praised later on this opening page as offering 'a language / to contain the essentials that matter, in all the flux of illusion.' The lines suggest the high stakes of Dudek's attempt as well as its philosophical suppositions: 'the flux of illusion' underscores the Heraclitean sense of time and space – and I will contend, of ego – that governs Dudek's aesthetic innovations. 'Accumulation' in fact quickly supersedes 'continuation' as the paradigm of poetic structure here: later, in a typical gesture of self-effacement and refusal of significance, Dudek remarks, 'to accumulate lines, is not that a pleasure? / To weave them into patterns, / is not that happiness?' (p. 13),[23] and later still he cries 'Accumulate, accumulate!' to swerve from a contemplation of the poet's nature ('One of God's handymen') to the poetic context that vitiates that nature: 'These industrial wastes, and the land we live in / ... with objectivity so hard to attain, and yet who wants it? / We put our pieties on paper' (p. 14).

The slippage from *continuation* to *accumulation* is striking. 'Continuation' implies a greater degree of linearity, or at least a greater awareness of past and future, lines written and lines in contemplation; 'accumulation,' the larger category from which the subset 'continuation' derives, is a refutation of arrangement in which 'adding to' is the point, not necessarily 'expanding on' or 'persisting with.' The poem's title, then, invokes situation, placement, whereas its functional term in the opening pages invokes mere contiguity. This contrast is analogous to the operative distinction in the Dudek passage I placed as epigraph to this section. There, Dudek acknowledges that his new species of poetic composition must still achieve 'art,' and that its doing so will depend upon a self-reflexive consciousness of the boundary between the *reality* and the *representation* of the poetic mind. 'Continuation' bespeaks Dudek's sense that we can indeed 'give an ever more convincing imitation' of mind: we gradually narrow the gap between representation and reality by comparing our past with our better present representations. 'Accumulation,' on the other hand, suggests a formal anxiety in this regard: that we do not in fact make forward progress in representing the mind, that we cannot *capture* mind's dance of meaning and incoherence without losing the awareness of the gap that makes 'art.'

Apart from their echo of Stephen Dedalus's view that the *integritas* of a work of art gives it 'selfbounded[ness],' distinctness from the object-world it represents, Dudek's remarks centre our attention on the parallels between the poetic structure of the *Continuations* and the structures of mentality that are chief among his objects of representation. Indeed it is evident that the same dualism is functional here, as it was for Klein and Layton, for mental as for aesthetic structures: in effect the poem asks, is the energy of mind 'continuous' (does it accrete meaning steadily onto an ever-expanding whole) or merely 'accumulative' and random? If the latter, what am 'I' who exist only in this discontinuous and fragmented form? Then: how might 'I' use poetic form – itself dangerously bifurcated on these same two principles – to represent mind in that indeterminate condition? *Continuation I* has much to say on subjects as diverse as Muzak and the number of atoms in the universe, but it is this relation between the principle of accumulation and the mind's desire for representation and continuity that should concern us chiefly at the far end of Dudek's career.

The accumulative, random, and juxtapositive poetics of *Continuations* constitute, I feel, the most highly fragmented and potentially incoherent of all Canadian long poems (Nichol's *Martyrology* not excepted; even the latter title tells us of a coordinating symbolism that Dudek's offhand title cavalierly refutes). The intensity of fragmentation in the poem is best observed, though the method is mundane, in the sheer brevity and number of poetic units accumulated: in 49 pages of text, Dudek displays 501 fragments of poetry, their 'continuity' with other fragments functioning only locally, and often even that degree of coherence denied them. I have counted, in effect, stanzas: units of verse without internal lines left blank to effect stanzaic rupture. Within these 'stanzas,' of course, fragmentation is also enforced: the predominantly aligned left-hand margin is sometimes ignored as words skim across the page to a right-hand, or medial, alignment; internal ellipses, parentheses, and dashes underscore sudden voltas within fragments. There is, however, a clear analogy implied between each unit of verse in the poem and units of mental activity, despite these internal tensions. A line left blank, enforcing fragmentation, always indicates a shift of some kind in the act of attention being recorded, even if a paradigmatic subject is maintained; very few units of thought, however ephemeral or indefinite, are allowed to end in a blank line without some kind of completion, whether by syntactic, epigrammatic, or imagistic closure. So the randomness we grant to poetic structure in *Continuations* is early on seen to reflect an interpretation of mental structure as well.

These (so far purely structural) effects of fragmentation and incoherence find resonance in the discursive and perceptual range and occasional obscurity of reference that functions in and among the units of verse as well. That the poem records a perceptual world like the poet's may be taken as a given: we see references to the life of literary criticism, to a multilingual and nationalist metropolis, to a 'Miss Collins' (presumably Aileen Collins, editor of *CIV/n* and Dudek's wife), and so on. These references create intimacy in the poem and anchor us firmly in the poet's experience, denying as they do any mediation between his experience and that of the speaking voice. The poet's local world, then, is offered as one possible perimeter for the energy of reference here. But the discourses of *Continuations* are hardly limited to the speaker's implied perceptual relation to his object-world. In recording the content of his own mind, he invokes the *données* of (among other disciplines) economics, astrophysics, aesthetics, epistemology, politics (especially Canadian), history, medicine, eschatology, optics, and journalism. Listed so blandly, the range of Dudek's references in the poem sounds manageable; returned to their emergence in fragments, these bodies of allusion promote difficulty, even obscurantism, and pull hard against the poem's chances of coherence and continuity:

> 'Sorry, I'm not a talker'
> A writer, not a talker
> (refuse all interviews, recordings, radio or TV)

In the twentieth century
the scientists were inventing anti-matter
while the humanists were inventing anti-life
One hurt in love loves no one,
Yet a bird is like a vital child

Do you have to relive through your son
all that you have suffered in youth?

Life is the great communion we share
Messiah became a simple man

Cordilla said to her quarreling lovers
'I cannot be divided, but I can be shared'

(p. 23)

The passage is clearly baffling if we ask for reasons for its arrangement, if we seek an aesthetic principle that tells us why one idea or image precedes another instead of following it. We may contend that a demand for such answers constitutes a limited response to Dudek's poetics, that we are prepared to be baffled, but what is a 'poem' if not an arrangement of words published in a certain order or disorder constitutive of meaning and affect? The poem demands, and I mean that its structurally arrogant poetics demands, an aggressive readership prepared to take vigorous mental action in response to such gestures.

Dudek's aphoristic, epigrammatic, and allusive propensities do not make the task any easier. Indeed the volume *Epigrams* that appeared six years before *Continuation I* may be taken as a lower-level staging ground for the principles of accumulation that reach their fruition in the later poem. There is little to choose in style, for example, between 'When the hypochondriac is sick he is twice as sick' (*Epigrams*)[24] and 'There's nothing wrong with God that a little atheism won't cure' (*Continuation I*, p. 15) that is not attributable to the effect of versification. Dudek may have written that '[e]pigrams are not the same as poems, you can't write a long epigram,'[25] but he also insisted that '[e]pigrams are one-line poems. A lot of them together are like a long poem.'[26] The half-contradiction can best be resolved if we agree to be more interested in the process of Dudek's mind than in the consistency of its results. His tendency to epigrammatic form – with its strongly projected closure and self-sufficiency – is very evident in *Continuation I*, in part because these philosophical one-liners contribute forcefully to a reader's awareness of the poem's moving forward on chiefly accumulative terms. The clever turn of phrase cuts off momentum; *Continuation I* pauses at a seeming, even false, conclusion; then it begins again, its disjointedness continually reaffirmed.

The poem's casual deployment of quotation and allusion has an analogous aleatory effect. Rifling through the pages, one will see a number of lines set off in quotation marks, as well as one long, apparently quoted passage – a parody of *Macbeth* V, v, 19–28 – indented and set in smaller type (p. 20). The intertextuality of these moments is disconcerting, especially if we have been breezing through a reading of the poem on the assumption that it is (as one of the quoted passages suggests ironically) 'a record of [the poet's] mind' (p. 33). If the quotations are exact, the illusion of mental process is troubled by it, for the exactness bespeaks scholarship, not the stream of consciousness. If the quotations are inexact, their placement in quotation marks is odd, for their misquotation makes them more truly the intellectual property of Dudek than of the original, now suppressed author who sparked his imagination. If quotation marks indicate not famous words, but overheard remarks from the 'outside' world, stream of consciousness can continue untroubled; but some of these passages are clearly literary rather than public in source. And if, finally, the passages quoted do not pre-exist at all? Dudek teases us with this possibility: 'You know, Eliot put quotations around lines we might recognize / I put some around a few / I thought too good as coming from me' (p. 15). Not then lines quoted from other poets, but lines the excellence of which embarrasses the self-effacing poet (but whose setting off in quotation marks, after this confession, emphasizes his great ability). The ambiguity of textual judgment in which we are placed contributes forcefully to the poem's drive towards incoherence and disorder. In the tradition of Eliot's *The Waste Land*, the fragments 'shored against' Dudek's 'ruins' do more to destabilize voice and referentiality in his long poem than to make it coherent in a literary or historical context; and Dudek provides no footnotes.

Missed quotations are the least of the reader's worries. Dudek's characteristically cryptic habit of allusion, intertextual reference without quotation marks, is signalled early on by a fragment on the first page: 'And the stratifications of silence / as Wayson S Choy put it, / the mute affirmations of space' (p. 11). Let us suppose a reader no more broadly educated than myself, who reads the line in utter ignorance of the identity of Wayson S. Choy.[27] What are the consequences of my ignorance, and what action is called for in response? First of all, the prominent notification of allusion is a red herring of sorts, for the fragment's phrases are not so much functional in the sense Choy gave them as in the poet's sense, to be activated in the imaginative reader's mind as metaphors. We can proceed, then, to connect 'stratifications' with 'silence' and 'mute affirmations' with 'space' (especially with our training in Imagist interpretation, which the *Continuations* poet tends to assume we have) and arrive at some functional *pro tem* meaning. In doing so we accord value and significance to even the most transitory and random of fragments from the speaker's consciousness, seeking to make them coherent, or at least as coherent as the consciousness which has, perhaps indifferently, cast them up. We are looking for common mental ground with the mind addressing us, and trying to fill in enough of its knowledge and habits that we may grasp the coherence of the infinite particulars and actions it appears ready to record. Reading *Continuations* is in this sense an act of portraiture, a drawing out of Dudek's personality from its own adumbrated archive.

The critical act of portraiture is difficult, though, and I do not want too readily to minimize the challenge with which we are faced by Dudek's poem. The coherence of these fragments remains, after long effort and much study, rather bewildering, even if we proceed so far as to chart recurrent ideas, note repeated imagery, measure variations in tone and so on; indeed, I would argue that to work in such a positivist manner, however briefly useful, would bring us no closer to the actual depth of experience available to us in *Continuations*. Certainly many of Dudek's familiar ideas are here (the rage against post-modern barbarism, the anti-commercialism, the curious blend of aestheticism and anti-aestheticism that is so characteristic of his mind), but just as many fragments point to new or alien conceptions we cannot safely neutralize as typical of Dudek, and so many others point to private or intimate experience that a simple response to *Continuations* as the embodiment in fragments of Dudek's consciously held *ideas* will prove shallow. This is not, finally, a poetry of ideas; it is certainly less 'functional' than the poetry Dudek called for in his *Delta* 'Proposal' of 1959.[28]

So, lacking a stable symbolism, a narrative or even narrative perspective, a consistent theme, a particular inquiry, the reader of *Continuation I* must accept one primary critical task: the discovery of some basis upon which to consider Dudek's poem sound, to consider it indeed *one poem*, under a single title, rather than 501 fragments. The title suggests that a complete suspension of the critical instinct for order would be inapt, or inept: something is 'continuing' throughout the whole and we should naturally wish to identify it. A surrender to utter flux in the poem would cheat Dudek of such minor gestures of rhythm, structure, provisional closure, and continuity as he has indeed planted – and of deeper forms of collectivity as well. On the other hand, it's clear that the identification of any grand foundational theme for the poem – the key, as it were, that would reveal the book's deep and pervasive coherence – would do the perhaps greater damage of subverting Dudek's accomplishment of a profound fragmentation and instability. Any claims we make for the poem's 'unity,' therefore, will have to derive from a model or cognate structure in which coherence is equally complex – but equally needful. 'It is still as lyric that the imagist long poem succeeds,' Dudek had claimed a year before *Continuation I* appeared, and the remark was partly self-critical.[29] The *Continuations* project is itself coherent – and only so – as a representation of the motion of content and phenomena in the poet's mind; specifically in Louis Dudek's mind, for the particularity of its references allows no other personality to materialize.

Adopting 'mind' as a principle of structural coherence for *Continuations* has the advantage of establishing singularity and *integritas* for this otherwise incoherent project, without the disadvantage of imposing a reductive model of 'unity' on a long poem that very apparently wants to flout or at least go beyond established forms of modernist poetic unity. Since the mind is at once one thing with which we may negotiate and an infinitude of fluctuating and unstable particulars, identifying the representation of mind as the Dudek project here respects both of the poem's thrusts: its centrifugal drive towards incoherence and randomness ('accumulation' in pure form) and centripetal drive towards order and stability (the desired 'continuation'). (That Klein's distinction of 'centrifugal' and 'centripetal' poetry is so tempting suggests how steeped this double thrust of Dudek's poetics is in forties intuitions of poetic order.) The duality in the constitutive metaphor of mind and poetics is available because of the accumulative principle maintained, for the most part with great rigour, in Dudek's poem. Had the poem's will-to-order exceeded its will-to-accumulate, tension would be lost and the credibility of its representation of mind would dissipate. To the extent possible in referential language, mind is not narrated in *Continuations*, but enacted. The energy of mental structure is processive and anti-causal: mind, yanked free of context, displays itself in pre-narrative form, an effect made possible only by the fragmentation and indirection of his modernist poetics.

Dudek alludes intermittently to his representation of consciousness in the volume: such references are often ironic and never harden into theory. Typical is the incorporated sarcasm of an unnamed interlocutor who says, halfway through the *Continuations* project, 'I don't want your fake poems / I want a record of your mind' (p. 33). The interjection is carefully distanced from the mental fragments surrounding it, placed as it is within quotation marks, parentheses, and its own stanza: Dudek has been at pains to mark off a separate voice, though the target of the quoted statement remains as indistinct as its speaker. Although it is possible that the interlocutor's demand was incorporated only to be ridiculed, he or she nevertheless spoke to the central question of this long poem's unfolding.

Other self-referential moments suggest a degree of anxiety about the potential for egotism and solipsism in the looked-for intersection of mind and poetic form. 'What's going on in that stupid head of yours?' another voice demands elsewhere, the rude comment once again set off in quotation marks to assert distinct vocality. Four lines later, but this time without quotation marks, a follow-up to the question surfaces: 'Who cares, does anybody care / about your precious mind and what goes on in it?' (p. 13). These dismissive (and mutually contradictory) assaults on the *Continuations* project – they function as such, whatever their original contexts – receive no response beyond the fact of their recording, but they must be of sufficient weight to explain the ironic self-image and hapless tone Dudek maintains in the volume. In a vague and apparently incidental correction of Wordsworth, for whom poetry was 'the language of a man speaking to men,' Dudek defines poetry as 'a man talking to himself // An old elephant, like a somewhat deflated balloon / he sits in his chair ...' (p. 25). *Continuations*, it seems, expects no audience, but the absence of an audience for poetry is one of its recurrent observations.[30]

Not all of the poem's self-reflexivity is so bashful. Scattered over the volume are a number of asides functionally definitive of its representational premises, such as the early remark that the 'real world' is 'Like the mind making poems / hid in the texture of language' (pp. 11–12). Dudek returns later to the implication of this metaphor that poem, world and mind are – in the *Continuations* aesthetic – one being:

> Necessity is the will of God
> What he wants most is to exist
>
> Wish you were here
>   having a good time
>
> I am the imagination that creates
>   an image of itself
>
> (p. 21)

The wry bathos of the middle stanza permits Dudek the otherwise grandiose equation of the world with the poem and the poet with God. As our *Continuations* poet writes, he brings into being both a world of phenomena and a palimpsest of himself, and the postcard cliché that links his stanzas on God's creation and his own self-creation suggests the ironic pleasure, as well as the loneliness, of the process. This contradictory experience of isolation and pleasure in the imagination's self-representation will later help to define 'the poem' as 'the soul in its lonely delight' (p. 29).

To pull these passages out of the poem's vortex is still to do some violence, however, to the apparent aimlessness of *Continuations*. The poem can hardly be said to make the project of self-representation clear. In fact, Dudek is a little scornful, elsewhere in the volume, of the premises I claim for him: he coyly parenthesizes, 'If you knew only my writing / would you really know me?' (p. 30). He also underscores the gap between any poetic representation of consciousness and the complexity of consciousness itself:

Keep it going, I said (we occasionally repeat)

The poetic stream
(at least to make it seem so
like all appearance)
– streams
of consciousness

(p. 40)

These lines endorse, evidently, the self-critique quoted earlier as epigraph, that 'there can be no poet's voice, no mimesis of a man thinking, that can be the exact equivalent of a human voice, or an exact replica of someone thinking.' The difference between the 'poetic stream' and its mere 'appearance' in a text is a necessary codicil to my identification of 'mind' as the poem's constitutive subject.

Consciousness cannot then be said to be simply an *object* of representation in *Continuations*, since mind is an uncloseable field of activity, with a great deal more content than is recorded and extending in time well beyond the last page of the published record. In an introductory note, Dudek calls *Continuation I* 'a poem without prescribed end or conclusion' (p. [7]); in effect it is the 'infinite poem' referred to but not quite, apparently, undertaken in the opening pages of *Atlantis* in 1966. Thus *Continuations* is to be continuous with the poet's life; as it is a second-level version of his living consciousness, it can only end – here again the comparison to nichol's *Martyrology* seems apt, sadly – with the poet's death, as Dudek acknowledges: 'And the poem is never finished / Death puts on the finishing touches' (p. 30). Nor can we argue that the representation of consciousness unites, fixes, or stabilizes the intense fragmentation and structural anarchy of *Continuations*, if mind is itself too extensive and indeterminate in structure and meaning to be presented as object.

On the other hand, recognition of the poem's *enactment* of consciousness means that we cannot simply identify 'Dudek' as the speaking *subject* of the poem, since to be the subject expressing a long poem is inevitably to have participated, *prior* to its expression, in its structural and thematic coherence, which the central voice here does not appear to do. My identification of consciousness as *the* cognate of *Continuations'* energy does nothing to weaken or regulate or dispel the poem's thrust towards randomness and incoherence, since it does not supply a thematic vantage point from which to make order out of this chaos; the order of mind is not a given. Instead mind offers a compelling cognate of this long poem's *integritas*: of the energy it enacts to mark itself off conceptually both from 'consciousness itself' and from the utter absence of poetic form that is the vanishing point of its radical aesthetics.

Continuations replicates, then, the mind's doubled status as subject and object of its own representations. But how precisely does the enactment of consciousness's 'stream' lend coherence to what is, after all, a dismayingly shattered poem? Dudek's statement on the issue is briefly helpful:

> *Continuation I* and *II* are simulations of the mind thinking. Of course it is not the actual content of any 'stream of consciousness,' for that would be chaotic, messy, absurd – no work of art. I accumulate in my notebooks only those lines and passages that come to me unbidden, that drop down from the blue, so to speak ... I find that the lines accumulated in this way have a peculiar connectedness in their progression, and I shape the whole sequence into a flowing, uninterrupted poem. It *corresponds*, as I see it, to something that is going on in the most erratic and vivacious area of my mind, and is therefore the stream that is truly poetry ...
>
> (pp. 140–1)

Emphasizing the spontaneous and unwilled emergence of the *Continuations* fragments and their 'correspondence' to – not representation of – mental energy, Dudek suggests both the *integritas* of the poem ('a peculiar connectedness') and its high randomness, its 'erratic and vivacious' motion. In his language is a profound, indeed Romantic, trust in the soothsaying of the unconscious mind, as well as a paradoxical validation of conscious creativity: in the small clause 'I shape' is expressed all his deliberate craftsmanship, an imposition of form on which he has not wished to comment at length. If there is paradox here, however, it is partly because Dudek's stakes are very high. He has two major goals in the project, potentially contradictory: to show the motions of consciousness in a form as close as possible to their unmediated rhythms, and to find in them a principle of poetic order that would sustain a significant long poem, without lessening our impression of the richness and freedom of mind it embodies.

Hanging fire in the latter phrase is another feature of *Continuations*, latent in Dudek's prose but acknowledged subliminally by him: the incipient egoism of the project. Not egotism, again, since the speaker of this poem does not celebrate and praise himself; but egoism: the experience of Dudek's consciousness is taken by him to be an appropriate motivation for readers of poetry. Despite the fact that the Dudek personality is put forward in the volume only in and among the collectivity of its fragments and is therefore much muted, everything we read in *Continuations* is referrable back to the qualities of Dudek's mind and experience. If 'he' is the only perimeter of the poem, as I have claimed, we are invited to inhabit his mind as we read, and he presumes the experience valuable. I think we accept this egoism because it is only implicit, for one thing; for another, because so much of the language of selfhood in the poem is self-effacing; for a third, because, whatever the force of ego in the project, the personality is rendered in so fragmented and ironic a manner – we are so constantly diverted from self-fixation – that we can hardly note it without conceptual effort and imagination. But just as Dudek can casually remark an 'area of [his] mind' that contains 'the stream that is truly poetry,' so can we acknowledge the force of ego in this most self-effacing of subjectivist narrations.

Indeed, surely it is a sign of ego to want, as this poet clearly wants, to sustain a higher degree of aleatory fragmentation than had been accomplished by any prior modernist epic. Dudek hopes to push poetic form right to the edge of incoherence and leave it there, without drawing back, but without slipping over into the 'chaotic, messy, absurd.' The pressure at this boundary is intense and the possible errors multiple: absurdity, yes; but also aesthetic flinching and a tendency to retreat into order, unity, clarity; as well as too full a delineation of mind to sustain the immediacy and mutuality of intellection he wants to pass to his reader. Flaccidity is another danger, of course: if the interest and vibrancy of the fragments are not in themselves sufficient to sustain readerly interest, an effect of ennui, shrugging indifference to coherence and to the reader, could savage the *Continuations* project. That Dudek does not shy off any of these dangers bespeaks a confidence in his project and in his ability to realize it that is not usually associated with his creative personality. In *Continuations*, self-effacement *is* self-affirmation: we can hardly read the poem if we do not accept the value of a mental encounter with Dudek.

These remarks on the structural and coherent effects of subjectivity in *Continuations* can best be exemplified and challenged by one of the most successful and then one of the least successful passages in *Continuations*. Quotation in full is necessary, lest the very possibility of incoherence be skirted by more economical reference:

Consider why even the best nations
may have a mad general for a head

Don't blame the Greeks, the Romans
Blame whoever it is
that acts the fool

They use the rest of us Nothing is true
but your own bent
Relax

What is it that concerns me?
Not egotism
(the 'tens of thousands' of Stalin statues)
money, or moonshine

The central ought

Poetry is an experience How you explain it
is something else

Like flying – and the theory

Just now, a man talking to himself

Driven to that by 'no philosophy' ... 'no development'
(Maybe just as well)

Who is there to talk to as poetry talks
The absent God
Don't push Don't push poetry
Even the book-published are far too many
Time is a mass grave
that ought to cure
us of vanity

That world's unimportant, that's why they erase it
constantly to make some other

'And He shall pu-ri-fy!'

To bring Zion with justice
                                        or an acropolis

Like catching a butterfly, a line
                                    while someone is talking
in the train (wh-at he gasped)
                                        Nothing

All thought   What you really are
Nothing out of nothing

Like a child's carlacue burnt in the night
                    written on darkness
Beautiful   So beautiful

(pp. 38–9)

Let us first imagine, if we still can, a reading in which reference of these fragments to the field of the speaker's consciousness, and the presumption of their coherence within his mind, were unavailable. After all, there is only one first-person singular pronoun in the passage (line 9); in any sense we are used to, no *persona* is characterized here. We will therefore perhaps be fairly baffled by the shifts of address in the passage, from the imperatives that open the first two stanzas, to the alternation of voice among 'us,' 'you,' and 'me' in the next two, and so on: there is no fixed point of view, no clear boundaries among the various identities invoked. We will also be confused, perhaps, by some of the connotation and a good deal of the denotation in the poet's lexical decisions: we do not know what we might 'blame the Greeks' for (l. 3), we can only guess at the connotation of 'moonshine' (l. 12; no familiar meaning fits, quite), and so on. We cannot know who is quoted at lines 11, 18, 29, 34. We can only guess whether 'the central ought' (l. 13) is something that 'concerns [him]' (l. 9) or a fourth thing that does not, after 'egotism ... money, or moonshine.' We cannot know what moment is referred to as 'Just now' (l. 17); by extrapolation, we have no real sense of the movement of these fragments in time, whether they are to be read linearly or 'spatially' (in Joseph Frank's sense). We can make no 'sense' of the third-last stanza at all (ll. 36–7): its three phrases have no syntactical relation to one another, and a number of sentences are possible from their conjunction, if we make the effort. A good deal of the passage is inaccessible to an impersonalist, objectivist reading.

Now we can posit the Dudek consciousness as the metaphorical field on which all these suggestive fragments glisten. How is our experience changed? The first thing to be remarked is that few of the above ambiguities are resolved: we have not imposed an arbitrary unity. Questions of address, perhaps, are suspended somewhat, at least in so far as our reference of the many fragments to a single mind tells us of a standpoint from which all the people mentioned are viewed or heard; though we know nothing more about the 'yous' addressed than we did before. Otherwise we have gained nothing, if what we are looking for is, indeed, a means of answering critical riddles and stabilizing ambiguities, of centralizing and fixing meaning in *Continuations*. Nevertheless something profound in our experience of the poem *has* changed. The energy of fragmentation, the ambiguity of reference, the subtlety of connotation, are now predicated as forms of mental energy, as motions of consciousness, and whereas our conscious desire for clarity remains frustrated, a new pleasure emerges *in that we are sharing the ambiguities and liberties of consciousness with another.*[31] We may not know, any better now, who gasped 'wh-at' on the train, but we share the partial and blurred memory of that experience with the unifying voice of our poet. When we are confused or baffled by the fragments cast up in his mental life, we have the notion of consciousness itself – specifically, our intimate contact with another consciousness – to which to appeal, and while incoherence is not eliminated, there is now a selvage to the poem's fabric, a perception of a finitude to this extension, density and ambiguity. We gain the pleasure of reference, not of a kind that leaves us safe in the lap of clear meaning, but of a kind that replicates our knowledge of ourselves by enacting a common mental life with the mind in which all these fragments are, in fact, deeply coherent. If we accept their coherence in Dudek's mind, much of our anxiety over meaning will be replaced by a new intuition of kinds of coherence not available to the reason. This is not 'unity,' if unity means erasure of difference among particulars; but it is wholeness, and we may come to find the experience of such *integritas* as valuable as the enjoyment of signification and statement.

The components of our readerly experience have now changed. We will perhaps replace the interpretation of metaphor, symbol, and utterance in which we have been trained with an ear for the rhythms of mental energy, such as, for example, the free associationism that accounts partially for forward motion here (as from 'the best nations' [l. 1] to 'the Greeks, the Romans' [l. 3]) and the recurrence to previous thoughts: the moment identified as 'Just now' (l. 17), for example, is referrable to page 25, on which the phrase 'a man talking to himself' first appeared before its repetition here. We will perhaps now be less interested in the placement of 'the central ought' in relation to the question 'What is it that concerns me?' than in the simple fact that such a phrase, fraught with centralizing and ethical judgments, occurred – not yet clearly positive or negative – not long after that question was first formulated in the mind. If we are willing to mull over these subtleties, it is because we find the mind we are experiencing to be worth such deep consideration; and if we are willing to suspend the will-to-clarity it must partly be because we recognize in this 'stream' something akin to the patterns of our own consciousness, and find in that a literary accomplishment as well.

The judgment of *Continuations* is thus inescapably personal. The poem leaves itself naked to critique by those who find Dudek's mind insufficiently interesting or his poetics formless and unsatisfying – an example, though, of their egoism and courage. And I do not mean to imply that this radical poetics is inherently 'good' merely because it intrigues *me*, since proof of a poem's quality is no more than critical consensus sustained over time. I do claim, however, that an appreciation of Dudek's project, if it *is* felt, will have to do with the poetics I have been articulating for this passage. This is not to say that the poem always lives up to the aesthetic project it realizes, particularly effectively, in the above passage; indeed, I think the failed passages in *Continuations* disappointing because of their sudden surrender of the ambiguous and courageous frontier just charted.

Nowhere is this surrender more disheartening than in Section IV, an extended rant against cultural barbarism of the late twentieth century, in which little of the delicate subjectivism just explicated survives. Quotation by excerpt should suffice to suggest the section's formal and coherent lapses:

> Why is there so little truth,
> so much crap, 'entertainment'
>   and other fake around?
> Are they all that stupid? inveterate liars?
> Is it self-interest? is it that lies pay off?
> Or are they scared – to show what they are? ...
>
> Mainly it's the grown-ups are bloody liars
> What are they trying to hide, anyway?
> The ravages of time, on heart and body?
>   The source of their filthy money?
> The sewage of commerce –
>   selling the crap they make
>   to cover the truth? ...

The media, spreading their shit music,
    shit talk, shit advertising
flowing with simple lukewarm consistency
        through the long hot afternoon
Voices of vanity, incurable vanity,
        of triviality,
become the real, the commonplace, the everyday! ...

Anything, to screw you through the back-door
Funiculi-funicula at the supermarket
                (murder with Muzak)
Salesmen with shit on their tongue   Can't stop
        lickety-click lickety-click lickety-click,
                        America
One half salesmen the other half suckers –
                    one of each born every minute
Land of the fuckin' free-for-all

(pp. 46–9)

I do not reproduce in the above quotation the Chinese ideogram opposite the first line of the passage, but it signals with fine irony the overweight presence of Ezra Pound in these lines; indeed, we are witnessing in part the possession of one fine mind by another damaged one, and the result is painfully destructive of Dudek's project. Note that the length of a typical 'fragment' has multiplied dramatically, from an average of a line or two to an average of six lines: as a result our sense of the poem's diaphaneity and Heracliteanism is much reduced. A similar inflation has occurred on the level of tone. With very minor exceptions, there is no withdrawal from vituperation in the section. Theme is (obviously) consistent. The context-world of the consciousness we were once following, in and out of perception and conception, is now a fixed and unidimensional world casting up only one kind of stimulus, to which the mind's response is more wholly unidimensional in turn. The speaker's sudden profanity is also embarrassing, not in itself, but in its unwieldy dissonance with the suggestive and at times vague diction we have experienced thus far.

The section's greatest fault, though, must be that my word 'speaker' above suddenly seems so much more appropriate to Dudek's poetics. The term did not function well in earlier sections: there was rarely any evidence of *someone* speaking, and even the concept of persona has to be strained to match the recording of consciousness Dudek achieved earlier. Now, however, it is hard to imagine these thoughts occurring so coherently and consistently in instantaneous mental form. At the very least, a prior decision has been made to allow the 'infinite poem' to focus on a finite theme for several pages, and that bespeaks a creative agent at one remove, suddenly, from the thoughts he chooses to record. There is no auditor or interlocutor for this speech. It is an intriguing irony that the passages in which the effect of consciousness is best achieved are better able to record the presence of others around the poet, whereas this passage – for which speech, not thought, is the cognate – shuts out all other voices in its relentless drive towards fixed meanings with which we are badgered into agreement, or out of reading further. We are now clearly cast as auditors; before we were overhearers. The relation is far less interesting. It is rather as if the suspended fragments of earlier sections, floating in time and paginally in space, were suddenly imploded by the vehemence of opinion into a hard kernel, without the interstices of meaning that invited us inward before.

My own hardened response to Section IV has a specialist motive, of course, and from another perspective (or finding it in another kind of poem) I could applaud its social vehemence and directness of speech. My interest here is, self-evidently, not the contents of Dudek's poetically embodied mind but the manner of its embodiment, and for that reason only the section's dissonance with the rest of Dudek's effort in the poem concerns me here. In fact, the section makes plain in reverse a number of vital features of the *Continuations* project: chiefly, that the kind of coherence sought in the better sections is a coherence that exists just at the edge of randomness, even of meaninglessness. It is the abandonment of that difficult tension in favour of fixed and utter meanings that vitiates Section IV. Section IV should also make plain the better subjectivism elsewhere in Dudek's long poem: it is self-representation, and self-affirmation, by self-effacement, by the bare adumbration of persona. If that delicacy of outline is not maintained, and the consciousness hardens into ego as intellection has here into speech, we encounter a degree of subjectivism that overflows ironic containment and spills into the egotism of cultural rectitude, a simplification I thought Layton to have risked in 'Whatever Else Poetry Is Freedom.' Finally, the tension between two formal impulses – the drive towards a pure random, and the complementary drive to give that randomness the minimum of form necessary to art – is essential to the late Dudek attempt; and, as I remarked, the possibilities of error are manifold.

They are also less interesting than the project itself, and the moments of its best realization. To summarize Dudek's intuitions as the *Continuations* project emerged in the course of the 1970s (the first unit of the long work was included in his *Collected Poems* of 1971), the modernist drive towards aleatory fragmentation was valuable, not only because of its reflection of a world whose coherence was not plain, but also because of the possibilities it opened up for the representation of the rhythm and density of human consciousness. It could be taken farther, in fact, than it had been taken, in an attempt to incorporate in the poetic text more – and more – of the phenomenal and the mental worlds: the 'infinite poem' can have only one main goal, in Ernest Buckler's phrase again, 'to get it all in.'[32] At the same time, Dudek affirms constantly the boundary between a text of pure accumulation and a work of art: he is concerned to find principles of aesthetic containment and structure that will integrate without unifying the highly aleatory work he proposes. Once the cognate relationship between the poetic text and the poetic mind is clear to him – and I do not suggest that this is a specific revelation at a specific moment in *Continuations'* conceptualization – he has the means at hand to 'complete' his infinite project, at least provisionally, volume by volume. He proceeds to draft fragments with enormous structural freedom, confident, as he says in his self-explications, that the resulting poem will be 'erratic and vivacious' because it will embody both the *integritas* and the infinitude of his mind. Conceptually at least, he is spared the potential egotism of this assumption by his maintenance of a highly ironic subjectivism, in which the stability and unity of the self are as much at question as those of the poem. We can refer the fragmentation and ambiguity of the poem to the Dudek mind and enjoy thereby a sense of an aesthetic perimeter beyond which, paradoxically, infinity cannot proceed into incoherence, but we cannot (for the most part) settle back into the fixed role of auditor to the fixed knowledge of Dudek.

The continuity of this project with the elements of forties poetics I have discussed throughout this book will be self-evident, and I will not bother to translate these remarks into the more specific terms I have relied on until now. Milton Wilson remarked early on that 'Dudek's later career is an interesting struggle to explore and expand and redefine, without ever quite repudiating, the kind of vision he began with,'[33] and that degree of intellectual integrity – with its cost in audience attention – suggests both the power of forties issues for Dudek's creativity as well as his centrality to the elaboration of those issues for later generations. It remains difficult to evaluate the effort, though the indifference of two or three generations of readers seems for many to have closed the matter. When Frank Davey explains Dudek's lack of recognition by remarking that 'Dudek does not try to make a commodity of his personality by using poetry to project a self-image which can be loved, hated, envied or reviled by the reader' (p. 54), he is correct in so far as he is comparing Dudek with poets like Purdy and Cohen. There is no sense indeed in which the egoist poetics of *Continuations* responds to an arguable marketplace for 'poetic' personalities. But Dudek does, certainly, 'project a self-image,' and while love, hate, envy, or revilement may not seem at first to be invited, a stronger reader reaction than Davey grants is one of the poem's *desiderata*, and might lie ahead; especially once the living mind is gone.

From *Europe* to *Atlantis*

If *Continuations* is indeed the natural outcome of Louis Dudek's poetic innovations over many years and several volumes, the span of creative action to which it sets a period obviously began with *Europe* of 1954. Most of the slender attention Dudek has received has been accorded *Europe, En Mexico* (1958), and *Atlantis* (1967), the three long poems that preoccupy Frank Davey, Dudek's best commentator. Few, Davey included, have sought to bridge the gap in Dudek's practice from the poetry of the forties to his sudden discovery of vocation in the long poem, and the present context invites a closer scrutiny of that lacuna, once the terms of poetic transition from the young post-Poundian of *Europe* to the originator of *Atlantis* are clearer.

The years 1953 and 1954 are critical for Dudek's development. In 1951 he returned to Montreal from New York, to take up his post in McGill's Department of English; coincidentally, 1952 saw the culmination and closing off of his forties work, with three volumes of his own poetry appearing (*The Searching Image, Twenty-Four Poems,* and *Cerberus* with Layton and Souster) as well as an anthology of Canadian poems edited with Layton (*Canadian Poems, 1850–1952*). In 1953 he made the trip to Europe that was pivotal, whatever lines we come to draw from the biographical to the poetic journey, in his focusing the subject of a long poem of cultural comment, *Europe* itself appearing the following year. The reincarnation was only partial, of course, and it makes no sense to speak of Dudek's 'middle period' until five years later, when 'Functional Poetry: A Proposal' (1959) and *En Mexico* had made plain the dominance of new ideas whose first establishment was in *Europe*. Nevertheless, one can hardly fail to remark that the same two or three years that silenced Page and Klein and gave dramatic new voice to Layton were critical years for Dudek's growth as well.

Alan Williamson charts American poetry through a similar period of culmination and transition in his *Introspection and Contemporary Poetry*. He deals with the various forms of confessional and subjectivist poetry appearing spontaneously in the American milieu in the early to mid-1950s and remarks the generational hostility with which they were at first received:

It is important, for one thing, to recognize that this poetry seemed so controversial and problematic partly because of its position in literary history – its impact on minds brought up on the Impersonal Theory and the New Criticism's polemical overemphasis on persona (a doctrine whose value, surely, lies in making us aware that character-creation through voice occurs in lyric as well as narrative poetry, and not in suggesting that 'I' in a lyric rarely means the author).[34]

Williamson is not much concerned to suggest the causes of this shift to the personalist mode in poets like Sylvia Plath and John Ashbery, although he does remark their common generational intuition of a failure of nerve in their inherited modernist ideas and precursors. The objectivist innovations of early modernism, not to mention Eliot, Auden, or Pound as individuals, had proven little able to comprehend a world in revolution and cataclysm, one whose foundations were so broken that the individual had little but the 'self' to fall back on for creative agency. As Williamson has it,'[t]he responses of the great Modernist writers to this [mid-century] history – wrong-headed, symbolic and personally driven as they often were – I suspect helped later poets conclude that *a psychology beginning at home was a necessary middle term between poetic sensibility and impersonal or ideological judgment.*'[35] Williamson's terms are vague here and remain largely undeveloped, but I take him to mean that American poets of the early 1950s felt the need to represent 'a psychology' of their own making if they wished to find the 'middle term' between objectivist impersonality – with its newly visible risks of misguided political judgment and historical interpretation – and a new subjectivism predicated on the 'poetic sensibility,' as both Layton's and Dudek's personalism would be. In Layton's case this new 'psychology' includes a candid and joyful embodiment of the subconscious and libido, a scorn of social nurture in favour of arbitrary nature, and a new understanding of identity predicated on multiplicity and procession, the 'murdered selves.' Interestingly, Williamson's poets lead him to a coincidentally much more precise anticipation of Dudek's weaving of psychology and poetry: 'he [the confessional poet] gambles that because the self seems to have an intuited order, the more candid he is, the more he surrenders to the accidents and nuances of experience, the more significant poetic order will emerge.'[36] Dudek did not come suddenly to this understanding as he turned away from his apprenticeship; it would take him over a dozen years at the long poem before he could truly be said to 'gamble' on the inherent order in the fragments of consciousness, in *Atlantis*. But *Europe* is his first attempt to respond, in a way that Williamson suggests is generational, to a felt need to transliterate the fact of consciousness into new and dynamic poetic forms.[37]

In the forties Dudek had shown particular gifts as lyricist and Imagist, as well as a somewhat ambivalent desire, typical of that decade, for longer poetic structures, in such largely social-realist meditations as 'East of the City.' I will have more to say of these early writings later. Their lyric and Imagist methods, whose paradoxical conjunction would be central to the long-poem aesthetics Dudek was to explore, did not fuse easily in the forties imagination, and there is in *Europe* – his first attempt at a long poem comprising sharply differentiated fragments united by the subjective central viewpoint – a high degree of formal stiffness. Davey, whose reading of *Europe* serves largely to anticipate the more proprioceptive methods of *En Mexico*,[38] registers in the earlier poem 'Dudek's inability to give up pretentious, decorative and rhetorical modes of writing' (p. 56), but he does not remark a similar self-consciousness in the broader organization of the poem. Davey feels that the poem's 'ninety-nine sections in no sense form a narrative; the *story* of Dudek's travels is not the subject of the poem' (p. 54), and later, that 'Dudek appears to have had no conscious plan when he began *Europe*, no outline of structure or plot' (p. 57). These remarks clearly help to anticipate Dudek's later, open-ended conceptualization of the 'long poem,' but they rather distort *Europe* in the process.

It is difficult to see the poem as unplanned or running counter to narrative when it opens with departure from Canada and closes with return to Canada, a clear European itinerary having intervened, whose stages are divided not only into numbered sections 1–99 but into five larger units, entitled in order to clarify an itinerary: 'Sea and Land,' 'England,' 'France,' 'The Warm South,' 'What Greece Has Given.' The single narrative perspective of the travelling poet-scholar also obviously contributes to the comparatively strong sense of structural coherence *Europe* projects. Still, a 'gamble' on the inherent order of consciousness is only rarely visible. Dudek had as yet little confidence that a sufficient poetic *integritas* could emerge from consciousness itself; hence the limiting need to number and title the fragments of his itinerary, a structural anxiety that would disappear entirely by the time of his second long poem four years later.

In keeping with this projected concern for his poem's coherence are the limits Dudek imposed on its force of fragmentation. The longer poem project evidently brought with it an intuition, to be rejected later, that sustaining poetic power over several dozen pages would require both constraints on fragmentation and a very conscious elaboration of the central imagination. Within numbered sections, the strong tendency is to a coherent and focused theme, a governing image or setting from the European vista, and a predominant tone; although it is true that some of the poem's best if not most characteristic effects occur in those passages where this pulse of strict coherence is allowed to lapse:

Paris, more stinking royal than any city:
    city of republicans, of the Conciergerie, Bastille!
(Some 10,000 visit Versailles on a Sunday?
    Nothing but sentiment. O the great age
        of the Roi Soleil!)
The city is filled with palaces and baroque horrors
and such filthy flambuoyant statues
  as deface the corners of the best cathedrals,
            even Chartres –
eighteenth century additions, twentieth century
    legs et dons.
And buried under Paris, under the Palais de Justice,
    under St. Germain and the Louvre,
you will find the stained glass
    of the Sainte Chapelle,
and a small Greek church of very early date,
and St. Séverin, perfect and harmonious, and quiet,
and the staring face of Notre Dame.[39]

Much of the 'France' section of *Europe* is taken up, in Davey's words, with 'the theme of artistic integrity,' and as section 48 opens we prepare for more condemnations of Europe's post-medieval aesthetic inauthenticity. And we get them, to be sure, for eleven vilifying lines. But the impressionistic *volta* at line 12 is one of the most delicately modulated in the entire volume, even if Dudek offers no correction of the earlier remarks in his sudden quiet praise of the vestiges of medieval Paris. The abandonment of the hectoring tone in favour of a more neutral aesthetic mood is perfectly achieved. The effect turns on the evocative power of random shifts in consciousness, and although Dudek is as yet unable to explore or embody that issue at length, the moment is rich with potential.

Note, however, even here, the high degree of formal coherence Dudek insists on. Like the passage just quoted, seventy-five of the poem's ninety-nine sections are single stanzas, and the bulk of those that permit internal stanzaic breaks occur, interestingly, in the opening section, 'Sea and Land.' There appears to be a correlation between the claimed authority of Dudek's cultural pronouncements in the poem, and the length and the solidity of his poetic units; when his views are muted or left uncertain, a greater degree of stanzaic complexity opens up, a cognate relation between form and theme that Davey, at least, who finds in *Europe* 'a wholeness, an integrity of vision' (p. 54) for its consonance of theme and aesthetics, will not find surprising. The poem's force of fragmentation, then, will have one or two restricted theatres of operation: in the fragmented relation between what the poet records and the range of European detail he actually saw as a traveller, and in the fragmented narration some readers might experience, who approached the volume expecting a more linear and coherent plot with clear transitions from episode to episode. Neither of these experiences of fragmentation in *Europe* is particularly potent in hindsight, though, certainly not in comparison to what lies ahead, from *En Mexico* to *Continuations*.

All this is to say that the problem of *integritas* is far less challenging to the poetics of *Europe* than it would be to all of Dudek's longer works thereafter.[40] It is no surprise, therefore, that the representation of consciousness – so vital later, in its ambiguity and fluidity, to the *integritas* of *Continuations* – is rather straightforward, one might say primitive, here. The relation of perceiving subject-speaker to the perceived object world is relatively clear and fixed. There is little or no interest in mental complexity and contradiction: the opinions expressed by the itinerant speaker are and remain those of the poem's management. There is also little interest in dramatizing formally the motions of consciousness: the poet's mind moves chiefly as his body moves, as on a pendulum between perception and conception. (See, for example, an interesting point at which the speaker 'close[s his] lids' and still sees 'arches' and 'marble colonnades' 'vibrating in the after-image their fixity has made' [p. 90]; the poet of *Continuations* would never pause so carefully to explicate the physical boundary between eyesight and insight.) While the fixed narrative viewpoint of *Europe* helps to affirm the already well-established coherence of the poem, it has not required any particular imagination or innovation on Dudek's part to represent that consciousness; the existing conventions of the cultural traveller – Ruskin seems so apt when he is finally invoked (p. 114) – were sufficient to the task of self-representation in *Europe*.

Interestingly, the best anticipations of the phenomenological manner towards which Dudek would later work are in the poem's first section, dominated by interwoven images of the sea and of his fellow passengers. Davey says that 'Dudek has only banalities to offer about the sea during his outbound voyage' (p. 57), and indeed nothing in the book's opening will rival the justly famous Fragment 95 near its conclusion, but it seems noteworthy that Dudek is best able to represent the fluidity and randomness of consciousness when he displays its voyage over the sea that was to become in *En Mexico* and *Atlantis* one of his favourite symbols of mind's flux and depth:

Bridge
parties in the lounge,
and tourist chatter:

Time's newest, flimsiest, cheapest crinkles
unwrapping Vacation Tours –
'Let's finish this hand'
'I've had enough'

(p. 7)

From eleven every morning the program reads 'Concert',
but it turned out to be Be-Bop
exclusively and German *Sehnsucht*
of Nelson Eddy vintage.
'How about Mozart?
Or the Messiah?'
piped an American collegian.
'Let's relax!'
The intellectual calibre (high on this voyage)
is about that of the *Sat. Eve. Post* ...

(p. 29)

The disjunctive effect of the interpolated snippets of conversation and the sharp shifts of the speaker's attention in a crowded ocean liner is vitiated, certainly, by Dudek's rather sneering tone; nevertheless in these passages the text is asked to function in both subjective and objective modes, with the boundary between the perceiver and the world somewhat problematized on the page. These interiors are circumscribed by numerous passages – also more Imagist than anything else in *Europe* – descriptive of the sea's power, languor, and evocativeness, and in the most famous of these (more than a 'banality') the sea becomes a cognate of literary energy:

The commotion of these waves, however strong, cannot disturb
the compass-line of the horizon
nor the plumb-line of gravity, because this cross co-ordinates
the tragic pulls of necessity
that chart the ideal endings, for waves, and storms
and sunset winds:
the dead scattered on the stage in the fifth act ...
The horizon is perfect,

and nothing can be stricter
than gravity; in relation to these
   the stage is rocked and tossed,
kings fall with their crowns, poets sink with their laurels.

(p. 27)

Nothing here suggests the sea as a metaphor of consciousness; there is no attempt to find a poetic form adequate to convey the flux and coherence of either. There is, though, a brief intuition that the forces of artistic form and of the sea are somehow intimate with one another, and though Dudek was to let go of the thought for the balance of this volume, it would stay with him, irrefutably, as he worked on. Nothing in *Europe* would again be so fragmented and Imagist in implication as the following Fragment 16, but its confident brevity bespeaks the poetics Dudek would go seeking hereafter:

The sea loves to move
   but it is in no hurry,
flops over languidly like an easy animal
waiting for storms,
   never still.

(p. 24)

En Mexico, a poem redolent of such languor and restlessness, would take up this post-Imagist manner, moving too 'in no hurry' away from the rather unambiguous methods of *Europe* into the density of fragmentation and *integritas* that would preoccupy Dudek for the rest of his career.

Dudek has written of the angst-laden process by which the newly fragmented poetics of *En Mexico* came into being:

I could not write any sustained poetry in Mexico. But I wrote bits and pieces, lines and clusters of lines, on separate bits of paper, and put them all together without any order or sequence. When I returned to Montreal I arranged this fragmented poetry, partly chronologically (as far as I could remember) and partly to make a pattern emerge. The result was the poem *En Mexico*, with its strange, sometimes broken, associative progression ...[41]

More critical arguments might suggest other causes of the later poem's radicalism: among them, a growing recognition of the inattention of his audience and a consequent unwillingness to order, mediate, and moderate his poetics to their apparent tastes. Dudek has elsewhere spoken of *Europe* as 'the culmination of the public voice, the voice that seemed to be related to the audience in a healthy kind of way,'[42] the clear implication being that *En Mexico* lacked that 'healthy' sense of audience and public purpose. Other likely contexts for the fresh discoveries of *En Mexico* include the useful rivalry with Layton in this period before their final rupture, Dudek's resurgent interest in the implications of Imagist poetics for longer forms (in keeping with contemporary experiment by Charles Olson, with whose career he was in close and sardonic touch),[43] and a not surprising maturing of his aesthetic sensibility, as the 'integrity of [moral and aesthetic] vision' Davey praises came to dominate his poetic imagination.

Whatever the cause, the centrifugal drive towards fragmentation is powerful in *En Mexico*. It is all the more striking because of the intensely meditative and sweetly ironic tone Dudek maintains. The journey through Mexico – for all that Dudek may have edited in a partial chronology – is not narrated, as action ordered in time: there is no sense of the travelogue available, although this is not to say that little of the visited milieu is represented. On the contrary, the spurning of narrative order seems to have released an intensity of image-rendering that *Europe* largely lacks:

The jungle has an oceanic luxury:
boys by a heap of papaya
(above, the cornfields,
                    maguey rows, cactus)
and thatched native huts
with little children in the puddles.
Rain, out of a solitary cloud,
then sun, more sun ...[44]

The Impressionist quality is achieved variously: by the italic font of the original edition, which suggests contradictory qualities of evanescence and intensity, as well as by the dramatic blank space around the fragments, each of which is set to a bottom margin. The fragments are not numbered, titled, or sectioned off in any way. Only one element in the volume serves at all to structure their free arrangement, and that is the illustrations of Zygmunt Turkiewicz, on pages 12 and 41, although I can find no functional sense of 'section' in the resulting three divisions of the poem.

My remark on the poem's participation in the post-Imagist continuity of which Dudek would form a major part in Canada[45] is as yet unsatisfactory, since I have insisted elsewhere that the mere fact of visual imagery or scene-painting in short free-verse poems is insufficient to a definition of Imagism's originality and specificity. Into such impressionistic renderings must come the juxtaposition and binarism of Pound's originary practice of Imagism if the latter term is to retain useful exemplary meaning. Sharp juxtaposition is strong in *En Mexico*, one feature that marks it off from the more rational methods of *Europe*:

It is most quiet
where it is most violent.
That's why we appear so good.

In a tropical cemetery
hardly a grave is to be seen,
so much is overgrown.

(p. 13)

Note that the fruitful juxtaposition in this brief fragment forces us to cross the boundary from intellection to perception, the same boundary that Dudek had so self-consciously rendered in *Europe* with the closing of his eyelids. The technique is clearly that of Pound 'In a Station of the Metro,' who similarly yanks his sympathetic reader to and fro on the subject–object boundary. Dudek's method is obviously more keen on the rationalist and denotative potential of the subjective mode, but the effect of juxtaposition is highly similar.

Perhaps more interestingly, Dudek is highly aware of the intensity and significance of startling juxtapositions, and comments on this feature of the Mexican journey frequently:

In a world of strangeness
all thoughts run together,
then come singly
like those bell-birds of Vera Cruz.

(p. 5)

Between cathedral spires
and the plum tree's pleasantness
there is no distinction.
Praise these.

(p. 36)

Such passages suggest, indeed, that a partial explanation of the return to his more Imagist practice lay in the fertility and density of imagery in Dudek's visual experience of Mexico. A world of such startling disorder – at least in the terms he brought with him, which we can imagine to be those of *Europe* – appears to have provoked his consideration, for the first time, of the kinds of coherence and meaningfulness that might inhere in a random structure. For the modernist poet writing in English, the search for such a poetics of randomness would have had to begin with the Imagist method, which Dudek had long been practising and would already have been teaching as the fundamental unit of modernist experimentation and aesthetic insight.

For Davey, such passages as the above are less interesting for their Imagist resonance than for their establishment of the 'proprioceptive' method of *En Mexico*. 'While the images appear superficially to be from an objective world,' he remarks, 'the rhythm reveals them to be thoroughly internalized: the objective is located within the subjective. The process of apprehension is now as much proprioceptive as perceptive ... the poet combines the elements of language – image, rhythm and denotation – to express a simultaneity of perception and response' (pp. 63–4). It appears largely on this basis that Davey finds *En Mexico* Dudek's most accomplished poem, an assessment with which Douglas Barbour agrees.[46] Davey's point is particularly clear in the contrast with *Europe*, in which to be sure both 'perception and response' are functional; the differences being that perception in *Europe* is rarely accorded the immediacy, the 'whatness,' of Imagist rendering, and response is heavily mediated by the organizing point of view of the traveller. In *En Mexico*, on the other hand, the percept is usually presented, with all the advantages of Imagist method, as if to the poet and to the reader simultaneously, just as the concept 'occurs' in the poet's mind and on the page – and hence in the reader's mind – simultaneously. Proprioception's attempt is to give the illusion of immediate contact with the experience of consciousness in another; *Europe*, on the other hand, is a story and a series of cultural contentions, both of a second or third order grasped well after the primary stimuli and responses have occurred.

For Davey there is no discontinuity between the phenomenalism of these findings and his persistent reading of Dudek as a poet whose chief attempt has been to 'restore [poetry] to the functions of *testimony* and process' (p. 81, emphasis added) by maintaining a 'projected authenticity' (p. 64) that allows him to speak directly to vital historical and cultural issues, the work that Dudek identifies in 'Functional Poetry: A Proposal' as the ground lost 'to prose ... over the centuries / in the subject matter of poetry.'[47] Dudek himself, however, appears to recognize that the increasing interiority of his poetry, while a form of authenticity, is also a possible absconding from an effective public duty. A more fruitful use of Davey's proprioceptive reading is to consider its effect on the reader's experience of the poem's particular kind of energy, especially since the relation between form and energy is one of *En Mexico's* prominent themes.

Given the conditions,
energy is given:
  water and sun –
    making the jungle.

Then walled haciendas
with all the animals under one roof.

And the temple
  of Quetzalcoatl.

(p. 18)

It is no coincidence that Dudek's proprioceptive tendency surfaces in a poem evincing the highest degree of structural fragmentation he or any other Canadian poet had yet attempted. I do not propose that he already understood the connection that *Continuations* makes plain between the establishment of an ambiguous subjectivity and the coherence of an intensely fragmented poetics, partly because I take him at his word on the difficulty and uncertainty in the composition of the poem. But it is in *En Mexico* that we first see Dudek attempt a representation of the rhythms rather than the results of consciousness, and those rhythms serve to establish the structural coherence of what might otherwise be an unsound and unremarkable poem.

The sheer fact of the poet's presence – an actual as well as a mental traveller, with food allergies, complaints about bus drivers and insects – foregrounds the fact that any vision of Mexico emergent here passes through the filter of a particularized individual, a being distinct from ourselves, with idiosyncrasies of observation, reflection, and diction. To speak rigorously, we learn nothing of Mexico in the volume, but a great deal of Dudek. The fragmentation of the poem is still not radical, and its components are rarely so opaque as to require great struggle (though in 1958 such a poem was a direct challenge to notions of poetic coherence and orderliness for most readers), but we are free at any point to refer both their clarity and their difficulty to the frame of that personality we are actually reading as we pass from item to item of his consciousness. I think, in *En Mexico*, that we rarely do so in frustration, surrendering all hope of a clear reading to the ambiguity of consciousness, as we are repeatedly forced to do in *Continuations*; but the possibility of such acts of reference is newly the point, and the Dudek persona is both consolidated and muted before our eyes. How much *less* insistent on his own presence, in fact, is this itinerant poet than that man in *Europe* whose habit was to insert himself and his responses into every scene he encountered; and yet how much more sensitively outlined for us, the very fact of his withdrawal as subject increasing, ironically, the tangibility of persona. The explicit mediating role of the *Europe* traveller is here made implicit and intermittent: some percepts receive comment, narrative context, intellectual meditation, and some do not, and the result is a flexibility of self-representation that the rigidity of *Europe* denied him. By standing back and blending the results of consciousness with a partial sense of the flux of mental life, Dudek has in fact given us a more intimate relation to himself, to the special coherence of his difficult mind, than he may have intended in composing *En Mexico*.

Davey is right, then, to emphasize the courage of the Dudek project. It shows most convincingly in the degree of intimacy he forges between himself as subject and the world as object, and between the reader as subject and himself as object, a network of relations enacted, not described, as he traverses a suggestively visual Mexico. It is telling that he takes from the Mexican experience an aesthetics newly submissive to the free flow of visceral energy; he reads into the density of jungle and ocean – or we may wish to say, he finds there – a principle of formal beauty that does not override but comprehends the incoherence of life. Two fragments juxtaposed near the centre of the poem lay out the terms of this discovery:

You may hate the jungle,
its inimical insects, flies,
and the chaos of growing
everything at once;
but we return for fertility
to its moist limbs
and vaginal leaves.

They grow over each other, overgrow,
and the whole thing, by elimination,
is also an order that exists.
Hence the necessary magnificence of all reality.
(Where an artist is only a pipsqueak
in a forest of mocking birds.)

(pp. 34, 35)

Newly approved of here are principles of 'chaos' and 'fertility' in which 'an order' is recognized. The search for a poetics, and an understanding of selfhood, that would account for and be able to embody such a chaos appears to begin with the recognition in *En Mexico* – in its difficult composition as well – that the most random 'jottings' of our experience may contain deeper understandings of order than the rational poetics of *Europe* were capable of.

Form is the visible part of being.
We know, the logic of its adaptations –
a signature of individuality,
an integrity,
the end of perfect resolution –
but not the inner stir.

Rest. Rest in that great affair.

(p. 75)

The new tone of submission is perhaps slightly misleading; it will be the 'inner stir' that preoccupies Dudek for the next quarter-century as he tries to find 'an integrity' that will give it form.

In *En Mexico*, then, we experience an almost ideal balance between the representation of consciousness and the dramatization of a journey in the object-world. In comparison with *Europe*, here we have moved sharply inward to a fuller register of the poet's mental life; in that sense, the recording of the external travel is reduced. On the other hand, it is possible to argue that that very inward turn makes a more authentic representation of the external world possible: that we have a finer intuition of Mexico here than our more self-assertive intellectual companion permitted us of Europe. In either formulation we remark Dudek's growing awareness that there can be no inquiry into the nature of the world – at least, not on the scale he desires – that is not beforehand an inquiry into self, and as the narration of journey disappears from 1954 to 1958, the enactment of consciousness emerges. Dudek would continue on this trajectory in the years following the composition of *En Mexico*. With growing alertness to the aesthetics he had discovered, he 'withdrew' further into a poetry of interior life, the object-world visited less and less clearly, and now contrasted ironically with an 'Atlantis' of the imagination. With a degree of relentlessness Dudek would pursue an interpretation of his poetry's destiny – seeking the natural form within himself,[48] as he had learned to do with the fragments from *Mexico*: for 'What / out of our living centre may we not create?'[49]

As we should now expect, the push onward into a fuller mimesis of consciousness in *Atlantis* has entailed on the poem an even greater degree of fragmentation in poetic structure and style. *En Mexico* looks aleatory, and the blank space around the fragments seems intended to show that effect off, but it remains a fairly short poem of 71 fragments, a minor structure in comparison with the extension and conceptual intensity of *Atlantis*. Here each of 151 pages, dense with ink, contains several fragment-stanzas, some working in concert to create longer units, others in utter isolation. Indeed, the breakdown of poetic form in *Atlantis* comes very close near the conclusion, as I shall remark later, to the completely alinear and dramatically aleatory method of *Continuations*, to be undertaken sporadically within a few years of this long poem's appearance. Another anticipation of the *Continuations* project is Dudek's occasional asides remarking the accumulative qualities of his composition of the 1967 poem:

It seems so easy
but about a page or so a day is what it comes to –
        no more. Sometimes better.

(p. 7)

These hours are of no interest –
                I sit and stare.
Wait for the words to come.

(p. 12)

Despite the reverse claim of inspiration in the latter verse-unit, with its ironic assertion of a Muse poetics, the *Continuations* injunction that the poet just 'Keep it going, day by day' (p. 31) is clearly taking shape in *Atlantis*. As the poetic process is thus foregrounded, the value of the poem as product is lowered: the final draft may be as random, broken, and opaque as the Muse, consciousness, itself.

Reflecting this accumulative aesthetics in *Atlantis* is a renewed tendency to catalogue, whose attraction for the 1940s poets I have repeatedly suggested. The most famous of these, justly so, is the poem's aquarium passage, incorporating both a list of Latin names of nineteen species Dudek sees, and his poetic rendition of their nature, highly aestheticized:

And I saw beautiful tiny sea-horses
        with a fin on the back
            vibrating like a little wheel

And a ghostly shrimp six inches long
                    light pink and white
and graceful as a star, or the new moon

And a whorl of delicate white toothpicks
And brown stems, with white strings like Chinese
            bean-sprouts, long and graceful.

(p. 33)

A less remarked catalogue occurs in an unnamed garden in London:[50]

Ilex Aquifolium, the pale-fringed holly.
The Strelitzia like a tropical bird,
            the hanging lamp of the purple fuchsia.
The rose Spiraea and the royal lily.
(And birds come to eat from your hand –
                    would you want to harm them?)

Gleditschia   Dietes   Regal Lily ...

The fruit of the Magnolia of Yunnan
                    opening their great pods
and the Cashmere Cyprus of Tibet
   that hangs like drapery, green and brown.

Nymphaea and tropical fish

But the rhododendrons were not in flower.
'The rhododendrons were not in flower!'
   'Ah, you must come back another time.'

To see the famous roses,
   Mme. Butterfly, Sutter's Gold, Masquerade,
      Christopher Stone, Misty Morn.

(pp. 131–2)

Similar acts of listing occur in the zoo at Rome (p. 54) and among the trees of (probably) Kensington Gardens (p. 122); in the Florence streets, the urge to catalogue is exerted in more regular poetic form, yielding a structure and style (though not an imagery) not unlike Page's:

> The crooked streets, the yellow zig-zag of houses,
> the chatter of the people, and the sound of clamor indoors,
> the quick vitality of the women, making love to the men:
> the white clouds, and the afternoon crowds
> walking, talking, or drinking apéritifs in the cafés.
> A musician among his friends
> singing *Vesti la giubba* from a chair ...
>
> (p. 61)

All these passages have their formal cognate, of course, in the poem's own accumulation of larger fragments: the principle of 'catalogue' is in fact a premise for *Atlantis*'s interpretation of consciousness.

Such catalogues bespeak the poet's desire for a highly inclusive rendition of his responses to Europe. The technique's vanishing point, as noted, is a *complete* list of the world, and Dudek's desire for a better and better encompassing of his mental life makes the catalogue a logical, if occasionally frustrating, choice for *Atlantis*. Davey especially has found the poem's technique inadequate: his first remark upon it is that 'lapses into commonplace increase' (p. 68) in such a method, although he acknowledges that 'Dudek would probably consider *Atlantis* a near perfect poem. The poem corresponds almost exactly to the aesthetic and moral theories it propounds' (p. 76). In the latter statement is Davey's primary premise for Dudek's entire importance as a poet (pp. 80–1), so his discomfort with *Atlantis* is a little odd; it may be accounted for speculatively by Dudek's resignation in the poem to intermittent eruptions of human brutality, a political and moral insight to which Davey's Marxist reading is inhospitable. Still, if authenticity of self-portraiture is a good, then the inclusion of commonplaces – authentic to Dudek's mind as to anyone's – must be a good as well.

It is nevertheless true that *Atlantis*'s fragmentation *is* extreme, and at times enervating. So much so in fact that Dudek felt compelled to restore the section divisions and numbering that had organized *Europe*. Apart from 'Prologue' and 'Epilogue,' suggesting an epic perspective, Dudek gives each of Italy, France, and England a distinct section marked off by Roman numeral and a quotation for epigraph. Each of these sections is in turn divided into three subsections with Arabic numeration, the trinity of trinities suggesting a strong urge towards symmetry in the midst of the poem's potential chaos. This structural imposition does little, however, to contain such a long and fragmentary poem: it is, for instance, extremely difficult to grasp a distinct mood or subject in any of the eleven sections thus created. Even the basic tripartite division modelled on the travelogue (departure, itinerary, return) has a limited effect on the formal coherence of *Atlantis*. Dudek's opening remarks on 'travel' as the poem's theme are careful to treat the journey metaphorically at best:

> Travel is the life-voyage in little,
>   a poem, a fiction, structure of illusion!
> And then you ask, 'What does it mean?'
>
> (p. 3)

> Like this ship leaving, gently, to silent tears
>   falling all around,
> the infinite poem begins ...
>
> (p. 5)

Other remarks seem to want to prepare us for the ephemerality of actual travelogue in the poem: 'Travel, to and from (the place does not matter),' he remarks (p. 3), and what's more 'I hate travel' (p. 10). After all these rather self-conscious notices, we should perhaps be prepared when Europe is hardly visualized, certainly not narrated, in *Atlantis*.

Dudek's Imagist ability is most visible in the Italian section, where a deliberate effort to reproduce the things seen is occasional:

> Ah, Napoli!
> Vesuvius and Somma in clouds,
> the climbing streets, white and light green in the sun,
>   lemon trees
> (in the afternoon, fireworks for the festa)
> children, tumblers of all ages,
> and below, the city – a pastel white – and the bay ...
>
> (p. 20)

Note the catalogic and paratactic structure ('streets ... and ... the city ... and the bay'), suggesting not so much a description of the scene as an unmediated imprinting of its unstructured detail on his mind. By the Paris section, the urge to describe is severely vitiated; only two or three passages fill in the whole of a particular setting, and they are desultory, and again catalogic, in the process:

> My favourite reading place in Paris
>   was a small park

by Saint-Julien-le-Pauvre
with the old church at the back
            and the cathedral in front,

the traffic passing by, and children at play
   (new ones asleep in their mothers' arms),
and languid lovers on the shady seats, holding hands.

(p. 100)

After this final gesture, about two-thirds of the way through *Atlantis*, the travelogue function of the poem is at best vestigial. England is not realized at all in scenes. We might glimpse the setting of a given incident or thought (though the uncertainty over London gardens indicates how indifferent Dudek now is to precision of location), but we have no passages like the two above, dedicated entirely to the rendition of a scene of beauty or interest. Such organizational force as the travelogue sectioning might seem to have offered is thus more than offset by the poem's drive inward.

The result is a degree of conceptual tension in *Atlantis*'s superficies, a fault perhaps in poetic terms, but arguably another measure of authenticity in the portrait of mind it now turns to attempt. It is as if Dudek halfway through had reconsidered the constitutive metaphor of his two earlier long poems – the journey of the body metaphoric of the journey of the mind – and decided that the real point of the comparison was its tenor of mental life, not the vehicle of travel in Europe, which could now enter the poem only in such minor-key gestures as were attractive to him in given moments of mental indulgence. This unevenness must bear some relation to the long period of the poem's composition; although Dudek has claimed that *Atlantis* was 'written in Europe'[51] in 1961, the poem did not appear until 1967, a six-year span commonly understood to be the period of its drafting and revision (Davey, p. 69). Although a good deal of the poem was drafted on site, was England farther away from the poet's memory when he turned to revise that section? Had therefore more of the image-rich Italian section been composed in the country it describes? Whatever the explanation of these modulations in the persona's degree and kind of attention in Europe, the impression is given throughout *Atlantis* of a distinct shift of attention from the phenomenal objective to the inner subjective world.

This steady removal into the representation of pure consciousness obviously links *Atlantis* and *Continuations* conceptually. The reduced representation of literal in favour of mental travel brings with it an efflorescence of intellectual material in the poem. Whereas in *Europe* the intellectual matter is almost entirely art-historical in nature, and in *En Mexico* largely ethical and aesthetic, in *Atlantis* a full outpouring of Dudek's interests is suddenly released, the result being a density of reference and discourse by and large congruent with the richness of *Continuations.* Since the reader encounters such concerns in fragments scattered over the length of a long poem, their connections are not immediately apparent, and none is taken up so consistently as to become integral in the poem as a whole. As Davey remarked of Dudek's more epigrammatic turns, moreover, these discursive fragments 'appear unconnected to ... the circumstances which originated them' (p. 71), and that lack of grounding in the fact of Europe denies causality to their appearance: bits of discourse occur on the page as in the poet's mind, nothing more. The interpretation of Europe begun in 1954 is now hardly the point of *Atlantis*; the interpretation of mind has superseded.

A greater self-consciousness about the uses of mind as *integritas* is visible in *Atlantis* than in *Continuations,* perhaps because the whole concept still strikes Dudek in 1967 as a potential egotism. There is, for example, an autobiographical passage with no parallel I know of in Dudek's poetry, beginning 'When I was a boy' and proceeding to relate a series of highly Wordsworthian childhood epiphanies over forty lines. (It occurs in the Paris section, but as usual has no visible relation to the traveller's time in Paris.) The sudden focus on the 'I' in this passage is disconcerting, whether we have been persistent in expectation of travelogue or pursuing more ambiguous modes of coherence in the poem. Dudek lets the matter drop indifferently, to keep the randomness of self-representation intact, but the episode bespeaks the remaining stiffness in his long and gradual turn towards a subjective field of poetic detail. Another feature of this self-consciousness is the frequent reference to the use of one's self as the organizing and coherent force in a fragmented poem. Most of these asides cast simultaneous light on the poetics of *Atlantis*:

What, then, if the forms we know
                    are sections of a full body
whose dimensions are timeless
                         and bodiless, like poems,
whose unseen dimension is mind?

(p. 13)

... there is one who looks with warm detachment
                    out upon the world,
and would create, out of that fury and violence,
                an order and a beauty that is all his own.

(p. 83)

Not that the poem doesn't have a meaning.
            It's what holds the thing together,
an invisible ghost.

(p. 131)

The first and third of these are perhaps particularly evocative of the present argument, in that Dudek is careful in them to underscore the ambiguous and fluctuating quality of consciousness he seeks to represent, a mind that is 'unseen,' a 'ghost' that 'holds the thing together.' But the second passage is more evocative of Dudek's hopes for *Atlantis*: that we recognize in our companion a 'warm detachment' and come to appreciate him for the 'order and ... beauty' he finds in the world.[52]

By 1967 Dudek accepts that it is in what he calls 'the sweet vortex of the "I"' (p. 120) and nowhere else that he will find new *integritas* to sustain his ongoing eradication of formal and stylistic decorativeness and convention in poetry. The long process by which he arrived at this conclusion, in preparing for and composing *Atlantis*, speaks to the natural uneasiness he felt, as a poet trained in the impersonalist 1940s, in taking modernism on to a fuller expression of subjective reality. His anxiety could only have been exacerbated by his sharp reaction against the poetics of Layton, in whom he found the expression of an egotism without boundary or aesthetic purpose. The extreme self-effacement with which Dudek learned to affirm selfhood in the long poem must have been in part a desire to avoid Layton's occasional extremes, but their aesthetics nonetheless have much in common. Both men, at their best, find in an ironically affirmative selfhood the basis for a reintegration of the incoherent fragments of experience and of the incoherent world around them. That they look so different in consequence of this common intuition, and so offended each other in the process, indicates to my mind not a fault-line in my suppositions about them, but the readiness of those suppositions to embrace markedly different poetic practices responding to common aesthetic and epistemological questions.

As I remarked earlier, late passages in *Atlantis* are distinctly anticipatory of the *Continuations* project:

Nothing is ever finished.
Hokusai, Hiroshige, Kuniyoshi
            (lightning like Japanese script)
and the Wm. Morris Co.

Modern artifacts, our Danish knives,
        lace, Wedgwood, china –

even a poet or two on the boards.
                                        Jazz.

'Electronic music should go with poems.'
'I'd like to try a harp and a drum.'
                                'An outdoor auditorium
with music tunneled underground.'

(pp. 137–8)

The growing brevity of interjection as *Atlantis* draws to a close, its juxtaposition of 'found' materials, the strongly aleatory passages emerging at this late moment, and the new emphasis on overheard conversation would be enough to let the last pages of the poem slip unnoticed into the later volume. Indeed, at roughly this point of *Atlantis* the poet and an interlocutor speak directly to the *Continuations* model just around the corner:

I said to my friend, 'Don't read this,
                                        it'll make you dizzy.'
But she read on, said she couldn't stop.
                'What is it?'
I said: 'The vertigo of freedom.' ...

Why stop at all, she said, why not go on? ...

'Of course I can't stop,' I said.

(p. 137)

'So let's continue' might have been the next line. Although *Atlantis* retains the longer focused passages that allow Dudek to speak at length on particular issues of concern to him, the way it ends suggests the inevitability of 'the infinite poem,' the concept it could not entirely realize in this form. One might also hear in these lines – not for the first time – the implicit egoism of Dudek's attempt. The poet who can describe his poem as inducing the very 'vertigo of freedom' is not so free of self-aggrandizement as Davey suggests. But the principles of fragmentation, randomness, and instability of reference that inhere in that poet's self-representation keep a firm check on self-delight, and the result is the 'warm detachment' for which he hopefully and correctly praised himself in an earlier passage.

There can be, and I wish there were, many narratives of Dudek's development from *Europe* to *Atlantis*. Mine has attempted to chart the poet's gradual sublimation in his own long poems, until the Dudek who is a sharply bounded character in *Europe* becomes an indistinct aesthetic premise in *Atlantis.* At the same time I have wanted to watch the three poems' cumulative endorsement of poetic fragmentation, their drive closer and closer to the limits of poetic coherence; and I have hoped to suggest that these two trajectories are enabling of one another. By 1967 Dudek had established his primary artistic purpose as the representation of consciousness in the fullest possible – and yet in clearly ironic – terms. While this decision entailed a gradual withdrawal from an elaborate mimesis of the objective world, it contradictorily recalibrated and reaffirmed a variety of Imagist *and* personalist methods that Dudek had explored in embryonic form as a young poet of the forties. True, Dudek was not much exercised, from the days of *First Statement* to the first trip to Europe in 1953, by the latent questions of forties poetic debate. It is ironic then that it was Dudek who appears to have pursued, and accomplished with the greatest integrity, the answers to questions that had been powerful and enervating to his confrères: what longer forms of poetry can draw on the Imagist example of fragmentation and juxtaposition without completely sacrificing the energy and wholeness a longer work demands? What basis is there for a return to subjective poetry that will circumvent the risks of subjectivism so fully inculcated by my modernist training? And are these two questions really one?

Dudek of the Forties

I remarked earlier that the poets of *First Statement* who were least receptive to the dominant styles of the early forties were Louis Dudek and Raymond Souster. Perhaps this is unsurprising: the two were youngest of the forties cohort, that much farther away from early modernist example, that much more open to emerging possibilities of voice and manner. Still, Dudek had to grow into his distinctiveness, and just as the P.K. Page we know from collections and criticism is not the Page of *Preview,* the Dudek poetry to appear first in *Unit of Five* in 1944 and two years later in *East of the City* – however unlike the mature work of the 1950s – was the result of years of apprenticeship, and it is such raw material, some of it clearly juvenile, that *First Statement* generally affords the scholar. One way through it is the consideration of Dudek's models for imitation, which in his first appearance in January 1943 arguably included, ironically, Page herself and A.J.M. Smith: the former in a poem called 'Offices,' whose 'typewriters stuttering to paper' are strongly reminiscent of Page's 'Stenographers,' which had appeared a few months before in *Preview;*[53] and the latter in an untitled poem whose concluding lines are redolent of Smith's early signature diction: 'And all the poems that sang in my heart / Turned to the same white, bitter salt.'[54] There is a good case for claims of 'influence' here, but its pursuit would be fruitless, since the young Dudek would move quickly away from this imitativeness as from these exemplars.

Dudek made it clear with his next appearance in *First Statement* that he wanted a different sound from contemporary poetry, in his awkward and self-conscious rendition of a member of the grammatical underclass:

> I'm over moral? Man! – If I had my way,
> I'd put up parlors in Dominion Square Building
> So's people could do things decent!
>
> ('Berger Street')

He realized more quickly than either Souster or Layton, though, that this voice was not his own either: the manner was fortunately abandoned as soon as attempted. An alternative formulated itself shortly after, with a species of sensitive visual poetry akin to H.D.'s 'Oread' but displaying little of the viscera of Imagism:

> Drop, drop, delicate pearl in water,
> Drop, delicate dancing pearl,
> Drop in sea of white water, chase dark-of-sunset, pearl,
> Up, delicate dancing pearl,
> Up, pearl, and light-fill the world.[55]

These lines 'In Praise of Sunrise' also make plain, however, a startling tendency to dandyism in the early Dudek: its preciosity is echoed in a number of Dudek's poems from the period, not only as here in mood and theme, but also in an unconsidered attraction to formal quatrains:

> Scarred roof of jade, starry spoon,
> Spread, once, for crazy hours of glee;
> Lucia's bridal veil, the flung festoon,
> Bee-swarms stinging till eyes cannot see ...
>
> 'Untitled ["Out of the silence ..."]'

I have elsewhere attempted a description of dandy poetry whose heyday was in the 1920s,[56] and this slight piece does not warrant its re-creation here, but it seems evident that the young poet was often charmed by a highly artificial vision akin to that of Robert Finch and Smith himself. Such imitations call into question Dudek's own version of his reaction in company with Layton to the superficial modernisms of the *New Provinces* group:[57] for a while anyway he was rather keen on some of their mannerisms, though these juvenile exercises do nothing to characterize his real poetic training.[58]

A more original form of juvenile imitation was Dudek's marked practice of the sentimental lyric:

Swift I brushed your hair aside,
Saw your eyelids open'd wide,
And kiss-devour'd a sound that cried,
Pleading mercy as it died.

'Untitled ["Snow drops glistened ..."]'

Possible influential explanations of this behaviour include the poetry of Edna Saint-Vincent Millay, whose popularity with A.J.M. Smith, for example, is little remarked. Dudek would also pen 'A Note on Isabel Ecclestone Mackay' for *First Statement* in early 1943, praising in her 'best poems' 'a rare touch of magic' and quoting accordingly:

I who have loved the rain,
Down with the rain I go –
Deep in the sweet, brown earth,
Quick with the pulse of birth,
I who have loved the rain
Press its cool lips again.[59]

We don't need to debate Dudek's judgment of the poet's quality, but his appraisal of her, contemporary with his own increasingly lyric and usually sentimental manner, is a useful footnote to his development. His juvenile lyricism is more significant than his other imitations, because a better self-representation will be key to his poetic development.

In fact, there is a fairly short course from the early sentimental lyricism to the emergence of a more ironic subjectivism whose implications are formal as well as thematic:

Let me lean here and breathe
Fantastic air,
Under buildings where blue ducts
Flow, and rats glide in gondolas, unskimmed

Rivers reek, of beetle skin,
Arachnida,
While vapours rise into the purple
Air like perfume, overcoming the senses.

('On a Bridge at Pt. St. Charles')

It is more than the poem's ironic comparison between 'Venice ... and The Bridge of Sighs!' and 'a bridge at Pt. St. Charles' in Verdun that leads me to compare this roughly cut poem to the later manner of the itinerant poet in *Europe*. The persona's role is much more muted here than in previous lyrics, and while a degree of dandyism persists, in company with images highly evocative of *The Waste Land*, his central function as fluid and spontaneous observer ironizes those allusions to reduce their derivativeness. The form is also more fluid, somewhat echoing the rhythm of the poet's moving eye; prominent enjambment suggests both the flow and the processive interruption of the speaker's thoughts. The eye and the imagination work simultaneously here in a manner that anticipates – certainly does not realize – the proprioceptive interests of later work. The inclusion of the spider's Latin genus as a sudden fragment of thought heightens the similarity, superficially, to Dudek's later method. My comparison is a little forced, and certainly Dudek would not show any further interest in such latent poetics for the better part of a decade. But it is to be noted nevertheless that the Dudek poems we still read today – if Robin Blaser's selection for *Infinite Worlds* is an indication – are just around the corner from these discoveries: Dudek's next poems for *First Statement* would be 'A White Paper' and 'Sound for Orchestra,' the former collected in *East of the City* and the latter in *Unit of Five*. Following shortly thereafter are 'Garcia Lorca' and 'O Contemporaries,' both notable in *East of the City*, and both written at the peak of his forties manner. In this sense, Dudek's apprenticeship in *First Statement* was swift and effective. That the much-matured poet of the mid-forties would refashion himself dramatically *circa* 1953 does not reduce the spectacle of his arrival in and prompt domination of the Montreal scene.

The two volumes just mentioned appeared with Ryerson on either side of the *Preview–First Statement* amalgamation, and by 1946 Dudek had every reason to think of his poetic career as well under way. This is perhaps why the drought of volume publication between 1946 and 1952 seemed to him as significant of failure and injustice as it appears to have done. Gnarowski noted above the prominent suspicion among Dudek, Souster, and Layton of their having been ignored by the Canadian publishers; Davey has it that both Souster and Dudek complained of a 'backlog' of poems that their two slim

Ryerson chapbooks of 1951 and 1952 did little to reduce (pp. 19–20). What exactly that backlog consisted of is hard to say; in Dudek's case it must have included a number of the previously unpublished poems that he eventually gathered at his own expense in *The Transparent Sea* in 1956, of which he says 'the earliest of these poems date from about 1942.'[60] The rhythms of composition, submission, and publication make the identification of Dudek's literal body of forties poetry difficult, of course. The poems in the five volumes which had appeared by the end of 1952 may all be dated firmly to the period of my present interest, however, and as those volumes also help to organize a version of Dudek's progress in the decade, I will take their offerings as a sufficient, if not an exhaustive, canon, pausing only to divide them in the remarks that follow between *Unit of Five* (1944) and *East of the City* (1946), on the one hand, and the three books of 1952, on the other.

The remarkable formal responsiveness that Dudek evinced in the days of *First Statement* is a persistent feature of his work in the middle forties. No other Canadian poet of the period dealt so easily with the traditions of English verse while staying quite so at home with its modernist renovation; in this period Dudek shows little formal consciousness or depth, none of the intense concern over form and style visible in Page, Klein, and the early Layton. His insouciance in this regard is refreshing, even if it is a sign, as Davey says, of an immature poet who had yet found no style or voice of his own (pp. 46–9); his amply 'eclectic detachment'– to borrow a Smithism[61] that seems curiously appropriate – is also a sign of an expansive creative will and a youth's refusal to enter the lists under the formalist angst that had been enjoined upon his modernist elders.

By the time the strong poems in the late *First Statement* period emerged, he had more or less given up his formal quatrains, but he put that training to good effect in free-verse lyrics whose flexibility does not call into question their elegance and mannerism. Most of these persistent lyrics deal with love and nature, and to that extent confirm a reading of the 1940s (like Comfort's, or Layton's of 1943) as a period of resurgent Romanticism:

Know, that as a rose unpetals in the morning
So your lips unpetal under my lips;

And also, like a bird sleeping with wings folded,
Your eyelids sleep under my kisses.[62]

There in the hills, we kissed.
In the streams, pebble-naked

– your body bread brown, then shining,
  shining with drops, bewildered with water –
your kisses bright as those berries I had,
kissed your lips like a rock, with mad water kisses.[63]

Dudek's attention to form, however lyrical, is still Imagist enough to permit the strained 'kissed your lips like a rock' to stand in its swirl of rhythm and euphony. The poems are delightful, if only because the Dudek they display is all but forgotten today. The love-lyric was not to take him far, though he reveals a telling honesty about sentimental emotion.

The contemporary poems of nature are somewhat more interesting to the present-day reader of Dudek, chiefly because they anticipate the 1950s fascination with natural energy and natural form that *En Mexico* will want to explore. A remarkable number of the opening poems in *East of the City* are about trees. The sentimental imagination is again operative, but now it is groping after an aesthetic dimension to natural growth:

Stately tree. See what moves
between you and me. Love.
For I have learned wisdom from trees,
have seen healed wounds in bark
made beautiful; hurt roots
by murderous stone, and branches,
the seekers, torn.

('Tree,' *EoC*, p. 7)

A far cry this from the vision of carnage and fertility in Mexico, but the voice is recognizable, and so perhaps is the quality of mind:

Someday we shall come again to the poem
as mysterious as these trees,
of various texture,
leaves, bark, fruit
(the razor teeth so neatly arranged,
so clean the weathered root).

(*En Mexico*, p. 69)

The precision of the vegetable eye and the willingness to learn of art from natural forms marks off these early nature lyrics from the balance of Dudek's forties poetry. They suggest that the search for an aesthetics adequate to nature and to the natural man was at least latent in his creative imagination very early on: and little else would be retained of his early style after the dramatic vocational decisions of 1953.

Dudek's Imagism was as yet undeveloped, however, at the period of 'Tree.' One or two of the early *First Statement* pieces, like the 'In Praise of Sunrise' quoted earlier, suggest some exposure to Imagist possibilities of visual irony, but their technique is both thin and self-conscious. *Unit of Five* shows little further interest in the method. By *East of the City*, however, a minor Imagist interest is visible, in two juxtaposed poems 'Evening' and 'Night Piece':

The moon floated down
a river between two clouds
melted the stone banks and they
were gone.
Never flew the stars
in pebbles so brilliant,
nor shook the sands
in such sediments!

('Night Piece,' *EoC*, p. 5)

Both objectivism and binarism give resonance to the poem and seem to indicate some greater exposure to and reflection on Imagism between about 1943 (during which the selection for *Unit of Five* would have been fixed) and 1946. Layton's Imagism surfaced in early 1943, and it is not too much to suppose that the then-close friends faced the early modernist school to some extent together. But Dudek (like Layton at that time) found little to develop in the Imagist method, and his visual sense was increasingly determined, limited, and reified by quasi-Marxist expectations of poetry's affective power, the famous 'social realism' of Canadian forties poetry.

'Social realism' has meant many things to critics of Canadian forties poetry, from vague expressions of sympathy with working-class life to the more doctrinaire expression of revolutionary responses. It is rarely considered as a primarily aesthetic orientation, in which the description of a particular kind of urban scene (or, less commonly, action) is arranged around an accumulation of visual details in an attempt to evoke class-poignancy in the reader. Its unspoken assumption is always that the reader does not usually, but badly needs to, see such places if he or she is to take the necessary ameliorative social decisions. Dudek's best social-realist practice partakes of the picturesque's tendency to arrange visual detail according to vertical planes; as his eye moves through the scene, his observing consciousness organizes it according to imaginative juxtapositions in space, the resulting sense of crowding and clutter functioning on both the visual and the stylistic levels. In this manner, social realism is not of much interest to Dudek in the *First Statement* period: he offers at best one or two poems that open with precise urban detail but veer away from it quickly into more fantastic or satiric modes of expression. 'On a Bridge at Pt. St. Charles,' quoted earlier, gives an indication of the habit, its Eliotisms quickly superseding the realist motive of the first stanza. 'The Mountains' (March 1944) also opens typically:

In streets, among the rocks of time and weather,
With the crisp noises around us, and the surrounding voices,
Hearing the steel of wheels repeatedly, like bayonets,
And the sound of guns from buildings, where the windows
Icily shut suddenly like visors, and men are marching ...

Note the accumulation of subordinate clauses in these first five lines; the poem will not be granted a subject and predicate ('I walk') until the ninth line, a syntax typical of Canadian social realism in practice.

Unit of Five shows the habit persistent, with poems like 'Sound for Orchestra' and 'A Factory on Sunday' opening up working-class urban views but struggling hard in subsequent lines to make them significant. In the latter poem, their significance is not social or political but archetypal:

That yellow chimney up against the sky ...

  is also the bossed bludgeon
Of the ape-man and barbarian ...

Then, most of all, it has the mystery
Of an occult Egyptian censer
Held in the hands of priests ...

(*UoF*, p. 10)

Note once again the accumulative parallel syntax that is prevalent in such depictions. The poem has a subliminal objectivist drive, sheer re-presentation, that tells against the political conviction with which the young poet would also like it to be soaked. It is only when Dudek trusts the objective details to carry their own political signification that his social realism matures, and that only occurs, on balance, during his first year or two in New York, in a few poems which would be collected in *East of the City*.

The volume runs counter not only to a conventional Canadian poetry, whose titles to that point had never acknowledged so bluntly the existence of urban life; it runs counter as well to some strains of the 'new' in poetry of the forties, such as the neo-Romanticism articulated by Comfort, who wrote (while expressing so much of the decade's consciousness), '... I believe that in essence art is the act of standing aside from society, with certain important qualifications.'[64] It is probably on this basis that a notice in the *Partisan Review* attacked the new Romanticism for a 'failure of nerve,' just prior to the appearance of *Art and Social Responsibility*.[65] Dudek would himself come to agree, however, that '[a] vivid picture of the city dump, or of the private dump of one's own conscious or unconscious, makes no poem.'[66] Nor indeed is Comfort's remark intended to absolve the poet of all social obligation; as he would go on to insist:

> ... artistic responsibility consists in taking all this upon our shoulders – in providing voices for all those who have not voices. The romantic ideology of art is the ideology of that responsibility, a responsibility borne out of a sense of victimhood, of community in a hostile universe, and destined like Prometheus, its central creation, to be the perpetual advocate and defender of Man against Barbarism, community against irresponsibility, life against homicidal and suicidal obedience.[67]

Thus the judgment of social consciousness in the forties is entangled, and when Dudek casts less obvious significance on his urban settings – when he objectifies them and spares archetypal comment – it is arguable that he shows greater, not less, social responsibility, and greater artfulness.

The impact of the social-realist impulse on *East of the City* shows the full range of possibility in the manner. Broadly speaking, the urban setting is marked; despite love lyrics and tree lyrics, the bulk of the work is set in cities, this alone making Dudek's first independent volume a landmark in Canadian poetry. The city figures in poems of self-promotion (the 'harbour bridge' and 'traffic' of 'Making Poems' [p. 1]), of love (when 'even the refuse in the streets / looks romantic' ['In Spring,' p. 16]), of nature (the 'traffic ... dynamos and steel' that cannot change a city tree that will not 'adapt itself to our tempo' ['Tree in a Street,' p. 10]). What counts in these surroundings is not their urbanism itself, of course, but Dudek's determination to represent the dingier urban details and play on their dissonance with more conventional materials. It is the 'shining morning' quality of *aubade*, Eos in the slums, that can give Dudek's social realism its powerful irony and beauty. Probably 'A Street in April' contains the best-known of such effects:

Neither the fire-escapes making musical patterns
nor the filigree of stone flowery and decorating
can now accompany young April; the iron grating
jars, someone dropped a kettle in the orchestrating.

(*EoC*, p. 25)

The rhythms of 'A Street in April' are really masterful, retaining as they do the quality of playfulness that conveys in this slum depiction the full incongruity with childhood and spring. In comparison with his *First Statement* social-realist efforts, Dudek has come far: here the scene and its significance are coeval, needing no help from the commenting poet. His withdrawal into the appearance of objectivity allows – as it would again later in his work – the full force of subjective experience to emerge.

Not all the varieties of social realism in *East of the City* are quite so happy. The pronounced sympathetic proletarianism of a handful of radicals in the 1930s – poets such as Dorothy Livesay, whose early attempts at a working-class poetics look so strained today – survives in a few Dudek poems that constitute a subspecies, dropped fairly quickly along with his Marxism in the later 1940s, of his social-realist period.[68] 'Basement Workers' is fairly typical and can be powerful:

... of roofs too near overhead,
of air sharp with particles, like gravel in sand,
boxes, and tables with torn fringe of metal,
blocked doors, stacks
of coffined cribs ready for crouching mummies,
paper to wrap around our pale corpses:
so these, dispersed, hang in the air between
  floor and ceiling ...

(*EoC*, p. 34)

Still, the opacity of some of the images (as in the fifth and sixth lines quoted) suggests a self-conscious effort on the poet's part, as does the opening line I suppressed: 'Let me give you reminders to keep the image clear.' I don't question the profundity of Dudek's sympathy, but only its enactment in the poem; it would be an interesting debate to compare the achieved degree of sympathy in this and in Page's 'The Stenographers.' Their radically different styles converge somewhat in the opaque imagery of Dudek's middle lines. Clearer imagery may not be poetically preferable, though, as 'Be Young with Me' suggests:

Sympathy like cords trips up the legs of youth
When he lifts the drunk from the sewage cover,
It ravages like measles the upright young daughter
Who fries her own face in the tenth drain of mazola.[69]

This poem opened, again, in high self-consciousness: 'Be young with me, have no pity for the poor,' and by the time the predictable inversion of this harsh sentiment surfaces it seems superficial, unearned, and full of bluster: 'Be young – / But carry an ax of stone to this murderous civilization.'

It is in the context of such varied success that 'East of the City' itself exemplifies the most successful and resonant of Dudek's social-realist methods. It does not deny but foregrounds and affirms his proletarian sympathy, by a firm muting of the personative function: no one needs to step in dramatically to claim identification with the subject workers. The poem opens with confident and powerful visuals in strong rhythm:

East of the city, under towering smokestacks
Where the railroad, brewery and tall bridge
Redden and drown our eyes with cinders,
Where the drumhead oilskin of the river wavers ...

Between the knees of the bridge, crouching
By a wall that gapes like a stupid face –
Pause, and see how heavy the corpses
Swing from the girders, how their shadows resound
As they shudder and fall from the beams.

(*IW*, p. 44)

No more than an 'our' is required to assert the continuity of the speaker's and the observed workers' experience: the effect is of understood community and shared exploitation. Dudek opens with a broad sweep over the setting and gradually draws the poem's visual focus downward; it is not only his eye moving (emphasizing detachment and objectification), but 'our' eyes that are told to move with his, our 'pause' demanded as we turn to look more closely. His aesthetics are like those of documentary film, with an opening wide-angle to establish setting and then a series of increasingly close shots until the specific action to be observed can emerge, in relative close-up:

The haggard labourers gather, muster together;
Dwarfed by the dark, they shrink in showers

Of light spat from the walls by the welders,
Then club-footed, hunched, they shoulder through
A cloud of golden atoms, shredded fireworks.
They sling their thumbs through their lax suspenders
On rags of shirt crossing their barren shoulders,
They wipe the wrinkles round their throats and ear-lobes,
And plod the streets together ...

(*IW*, p. 44)

The visual technique has the advantage of a steadily increasing identification with the workers portrayed, and it places the action that follows – a narrative of several disjointed tasks and events in their labouring day and restless evenings – in both aesthetic and economic contexts.

Ensuing stanzas flesh out the portrait of workers' lives and emphasize its soullessness:

Then late, on stairs like a broken accordion
They mount to the two-room flat, smelling a cloth
That wraps their faces and tangles at their feet;
They eat the cold supper, leaning on their elbows
And grousing, while the wife tense in the kitchen
Waits with lukewarm water, and the fecal dishes.
Afterwards, leaning limp out of windows
They look at life in the street, wait for bedtime ...

(*IW*, p. 45)

In contrast, and perhaps with unwitting irony, later stanzas showing the men at work in the factory have a high degree of visual and emotional energy and excitement: the job has made a 'chesty gorilla' of a young man into a 'gaunt old man ... phthisic,' but the work is done with pride, even a sense of purpose. This is because Dudek wants his usual note of uplift with which to conclude even this long poem, so he has to demonstrate that when the men work together (which they can be shown to do, in this realist aesthetic, only in the factory itself), they can bring about radical social change:

But look, how forceful with facts, the sullen slaves
Here powerful and proud, stand up as leaders.
No thread runs in the rounded wheel without them.
The wheel of society, steel-bright with the future,

Is wrought by the people, its only revolutionists.
See, how the war clouds boil around the factories ...

(*IW*, p. 46)

The sententiousness slipping in here seems an inescapable feature even of the best social realism. At least Dudek mutes it with the sentimental freshness and sense of open possibility with which he concludes the poem:

Drive out
Through factories, and brick walls of buildings
To the east, to the fields sweet with clover ...
For this, take up a handful of green grass for hope:
Walk out tomorrow, talk to the world and the people.

(*IW*, p. 46)

Despite the imperative mood, the poem's closure emphasizes the need to know more of 'the people' than the poem has been able to incorporate. Few social-realist poems in *East of the City* admit as much. 'East of the City' is among the best examples of mid-century social realism, for the precision and vividness of its images, for its relative control over sympathy and aesthetic distance, for its difficult attempt to balance optimism with realism. It has been too little noted: a remarkable period-piece.

'East of the City' also shows, however – despite the enormous difference of style and perspective between this and Page's 'Photos of a Salt Mine,' for example, or Layton's 'Proof Reader' – the ineluctable force of the debates over poetic style and structure that I have identified in the transition of poetry in Canada in the forties. Its heavy reliance on the '*a of b*' formula for image-making that Page first showed us (out of Anderson and Thomas) is, for example, remarkable. In the poem's three pages there are some two dozen sightings of the method: 'the drumhead oilskin of the river,' 'the knees of the bridge,' 'shattering bells / Of hammers and cranes,' 'the giggle of gargoyles,' and so on (*IW*, pp. 44–5). Certainly, Dudek's conjunctions of noun with noun around the operative 'of' are not as startling, as showy, as Page's and Anderson's characteristic effects ('the bivouac of Sunday' and so on), but the reliance on juxtaposition, derivative of Imagism, is the same. Nor does Dudek crowd his '*a of b*' formulations intensively in an attempt to override the reader's will to clarity. He does, however – and this seems inherent in most kinds of forties poetry – invoke a principle of accumulation to organize details, a tactic we have already seen syntactically in other social-realist work from his hand.

In the opening lines, already quoted, there is the same tendency as in Page to accumulate several subordinate clauses prior to the long-deferred arrangement of an independent clause: 'East of the city,' 'Where the railroad,' 'Where the drumhead,' 'And in the damp,' and 'Between the knees' all open subordinate clauses, each one offering a central striking image, prior to the imperative 'Pause' in the tenth line that actually initiates action in the poem. In the second stanza, this syntactic accumulation is replaced by the accumulation of images, largely isolated from one another:

> Out of the ruptured cauldron, the green factory
> Whose ogre eyes gleam in the sooty night,
> Railed wrists stretch over hard, broad hills,
> The cold coal and straight strata, iron and steel;
> The belly boils, and peal its shattering bells
> Of hammers and cranes, flying their halleluyas.
>
> (*IW*, p. 44)

Note the relative syntactic obscurity of this sentence, the difficulty of construing an antecedent for the appositive 'straight strata,' the uncertainty of subject for the plural predicate 'peal,' not to mention the generally higher degree of difficulty in its imagery. The good effect of these techniques is Dudek's embodiment of the incoherence, even the violence, of the factory's mechanic energy; the poetic effect is his closer approximation of the typical forties style.

The accumulative force of 'East of the City' is beautifully contained by the documentary eye that structures its details, by the use of a typical worker's evening, night, and morning as a temporal structure and (for better or worse) by the rather ponderous political optimism of its closure. The poem's realist aesthetics do not allow a prolonged vagary into the obscurity and density, the high stylism, of Page's social poems. But the poem's assumption that social realism demands a documentary depiction of details of the workers' lives indicates the proximity of Dudek's representationalism to the catalogic mode of thirties and forties discourses, from the archival reports of Mass Observation to the obsessive notation by Klein of each detail of Joyce's *Ulysses*. Social realism presumes the need for an archive of the working-class world, and the goal is not so much to get at the essence of that world in a brilliant poem as it is to gather, over years of 'research,' a grouping of poetic insights whose collective effect is the reconstitution of a disempowered milieu and class. In this sense, the project anticipates a sufficient catalogue as its culmination; again, the vanishing point of such aesthetics is the 'infinite poem' of social detail.

Indeed it is not unlikely that Dudek came to this best version of his social-realist incarnation to some degree under the *Preview* influence. As the *First Statement* material makes plain, the young poet had social conscience early on, but no certain poetics to make it effectual; from 1942 to early 1944, while the urban setting is visible and a satiric voice intermittent, there is little that may be thought realist in Dudek's social poetry. It is only in poems like 'The Mountains' (March 1944) and 'O Contemporaries' (Feb./March 1945; *IW*, p. 43) that the 'East of the City' technique emerges. Remembering the early Dudek's inspiration as sentimental lyricist, it becomes necessary to account for the increasing attention to social realism *circa* 1945 and to some extent to contextualize the kinds of social realism he attempted in relation to the kinds then effective for other poets. It would hardly be surprising for him to have considered the *Preview* attempts at social realism, dismissed their artifice and formalism, but responded favourably to their models of catalogue and accumulation. It is also important to note the chronological overlapping of Dudek's inquiries into social realism and Imagism: for reasons as yet difficult to hazard, the two became attractive to him at roughly the same time, a coincidence that may at least suggest some deep continuity in the two apparently opposed projects.

The motive of these remarks will not be clear to those unfamiliar with the sudden, strange, and brief episode of Dudek's poetry in the books of 1952. In *Twenty-Four Poems*, one of the first books off the Contact Press, Dudek's Imagism is (apparently suddenly) prominent and highly skilled; and in *The Searching Image*, a Ryerson chapbook, his poetry appears to have taken a sharp turn towards the stylism, artifice, accumulation, and obscurity of Page, Anderson, some Klein, and the early Layton, a manner in which his best-known accomplishment is 'The Pomegranate.' Social realism is invisible in both books. This remarkable dual swerve indicates, tellingly, the deep connection between Imagist methods and the forties style dominant in *Preview*. It demands some accounting, moreover, that will help us understand how the emerging social realist and persistent lyricist of 1946 could have become, by 1952, a stylist and objectivist. Dudek referred to these as 'poems from the 1940s or early 1950s that might illustrate the road not taken' in his later work,[70] so a second accounting will need to explain the transition from such poetics into the far more discursive manner of *Europe* only two years later. My attempt to discern the accumulative and '*Preview*ish' qualities of Dudek's social realism was a first attempt to narrow the gap between Dudek's better-known trajectory from social realism to social and cultural comment (*East of the City* to *Europe*) and the brief flaring anomaly of the 1952 publications.

When Dudek returned to Montreal in 1951, he had surrendered any radical Marxist propensity to his general political leftism, a disillusionment explained variously[71] but one which no doubt helped his quick affiliation with F.R. Scott and Scott's more moderate socialist circle upon his return. He now kept company with Scott, Klein (briefly of course), and Neufville Shaw of the *Preview* group; shortly after, his famous 'Poetry Grapevine' would keep him in touch with most of the published Canadian modernists, including Page and Wreford of *Preview*, and Smith, E.J. Pratt, and Robert Finch of *New Provinces* (Davey, p. 12). His poetry contacts had expanded to include the widest possible range of Canadian voices, and he evidently welcomed involvement in the dominant formalist trends of mainstream Canadian modernism of the 1950s. On the other hand, his *First Statement* friendships were on the wane: his first rupture with Irving Layton would prevail until January 1952, and their reconciliation was coincident with John Sutherland's departure from Montreal for Toronto. At a distance it appears likely that Dudek's formalist and Imagist practice of the early 1950s was consonant with, if not furthered by, new creative friendships.

Considerations of the high artifice of Dudek's style in *The Searching Image* will have to take into account the possibility of strong publisher intervention in the volume's selection, but *Twenty-Four Poems*, with its efflorescent Imagism, was entirely under Dudek's control with the Contact imprint. The volume's Imagism has a Poundian classicism to it, as in 'Sunset,' that suggests Dudek's Poundism may well have been operative in the sudden Imagist concentration of his poetry:

Spurs, hoofs in the mud branch,
blood on the dew, and dawn!
Love's O opened among the spearheads,
among the dead arrayed
                    in faggoty designs;
the long light touching the foreheads
of the old and the young – too warm to be so dead.[72]

The Pound influence (I am obviously thinking of 'The Return') cannot be accurately dated; Dudek claims to have been reading and admiring him as early as the mid-1940s,[73] and whatever influences began on that first encounter were certainly demonstrated and deepened in the period of Dudek's visits to Pound in St Elizabeth's Hospital from 1949 to 1951: *The Searching Image* would be dedicated to him. Pound is functional of course as a plausible point of contact between the Imagist work of the early 1950s and *Europe*. Dudek's Imagism also shows, perhaps more suggestively for present purposes, the dominantly accumulative aesthetics of the forties:

Moss, green gold, the glory of an old bronze monument,
gilding the nameless rocks,
red leaves, gardens of them among the barer shrubbery,
berries, black priceless beads in couples
and triples, sunlit on the scattering stems,
a fountain of white branches falling out into the world,
banks of simple grass, green transparent leaves,
stones, trees, a pattern of criss-crossing twigs,
the sun shining on these decorations,
parks, walks of them,
and the crystalline texture of pebbles always at your feet ...

('A Morning Walk,' *24P*, p. vi)

Few Dudek poems thus far have made the accumulative method more obvious, or given a more casual impression of the poet's eye falling from object to object as his hand moves in reportage across the page.

Other Imagist or post-Imagist poems in the volume suggest how readily the Imagist impulse can lead to the peculiarities of form and style that had once been – in Dudek's view – so prominent and so vitiating in the *Preview* poets. Note the return of the '*a of b*' formula in 'Midnight,' for example, with its 'Bauer balls of light,' '"skoal" of giant glasses,' 'green plums of go-lights' and so on (*IW*, p. 63). 'Local Colour: Night Lights' recalls the tendency in Page to a lapidary, enamelled imagery that has its impact on style (as in her 'Photos of a Salt Mine'):

Undersea, a green cone of colour,
grapes, emerald, red, around a white
willow, in lime and blue luminous neon;
pearl splash of eyes weeping an anguished amethyst
glowing across a criss-cross diadem of crimson ...
green, shining on oyster sidewalks,
streets of shell, on which effeminate fish
upright on tiny tails, blackly balooning [*sic*]
among rocks in water, with ghostly gills of amber ...

(*24P*, p. xxii)

Note once again the highly accumulative method: there is no syntax *per se* in the poem, these subordinate clauses never serving to modify such minimal predication as Dudek offers for its closure. There is more to say about *Twenty-Four Poems*; Robin Blaser's selection for *Infinite Worlds* found little worth keeping in its Imagist work and much of note in such poems as 'Panta Hrei,' 'An Air by Sammartini,' and 'Spilled Plaster,' all of which help to anticipate the long-poem themes of the later and better-known Dudek. But the dominant Imagism of the volume, in which such speculative poems are the distinct exception, seems more challenging to a coherent reading of Dudek's progress, who looks more like a stereotypical *Preview* poet in this volume of 1952 than a reader of *East of the City* could have thought possible.

The contemporary *The Searching Image* has little of the companion book's Imagism; it is vestigial at best in 'Clouds' (p. 2), which also shows the (perhaps) last gasp of Dudek's social realism, and 'Acropolis' (p. 7), reminiscent in its open form of the more Poundian pieces in *Twenty-Four Poems* but lacking their precise visualizations; if anything, 'Acropolis' anticipates the ruminative style of *Europe*, with its fragments of Greek and Renaissance art and scholarly sensibility. Instead, *The Searching Image* is far more indebted to Anderson and to Page than it is to Pound. Only one of its poems has maintained its readership, 'The Pomegranate,' a decorative and formalist piece that seems to substitute stylistic vigour and complexity for significance of subject, 'reading' the piece of fruit in an effort of bardic uplift reminiscent of Klein in the Quebec poems:

> The jewelled mine of the pomegranate, whose hexagons of honey
> The mouth would soon devour but the eyes eat like a poem,
> Lay hidden long in its hide, a diamond of dark cells
> Nourished by tiny streams which crystallized into gems.
>
> (*IW*, p. 49)

The '*a of b*' is fainter, but present. The poem opens with self-reflexive remarks about its own aesthetics, by which the eye eats instead of the mouth; lapidary imagery is present, suggesting a high degree of aestheticization. The persona is fascinated by the pomegranate's secret innards: he just spoke of them as 'hidden,' and he goes on to note that 'The seeds [are] nescient of the world outside,' that the fruit's interior is a 'place of no light' where 'grenadiers' – the seeds again? – 'Gleam ... without a sun' (*IW*, 49). His exclamation towards the end of the third stanza explains the fascination: 'what art were no eyes were!' To some extent this is the Dudek of the 1950s and after, finding in natural form principles of beauty and structure that the wilfully seeing artist cannot follow. Indeed there is a suggestion of tragedy in the moment at which his eyes do pierce the fruit's skin, 'broken by my hand, this palace of unbroken tears.' After this boundary is penetrated, the poem offers its most difficult juxtapositions:

To wedding bells and horns howling down an alley,
Muffled, the married pair in closed caravan ride;
And then, the woman grown in secret, shining white,
Unclothed, mouth to mouth he holds his naked bride.

And there are days, golden days, when the world starts to life,
When streets in the sun, boys, and battlefields of cars,
The colour on a bannister, the vendors' slanting stands
Send the pulse pounding on like the bursting of meteors –

As now, the fruit glistens with a mighty grin,
Conquers the room; and, though in ruin, to its death
Laughs at the light that wounds it, wonderfully red,
So that its awful beauty stops the greedy breath.

(*IW*, p. 49)

Much of the difficulty of 'The Pomegranate' can be referred to its broad but vague Freudianism, though the vestigial urban realism of the middle stanza quoted here isn't helped into coherence by such an appeal, and the poem's Dantean conclusion about the fruit's significance still seems overstepping: 'The movement of the stars is that, and all their light / Secretly bathed the world, that now flows out of flesh.' The secrecy theme persists, and it, too, helps to make coherent what is otherwise a rather jumbled meditation on an aesthetic object.

The predominant stylistic quality of 'The Pomegranate' though is the density of its metaphors. Though individual images tend to be fairly accessible throughout, the poem is certainly showy, each line expected to live up to the intense visual and suggestive qualities of the opening 'hexagons of honey.' It seems likely that the 'aesthetics' of the pomegranate have been enjoined onto the poem, now offering a skin which we can penetrate to see dense 'honey' and 'blood' within. The effect is made particularly striking – and, for followers of Dudek, particularly anomalous – in comparison with the late urban stanzas, quoted above, in which the degree of metaphoricality plummets, as if to assert the incompatibility of such delicate imagery with the political grounding of the social-realist poem. These forces seem unresolved in 'The Pomegranate,' an ambivalence which to my mind helps to account for the effort of bardic closure. The poem's instability is not, obviously, profound; it forecasts Dudek's need for a coordinating perceptive consciousness in which the aesthetic object, the social perspective, and the philosopher's conclusions might all be integrated, but it is not in the same danger of conceptual or imagistic excess that its exemplar poems of the forties, such as Page's 'T-Bar' and Klein's 'Bread,' routinely risk. Still, considering the styles out of which this poet has emerged, and the vigour of his *First Statement* polemics against verbal decoration and obscurity of metaphor, 'The Pomegranate' of 1952 is a startlingly *forties* Dudek poem.

Were 'The Pomegranate' the only stylized poem in *The Searching Image* it would be a far less remarkable Dudek volume, but the technique here is practised often in the fourteen poems Ryerson could afford to print. 'The Bee of Words,' the volume's introductory poem, is like 'The Pomegranate' in its vigorous metaphoricality and its dense structure:

> Her mouth opening in lovely speech is the wet leaf
> of a flower, her voice the bee's soft sound in the air
> bringing the sting of desire; under the light of her hair
> the bee of words runs and robs like a loaded thief.[74]

Dudek again avoids, for the most part, the deliberate difficulty of comparison that characterized the poetry of Anderson and of Page, whose delicacy of perception and intensity of imagination he nevertheless approximates here. This relative restraint is ruined, however, by the highly rhetorical ending, the 'worn rhetorical gesture' that A.T. Tolley remarked to be characteristic of closure in forties poetry:[75]

> What generation of smoke turning to golden clouds
> does love make of a warm mouth and its own burning?
> What lands of love, for which those waxen wings are yearning,
> will yield them honeyed fields and apples breaking the boughs?

For closure's sake the metaphorizing spins exponentially out of control: 'love' makes a 'mouth' undergo 'burning' that yields 'smoke' (a 'generation' of it) that turns into 'clouds.' The hollow effect suggests the dangers of Dudek's short-term rededication to lavish lyric styles.

'Christmas' (*SI*, p. 3) repeats these gestures to an extent that makes the comparison with Page and Anderson unqualified. Its metaphors are highly cluttered, heavy with excess and obscurity:

> I cannot lay a rail across a slum reeking
> Lifted on silver studs, with flasks for pylons,
> To Jesus' simple straw and lambs crying 'love'
> And a small star shining the wise men home;

But kicking the tinsel, tearing receipts with teeth,
The bit lip spitting at the collector's teapot,
With canaries bled in my dreams and snow like fire
I celebrate the season bringing forth a god.

Note the elaborate and overworked syntax, uncharacteristic of the poet on either side of this anomalous few years, as well as the strain it imposes on referentiality: what is 'reeking'? What is 'lifted on silver studs,' apart from (metaphorically) Jesus? 'Flasks' of what? What 'collector's teapot'? The pedantic demand for clear antecedents for these brittle images seems ungenerous, but by any standard Dudek has raised as a critic or poetic theorist, such questions have to be asked of any poem. The much deeper question of course is, what has happened to Dudek's style? 'Christmas' is a minor and unreprinted poem, granted, but as the farthest point reached on an aestheticized 'road not taken,' it is telling us something vital about Dudek's pivot from the forties to the fifties, a three-period refashioning whose key events and outcome may now, in retrospect and context, be a little clearer.

Participation in the F.R. Scott and McGill circles must at least have encouraged Dudek's efforts in the forties mannerisms. *The Searching Image* contains a response poem to Scott's famous 'Overture' (and perhaps his 'Old Song') called 'Old Music' (pp. 1–2), its title and a number of its metaphors alluding to the precursor works, though the execution is faulty and suggestive of a degree of self-conscious effort in his new affiliation. To such suggestive but unproveable explanations we would want to add a greater knowledge of Dudek's personal life *circa* 1950, a fuller catalogue of his reading in the period, a detailed rendition of his intellectual relations with Pound, and so on. I find it highly telling that Dudek in the retrospect of later life could admit that '[w]hat drew me to Pound was his aestheticism and his revolutionary modernism in principle,' or remark upon 'the positive aspects of [Pound's] aestheticism and his pursuit of enlightenment.'[76] As one who has long been interested in the relations between Aestheticism and modernism, I am particularly intrigued to see an interpretation of Dudek's 'Poundism' that helps to explain not only the cultural inveighings of *Europe* but the delicacy of formalism in *Twenty-Four Poems* and *The Searching Image* as well. This for another time.

The implications of the anomalous styles of 1952 are more interesting, though, than their explication. First, Dudek's social-realist poetry was not among his original impulses: he was originally inspired as a lyricist and only turned to social realism, in a catalogic and accumulative mode appropriate to his forties models, in his mid-twenties, to abandon it substantially, along with his Marxism, by about the age of thirty. That abandonment was coincident with an increasing formalism, reminiscent of earlier forties styles, in his work; the representational goals of his social poetry were retained, but their aesthetics stylized, in a corollary efflorescence of Poundian Imagism. These tendencies reached their mutual apogee in collections of 1952. Shortly thereafter, Dudek began his exploration of the modernist long poem, eventually pushing its fragmentation, extension, and structural incoherence farther than any other Canadian poet, and at the same time exploring with rigour and method the extent to which the subjective consciousness, rendered with irony, may provide its own principles of *integritas* and significance to aleatory poetic styles.

Next, it seems to me that this set of circumstances suggests, ironically, both the deep incompatibility of social-realist and formalist aesthetics *and* their curious partnership, in the forties, in a tendency to accumulative catalogue, the former taking its components from the phenomenal and social world, the latter from the fretful juxtapositive imaginings of the poet. They suggest as well that Dudek was a fundamentally subjective poet from the start: that the social-realist and the formalist periods are *equally* anomalous to a narrative of his development that sweeps from the *First Statement* lyrics through *Europe* to the mental field of *Continuations*. I have argued that Dudek works out in his long poems the fullest theoretical answer offered by anyone to the problems of forties poetics, and that in his best poems and passages that theory is embodied in strongly affective form; I now find it telling that before initiating that 'research' he dallied with the mannerisms of his forties confrères, mannerisms that he had scornfully rejected five to ten years earlier. That his two primary experiments of the pivotal 1952 had their roots in Imagism and in the mannerism of Anderson and Page suggest the fundamental connection between those two styles. I think we must also presume of the 1952 styles their coherence with his self-reincarnation in *Europe*: that there is some sense in which this period of forties training was *necessary* to his forward progress.

Dudek's increasing breadth of reading and study during the New York years clearly made him far more concerned than he had once been to identify the poetic issues of debate in his time and gave him important new contexts for his assessment of the style he had heretofore associated solely with *Preview*. As his Marxism waned, and took with it his poetic attachment to social-realist catalogues of the urban scape, the mannerism of his former rivals briefly appealed to him as a method by which he could pursue the interrogations of poetic subjectivity and of structure and style that were beginning to surface in and characterize his increasingly intellectualized mind. His first period of experiment with this new consciousness of form and its relation to meaning was understandably retrograde: he worked through, almost as a scholar might, the available formalisms of his period of apprenticeship, but quickly found them inadequate to the complexity and urgency of his inquiries into the creative nature, into civilization instead of society, and into broader modernist forms. But the 1952 publications reveal nonetheless that the forties styles were not – as Dudek himself would later suggest – aberrations, but fundamental practices arising from the central legacies of modernist poetic change. When Dudek asked Souster in 1951, as he was preparing *The Searching Image* and *Twenty-Four Poems* for the press, 'Can anything be done to sew the earth together?',[77] he was asking the fundamental question of mid-century modernism as its adherents tried to move from the fragmented objectivism they had inherited to new forms of *integritas* and order incipient in the creative mind.

Nothing can account fully, however, at least not in literary-historical perspectives, for the long poems that began their appearance so soon after this brief period of Dudek's middle apprenticeship. It is one thing to say in retrospect, as I do conclude, that Dudek's brief flirtation with a highly decorative formalism was a necessary stage in his departure from a fairly superficial social poetry to a deeper penetration of human culture, that his formalist experiments of 1952 show him engaged with questions of poetic voice, form, and structure that had contextualized but not interested his youth and would largely determine a direction for his creative maturity. It is entirely another to try to explain *how* precisely a particular poet *did it*: what moments of brief and partial illumination culminated in the decision to write *Europe* so soon after 'The Pomegranate.' Retrospect can never re-create the uncertainty of prospect, nor criticism the intangibles of creativity. For those for whom my last sentence is still true, Dudek is a far more fascinating poet and important champion than we have realized.

First Conclusions

Dudek's development confirms, then, that there was a forties period style, close in kind though not always in degree to the dense and often difficult post-Imagist practice of *Preview* poets P.K. Page and Patrick Anderson; and that this period style engaged powerful and inevitable questions that kept its mannerisms alive throughout the 1940s. Irving Layton took until about 1953 to escape their practice entirely: in the course of the 1940s, he remained more fully in the orbit of the *Preview* pantheon – Thomas, Auden, the Surrealists – than has been recognized. But it is Dudek's case that shows with the greatest complexity the power of that dominant poetics, whose force he proves by both example and exception. That a poet who had largely shunned the prevalent manner throughout the 1940s should find it newly suggestive and still powerful enough *circa* 1950 to initiate a new albeit brief period of his own apprenticeship would seem to suggest that no poet of the era, not even one of its most particular voices, could refuse to deal with the conundra that that poetics had attempted to resolve, or the others it would cast up for poets of the next generation.

The lyricist, satirist, and emerging social realist Dudek of *First Statement* does indeed help us to see important local distinctions between his and the rival magazine *Preview*. In company with Souster, Dudek allows us to remark that *First Statement* was attractive to a few poets who in their salad days had no particular affinity with the forties period style, as it was to others who had certainly felt its influence; whereas *Preview*'s editorship was stricter – not different – in its adherence to that dominant manner and attracted no durable alternatives. Some will persist in calling Dudek's and Souster's contributions to *First Statement* that characteristic note of forties poetry that shows the favoured magazine's responsiveness to literary change; but they must be asked, what exactly is the *First Statement* note? Is Dudek's sentimental lyricism, his Scott-ish satire, his latter-day social realism the 'forties' poetry they want to admire? If so, why did each of these styles have to be abandoned by 1952 in favour of the supposedly outmoded style of his *Preview* friends – to be reconfigured in turn in another dramatic swerve in 1953? I have said that the polarization of the two little magazines cannot help us with any fresh critical questions about these poets. Dudek's case makes plain that we need both *Preview* and *First Statement* references if we are to understand the currents and counter-currents that influenced young poets in the decade. He makes plain as well that those two little magazines had a great deal more fruitful common ground than antagonism. Their richness lay between them; inarguably for Dudek.

And yet it is ironically Dudek the critic to whom we must turn as the source for most of the prevailing and less than adequate narratives of Canadian forties poetry. While he occasionally modulated the details of the narrative, it has been his polemics and commentaries – from the *First Statement* essays until the late 1980s – that have established, hardened, and rendered stereotypical the bifurcated and little-magged literary history of the Montreal forties that persists today. I need not repeat here the polemical viewpoint of my introduction. It does bear repeating, though, that the bulk of forties narratives has a family intellectual connection to Dudek's own polemics: forties commentators Gnarowski, Francis, Fisher, and Norris were all either supervised or mentored by Dudek or supervised by one of Dudek's students. They did not much distance themselves from his inevitably self-interested narratives of the period of his apprenticeship, and their writings have been constitutive of a successful orthodoxy. That another Dudek student should make these remarks renders them ironic but is not necessarily prejudicial to their accuracy. We can hardly be surprised to find that the single perspective of a man who both participated in and offered scholarship on a given period of poetic transition should be both dominant and suspect. I hope here to have separated the forties commentator from the poet, at least briefly, so that the poet comes a little clearer of significance and the commentator drops back – a little – into the shadows: a curious way of paying an intellectual debt.

Conclusion: The Generation of the Forties

When I reject little-magazine-based narratives of Montreal poetry in the 1940s, I am left with the problem of *integritas*: how to present a strong and whole image of four major Canadian poets without suppressing significant differences among them. If anything, I have erred on the side of too much unity, although my four chapters' relative avoidance of narration in literary-historical time may lead some to disagree. It may be that I have asked the same Imagist abilities of my readers as the poets I have considered asked of theirs. If that is so, I have now a last opportunity to integrate these fragmented perspectives, or indeed to fuse them too anxiously. *Integritas* is a fine line; unity need not be.

P.K. Page shows us the forties period style in its clearest form, redolent at once of intense sensual power and stylistic verve, and of risks of exhaustion and alienation from relations of sympathy with those she represents or with her readers to whom she represents them. She makes plain the surviving Imagist drift of modern poetry in the 1940s, in the juxtapositive force of her early metaphoricality (the '*a of b*' formula that we saw briefly in Klein, Layton, and Dudek too), as well as in the concise Imagist fragments recuperable at the heart of her more discursive poems. She also shows in her forties work the decade's common tendency to accumulation (with little subordination) of such post-Imagist fragments as the structural basis of longer poems; in some cases a style productive of entropy, flaccidity, enervation, in others of an astonishing radicalizing of perception and our grasp of beauty. On the solid Imagist ground of her dense style, she has perhaps greatest affinity with Louis Dudek of the post-*Europe* years: what is in Page the fundamental Imagist technique of dramatic visual perception in its relation to glimpsed essential truth, is in Dudek the fundamental Imagist inquiry into the processes and limits of consciousness, perception shading for him into proprioception, but the relation between *insight* and the phenomenal world fascinating both poets for their entire careers.

Page's early poetry also lends new vividness to our ideas of modernist impersonality. It was, in part, a dogma, and it appears largely to have been inherited as such by Canadian poets (although Klein showed us a more delicate and thoughtful negotiation with the idea, and its cognate 'anonymity,' in the course of his poetry and fiction from the late 1930s to the final silence). Calling an idea a dogma makes that idea easier for us to dismiss in the 1990s. But Page helps us to see that the idea of impersonality was not only powerful, hegemonic, as she began to write poetry, but *attractive*. Clearly she saw in impersonality's goal of objective rendition, and its neutralization of superficial differences that divert us from communication and negotiation with others, the possibility of stable representations and sociohistorical analyses that pre-modern subjectivist poetics had left obscure or mystified. Spending her teens and young adulthood in a global climate of anxiety and anticipation of violence – Samuel Hynes says that as early as 1928 the 'postwar' generational consciousness was largely replaced by a 'pre-war' alertness among young writers[1] – the idea of a sublimation of personal desire and definitive ego in a new poetics of objectivity and aesthetic distance was naturally heady matter. That it also entailed a degree of self-erasure she eventually found costly – and that, in part, in relation to her sex – speaks more to her willingness of sacrifice than to modernism's exclusion of her particular voice.

Most narratives of 1930s and 1940s poetic history emphasize the atmosphere of resignation and withdrawal that permeated local cohorts in the West when Joseph Stalin signed his non-aggression pact with Adolf Hitler in August 1939, guaranteeing the Wehrmacht a single front should the Allied European powers choose to resist German expansion into Europe. Hynes suggests that the poets of the 1930s did not go on to write 'war poetry' because their real war – the *avoidance* of a conflict with Fascism by a reconstitution of society on internationalist leftist principles – had been lost as soon as literal war was declared. In this context it is not difficult to understand that the positive orientation of modernist impersonality should gradually be lost on a new generation of poets trying to remain politicized and effectual in the midst of that global conflict. During the 1940s the dogmatic aspects of impersonality became more apparent, and its aspiration towards a universalizing inclusiveness less so, and some of these tensions are visible in Page, for whom impersonality remained so forceful until 1954 that it eventually stymied her equally powerful inclination to the expression of compassion for those who found themselves eccentric to the regimens of a world at war. We saw her lament to Floris Clarke McLaren the supervention of a 'poetic idiom so different from [her] own,'[2] and it is true that the Americanization of Canadian English had begun as she wrote; but the deeper idiom she surely could not share was that of the expressive subject, though her two attempts in the new *integritas* of the 1950s will remain among her masterpieces: 'Arras' and 'After Rain.'

A.M. Klein's case made a plainer connection, though, between the problem of *integritas* and the representation of coherent personality in the forties poem. His own impersonality was not strict until that point in his development at which, apparently, he found it impossible to continue writing poems comprehensive of his people and their traditions. The exemplary inclusiveness of his poetic aspiration and of his creative sensibility showed, not long after the Holocaust images began to precipitate in his mind, the first signs of insufficiency to historical pressure, and a new poetry in the forties manner diverted him briefly from the epic responsibility he had earlier welcomed. In the poems of *The Rocking Chair*, still, despite their broad closing out of Jewish Montreal (and of the Jew who was speaking of Montreal), Klein retains a few fitful gestures of self-centralizing, the 'chiefest, I' who reminds us only vaguely of the poet 'who unrolled [his] culture from his scroll' in earlier incarnations. It was in the mid-1940s that Klein's curious ambivalence between self-revelation and self-concealment – and it was he who first made that typically forties hesitation plain to me – reached its most acute period. That the post-Holocaust poetry should have demanded so thorough an impersonality of Klein suggests again the attraction of that modernist idea at a time of personal and historical crisis: the difference of the Jew may disappear from the surface of the poetry, but by so sublimating himself he retains his creative authority. A more critical view of impersonality – in which we condemn modernism's inelastic response to Klein's cultural particularity – seems shallow and unreflective of Klein's own recognition of a brief safety within its neutral borders.

On these grounds alone it would be possible to pursue the connection between subjective and structural *integritas* in the poetry of Klein, without looking forward (as many will not have wished to do) to the conclusive destructive phase of his private self-rendering. It was Klein, after all, who penned the most direct Canadian appreciation of the force of *integritas* I claimed early on to be a fundamental goal of forties poetry. It was also *his* habit – not Layton's, and not Dudek's until much later – to find his most resonant images of poetic energy and innovation in the processes of mind and imagination that generated poetic structure in the first place. He is in that regard a prototypical figure for his forties colleagues, and perhaps as a somewhat older poet who resisted clear affiliation with any of the partisanships into which they had formed his example was compelling. His fundamental recognition of the deep analogy between the structure and process of consciousness and the form and energy of poetry has clear echoes: in Page's ultimate realization that an image-manner deflecting one's sympathies into stylism was self-defeating; in Layton's intuition that the lyric subject could be redrawn in modernist poetry if the randomness and doubling irony of that subject were retained and heightened structurally; in Dudek's prolonged merging of self-representation and poetic composition. While it does seem apparent, as Layton thought, that Klein learned more from his forties companions than did they from him, it remains true that his story is the *ur*-text of the mid-century drift from impersonal impassivity to renewal of testimony in Canadian modern poetry. That he reversed the forties swerve to close his own creative life only makes this narrative of poetic transition and its attendant pressures more resonant.

It is by attending to Klein, too, that we can make the 'war context' of these poets' early years into a visceral and frightening reality. Not that he dealt willingly or even openly with the war's impact on European Jews in his poetry; he reserved full response for the prose of *The Second Scroll*. But because Klein has been so well served recently by his bibliographers, biographers, editors, and critics, we can shade the picture of his response to the war more accurately, and we can imagine through him some part of the personal violation and loss of creative force that each of these poets must have experienced to different degrees, and in different disruptive images. The situation of Klein in the burgeoning field of Holocaust studies needs a much fuller articulation than I have been able to gather together. That such historical context is inseparable from the less impactful analysis of poetic styles within my expertise is newly evident, however, and it gives to Klein's forties emulation of the styles of Anderson and Page new significance. If I were to start the book again, now, having this preliminary work behind me, I might phrase its central question differently: since all four of these *Preview* and *First Statement* poets showed some degree and extent of attraction to the 'forties period style,' to what broad historical and private conditions as non-combatants in wartime were they all responding? Klein, I think, would be the central figure of that very different discussion. Here he has served to show the fundamental inseparability – for all the decade's poets – of subjective and of poetic *integritas*, and to show that that relation is essential to poetic change in the final decade of his art.

Before closing this reflection on impersonality, and on those two poets who grasped its opportunities most persistently and suggestively, I want to underscore the present study's rejoinder to postmodern critiques of that precise modernist idea. Note preliminarily that there is no clear distinction on this ground between the *Preview* poets and the poets of *First Statement* until the 1940s were well over. Layton's withdrawal late in the decade from his own juvenile impersonality is a gradual and uncertain one at best; only in 1953 would he fight his way fully clear of its prescriptive force. Dudek dropped his early lyricism and sentimentalism at the turn of the decade in favour of brief impersonalist devotions; his poetry would never return to the naïve subjectivism of the 1940s. Page and Klein, to approach the old distinction from the other flank, show the inseparability of modernist objectivism from the period's many inquiries into the new grounds of subjectivity in the post-Marx, post-Freud, post-Bergson, and post-civilized world. As Eysteinsson had it earlier, 'what the modernist poetics of impersonality and that of extreme subjectivity have in common (and this outweighs whatever may separate them) is a revolt against the traditional relation of the subject to the outside world.'[3] Any strict polarization of impersonality and subjectivity, or any assignment of those modes to this or that poetic camp in Montreal, will falter against close examination of the issues of voice and personation in all four poets considered here. The real distinction, and the negotiation of its ambivalences, lay with the individual, not with the little magazine.

Still more significant, the poets who also adhered to impersonality in its less compelling form – the general avoidance of direct lyric expression – and found it most difficult to imagine themselves into the new subjective emphases of poetry in the 1950s – Anderson, Page, Klein – help us to see that there is no inherent connection between impersonality's ideal sublimation of the individual's particularity and the disempowerment of poets on the margins of authorial or societal power. Indeed, it is perhaps newly prominent among the demographic details that have dominated little-magazine scholarship in Canada that the forties poets who were most clearly drawn to an impersonalist poetics were also those whose marginality – by today's scales of cultural significance – was most marked. Anderson's homosexuality obviously did not find needed expression in his forties poetry, but it is equally true (as Robert K. Martin has shown) that a good deal of his homosexual desire did, at least subliminally; and this is in part because impersonality theory helped him to forge a socially compulsory distance between such textual desire and his own private preferences.

It is analogously true that P.K. Page could not give direct feminist voice to those stenographers, 'young girls,' and seaside daughters who peopled her imagination in the forties. Her shunning of lyric – from a half-century's retrospect – may seem to have been imposed by a regulation against personal expression that was ideally timed to silence the women who were entering the poetic community more fully than ever before. This is the *No Man's*

Land view of impersonality, Sandra Gilbert and Susan Gubar's. But it is more plausible – and more in keeping with Page's emphatic rejection of the subjectivist idiom even after it grew dominant – that her poetry was able to include such precisely nuanced representations of women specifically because (to a patriarchal readership ready to ridicule women's judgments and emotions as 'sentimental'– see Suzanne Clark) she did not authorize her insight by reference to her private experience. Because today such a negative patriarchal readership is much muted (perhaps gone altogether?), we may lose sight of *her* dilemma and regret that she could not find early on a more expressive means of witness in her eccentric vision; and then blame impersonality for *our* discomfort. But it seems short-sighted to deny partial credit to a key modernist technique that allowed Page to set the terms of her proto-feminist aesthetics in a cultural period in which their candid declamation could have denied her her appreciative readership, if not publication itself.

Klein's minority responses to the idea of modernist impersonality have already been a subject of discussion and need not be re-enacted. The network of interdependences among his Jewish identity, his desire for a central place in the poetry of his own people and in the poetry of his chosen creative language, his willingness to sublimate his own identity in order to speak for representative Jews of a threatened cultural past, and the self-erasure that was a condition of his creativity's waning, is far too densely woven to permit brief peroration. But he confirms the case that young poets with a keen sense of their ethnic, sexual, or gendered distinctness from a mainstream poetic tradition approached the impersonalist orthodoxies of their period more or less willingly, and held on to them most persistently even after their broader discrediting in the poetry around them, and in the process found vital means for the expression of the particular subjective commitments for which we now might chiefly value them.

That impersonality could not long restrain the poetic exuberance of an Irving Layton does not substantially alter these remarks. That he did not find as a Jewish poet a *modus vivendi* in impersonality does not mean that parallel means of self-erasure, or at least erasure of demographic difference, were not needful to him. The Israel Lazarovitch who emerged as Irving Layton would write poetry for the better part of two decades before his Jewishness would become explicit in his poetic vision. For him, ironically, it is not impersonality that appears to have suppressed his cultural distinctness from mainstream traditions, but subjective expression itself. Still, the pattern appears, that the articulation of difference at mid-century was easier in the impersonalist mode and more difficult in the lyric. This view is not in keeping with much current assessment of modernist impersonality.

To return now to more general summary remarks. Layton's exemplary turn *circa* 1953 to a fully developed subjectivist poetics will remain the signal of the new Canadian poetry's birth, and the forties manner's rather abrupt dissolution. No one emergent from the 1940s made plainer the value of subjective expression within late modernist poetics, and no other forties poet recovered personalism with Layton's messianic intuition of the validity of his swerve. In the wind-beaten maelstrom of 'The Cold Green Element' is a self-focusing of such intensity and splendour that its effects seem entirely unprepared for by the debates over poetic style that preoccupied the forties, and we might be so caught up in that whirlwind as to forget, even fail to reprint, the poems of his prolonged apprenticeship in the forties. If it is true that Layton's violently subjective experience of reality and his brimming ego could not have been turned to impersonalist service – and in that thought I am reminded that some good part of literary history is explicable only by the coincident self-discovery of particular personalities at random crossroads – it is equally true, and freshly visible, that the forties style held sufficient orthodox authority *and* stylistic excitement to restrain even such a personality's vocalization for some dozen early years of composition.

More could in fact be claimed. Arguably the saving grace of Layton's self-celebratory poetics – the containing force that prevents their joyful egoism from spilling over into narcissistic egotism – derives from the *integritas* forged between identity and poetic structure in the course of the forties. If I am right that the 1950s masterpieces justify their egoist effusiveness by delineating a collective of forces that objectify and ironize the Layton persona, we can trace the stylistic and formal cognates of such forces rearward to the post-Imagism of the previous decade. The intensive fragmentation of the garden in which the *Übermensch* dances in a random flow of images, associations, and dissolutions of selfhood is not readily separable from the forties manner's insistent poetics of accumulation and sublimation of the coherent focal self. If Layton had learned by 1953 that he could record the fulsomeness of subjective feeling only within the ironic limits established by an impersonal *integritas* more comprehensive than that of the celebratory persona, it was in part because he had spent the forties, however grudgingly, schooling in that tension. The poems' persistent postulation of an objective plane from which we are to view the mistaken poet suggests both the ironies Layton understood to be needful in the representation of subjectivity and the formal multiplication of points of view inherent in the post-Imagist poetics he had inherited. In turn, the poems in which that ironic containment is less tangible are less random and accumulative in their coordination of vital images: the centring force of ego is so powerful in 'Whatever Else Poetry Is Freedom,' for example, that the ironic fragmentation and randomness of insight enforced by his aleatory post-Imagist poetic style are reduced, pressured into a more coherent versification and syntax through which our ironic eyes find it increasingly challenging to pierce.

In the poems following 1953, Layton also fights clear of one of Klein's most disturbing forties intuitions: that the mind is as permeable, as subject to invasion, dissolution, and murder, as the body. Layton surmounts Klein's paranoia not by shoring up the boundary between mind and body, but by utterly confounding them: in Layton it is the 'self' that can be 'murdered,' an alternative reading that may be more terrifying, but that leaves open the possibility of successive reconstitutions, as the death of the body does not. This idea would appear critical to Layton's establishment of a new egoist poetics. In his alertness to the processive and multiple conditions of mental life, he was to some degree imaging the mind of his mentor and formulating a personative elasticity that would spare his poetry the same shattering that he had witnessed in Klein's. It is perhaps this idea, with its implications for an associative, transformational poetics, that he most palpably surrendered in the 1960s: in the later dispensation, that of the clearly superior poet-prophet, denunciation was paramount, and the incorporation in a fragmented poetics of the poet's vulnerability to the random violence of ignorant society was no longer possible. His typical forties willingness to promulgate a wavering, Heraclitean notion of the self in the poem was not durable, although it may in retrospect look more attractive to those whose present models of selfhood are themselves less robust than Layton's.

In fact it was Dudek, not Layton, who would radicalize *and* sustain the Kleinian instability of poetic selfhood, in his gradual fusion of the consciousness's openness to invasion – by other voices, texts; by ruins, cathedrals, moments of sunlight – and the poem's. It is only my critical choice to read *Continuations* and, to lesser degrees, the earlier long poems as embodying the mental life of the poet, and those who want a more objectivist reading of Dudek's long poems have their evidence. Still, if I look for the poetics in which the forties techniques of Imagist rendering, accumulative aesthetics, and sublimation of the poet's mind into the energies of the text are melded most fully with the more openly subjectivist modes of the 1950s – and in which that melding could be sustained into the 1980s and beyond – I find it more rigorously achieved in Dudek's experimental long poems than elsewhere. No one else from the Montreal forties went looking as patiently as Dudek for an *integritas* in which the objectivist dicta of modernism in his youth and the personalist freedoms of his early maturity could be sustained, interdependent, at the highest degree of imaginative and structural tension.

Dudek's early lyricism was markedly idiosyncratic in the overwhelmingly impersonal poetry written in Montreal in the 1940s. His brief experiments with Imagism in the little-magazine and war period cannot really outweigh the obvious urgency with which this young poet was compelled to set down his private emotions and observations. But lyricism of so immediate and unexamined a kind did not offer Dudek a meaningful route forward from the forties. We can guess at but not re-create with entire satisfaction the reasons for his sudden return to the forties period style and its objectivist methods at the turn of the 1950s. What we can observe with greater precision is his consequent search for an objectivist frame around his subjective perceptions and insights, in *Europe* and after. He helps us to see, in a way that Layton, for whom the forties period style seems to have been more compulsory *and* inviting in the 1940s, cannot, that some such period of training in the objectivist goals and techniques of the 1940s was a predicate of poetic change as the 1950s got under way. If in the later long poems Dudek is more Imagist, his structures more fragmented, more densely juxtaposed, if his coordinating persona gradually dissolves until it blurs with the fragments it registers and casts onto the page, the advance seems tied to his brief imitation of Page, Anderson, even Klein, in *Twenty-Four Poems* and *The Searching Image*. He called those books' poems 'the road not taken,' as we saw; but the two forks in his path in 1952 were to merge in *En Mexico* six years later, where he restored the subject to modern Canadian poetry by writing himself, though no more than a palimpsest, into the suspended fragments of his private experience.

Dudek's case is furthermore a reminder that there is no necessary connection between robustness of private ego and a 1950s swerve to self-expressive poetics. His poetic persona is as thoughtful, cautious, even diffident, as Layton's is abrupt and intuitional. It is difficult to say, in fact, why the forties search for a new *integritas* in the modern poem should have led a generation of poets to the renewal of ironic subjectivism as opposed to some other coherent poetic force. In thinking this through I have at times relied, as have others, on the assumption of war-consciousness and the inescapable duties of testimony and historical witness – a stepping forward when called – that that consciousness entailed. This explanation seems compelling but partial. I also just noted the sheer coincidence we must submit to as literary historians, in the gathering together of particular poetic personalities at focal moments of cultural change: to fail to acknowledge that random luck would be hubris, but its explanatory force is, likewise, partial. The present context allows me to hazard a third, also partial, explanation; as we seek and juxtapose these fragmented historical ideas, we may begin to close in on the absent truth around which they circle.

As dedicated modernists, these poets would not have found desirable an *integritas* that merely regressed to the formal, stylistic, and vocal stabilities of pre-modern poetry. Clearly each of them thought the experimental tension and difficulty of modernist structures delightful; each of them, even Klein, found the goals, if not the methods, of Imagism exemplary. They were excited, point-blank, by the early modernist revolution of the word, and if some of its stringency and authority had been lost, its formal revelation remained definitive of their idea of poetry. Sensing differently but commonly the need for a next wave, they began to incarnate in their poetics the mid-century's renewed fascination with the record of human character. Patrick Anderson was among the most personative of the little magazines' poets in the 1940s, and if he did not find an adequate fusion of subject and object in his poetry of the period, he did at least intuit the emerging compatibility of those modes. Page's preoccupation with the eccentric verse portrait suggests that she grasped early on that a renewal of modernist poetry would depend on a new representation of consciousness. Dudek remarked to Layton as early as 1942, 'The man behind the poem is the thing – no matter what his form, his methods or his tools ... Character – strong and healthy character – is the essential quality of all good poetry.'[4] As all of these poets sifted through the possibilities of poetic transformation in the forties, they deduced the need for an *integritas* that would grant the aleatory modernist poetics sufficient coherence and force to be of value in a war-driven world *without reducing modernism's exemplary embodiment of that world's fragmentation, dissonance, and violence of style.* I risk the conclusion that it was only in an image of consciousness itself – taken by them to manifest exactly such aesthetics of fragmentation, juxtaposition, ambiguity of outline, and distinctness of being – that their search could be satisfied.

It is not difficult to see, in retrospect, why Page and Anderson should have found it hard to join the sudden subjective chorus of the early 1950s. Quite apart from their early modernist training and their strong attachment to impersonalist ideas – abstractions it is easy to posit but difficult to quantify at this ironic distance – the idea of speaking subjectively had been politicized needlessly for each of them. Page would not have to have been the most delicate register of patriarchal nuance to grasp the anti-feminist implications of many reviewers' remarks on her early poetry. To respond with a more aggressively lyric feminist manner, however ironized by her modernist gift, would have been foolhardy, to say the least, and with her hauntingly sardonic insight it would not have been lost on her that the new subjective emphasis was proving itself chiefly powerful for male poets safe from gender recrimination. Anderson, too, could hardly have trusted a new expressive manner when such minimal private content as *had* percolated in his own impersonal poems had led John Sutherland to a flat declaration of his homosexuality. In this context it is newly apparent why Anderson's threat of libel against Sutherland and *First Statement* should so stand out in the little-magazine narrative: not because it helps us firm up the battle lines with *Preview*, but because it pivots precisely on the question of self-revelation and self-concealment in mid-century modernist poetry. Apart from the violation he was wreaking, Sutherland was demanding a sharp polarization of the impersonal poem, in which such private implications would not at all appear, and the wholly subjective poem, in which Anderson would presumably exit the closet wholeheartedly. Sutherland certainly did not understand that the two 'choices' were beginning to collapse; it was not in his Manichean critical character.

Still, a critical imaging of the forties generation that chastened or excluded Sutherland would be of no use now. If I have correctly argued that a generation is better defined by the questions it asks itself than by the answers its separable members indoctrinate, Sutherland's terms of reprobation for the poetry of Page and Anderson indicate a critical mind turning over and over the issues of poetic structure, soundness, and subjectivism that were definitive of artistic inquiry for the poets of his generation. And if in his rush to judgment on such questions Sutherland took up the role of chief nay-sayer in the transition in Canadian poetry in the forties, he is no less significant of a generational consciousness for all that. The poets of the period constituted a generation; we can be emphatic at this point. But they do not so constitute themselves by reason of coincident birth, nor by clear assignment to the margin or the centre of Canadian literary activity, nor by any other demographic means. They do so instead as gifted and intellectual individuals facing in common a plenitude of challenges to their personal and artistic progress, from the most terrifyingly historical to the most intangibly unconscious, and arriving at a set of poetic chances that focused for them that multiplicity of experience. In trying to explicate that commonality I have sought to maintain a due sense of their vivid differences, and in that attempt, if not in its methodological consequences, this book has had a modernist aesthetics at its heart. In every stage of the argument I have assumed, and often enough tried to prove, that the modernist poem seeks dynamic structural tension by steadily heightening two of its formal thrusts: the one towards fragmentation and dislocation, the other towards coherence and order. In that dual *integritas* lies, to my mind, the astonishing and eccentric beauty of modernist art. If it remains difficult to align P.K. Page and Irving Layton as partners in a particular kind of manifold inquiry, that difficulty is welcome, for it is not vitiating of my claim that they are of a single generation, a term I can think useful only if it allows me to sustain a clear vision of the differences as well as the similarities among such diverse creative personalities. The four major poets of the 1940s circle in this book somewhat randomly, somewhat stringently, and that is the work's own problem of *integritas*. As of all modernist structures, our intuitions of its sufficiency will doubtless differ. We can always dispute resolutions: but perhaps now we have a good new set of questions.

The first wave of Canadian modernist studies petered out in the course of the 1980s. In the retrospective light of happy recent accomplishments of contemporary Canadian writers, and of the critics who observe their reputations, the poets who gave us our original modernisms will often look unprolific, sparse, abashed. They are not. They are, certainly, underserved by *their* critics, by and large, and their poetry often comes down to us in narratives to which we are habituated – by which we may be bored. But there is no period of Canadian literary history readier for our critical service: no period so tempting in its combination of surviving generality and platitude on the one hand and undiscovered resources and riches on the other. I took three basic polemic positions in order to mine this archive: I rejected a dominant narrative frame for 1940s period study, the little magazine; I forced the Canadian poets as far as I could into international contexts; and I refused the negative image of modernism's styles and purposes, taking it for granted instead that all my poets were critically alert and deeply feeling individuals who would not have been attracted by modernism had it appeared to them rigorously exclusive of sympathy and difference. How many other decisive swerves are possible? What we're after is a field of free disciplinary play in which new intuitions are visible, horizons hazy in the distance, and modernism's freshness and spontaneity recuperable.

Notes

Wherever possible I have cited parenthetically from a recent selection or collection of the poet's works, such as P.K. Page's *The Glass Air* (1985) or A.M. Klein's *Complete Poems* (1990), as long as no significant revision has been made to the quoted passage from its forties version. Many poems treated here, however, are not available in recent compilations. In such cases, I cite a contemporary appearance in volume form (for example, Irving Layton's *Now Is the Place* [1948] or Louis Dudek's *The Searching Image* [1952]) or, lacking one, the original appearance in a magazine. Poems and other materials *of no more than a page* quoted from the various magazines and not gathered into a readily available volume are cited fully from the magazine in question in the bibliography. They are not cited further in these notes, as no page reference is needed. (In a few such instances where author or title requires clarification, a short title is provided in parenthesis in the text.) Such materials *of more than a page* are noted conventionally, and page numbers specified. For the reader's convenience, poems that do appear in later volumes are cited in the notes, by page number in the volume; however, for interested readers, the original *Preview* or *First Statement* source is also indicated in the individual entry in the bibliography.

Introduction: Reading the Forties Poets

1 See Robert K. Martin, 'Sex and Politics in Wartime Canada: The Attack on Patrick Anderson'; Justin D. Edwards, 'Engendering Modern Canadian Poetry: *Preview, First Statement*, and the Disclosure of Patrick Anderson's Homosexuality'; and David Leahy, 'Patrick Anderson and John Sutherland's Heterorealism: "Some Sexual Experience of a Kind Not Normal".'

2 See, for example, Laura Killian's new reading of Page in light of recent feminist responses to modernism, 'Poetry and the Modern Woman: P.K. Page and the

Gender of Impersonality,' and Diana M. Relke's 'Tracing a Terrestrial Vision in the Early Works of P.K. Page.'

3 Layton's best critic has been Wynne Francis, and she is at *her* best when providing a challenging and scrupulous reading of a major Layton poem. See '"The Birth of Tragedy": A Nietzschean Reading' and 'Layton's Red Carpet: A Reading of "For Mao Tse-Tung: A Meditation on Flies and Kings".' Her 'Layton and Nietzsche,' the first prolonged account of the influential relation between the two authors, remains standard reading, despite having been strongly supplemented by Kurt Van Wilt's 'Layton, Nietzsche, and Overcoming.' That only one or two Layton poems have received such attention remains, however, my point here.

4 See Louis Dudek, 'Academic Literature,' *passim.*

5 Robert Kroetsch, 'A Canadian Issue,' *Boundary 2* 3.1 (Fall 1974); qtd. in Ken Norris, *The Little Magazine in Canada*, p. 1.

6 In 1994 Dennis Denisoff, then a doctoral candidate at McGill University and my research assistant, surveyed the critical reception from 1970 to 1993 of fourteen Canadian modernist poets: Louis Dudek, John Glassco, Leo Kennedy, A.M. Klein, Raymond Knister, Irving Layton, Dorothy Livesay, Anne Marriott, P.K. Page, E.J. Pratt, W.W.E. Ross, F.R. Scott, A.J.M. Smith, and Raymond Souster. Figures who might have received recent attention as postmodern writers (Margaret Laurence, Phyllis Webb, and Leonard Cohen) were excluded. All existing bibliographies were consulted; the statistics include scholarly articles, monographs, collections of essays (if reprinted essays, counted as one item), and biographies; they do not include interviews or items in the popular press. Between 1970 and 1979, 134 critical pieces on such poets were published, roughly one per poet per year. From 1980 to 1989, the number of such materials slumped by over 40 per cent, to 78 items (roughly one per writer per two years). Major figures like Klein, Layton, and Pratt received the vast bulk of this attention, so the less-known modernists were given very little or no consideration in the 1980s. By 1993 an additional 43 such items had appeared, an increase that suggested that the 1990s as a whole would prove slightly more hospitable to Canadian modernist studies than were the 1980s, but the broad decline of interest after the 1970s remains. Curiously, women modernists appear to be suffering most from this ongoing decline: the drop in critical discussion of Dorothy Livesay, Anne Marriott, and P.K. Page from the 1970s to the 1980s was only 22 per cent (compared with 45 per cent for men), but from the 1980s to the 1990s (assuming a stable rate of attention through the decade to 1999), a further drop of 26 per cent is likely. Male modernists account for the minor 'renewal' of attention in the 1990s. At current rates, criticism of their writing will jump better than 50 per cent from the 1980s through the 1990s: this at precisely the scholarly moment at which studies of Canadian women modernists

should logically be expanding. My thanks to Mr Denisoff for hours of painstaking and productive statistical labour.

7 I emphasize 'favourable' because a recent piece on Smith and Scott by D.M.R. Bentley constitutes the kind of 'counter-modernist' research I consider later. Bentley claims in '"The nth Adam": Modernism and the Transcendence of Canada' that 'the simplification, devaluation, and decontextualization of reality that is widely evident in high Modern Canadian poetry participates in the industrial and capitalistic enterprise whose most obvious effects in the present century have included the degradation and homogenization in Canada and elsewhere of distinctive natural and social environments ... The lack of national and local specificity in, say, [Scott's] "Lakeshore" or [Smith's] "Swift Current" is part of the movement that has placed the united colours of Benetton in every shopping centre of any size in the consumer-capitalist world. The golden bough and the golden arches have more in common than may first be apparent' (*Gay] Grey Moose*, pp. 264–5).

8 John Sutherland, 'The Writing of Patrick Anderson,' p. 4.

9 Louis Dudek, 'Poets of Revolt ... Or Reaction?' p. 4.

10 Dorothy Livesay, 'Review of *News of the Phoenix*,' pp. 18–19.

11 Irving Layton, 'Politics and Poetry,' pp. 18–19.

12 John Sutherland, 'Critics on the Defensive,' p. 67.

13 Dudek remained variously active on the home front, preparing surveys of Quebec's involvement in the war for Maurice Hébert, father of poet Anne Hébert, and assisting in conscientious-objector research in malaria control, though not himself a conscientious objector (personal communication).

14 See Joan McCullagh, *Alan Crawley and* Contemporary Verse, pp. xix–xx.

15 See Lynn Harrington, *Syllables of Recorded Time: The Story of the Canadian Authors' Association*, especially pp. 70–3.

16 Seymour Mayne, 'A Conversation with Patrick Anderson,' p. 70.

17 Ibid., p. 76.

18 Dudek's memory of Anderson is roughly typical: '... at the head of *Preview* stood Patrick Anderson, and he was a visiting Britisher in Canada, and around him were people who felt a strong attraction to this kind of cultural representative. And that's the crucial thing about it, that one magazine, *Preview*, was associated with what I think of, historically, as the colonial attachment of Canadian literature: their poetry had affinities with the English poetry of the preceding decade – especially Auden and Thomas – whereas the *First Statement* people were more related to contemporary American poetry ... And therefore what you had in these two magazines was a significant confrontation between the colonial pull toward British literature and the new native strain that would come right out of Canada'

(Nause and Heenan, 'An Interview with Louis Dudek,' p. 31). Anderson's birthplace slips readily here into a critical comment on *Preview.* We might also note the irony of Dudek's view that the new poetry 'that would come right out of Canada' was written by 'people [who] were more related to contemporary American poetry.'

19 The five scholarly articles that appeared in the subsequent twenty years show our persistent but low-level interest in Anderson: see Patrick Campbell, 'Attic Shapes and Empty Attics: Patrick Anderson – A Memoir'; Michael Gnarowski, 'New Facts and Old Fictions: Some Notes on Patrick Anderson, *1945* and *En Masse*'; Robert Martin, 'Sex and Politics in Wartime Canada: The Attack on Patrick Anderson'; Patricia Whitney, '*En Masse*: An Introduction and an Index' and 'From Oxford to Montreal: Patrick Anderson's Political Development.' As noted above, two recent articles in *Essays on Canadian Writing* (62 [Fall 1997]) have expanded the Anderson bibliography by pursuing Martin's gay-studies approach and findings in greater detail. These new methods notwithstanding, the biographical emphasis of Anderson research is obvious.

20 Mayne, 'A Conversation,' p. 60.

21 Miriam Waddington, 'Introduction,' pp. 13, 10, 11.

22 See Louis Dudek, 'A Letter re "First Statement" [to Michael Gnarowski],' pp. 213–16.

23 Frank Davey, *Louis Dudek & Raymond Souster,* p. 3.

24 These biographical details from Whiteman's 'Introduction' in *The Letters of John Sutherland,* pp. ix–x.

25 Waddington, 'Introduction,' p. 7.

26 Elspeth Cameron, *Irving Layton: A Portrait,* p. 206. The remark is speculative, or at least uncited.

27 Whitney, 'From Oxford to Montreal,' p. 44.

28 Lorne Pierce to Patrick Anderson, 24 Aug. 1945, *Pierce Papers,* Box 11, Folder 6, item 14.

29 Earle Birney, Reader's report on Patrick Anderson's *The White Centre* manuscript, *Pierce Papers,* Box 13, Folder 5, item 15.

30 See Earle Birney, 'Struggle against the Old Guard: Editing the *Canadian Poetry Magazine,*' pp. 15–16. Anderson apparently sent Birney his appreciation of the review.

31 Lorne Pierce to Patrick Anderson, 24 Aug. 1945, *Pierce Papers,* Box 11, Folder 6, item 14.

32 See, among other correspondence, Patrick Anderson to Frank Flemington, 20 Apr. 1946, *Pierce Papers,* Box 13, Folder 5, item 19.

33 Peggy Doernbach Anderson to Lorne Pierce, 31 Oct. 1946, *Pierce Papers,* Box 13, Folder 5, item 28.

34 Patrick Anderson to A.J.M. Smith, undated, *Anderson Papers*, Folder 7 (Correspondence 1945), p. 1.
35 Patrick Anderson, 2 Feb. 1946, *Anderson Papers*, Folder 8 (Correspondence 1946).
36 Whitney, 'From Oxford to Montreal,' pp. 44–5.
37 Mayne, 'A Conversation,' p. 47.
38 John Sutherland, 'Wagner and Zarathustra,' p. 15.
39 John Sutherland,'Why George Left College [pseud. "Jack Hakaar"],' pp. 15–16, 17.
40 John Sutherland,'Why George Smokes a Pipe [pseud. "Jack Hakaar"],' p. 6.
41 See, for example, an undated entry late in the journal for 'Summer 1936': 'I love boys, and the excitement of boy's names – Johnny, David, Tom, Tony. But there is something specially appealing about Johnny. I like the wild, the ruthless; the ruffled locks, the brown hair streaked with yellow: the constant movement and fire of legs, even, perhaps most, when still. You can't put it down, perhaps, least of all in pornography. And the more you think of boys, the more you feel old, like a salacious old man looking at some Ganymede ... I haven't had a romance since David. But I am not too old yet. Must do my exercises, and go to sleep. Last night I dreamed I was shot in the stomach' (*Anderson Papers*, vol. 3, n.p.). The sudden violence of the latter image is horribly echoed in a number of marginal illustrations Anderson scattered through his journals, showing male figures with simple drawings of lightning, knives, or wounds where their genitals should be.
42 Whitney, 'From Oxford to Montreal,' pp. 32–3.
43 Martin, 'Sex and Politics,' esp. pp. 114–17.
44 Whitney usefully quotes artist Mary Filer, who met Anderson and Gearing at about this time; Anderson, she says, 'seemed so much more composed, I think it meant everything to him to have this new companion' (p. 47 n. 36).
45 Quoted by Whitney, 'From Oxford to Montreal,' p. 45.
46 Ian Young to Patrick Anderson, 14 May 1972, *Anderson Papers*, Correspondence 1972, Folder 1 of 2. Anderson's reaction is curious, considering that he had himself edited *Eros: An Anthology of Friendship* with Alistair Sutherland in 1961, a pioneer publication to which Young referred with praise.
47 Whiteman, 'Introduction,' in *The Letters of John Sutherland*, pp. xxix–xxxi. The notebook entry is quoted by Whiteman from Hilda Vanneste, *Northern Review, 1945–1956: A History and an Index*, p. 158.
48 John Sutherland to Anne Wilkinson, 9 Mar. 1952, *Letters of John Sutherland*, ed. Whiteman, p. 230.
49 Waddington, 'Introduction,' p. 14.
50 John Sutherland, 'Editorial,' *First Statement* 1.1, p. 1.
51 John Sutherland, 'On a Story Published in Preview Magazine,' p. 5.
52 John Sutherland, 'First Statement Opinions,' pp. 6–8.

53 John Sutherland, 'Mr. Coulter and the Canadian Landscape,' p. 7.
54 John Sutherland, 'Introduction,' in *Other Canadians*, p. 10.
55 John Sutherland, 'The Past Decade in Canadian Poetry,' pp. 73–4.
56 'I, of course, respect genuine religious poetry ... and I have written some poems, well done enough to fool people into thinking they are genuine, but they aren't. I'm not sure if it's wise to let the cat out of the bag like this' (Smith, typescript annotations of his own poems, *Smith Papers*, Box 1, Folder 12).
57 Mayne, 'A Conversation,' p. 63.
58 Sutherland, 'On a Story Published,' p. 4. It is Sutherland, of course, who translates verbal style into physical aggression, not Bruce Ruddick of *Preview*, whose short story 'Vi' occasioned Sutherland's remarks.
59 John Sutherland, 'Introduction,' in *Other Canadians*, p. 11.
60 Waddington, 'Introduction,' in *Essays, Controversies and Poems*, p. 7.
61 See Allan Anderson, 'A Communication,' and Patrick Anderson, 'A Reply.'
62 Patrick Anderson to A.J.M. Smith, undated, *Anderson Papers*, Correspondence 1945, Folder 7, p. 2.
63 Louis Dudek, 'The Role of Little Magazines in Canada,' p. 208.
64 Louis Dudek to Raymond Souster, 26 Nov. 1951 and 16 Jan. 1952; qtd. in Davey, *Dudek & Souster*, p. 13.
65 Waddington, 'Introduction,' p. 11.
66 'Montreal Journal 1,' *Anderson Papers*, vol. 1, pp. [44–5]. Whitney quotes the same passage; see 'From Oxford to Montreal,' pp. 34–5. A letter from Anderson to Page of 15 November 1973 strikes a retrospective conciliatory tone; he remarks having recently reread this passage of his journal with faint irony, and then describes points of affiliation he finds between his poetic vision and that of Page (*P.K. Page Papers*, National Archives, Ottawa, Ontario, vol. 6, 'Patrick Anderson' dossier).
67 Usher Caplan, *Like One That Dreamed: A Portrait of A.M. Klein*, p. 96.
68 'Montreal Journal 1,' *Anderson Papers*, p. [43].
69 Whitney, 'From Oxford to Montreal,' pp. 36, 40–1.
70 A.M. Klein to A.J.M. Smith, 1 May 1948, *Klein Papers*, vol. 1, pp. 385–6.
71 Mayne, 'A Conversation,' pp. 54, 62.
72 See for instance 'From Oxford to Montreal,' p. 37, containing a vignette by Page: 'Patrick never made a secret of his sympathies, but he was careful. I remember one night walking home late along Sherbrooke Street singing some of the songs from the Spanish Civil War and Patrick divorced himself from us. I would guess it had to do with his Selwyn House job.' Similarly, Anderson had to hide his friendship with the social-democrat Klein during the meetings for *En Masse*, a short-lived Communist organ (pp. 40–1), and presumably had to mute his communism somewhat in the company of the socialist Klein and F.R. Scott.
73 Perhaps a related feature is the use of the pseudonym 'Jack Hakaar' for the publi-

cation of 'Why George Left College,' the first of the two sketches: 'Jack' is readily translatable back into 'John,' and 'Hakaar' might be thought to play on 'hacker' and 'catarrh,' both words easy to associate with a tubercular condition. The verbal play is evocative of A.M. Klein's self-revelation and self-concealment in the pseudonym 'Avram Haktani,' whose translation into Abraham Little, or Klein, is now very familiar.

74 Sutherland, 'Writing of Patrick Anderson,' p. 4.

75 Ibid.

76 Martin's belief that as a result of Sutherland's article 'the public viewed Anderson as a poet whose dishonesty about his sexuality prevented him from accomplishing major work' ('Sex and Politics in Wartime Canada,' p. 110) is surely an exaggeration: both Ryerson Press and McClelland & Stewart were to publish Anderson's poetry thereafter, to more or less auspicious reviews.

77 Bruce Whiteman, ed., *The Letters of John Sutherland, 1942–1956*, pp. 53–5.

78 John Sutherland, 'Role of Prufrock,' p. 19.

79 Whitney, 'From Oxford to Montreal,' p. 33.

80 See Anderson, 'Love Poem'; Sutherland, 'Three New Poets – Editorial,' p. 3. The actual lines from Anderson's poem are: 'Yet stand. You are tall as Europe. / Yet stand. I am tall as Asia.'

81 John Sutherland, 'The Great Equestrians,' p. 79.

82 Sutherland, 'Writing of Patrick Anderson,' p. 5.

83 Sutherland, 'Role of Prufrock,' p. 19.

84 Sutherland, 'Why George Left College,' pp. 15–16.

85 John Sutherland to P.K. Page, [1947], in Whiteman, ed., *Letters of John Sutherland*, p. 47.

86 'Poetry of P.K. Page,' pp. 13–23, as cited by Whiteman.

87 Sutherland, 'P.K. Page and *Preview*,' p. 8.

88 Sutherland, 'Earle Birney's "DAVID",' p. 6.

89 Sutherland, Review of *Unit of Five*, p. 31.

90 Allan Anderson, 'A Communication,' p. 1. Note the phrase 'private circus,' one which Sutherland would also borrow from Anderson's poetry in the libellous article two years later (just quoted). The coincidentally named Allan Anderson remains unidentified – Miriam Waddington mentions Allan Anderson as a *First Statement* contributor (p. 12), but he does not appear in the little magazine – though Patrick refers to him as the 'incipient editor of a progressive paper' in his 'Reply.'

91 The dates are not utterly clear; *First Statement* 1.4 may have appeared just before *Preview* 8, or just after, but in either case it is very apparent that the two editorial boards read and responded to each other issue by issue. P.K. Page, for example, criticized *First Statement* for its 'rather wide-eyed uncertain policy of inclusion,'

in 'Canadian Poetry 1942,' p. 8. The next *First Statement* closed with a 'brief statement' of its editorial policy: 'We do wish to include a variety of Canadian writers' (1.5 [Oct. 1942], p. 9). The note is in obvious response to Page's remark.

92 Anderson, 'Introduction,' in *Preview*, p. iv.

93 Patrick Anderson, 'A Poet Past and Future,' p. 13.

94 John Sutherland, 'The Role of the Magazines,' p. 1.

95 Whitney, 'From Oxford to Montreal,' p. 45.

96 Mayne, 'A Conversation,' p. 67. Anderson was also typically honest with Mayne about the 'war neurosis' – that is, draft-fear – that also propelled him into the pacifist ranks of the Communist Party (p. 51).

97 Philip Kokotailo,'The Bishop and His Deacon: Smith vs. Sutherland Reconsidered,' p. 63. Kokotailo suggests that Sutherland's influence on Smith was such that the younger man was the older's 'precursor,' an inversion of poetic precedence theorized by Harold Bloom in *The Anxiety of Influence*.

98 Sutherland, 'P.K. Page and *Preview*,' p. 8. Anderson incidentally points out that 'it was an American critic, Cleanth Brooks, who first taught me the functional nature of metaphor and it was an American poet, Hart Crane, who showed me the varied use of symbol ... The fact that I acquired my "modernism" during two years in New York is often forgotten' ('A Poet Past and Future,' pp. 14–15).

99 John Sutherland to Desmond Pacey, 23 Dec. 1952, in Whiteman, ed., *Letters of John Sutherland*, p. 275.

100 See Davey, *Dudek & Souster*, p. 14.

101 Patrick Anderson, *The White Centre*, pp. 29–45.

102 Patrick Anderson, *A Tent for April*, n.p.

103 See Brian Trehearne, *Aestheticism and the Canadian Modernists: Aspects of a Poetic Influence*.

104 Davey, *Dudek & Souster*, pp. 4–5.

105 Dudek, 'A Letter re "First Statement",' p. 216. Dudek also felt that 'the case could very well be made that the aggressive direction often attributed to *First Statement* was chiefly the contribution of Layton, Souster, and others (including myself), not of John Sutherland' (p. 215).

106 Sutherland, 'On a Story Published,' p. 5.

107 Patrick Anderson, 'Ourselves,' p. 11.

108 Dudek, 'A Letter re "First Statement",' pp. 215–16.

109 *First Statement* 1.12 [Feb. 1943]; *Preview* 11 (Feb. 1943).

110 George Woodcock, 'On Patrick Anderson,' p. 163.

111 Milton Wilson, '*Other Canadians* and After,' p. 80.

112 Sutherland, 'P.K. Page and *Preview*,' p. 7.

113 John Sutherland, 'A Note on the Metaphor,' pp. 9–10.

114 Louis Dudek, 'Geography, Politics and Poetry,' p. 3; 'Academic Literature,' pp. 17–18.

115 John Sutherland, 'The Master.' Waddington gives no source for the poem. Her ordering of Sutherland's poems is not chronological, but perhaps by juxtaposing 'The Master' with two other early 1950s poems she indicates the piece's relative lateness.

116 Sutherland, 'Writing of Patrick Anderson,' p. 3.

117 Sutherland, 'Introduction,' in *Other Canadians*; quoted earlier from Davey, *Dudek & Souster*, p. 5.

118 John Sutherland, 'On Thomas Wolfe,' p. 15.

119 Anderson, 'Introduction,' in *Preview*, p. iv.

120 See Trehearne, *Aestheticism and the Canadian Modernists*, pp. 261–9.

121 Waddington, 'Introduction,' p. 8.

122 See Trehearne, 'Critical Episodes in Montreal Poetry of the 1940s,' pp. 31–3.

123 Patrick Anderson, 'Night Out,' p. [4]. Readers will notice the use of 'zero' as a marker of ultimate inanition both here and in the earlier-quoted Sutherland poem 'Triumph.' It also shows up in A.J.M. Smith's earlier 'Son and Heir 1930,' where 'zero's shears at paper window-pane' are indicative of imminent social exhaustion (*Poems New and Collected*, pp. 114–15). Unless they all had another source of which I am unaware, Anderson and Sutherland may have been reading their Smith with attention.

124 Waddington, 'Introduction,' p. 7.

125 The *Page Papers* contain a moving letter from Orlando Gearing to P.K. Page dated 17 March 1979, in which he describes the trauma of tending to Anderson in his final illness. Written across the bottom by hand is the searing notice that 'P has just died ... In all ways I've never known a more destructive year and it isn't even Spring ...' (vol. 6, 'Patrick Anderson' dossier).

126 Patrick Anderson, *A Visiting Distance*, p. 7.

127 Dudek, 'A Letter re "First Statement",' p. 216.

128 Milton Wilson, '*Other Canadians* and After,' p. 91.

1: Imagist Twilight: Page's Early Poetry

1 The date is indicated by an exchange of correspondence between Page and Floris Clarke McLaren beginning in January 1955 (conceivably 1954; see below, p. 101): in late 1954 (conceivably late 1953), McLaren had been sent a draft of the poem largely in its present form. This information mildly contradicts 'After Rain's' placement among the poems of '1955–1967' in *The Glass Air*; see also Cynthia G. Messenger's remarks on the unreliability of dates in the second edition of *The Glass Air*, in 'Selecting P.K. Page,' p. 116.

2 Rosemary Sullivan, '"A Size Larger Than Seeing": The Poetry of P.K. Page,' pp. 32–42.
3 P.K. Page, *The Glass Air*, pp. 76–7. This volume hereinafter cited parenthetically as *GA*.
4 Diana M.A. Relke has a similar treatment of 'After Rain' in 'Tracing a Terrestrial Vision in the Early Works of P.K. Page,' p. 26.
5 See P.K. Page, 'Questions and Images,' in *GA*, p. 191.
6 This is perhaps not surprising in a poet who so frankly admits to being a 'Muse poet,' that is, one who must wait as if passively for the intermittent gift of poetry. See Jon Pearce, 'Fried Eggs and the Workings of the Right Lobe: An Interview with P.K. Page,' p. 32.
7 Samuel Hynes, *The Auden Generation: Literature and Politics in England in the 1930s*, p. 12.
8 Astradur Eysteinsson, *The Concept of Modernism*, p. 50.
9 A.T. Tolley, *The Poetry of the Forties in Britain*, p. 9.
10 Indeed, the significance Tolley finds in Auden's and Isherwood's departures from England is reflected in the various dispersals of Canadian modernist poets in the twenties and thirties: from the diaspora of the post-McGill years (Smith to Scotland, Kennedy to the United States, Glassco to France) to the smaller but persistent dispersals of the Depression: Smith to the Midwestern States and a succession of temporary academic positions, Klein to Rouyn in 1937, Livesay to New Jersey, and so on. Kennedy's letters to Klein represent this sense of divided ways keenly, not only in the spat that erupted between the two poets in March 1940, but perhaps more tellingly in Kennedy's offhand remark on 26 October 1940 that A.J.M. Smith lived only thirty miles from his home in Detroit and that he, Kennedy, 'ought to get in touch with him.' (See Kennedy to Klein, 8 Mar., 20 Mar., and 26 Oct. 1940; and Klein to Kennedy, 15 Mar. 1940, in the *Klein Papers*, vol. 1, pp. 77–80, 100–1.) Whatever friendships underpinned the literary affiliations of the earlier poets, there were distances enforced by work and age that by 1940 had served to weaken the generational coherence they would present to their younger compatriots.
11 Quoted by Sandra Djwa in *The Politics of the Imagination: A Life of F.R. Scott*, p. 212. Dudek's retrospect belies his own poetic practice in early *First Statement* submissions; see below, pp. 283–97.
12 D.M.R. Bentley and Michael Gnarowski, eds., 'Four of the Former *Preview* Editors: A Discussion,' pp. 110, 111.
13 Needless to say, the preface written by A.J.M. Smith and rejected by E.J. Pratt and Robert Finch as too incendiary would have sounded a much more assertive note; Michael Gnarowski's reprint of *New Provinces* wisely incorporates the lost preface.

14 Michael Gnarowski, 'Introduction,' in *New Provinces*, p. xxi.
15 Louis Dudek, 'Questions – Some Answers [an interview with George Bowering, Frank Davey, Steve McCaffrey, and bp nichol],' pp. 292–3.
16 See Brian Trehearne, *Aestheticism and the Canadian Modernists: Aspects of a Poetic Influence*.
17 Neufville Shaw, 'The Maple Leaf Is Dying,' p. 3.
18 See Brian Trehearne, 'Critical Episodes in Montreal Poetry of the 1940s,' pp. 42–4.
19 John Sutherland, 'P.K. Page and *Preview*,' p. 7. Hereinafter cited parenthetically.
20 See especially Suzanne Clark's introductory remarks in *Sentimental Modernism: Women Writers and the Revolution of the Word*; see also, for a less reasoned summation of male reviews of women's modernism, Susan Gilbert and Sandra Gubar, *No Man's Land: The Place of the Woman Writer in the Twentieth Century* (3 vols.), especially vol. 1, *The War of the Words*; and see Bonnie Kime Scott's useful anthology of women's modern writing and literary theory, and male modernists' responses to these, *The Gender of Modernism*, as well as her more recent *Refiguring Modernism*.
21 See Waddington to Sutherland, in 'First Statement Opinions.' Layton's response ('First Statement Opinions') follows. An editorial note entitled 'First Statement Groups' referring to Page follows Layton.
22 John Sutherland, Review of *Unit of Five*, p. 31.
23 Apart from a single poem, 'The Sleeper,' that appeared in the following issue (1.7 [Nov. 1942]) and that had no doubt been submitted and accepted before the disparagements of 'P.K. Page and Preview' appeared.
24 Without doubt written prior to his marriage in November 1943; see Sutherland to Page, n.d., in the 'Sutherland, John' dossier of the *Page Papers*, vol. 8. The letter following these declarations in the Sutherland dossier refers to the courses he is taking at McGill University, so (if it was indeed written later) Sutherland's attempt at a greater intimacy must have occurred during or prior to fall 1942, when he briefly registered in Arts at McGill.
25 As Sutherland puts it most revealingly, in 'The Poetry of P.K. Page': 'the new awareness has precipitated a conflict, and Miss Page cannot make up her mind about those who "cry for love"' (p. 105).
26 John Sutherland, 'Earle Birney's "DAVID",' p. 6.
27 See again the opening paragraph of this Sutherland article, with its emphasis on the collocation of 'strangeness' and 'beauty' in *Preview* aesthetics, quoted in the introduction, p. 30, above.
28 See Trehearne, 'Critical Episodes,' and above, pp. 32–3.
29 Havelock Ellis's translation of Paul Bourget, quoted in R.K.R. Thornton, '"Decadence" in Later Nineteenth-Century England,' pp. 19–20.
30 See Smith's review of Page's *As Ten As Twenty* and Anderson's *The White Centre*,

in *The Canadian Forum* (Feb. 1947); Sutherland's letter to the *Forum* editor in defence of Page and Anderson (Apr. 1947); and Smith's response to Sutherland's letter in another letter to the *Forum* editor (Apr. 1947).

31 Milton Wilson, '*Other Canadians* and After,' pp. 80, 81 (emphasis added).

32 David Perkins, *A History of Modern Poetry,* vol. 2, p. 32.

33 In *Aestheticism and the Canadian Modernists,* I argue at greater length the need to distinguish between the school *per se* and the styles it may have influenced (pp. 39–47). Behind my argument there and here lies John T. Gage's *In the Arresting Eye: The Rhetoric of Imagism,* which demonstrates with much greater detail and specialization the gradual stages through which the Imagist doctrine passed after Pound's management ceased.

34 Perkins, *History of Modern Poetry,* vol. 2, p. 420. Perkins's suggestion that Imagism finally passed with the close of the 1940s will seem self-evident later in this section.

35 Ibid., p. 33.

36 Ibid., p. 41.

37 Ibid., p. 120.

38 Gage, *In the Arresting Eye,* p. 7.

39 Graham Hough, *Image and Experience: Studies in a Literary Revolution,* p. 9.

40 Ibid., pp. 16–17.

41 Paul C. Ray, *The Surrealist Movement in England,* p. 28.

42 Gage, *In the Arresting Eye,* p. 130.

43 Perkins, *History of Modern Poetry,* vol. 2, p. 179.

44 Dylan Thomas, *The Collected Poems of Dylan Thomas, 1934–1952,* p. 69 ('Foster the Light').

45 Seminal discussions of the phenomenon from which my knowledge of it is drawn are in Hynes, *The Auden Generation,* pp. 284–7, and in Kathleen Raine, *Defending Ancient Springs,* pp. 47–9.

46 The project's most easily accessed result is *May the Twelfth: Mass-Observation Day-Surveys 1937,* a fascinating compendium of the reports of various Britons on the events of the Coronation Day of George VI.

47 Hynes, *The Auden Generation,* p. 284.

48 Charles O. Madge, 'Oxford Collective Poem,' p. 19.

49 My thanks to David Pocock, director of the Tom Harrisson Mass-Observation Archive, University of Sussex, Brighton, England, for prompt and helpful responses to inquiries.

50 Raine, *Defending Ancient Springs,* pp. 47–8.

51 Michael Heenan, 'Souvenirs of Some: P.K. Page Responding to a Questionnaire,' p. 100.

52 It would be a mistake to take the forceful exposure by Suzanne Clark in *Senti-*

mental Modernism of 'sentimentalism' as the standard charge levelled by male modernist reviewers against their female rivals to mean that we should no longer disparage certain works as 'sentimental.' Clark herself vacillates, in my view, between a *denial* of sentimentalism in the women she studies – the term remaining pejorative – and a valorization of their sentimentalism in which the term becomes complimentary.

53 Hough, *Image and Experience*, p. 17.

54 Ezra Pound to Ford Madox Ford, 7 Sep. 1920, quoted in Brita Lindberg-Seyersted, *Pound/Ford: The Story of a Literary Friendship*, p. 43.

55 See Gage, *In the Arresting Eye*, p. 112.

56 Yvor Winters, 'The Testament of a Stone, Being Notes on the Mechanics of the Poetic Image,' pp. 213–14.

57 Joseph Frank, 'Spatial Form in Modern Literature,' p. 10.

58 Ibid., p. 4.

59 Cecil Day Lewis, *The Poetic Image: The Clark Lectures Given at Cambridge in 1946*, p. 82.

60 Ibid., pp. 50–1.

61 Ibid., p. 115.

62 Ibid., p. 125.

63 Ibid., p. 115.

64 Ibid., p. 75.

65 Henry Treece, *How I See Apocalypse*, p. 75.

66 Ibid., pp. 59–60.

67 Quoted in ibid., p. 75.

68 Ibid., p. 82.

69 Ibid., p. 63 (emphasis his).

70 Ibid., p. 79.

71 The poem's apocalyptic vision is characteristic: 'Bestow the sun to belch a vacant hell / And no more lamp our life-sized life. / We will exist as bats deep down a well ...' Of equal interest is the poem's registration of the Apocalyptic demand for a new spiritual wholeness: see below, pp. 180–5.

72 John Sutherland, 'Writing of Patrick Anderson,' pp. 5–6.

73 Sutherland, 'The Poetry of P.K. Page,' pp. 110–11.

74 Eysteinsson, *The Concept of Modernism*, p. 9.

75 Morse Peckham's brilliant rendition of the pressures on poetic style from the late nineteenth to the early twentieth century is so formative of my remarks as to be inextricable from them. See his 'Aestheticism to Modernism: Fulfilment or Revolution?'.

76 Day Lewis, *Poetic Image*, pp. 127, 115.

77 James Joyce, *A Portrait of the Artist as a Young Man*, p. 212.

78 Eysteinsson quotes the same passage in *The Concept of Modernism* (pp. 9–10) and emphasizes the central function of Joyce's aesthetics in long-standing definitions of modernism. Eysteinsson's larger purpose in dismantling such appropriations of Dedalus on Aquinas is to demonstrate that the notoriously autonomous modernist art-object cannot in any meaningful sense exist.
79 Charlton T. Lewis, *A Latin Dictionary for Schools*, p. 538.
80 Hugh Kenner, *The Pound Era*, p. 186.
81 Laura Killian, 'Poetry and the Modern Woman: P.K. Page and the Gender of Impersonality,' p. 95.
82 Eysteinsson, *The Concept of Modernism*, pp. 27–8.
83 Maud Ellmann, *The Poetics of Impersonality: T.S. Eliot and Ezra Pound*, p. 4.
84 Perkins, *A History of Modern Poetry*, vol. 2, p. 111.
85 Quoted in Barbara Everett, 'Eliot's "Four Quartets" and French Symbolism,' p. 7.
86 P.K. Page, *The Metal and the Flower*, p. 19 ('Green Little Corn'). Hereinafter cited parenthetically as *MF*.
87 Sutherland, 'P.K. Page and *Preview*,' p. 8.
88 Wilson, '*Other Canadians* and After,' p. 80.
89 See Constance Rooke, 'P.K. Page: The Chameleon and the Centre,' pp. 177–8.
90 As A.J.M. Smith remarked, in 'The Poetry of P.K. Page,' p. 19.
91 P.K. Page, letter to Patrick Anderson, 14 Oct. 1973, *Page Papers*, vol. 6, 'Patrick Anderson' dossier. Page went on to agree with Anderson's proposal for a reprinting of the complete run of *Preview* nevertheless.
92 In *First Statement* as 'Landscape of Love.'
93 I accept here the title and slightly revised conclusion that appeared in *As Ten As Twenty* of 1946. The *First Statement* ending of this poem read 'scanned by the valvular heart, / the field-glasses.'
94 See, for example, 'Panorama' and 'Divers.' A startling exception that perhaps proves the rule is 'Adolescence,' with its confetti-storm of personal pronouns – twenty-two in fact in twenty-two lines of poetry.
95 Tolley, *Poetry of the Forties in Britain*, p. 63.
96 P.K. Page, *As Ten As Twenty*, p. 20. Hereinafter cited parenthetically as *ATAT*.
97 One might add that volumes of poems that relied too heavily on eccentric portraits could themselves become a kind of metapoetic album of accumulated persons, thus lacking a larger unity and integrity of creative vision. This is an arguable weakness of Page's *The Metal and the Flower*, in which the portraiture impulse was becoming excessive.
98 In an interview with Sandra Djwa in 1996, Page remarks of Atwood's poetry that '[o]ne of the things that interested me ... was how we both used so many of the same images, although she used them differently' ('P.K. Page,' p. 54). Compare,

for instance, Atwood's well-known 'This Is a Photograph of Me' with the opening of Page's 'Photograph':

> They are all beneath the sea in this photograph –
> not dead surely – merely a little muted:
> those two lovers lying apart and stiff
> with a buoy above which could ring their beautiful movements ...
>
> (*GA*, p. 55)

Page's interest in surreal experiences and often cool formalism produces numerous such effects and seems to confirm that, with Atwood and the 1960s, Canadian poets began, finally, carefully, to read one another. See below regarding 'Arras,' p. 94.

99 A useful and stimulating adjunct to any reading of 'The Stenographers' is Page's prose piece 'Stenographers.' Among its contributions is a helpful gloss on the poem's difficult and sexually suggestive phrase 'boyfriends of blood.' The prose commentary, part of a *Preview* issue called 'Some Aspects of the War: A Civilian Report,' makes plain that many of the women in Page's office had male partners in the various Canadian forces in the war. The piece's depiction of other aspects of the stenographers' blighted days in an institution of intense and inane regulation constitutes a surreal, even blackly humorous, cognate of the best-known Page poem.

100 Wilson, '*Other Canadians* and After,' p. 82.

101 Indeed, Smith thought *The Metal and the Flower* her better volume. In the biographical note on Page in the third edition of *The Book of Canadian Poetry*, he wrote that *The Metal and the Flower* 'has greater unity, intensity, and perception and thus marks an advance even on the finest things in her first volume ...' (p. 446). See also his 1971 article 'The Poetry of P.K. Page,' where he reads her chiefly as 'metaphysical' poet in his own tradition.

102 Desmond Pacey, *Creative Writing in Canada*, p. 161.

103 Desmond Pacey, 'English Canadian Poetry, 1944–1954,' p. 167.

104 See Killian, 'Poetry and the Modern Woman,' p. 103, n. 13.

105 Anonymous, 'Reader's Report on P.K. Page's "The Untouched Hills",' *Pierce Papers*. This manuscript was the collection of poems that Ryerson eventually published as *As Ten As Twenty*.

106 Henry W. Wells, *Where Poetry Stands Now*, p. 55.

107 Ibid., p. 8. Wells especially associated the weaknesses of 'personalist' (our 'impersonal') style with women poets.

108 Ibid., p. 56.

109 Wilson, '*Other Canadians* and After,' p. 80.

110 'We all felt that if we could make it easier and pleasanter for people to come to our poetry, we should certainly do so. At the same time we thought it necessary to stress that an explanation or a paraphrase is only a guide and, usually, a dubious one, to the poem itself. As we know from our days at school, notes and paraphrases can do a great deal of harm, if taken too seriously' (p. 1).

111 Page to Anderson, 14 Oct. 1973, 'Patrick Anderson' dossier, *Page Papers,* vol. 6.

112 Page to McLaren, undated [early 1955?], 'Floris Clarke McLaren' dossier, *Page Papers,* vol. 8.

113 Page to Corman, 25 Feb. 1953, 'Cid Corman' dossier, *Page Papers,* vol. 6.

114 See Page to Corman, 16 Jan. and 25 Feb. 1953, and Corman to Page, 21 Jan. 1953, 'Cid Corman' dossier, *Page Papers,* vol. 6.

115 Perkins, *A History of Modern Poetry,* vol. 2, pp. 125–6.

116 Wilson, '*Other Canadians* and After,' p. 91.

117 Page to McLaren, n.d. [1955?], 'Floris Clarke McLaren' dossier, *Page Papers,* vol. 8.

118 McLaren to Page, 19 Apr. [1955?], 'Floris Clarke McLaren' dossier, *Page Papers,* vol. 8.

119 Chiefly by identifying the woman reflected in the window as the speaker herself, rather than as another party reflected at an angle. Granted the poem's rigorous third-person handling of the woman reflected belies my claim, as does Douglas Freake, who thinks the reflected woman clearly an other ('The Multiple Self,' pp. 100–1). I persist in my view partly because (as Freake suggests) the boundaries of self and other are rarely rigid in Page's early poetry, and her representations of apparent others are often suggestive of self-division (see 'If It Were You,' 'Cullen'). Freake himself supplies a superbly apt passage from Alan McGlashan's *Savage and Beautiful Country: The Secret Life of the Mind* (1966), a book referred to by Page in 'Questions and Images': 'the Dreamer constantly and effortlessly performs the rationally inconceivable feat of being both the experiencing subject and the observed object at the same moment and to the same degree' (qtd. p. 108). In my view, 'Reflection in a Train Window' is best articulated in light of McGlashan's insight.

120 P.K. Page, 'Questions and Images,' p. 187.

121 Still, it is fascinating to think now of Page's recent attraction to the *glosa.* Four-line fragments dis-integrated by Page from other poems and poets – with whom she obviously felt some powerful sympathy – are themselves fragmented into single lines, then integrated into four new stanzas by Page's lines of response. At the end, a new whole poem emerges which is neither Page's nor the prior poet's, entirely; in which the *integritas* of the borrowed quatrain and that of Page's new poem exist in ideal harmony.

2: The Poem in the Mind: The *Integritas* of Klein in the Forties

1 By the time of the amalgamation, Klein had sent 'Variations on a Theme,' 'Actuarial Report,' 'Commercial Bank,' 'Bread,' 'Dentist,' 'Montreal,' 'The Library,' 'The Green Old Age,' to *Preview,* while *First Statement* had printed three of the psalms from the eventual 'Psalter of Avram Haktani,' two substantial excerpts of 'The Hitleriad,' and 'Pawnshop.'

2 A.M. Klein to A.J.M. Smith, 4 Jan. 1944, in 'Some Letters of Klein to Smith,' p. 11. Smith had evidently written to Klein to complain about Neufville Shaw's disdainful review of *The Book of Canadian Poetry,* and of his own poetry in it. Interestingly, Klein's invective precedes his joining the editorial board of *Preview* by only two months. D.M.R. Bentley makes use of the same passage to elucidate the anti-coterie sentiment in 'Portrait of the Poet as Landscape': see his 'A Nightmare Ordered: A.M. Klein's "Portrait of the Poet as Landscape",' p. 44, n. 30.

3 Certainly Klein was not always easy under his mantle as Jewish poet. In January 1943 he had remarked firmly to A.J.M. Smith that Smith had included too much of Klein's Judaica in the manuscript of *The Book of Canadian Poetry,* and (in Usher Caplan's words) 'complained bitterly about how the Canadian critics E.K. Brown and W.E. Collin tended to define him in terms of his Jewishness. "Lord, O Lord," he cried, why did they both have to go "flaunting my circumcision? I am not a poet because I'm a Jew ..."' (*Like One That Dreamed: A Portrait of A.M. Klein,* p. 102). Typically, Klein was at roughly the same time chiding American poets like Karl Shapiro for not expressing their Jewishness enthusiastically enough, a paradox also remarked by Caplan. See 'Annotation on Shapiro's *Essay on Rime,*' in *Literary Essays and Reviews,* pp. 169–77 (hereinafter cited as *LER*), and the exchange of letters between Klein and Shapiro, discussed by Caplan, pp. 150–1.

4 A powerful indication of the difficulty of Klein's dual vocation is 'Ave Atque Vale' of 1931, in which Pollock correctly notes 'some strain in the poem's unremitting air of good cheer: perhaps Klein protests too much as he tries to convince himself, as well as his audience, that he is part of a vital community with roots reaching far back into history' (p. 52). To this reading might be added the stress tangible in the poem's attempt to harmonize the poet's English verse exemplars with his rather overworked (and newly researched) affiliation with Jewish Talmudic folklore. The strain is notable in his Chaucerian imagining of that 'parfait jolly company,' as it is in his codicil claim that he 'forsakes ... Shakespeare' only 'for a space' (qtd. in Pollock, p. 52).

5 To Smith's request for 'a brief statement of [his] attitude towards [his] art,' Klein replied, 'I am surprised that you ask it. You know that such questions elicit only the sheerest of arrogant balderdash. What shall I say in reply: "I sing because I

must!" – How phoney ... Me, I will have none of that cant' (A.M. Klein to A.J.M. Smith, 21 Jan. 1943, in 'Some Letters of Klein to Smith,' p. 3).

6 These materials all appear in an undated dossier entitled 'Marginalia' in the *Klein Papers;* Steinberg and Caplan have reproduced them under that heading in *LER*, pp. 182–92; see also *Notebooks*, pp. 103–24 (hereinafter cited parenthetically as *NB*).

7 In 1948 Klein endorsed this linkage of Judaic proscriptions and literary expression: 'the whole vocabulary of the Bible is part of an attempt to escape from the aesthetic suppressions occasioned by the Second Commandment: "Thou shalt not make unto thee any graven image, or any likeness of anything that is in heaven above, or that is in the earth beneath, or that is in the water under the earth" ... But the soul, it would appear, hungers toward such creativity; where such creativity is impeded, frustration ensues. But frustration always seeks some way out. For the ancient Hebrew the way out of the prohibition of the Second Commandment was – to make images in words' ('The Gesture of the Bible,' *LER*, p. 132). My thanks to Michael Abraham, whose doctoral research into Klein, Layton, and Cohen brought this passage to my attention.

8 '$x^2 + 2xy + y^2$,' in 'Marginalia,' *Klein Papers*, vol. 5, p. 5224; *NB*, pp. 116–17.

9 *Klein Papers*, vol. 5, pp. 5228–30; *LER*, pp. 183–4.

10 Bentley, 'A Nightmare Ordered,' pp. 39–40.

11 'Centripetal poetry' draws the reader ever deeper within its complexities, which Klein here refers to as a 'vortex'– a noticeable borrowing from Pound in Klein, whose distaste for him is everywhere else very clear. 'Centrifugal poetry' raises readers to a level of excitement that throws them off at the poem's end to a contemplation of the world outside the poem – of the meanings of that world that the poem has gathered for us.

12 I know of no evidence that Klein encountered Frank's essay. Because it appeared just as he began his courses on modern poetry at McGill, however, and referred at length to *Ulysses*, with criticism of which Klein was extremely familiar, there seems a very good likelihood that an encounter with Frank's language germinated in the 'Marginalia.' Klein's exegetical technique for *Ulysses* suggests a grasp of its details very like a dense atomic structure; see below, p. 121, and n. 21.

13 Bentley, 'A Nightmare Ordered,' p. 8.

14 Louis Dudek, 'Emile Nelligan,' p. 20.

15 I am grateful to David Bentley for a conversation in which he focused the idea of personal integrity for me in a way that resonates here and throughout this chapter.

16 Norman H. Holland argues for an aesthetics of selfhood in his *The I*. He contends that Freud's methods entailed an essentially aesthetic (in fact New Critical) approach to psychological interpretation: by gathering up the details of a personality as a literary critic might gather up the fragments of a modernist poem, Freud

would glean among them a central meaning repressed by the patient. In his Part I, 'The Aesthetics of I,' Holland demonstrates Freud's reliance on the technique in a number of case-histories, and I have emulated it here, although without the nice expertise of Holland, nor evidently of his intellectual parent.

17 Caplan quotes an earlier version for the title, which he has as 'A psalm of Abraham of that which *is* visited upon him' (emphasis added). The poem is reprinted on page 180, and gives Caplan's chapter 12, 'A Prowler in the Mansion,' dealing with early signs of Klein's later crisis, its title.

18 I quote the version from Zailig Pollock's edition of Klein's *Complete Poems*, pp. 510–11. Hereinafter cited parenthetically as *CP*.

19 In 'The Psalter of Avram Haktani,' which is Englished into 'Abraham Little,' or, in Yiddish, Abraham Klein. Klein's playfulness with pseudonyms and its implication for his sense of selfhood is of interest below, pp. 133–4.

20 Klein writes, in a past tense suggestive of fictionalizing,'At last I had decided upon it. My mind was set, frozen into the shape of its decision. The debate, the argument and counterargument now belonged only to a theorizing and vacuous past. All the compelling truths which I had myself mustered against my [nadir?] would now have to be ignored ...' In subsequent lines 'Kay' considers killing himself by knife, by gas oven, by razor blade, but finally settles on sleeping pills as the least painful solution. See the *Klein Papers*, pp. 3509–13, and *NB*, pp. 29–31; see also Pollock, p. 135.

21 A letter of 17 July 1948 to one Henry Allen Moe of the Guggenheim Foundation (*Klein Papers*, vol. 1) renders the daunting enormity of Klein's critical goals for the novel:

> What I want to do – and have up to page 210 of Random House text already done – is to annotate the book, *paragraph by paragraph*. If ever there was reason required to revive the tradition of exegesis which prevailed in the 19th century, a tradition which was exercised upon classics both English and Latin–Greek, Ulysses provides that reason. Accordingly, my commentary treats of every difficult phrase, every obscure allusion, every elusive thought sequence. Then, each Homeric Parallel is exemplified; then, its literary techniques are illustrated. When the chapter is finished, nothing remains not understood (that is, by him who reads and does not run) – and what appeared at first as [chess?] and charade is seen to be the result of the order and reason of the most fertile mind of our century.

Klein himself may have recognized the project's power over him and responded with later anger; Caplan notes that 'Klein's unfinished study of Joyce is the most obviously missing part of the [Klein] collection [in the National Archives] and probably the only major part that he deliberately destroyed' (p. 218). See also Harold Heft, 'The Lost Klein Guggenheim Application.'

22 See especially his pp. 196–204 and the reading of *The Second Scroll* in his penultimate chapter, 'Keri' (pp. 233–52). For a rare earlier treatment, see Rachel Feldhay Brenner, 'A.M. Klein's *The Hitleriad*: Against the Silence of the Apocalypse,' a positive rendition of the accomplishment of *The Hitleriad*.

23 Klein's apparent lapse does not seem, perhaps surprisingly, to have been a prominent source of anxiety for him. To be sure there is the well-known passage of 'The Cripples,' with many echoes in other poems, in which a speaker observes the worshipful praying their way up the stairs of Saint Joseph's Oratory in Montreal and remarks, 'And I who in my own faith once had faith like this / but have not now, am crippled more than they' (*CP*, p. 648). And it may be that the journey to the new Israel – as some passages of *The Second Scroll* suggest – revived his piety for a long-enough period that subsequent renewal of disillusion was costly. But it is also known that Klein's attendance at synagogue was very limited and that his practice of ritual was 'vestigial' and 'perfunctory' (Caplan, p. 141). Even more revealing is the ease with which he could admit to himself his own limited and secularized observance of the faith while chastising Jewish writers like Karl Shapiro for their inattention to the tradition and belief that was inescapably a part of their creative consciousness; 'to Klein,' as Caplan notes, 'there was no great contradiction in the fact that he veered from religious tradition in his private life while at the same time insisting on the integrity of the tradition in public' (p. 141). Such a casual reconciliation of what might have been a profound awareness of hypocrisy suggests that the cost of his scepticism was minimal.

24 Tom Teicholz, in *Conversations with Jerzy Kosinski*, asserts that 'there is a central drama to the subject of a Holocaust survivor taking his life ... I imagine Kosinski would probably have replied that he took his life, as any person has the power to take his own life, Jew or non-Jew, Holocaust survivor or not. He would insist, I believe, that he did not take his life as other survivor/authors Bruno Bettelheim or Primo Levi did, or for that matter as Goebbels did. No, I imagine the important thing for Kosinski was that it was he, himself, not the Nazis and not heart disease, who was the determinant' (p. xiii).

25 Original formulations of this dichotomy are in Elie Wiesel, *One Generation After*. Saul Friedlander offers a powerful contemporary formulation in his introduction to the essays in *Probing the Limits of Representation: Nazism and the 'Final Solution'*: 'Our central dilemma can be defined as confronting the issues raised by historical relativism and aesthetic experimentation in the face of two possibly contrary constraints: a need for "truth," and the problems raised by the opaqueness of the events and the opaqueness of language as such' (p. 4).

26 See, for example, 'The New Order: Murder and Ransom,' 27 Nov. 1942

(pp. 173–5); 'The Slaughter of the Children,' 11 Dec. 1942 (pp. 176–7); and 'The Warsaw Ghetto,' 21 May 1943 (pp. 189–90), in *Beyond Sambation*.

27 Caplan says that the first fragmented news of the genocide reached North America in spring 1942 (p. 102). Otto Friedrich, in *The End of the World: A History* says that 'by the summer of 1942, the Allied capitols had received reports of mass slaughters, from the camps themselves, from neutral observers, even from anti-Nazi Germans. The London Daily Telegraph reported that June that more than one million Jews had been killed in the east' (p. 317). Arthur Morse notes in *While Six Million Died: A Chronicle of American Apathy* that later 1942 brought the first realizations that the Nazi genocide would be systematic; in early 1943, news of the 'death camps' was increasing in quantity and detail (pp. 23–64). As I write, an Associated Press news report (20 May 1997) indicates that Sir Winston Churchill knew of the Nazi genocide as early as late 1941.

28 I cannot square the *Collected Poems* dating with Pollock's reference in *A.M. Klein* to 'three dozen poems' written 'between completing *The Hitleriad*, towards the end of 1942, and beginning "Portrait of the Poet as Landscape," towards the beginning of 1944' (p. 113). Since in the subsequent discussion he includes 'Autobiographical' (1942) and 'Sonnet Unrhymed' (1945), I take it that all but three of these three dozen poems were written in either 1942 or 1944 and thereafter.

29 Pollock reads a number of the Quebec poems for their buried, even subliminal, references to Klein's Judaism, and the effort is worthwhile, if a little strained. When Klein changes 'antique ballad' to 'Anjou ballad' as he approached the final draft of 'The Rocking Chair,' for instance, he 'completes his invocation of the tradition that binds together the community of Quebec by inscribing, at its very heart, the word "Jew"' (p. 179). Such suggestions help us to credit Klein's own rationalization that he was not abandoning the Jewish subject but 'travelling incognito' among the Québécois (qtd. in Caplan, p. 149). Nevertheless, the very delicacy of articulation such resonances require of Pollock suggests the more obvious truth: Klein worked hard, perhaps harder than he knew, to obscure the palimpsestic Jewish references in these poems.

30 The full force of this break in Klein's poetry was not brought home to me until Mark Cohen, then pursuing a Master's paper on Klein under my supervision, exploited Pollock's chronology in a sensitive and disturbing reading of Klein's development. I am grateful for the chance our relationship gave me to focus more sharply on Klein's role in forties poetry.

31 Michael Greenstein's 'Canadian Poetry After Auschwitz' provided and contextualized this quotation for me, and the essay that contained it has been very helpful in my attempt to bring these issues once again to bear on Klein. See his *Third Solitudes*.

32 J.M. Kertzer, 'Personality and Authority: A.M. Klein's Self-Portrait,' p. 31.

33 Quoted in Malcolm Bradbury and James MacFarlane, eds., *Modernism, 1890–1930*, p. 148.
34 Untitled entry, 24 Sep. [1942], 'Raw Material' dossier, *Klein Papers*, vol. 5, p. 3465; *NB*, p. 4. 'In incognito dight' originally appears at the end of the final sentence, after the illegible word 'proud' (which I read as such on the editors' authority). The phrase has, however, been circled, and an arrow places it between 'ego' and 'and doubly.'
35 Ellmann, *Poetics of Impersonality*, p. 7.
36 In 'Marginalia' (*LER*, p. 182).
37 In ibid. (*LER*, p. 183).
38 After 1948, despite the five years still to pass before his nervous breakdown, he wrote only five more poems and thirty-three generally bitter little epigrams, and in 1951 refused Lorne Pierce's interest in the possibility of another volume (Caplan, pp. 195–6).
39 *The Second Scroll*, p. 78. Hereinafter cited as *TSS*.
40 A subtext of this pattern was Klein's occasional habit of speaking of his pseudonymous alter-egos in the third person, and discussing their writings as a critic: for example, he berates the columnist 'A.M.K.' for his verbal prolixity and density of reference in 'Verbum Sat,' an early 'McGilliad' column (*LER*, pp. 155–7). Of more immediate interest is his response to criticisms of 'The Psalter of Avram Haktani' in a letter of 7 Aug. 1942 to Louis K. Levinthal, of the Jewish Publication Society of Philadelphia: here he speaks of 'Mr. Haktani' in the third person and reports his objections to the Society's editorial interventions (*Klein Papers*, vol. 5, pp. 177–88) as if on behalf of another.
41 Pollock also notices the echo (p. 200).
42 See especially vols. 3, 4, 20, and 33 of *The Patrick Anderson Papers* (National Archives of Canada, Ottawa), containing the voluminous journals of Anderson's early life.
43 Diction borrowed, obviously, from 'The Rocking Chair,' in which the chair's rocking is compared to the alternation of the words '*invoke, revoke*' – an allusion to the governing discourses of church and law in Quebec society.
44 *Klein Papers*, vol. 5, p. 5244; *NB*, p. 123.
45 Since Pollock's meticulous textual notes do not record variant punctuation of the second of these lines, and since it appears in *The Rocking Chair*, his copy-text, with a comma after 'trick,' the absence of which Pollock does not remark in other manuscripts, I have restored the comma here.
46 Hans Natonek wrote in *In Search of Myself* of his 'experiences as an unknown writer confronting a materialistic and self-satisfied society with no interest in what he has to say ...' (*CP*, p. 1001). The connection to 'Portrait' is compelling, despite Klein's more general dislike of the book.

47 John T. Gage, *In the Arresting Eye: The Rhetoric of Imagism*, p. 112.
48 Ernest Buckler, *The Mountain and the Valley*, p. 254.
49 Caplan remarks that the younger forties poets 'tended to think that [Klein] learned more from them, by way of example and criticism, than they learned from him' (p. 100), and that seems likely, if we remember that Klein wrote little but juvenilia, satire, and Judaica prior to his contact with Page and Anderson. Nevertheless, in an interview with Michael Heenan, P.K. Page remarked emphatically that Klein's 'elaborate use of language, of image, the embroidery of his work, to say nothing of the metaphysical content, all had a very great effect upon me' ('Souvenirs of Some,' p. 103).
50 The poem's subtitle, '(For Camillien Houde),' did not appear in its original publication in *The Canadian Forum*. As Pollock notes, despite the savagely ironic treatments of the poem, Klein was an apparent admirer of Houde's and sent him a copy of 'The Rocking Chair'; Houde responded, in one of biography's lovely ironies, by singling out 'Political Meeting' for particular praise. See *CP*, pp. 1010–11, and *A.M. Klein*, pp. 186–8.
51 *Klein Papers*, vol. 1, p. 376.
52 Pollock characterizes this closure as 'a centripetal return inward, towards a centre, a One, which unifies and gives meaning to the many' (p. 16). That is perhaps Klein's hope for the passage. But such positivist readings have a rejoinder in Klein's earlier noted disdain of the Marxism of his fellow *Preview* editors: 'these people think that having discovered that bread is vital, they have found the last word in human thought ...' (see note 2, above).
53 Much of this language and most of its inspiration comes from Maggie Kilgour's *From Communion to Cannibalism: An Anatomy of Metaphors of Incorporation*, an exuberant study of selfhood and its alimentary relation to otherness.
54 T.S. Eliot, 'Tradition and the Individual Talent,' p. 5.
55 Dismemberment was a minor fascination throughout Klein's career, but perhaps especially so in the 1940s; see, for example, 'Desideratum' of 1942 (*CP*, pp. 569–70) and 'Address to the Choirboys' of 1944 (pp. 613–15).
56 Compare the structuring force of the words 'Again' and 'still' in 'Autobiographical,' a pivotal poem in Klein's development, balancing as it does the Judaic inspiration of earlier poems with the modernist catalogues of *The Rocking Chair*.
57 See Earle Birney, 'Canadian Jewish Poet.'

3: Image and Ego: Layton's Lyric Progress

1 The remark was made in a letter to Cid Corman of 18 July 1953, quoted by Elspeth Cameron in *Irving Layton: A Portrait*, p. 206.
2 Major items in this critical tradition include P.K. Smith's 'Irving Layton and the

Theme of Death'; Wynne Francis's 'Layton and Nietzsche,' '"The Birth of Tragedy": A Nietzschean Reading,' and '"The Farting Jesus": Layton and the Heroic Vitalists'; and Kurt van Wilt's 'Layton, Nietzsche, and Overcoming.'

3 Francis concludes that the Nietzschean impact on Layton's poetry did not occur until the early fifties ('Layton and Nietzsche,' 273), but Louis Dudek has noted that Nietzsche was common fare for the members of the *First Statement* group from the earliest days (John Nause and Michael Heenan, 'Interview with Louis Dudek,' pp. 36–7). Miriam Waddington says that John Sutherland was reading Nietzsche as a 'favourite author' by 1943 ('Introduction,' p. 8), and his two articles on Nietzsche in *First Statement* in 1944 were the first by any member of the group ('Wagner and Zarathustra,' 'Convalescence and Writing'). At the same time, according to Waddington, Layton was trying to improve Sutherland's Marxism ('Introduction,' p. 8); since Layton's celebration of the superior man, arising from his interpretations of Nietzsche, would eventually undermine the integrity of his Marxism, Sutherland may have been the better-read Nietzschean of the two *circa* 1944. Layton, however, claims to have 'come upon Nietzsche long before [he] had met Sutherland' (*Waiting for the Messiah*, p. 223). Layton mentions Nietzsche in his 1946 Master's thesis ('Harold Laski: The Paradoxes of a Liberal Marxist,' p. 37), albeit in a manner, as Cameron remarked (*Irving Layton*, p. 159), that leaves his real knowledge of the philosopher at that time suspect.

4 The phrase is A.J.M. Smith's, from the self-disparaging final lines of 'My Lost Youth.' See below, notes 30 and 37.

5 In a vituperative letter responding to Margaret Avison's review of *Here and Now* in *The Canadian Forum* of June 1945, pp. 64–5, Layton cited 'Newsboy,' 'The Swimmer,' and 'Proof Reader' as the proof of his poetic talent (qtd. in Cameron, *Irving Layton*, p. 152). In later retrospect he narrowed the body of evidence to 'The Swimmer,' the rapturous composition of which he related in the 'Preface' to *The Laughing Rooster* (rpt. in *Engagements*, p. 112), and again in *Waiting for the Messiah*, pp. 228–30. In these narratives it was the force of inspiration he felt as he wrote 'The Swimmer' in 1944 – and its excellence – that convinced him of his poetic vocation.

6 'Introduction,' p. 14.

7 Anne Compton has an excellent summary of the controversy and its later echoes in her *A.J.M. Smith: Canadian Metaphysical*, pp. 164–5.

8 See 'The Recent Poetry of Layton.'

9 See Louis Dudek, 'Layton Now and Then: Our Critical Assumptions.'

10 Dudek, 'Patterns of Recent Canadian Poetry,' p. 109.

11 Louis Dudek, 'Layton on the Carpet,' p. 137.

12 Ibid., p. 138.

13 Louis Dudek, 'The Transition in Canadian Poetry,' p. 133.

14 These include his participation with Dudek and Raymond Souster in *Contact*; his correspondence with American poet Robert Creeley, then in Mallorca; the first signs of tension in his marriage with Betty Sutherland (Cameron, *Irving Layton*, pp. 224–5); as well as the sudden astonishing increase in his poetic output and publication of volumes after the appearance of *Cerberus* in 1952.

15 See Brian Trehearne, 'A Partial Correspondence.' Review of *Irving Layton and Robert Creeley: The Complete Correspondence, 1953–1978*, eds. Ekbert Faas and Sabrina Reed.

16 See Irving Layton to Robert Creeley, 16 Aug. 1954, in *Irving Layton and Robert Creeley: The Complete Correspondence, 1953–1978*, ed. Ekbert Faas and Sabrina Reed, pp. 118–19.

17 Erwin Wiens, 'From Apocalypse to Black Mountain: The Contexts of Layton's Early Criticism,' p. 4.

18 See the introduction, pp. 4, 32, and Trehearne, 'Critical Episodes in Montreal Poetry of the Forties.'

19 Wiens, 'From Apocalypse to Black Mountain,' p. 4.

20 Ibid., p. 12.

21 Henry Treece, 'How I See Apocalypse,' in *How I See Apocalypse*, p. 80.

22 Irving Layton, *Music on a Kazoo* (1956); in *Fornalutx*, p. 117.

23 Treece, 'How I See Apocalypse,' p. 82.

24 Ibid., p. 75.

25 Henry Treece, 'More Notes on the Image,' in *How I See Apocalypse*, pp. 59–60.

26 Ibid., pp. 62–3.

27 Louis Dudek to Alan Crawley, 15 Dec. 1951, *Crawley Papers*, Folder 7, p. 2.

28 The Canadian journal *here and now* was published in Toronto from 1947 to 1949; first appearing two years after Layton's volume, it cannot have given him a title for his first collection. The title phrase was obviously appealing to a wide range of literati at the time.

29 See above, p. 182.

30 Nevertheless, only a handful of short lyrics betray the undergraduate sensibility of cleverness and affectation which mars, for instance, some of the work by famous Canadians in the *McGill Fortnightly Review*. The four 'Epitaphs' (all written by early 1942) in the volume are difficult to distinguish from A.J.M. Smith's efforts in the same genre in the early twenties; 'Church Parade' and 'Lady Remington,' both from 1943, with their coy rhymes and conventional expressions of the outrage of war, are predictable. 'My Father,' with its impersonal and faintly satiric portrait of an ageing Jew obsessed with 'the ways of God' and 'with kings,' looks like a homage to Klein's manner; there is even a short squib called 'Night,' the dandyish metaphors of which would have pleased any sixteen-year-old editor of a school rag. To dwell on such entirely unrepresentative pieces would be fruit-

less; but they require acknowledgement in a survey of Layton's forties creativity: he still valued them enough, whatever their provenance, to collect them in his first volume.

31 In Irving Layton, *Selected Poems, 1945–1989: A Wild Peculiar Joy*, p. 16. Hereinafter cited parenthetically as *WPJ*.

32 Irving Layton, *Waiting for the Messiah*, pp. 228–9.

33 My dating of Layton's forties poetry has been immeasurably assisted by Joy Bennett's and James Polson's *Bibliography of Irving Layton*.

34 Vol. 2 (1943), n.p.

35 Irving Layton, 'Words Without Music,' p. 23.

36 Ken Norris, *The Little Magazine in Canada: Its Role in the Development of Modernism and Postmodernism in Canadian Poetry*, pp. 40–1.

37 Nor, apparently, should A.J.M. Smith's influence be thought to have worked solely on *Preview*. Early Layton poems in *First Statement* bear a distinctly Smithian quality:

> Since like a sunbeam on a blind man's eyes
> Is useless death, what mad surprise
> Shall gender beauty from the broken plain?
> ('Accept This Day')

> Yet so an ancient malison
> Is acknowledged here,
> For where the moon was cruelly stabbed
> A red stain will appear.
> ('Day')

The language and imagery of the former is reminiscent of Smith's uncollected 'Testament,' whereas 'Day' smacks of some of Smith's earlier Imagist material: see, for example, his 'To the Haggard Moon' and 'What Strange Enchantment,' in *Poems New and Collected*, pp. 27, 60. All four pieces have a persistently undergraduate quality, and their other sources are many.

38 Irving Layton, *Here and Now*, n.p.

39 See Trehearne, *Aestheticism and the Canadian Modernists*, pp. 39–47.

40 Beginning with Harry Roskolenko, in his double review of *Here and Now* and *Now Is the Place*.

41 Layton, *Here and Now*, n.p.

42 Ibid.

43 Ibid.

44 Ibid.

45 Ibid.

46 This *First Statement* version of the poem was entitled 'April.' The revision noted below is the only other change before its inclusion in *Now Is the Place*, n.p.
47 Layton, *Here and Now*, n.p.
48 Louis Dudek, candidly admitting that he 'may be seeing everything through the magnifying glass of [his] own ego,' feels that in Canadian modern poetry 'the possibilities of open form ... the problem of consciousness, of deep subjectivity, and a kind of poetic exploration of the theory of knowledge ... of the *Tish* movement in Vancouver in the sixties ... and other far-out experimenters ... was essentially made possible by the opening up of the forties' ('Poetry of the Forties,' pp. 287, 299). That 'opening up' was stereotypically *First Statement*-ish in orientation: 'the younger poets in the forties cultivated a kind of brashness, vulgarity, and directness of realistic approach. "The flat of the platitude" became their *forte*: invective, even cynicism, and an oratorical style replaced the New-Critical tightness of the metaphysical moderns' (p. 294). Frank Davey, *Tish* original, more or less endorses this lineage throughout *Louis Dudek & Raymond Souster.*
49 'Proof Reader' joins 'The Swimmer' and 'Newsboy' as indisputably poetic in Layton's angry response to Margaret Avison's review of *Here and Now*; see above, p. 344, n. 5.
50 Layton, *Here and Now*, n.p.
51 See above, regarding P.K. Page, pp. 72 and 97.
52 Layton, *Here and Now*, n.p.
53 Daniel Albright, *Lyricality in English Literature*, p. 225.
54 The term used by Milton Wilson to describe the early poetry of P.K. Page and Patrick Anderson. See '*Other Canadians* and After,' pp. 80, 81, and above, p. 54.
55 Irving Layton, *Now Is the Place*, n.p.
56 It is true nonetheless that, in order to make his real leap forward from this poem's rather hesitant personation, Layton had to turn away from the poor, east-end setting of his forties poetry. As we will see, the masterpieces of the 1950s are loosely pastoral in setting, and the slum world – even, in large part, the urban world – will not be much visible in his best work. Finally, Layton's gifts were not those of a social realist, and it appears that his familiar persona could not emerge until his early urban devotions had been paid and put aside.
57 Layton, *Now Is the Place*, n.p.
58 Ibid.
59 Ibid.
60 Ibid.
61 Irving Layton, *Balls for a One-Armed Juggler* (1963); rpt. in *Fornalutx*, p. 20.
62 Al Purdy, 'The *Collected Poems* of Irving Layton,' p. 149.
63 See, for example, 'After the Chinese' and 'The Way of the World' in Irving Layton, *The Bull Calf and Other Poems*, pp. 30–1, 40–1.

64 Samuel Hynes, *The Auden Generation: Literature and Politics in England in the 1930s*, p. 226. See also Jacqueline Chenieux-Gendron, *Surrealism*, especially pp. 60–70, 'Theories of Image and Collage'; and see Paul C. Ray, *The Surrealist Movement in England*, especially pp. 38–50, 'The Surrealist Image.'
65 Faas and Reed, eds., *Irving Layton and Robert Creeley*, p. 9.
66 From the opening stanza of 'Whatever Else Poetry Is Freedom' (*WPJ*, pp. 65–6).
67 Herbert F. Tucker, 'Dramatic Monologue and the Overhearing of Lyric,' pp. 241–4. Tucker rejects 'the mystification inherent in the critical fiction of the speaker' (p. 241) but admits that its persistence is best explained by its inescapability in the classroom, among students with little or no concept of a possible ironic gap between a poet and a first-person poetic voice.
68 Faas and Reed, eds., *Irving Layton and Robert Creeley*, p. 15.
69 He had used a very similar argument ten years earlier – the period of his prose allusion to the Apocalyptics – when his short story 'A Parasite' was attacked in a long sneering letter from Patrick Waddington to John Sutherland as editor of *First Statement*. Waddington's premise for his intense dislike of Layton's representative titular character in the story is modernist and impersonalist: 'the extension [of] emotion which is permissible in the third person is not in the first; it [is] too close to us.' Layton's response (and tone) would become habitual: 'I am sure that Mr. Waddington's friends will point out to him the egregious asininity of confusing a drawn character with the author who drew it.' The entire exchange is somewhat whimsical, Waddington of course having been among the contributors to *First Statement* and Layton at least officially among his 'friends.' It suggests, nonetheless, that Layton had a needed grasp on the links among personation, ethics, and criticism well before their flowering in his poetry and letters to Creeley in the early 1950s. See Layton, '*First Statement* Opinions.'
70 Layton to Robert Creeley, 16 Aug. 1954, in Faas and Reed, eds., *Irving Layton and Robert Creeley*, p. 119.
71 To borrow Wynne Francis's disparagement of Patrick Anderson's manner; see 'Montreal Poets of the Forties,' p. 43.
72 See Norman H. Holland, *The I*, especially Part I: 'The Aesthetics of I.'
73 James Joyce, *A Portrait of the Artist as a Young Man*, p. 212.
74 Chénieux-Gendron, *Surrealism*, p. 5.
75 Treece, 'How I See Apocalypse,' p. 80.
76 Hugh Kenner, *The Pound Era*, p. 186.
77 This phrase is meaningful because of James MacFarlane's delicate articulation of the ambivalent modernist response to dualism, in Bradbury and MacFarlane, eds., *Modernism, 1890–1930*: 'What is distinctive – and difficult – about the Modernist mode is that it seems to demand the reconciliation of two distinct ways of reconciling contradictions, ways which in themselves are also contrary ... the Modernist

purpose ought to be defined as the resolution of Hegel with Kierkegaard; committing oneself neither wholly to the notion of "both/and," nor wholly to the notion of "either/or," but (as it were) to both – and to neither. Dauntingly, then, the Modernist formula becomes "both/and and/or either/or"' (p. 88).

78 See Brian Trehearne, '"Scanned and Scorned": Freedom and Fame in Layton,' pp. 139–50.

4: Forties Continuations: Dudek's Long Poems and the Period Style

1 Alex Comfort, *Art and Social Responsibility: Lectures on the Ideology of Romanticism*, p. 19.

2 Irving Layton, 'Politics and Poetry,' p. 20.

3 Anonymous, 'Correspondence,' p. 20.

4 Frank Davey, *Louis Dudek & Raymond Souster*, p. 102. Hereinafter cited parenthetically.

5 Dudek to Souster, 9 Feb. 1952; qtd. in Davey, ibid., p. 18.

6 John Sutherland, 'Introduction,' in *Other Canadians*, p. 19.

7 See Davey, *Dudek & Souster*, p. 14, especially Dudek's letter to Souster of 7 June 1951, ridiculing Sutherland's judgment of Katherine Mansfield in a recent issue of *Northern Review*: 'My theory is that looking for "native quality" just shuts the eyes to what is new and different and alive ... We've got to *belong to the European tradition!!!*'

8 See Louis Dudek and Michael Gnarowski, eds., *The Making of Modern Poetry in Canada: Essential Articles on Canadian Literature in English* (1967). This invaluable scholarly compendium, which revealed for the first time the documentary richness of Canadian modernist writing, has not been adequately critiqued for its partial determination by Dudek's own interests as a participant in the debates he represents.

9 Michael Gnarowski, *Contact Press, 1952–1967*, n.p.. Gnarowski also notes, contrary to the mythos surrounding *Contact*'s activity in the 1950s, that it was not established at a time of declining Canadian activity on the part of mainstream publishers, and Davey makes it plain that a chief function of Contact Press for Souster was its opportunity for self-publication (p. 24).

10 Wynne Francis, 'A Critic of Life: Louis Dudek as Man of Letters,' p. 10.

11 Elspeth Cameron, *Irving Layton: A Portrait*, pp. 196–200.

12 John Nause and Michael Heenan, 'An Interview with Louis Dudek,' pp. 34–5.

13 Michael Darling, 'An Interview with Louis Dudek,' p. 12. See also Dudek's recent autobiographical piece ('Louis Dudek') for the *Contemporary Authors Autobiography Series*: 'Democracy was not achieved to make us all mediocre, but to make us free and superior, each in his own way. Elitism is a good thing, and highly

democratic, if rightly used, on behalf of the majority' (p. 124). Of course, the most virtuous elite in Dudek's imaginative world is made up of 'the citizens of Atlantis,' that cadre of artists, philosophers, and intellectuals who perpetuate the values of culture and civilization throughout eternity.

14 Comfort, *Art and Social Responsibility*, p. 16.

15 For which see any of Layton's forewords to his volumes of poetry from about 1958 on, collected in *Engagements*; the most developed of Dudek's statements on 'barbarism' comes in the prolonged 'Questions – Some Answers' exchanges with George Bowering, Frank Davey, Steve McCaffrey, and bp nichol that opens the special Louis Dudek issue of *Open Letter*, esp. pp. 10–20.

16 See Layton's introduction to his poems in *Cerberus*, p. 46.

17 Davey remarks that 'Souster's aesthetic has not changed much since it first appeared in *Direction* in 1943' (p. 106). Bruce Whiteman says that Black Mountain poetics had in fact little effect on Souster's style, and that William Carlos Williams should be seen as the last significant influence on his poetry ('Raymond Souster,' pp. 241–2). Souster was introduced to Williams's poetry by Dudek in 1951, when he was thirty (Davey, *Dudek & Souster*, p. 11), and so the poet has written for the subsequent forty-five years without any substantive growth or reconsideration of his form. Souster himself candidly admitted that the exposure to Williams gave his 'world of poetry ... its present shape' (qtd. by Michael Gnarowski in *Contact, 1952–1954: Notes on the History and Background of the Periodical and an Index*, p. 1).

18 Norris, *The Little Magazine in Canada*, pp. 34–5.

19 Terry Goldie, 'Louis Dudek,' p. 76.

20 See Louis Dudek, 'Louis Dudek,' p. 128.

21 Ibid., p. 137.

22 Louis Dudek, *Continuation I*, p. 11. Hereinafter cited parenthetically. I shall call the speaking consciousness, the *persona*, of the *Continuations* 'Dudek' in the remarks that follow: not because I wish to collapse the poem's speaker-recorder and the poem's creator (rather, I lament the lack of an aware personative criticism of Dudek's long poems), but rather to suggest that Dudek the creator of the text toys deliberately and destructively with the New Critical mantra that the historical poet and ahistorical or textual speaker must never be conflated. In *Continuations*, arguably, we are listening to Louis Dudek in an unmediated fashion; that is the poem's desired effect, anyway; and to insist rigorously on a speaking persona who is 'not Dudek' will confound us when the historical poet playfully flings his own private life down on the page. Unlike Layton, Dudek has never taken shelter from the implications of his own poetic statements behind the 'I is another' of Rimbaud.

23 Dudek has kindly pointed out to me that these lines echo Ezra Pound's translation

of Confucius (from the *Analects,* the opening lines of Book I): 'Study with the seasons winging past, is not this pleasant? / To have friends coming in from far quarters not a delight?' (p. 10). The Confucius–Pound echo in the Canadian poet's mind and its alteration as a means of explicating his own poem's aesthetics give a particularly clear example of the interweaving of memory, association, and perception in the *Continuations* project.

24 Louis Dudek, *Epigrams,* p. 49.

25 Ibid., p. 12.

26 Ibid., p. 38.

27 Wayson S. Choy published an article in Dudek's little magazine *Delta* in October 1962 and an award-winning novel, *The Jade Peony,* in 1995, fourteen years after *Continuation I* was published.

28 In an entry in his recently published *1941 Diary,* Dudek writes, 'I was discussing yesterday with Layton the relation between personality and truth, trying to describe the view I hold, in art especially, that it is not the doctrine which is the essential truth but the personality. There is truth in the man, not in his ideas alone' (23 Apr. 1942, p. 40). If my reasoning about the *Continuations* project is fair, the fragmentary thought anticipated several decades' worth of Dudek's poetry.

29 Louis Dudek, 'The Theory of the Image in Modern Poetry,' p. 276.

30 See, for example, p. 50: '.0001 per cent read poetry, / 200 out of twenty million ... Point o-o-o-one – as many as get killed / on a good holiday week-end.'

31 Louis Kampf claims, counter to a more contemporary view of modernism's elitism and aloofness, that such profound connection between the reader or viewer and the consciousness of the artist is one of the chief goals and effects of modernist art. See his (now too little known) *On Modernism: The Prospects for Literature and Freedom.*

32 See Ernest Buckler, *The Mountain and the Valley,* p. 254; and see p. 150, regarding A.M. Klein.

33 Milton Wilson, '*Other Canadians* and After,' p. 84.

34 Alan Williamson, *Introspection and Contemporary Poetry,* p. 7.

35 Ibid., p. 2 (emphasis added).

36 Ibid., p. 12.

37 In a letter to Layton in the year *Europe* was published, Dudek attempted to reconcile the subjectivist drive of his new poetry with the still-forceful rhetoric of impersonality:

> Herein lies the paradox of all art, never to be removed. It is on the one hand by its very nature the personal equivalent in knowledge and experience, and at the same time it desires to become *true* in an impersonal absolute sense.

> The artist therefore works all his life to free his work of eccentricity, and to lay out his proof with absolute conviction. The result is a fine impersonality, of surface. And yet it is a permanent example of a personal vision of reality.

See the Dudek dossier in the Correspondence section of the *Irving Layton Papers*, 23 Aug. 1954.

38 'In *Europe*, except in the best passages, perception and response were divorced; passages of externally focussed description were opposed by passages of self-conscious rational analysis. The gain in projected authenticity which Dudek achieves by the unified proprioceptive methods of *En Mexico* is both large and striking' (p. 64).

39 Louis Dudek, *Europe*, p. 62. Hereinafter cited parenthetically. I cite the original edition of the poem rather than its recent reprint with emendations by Dudek himself, in order to explore *Europe's* exemplification of his poetic practice to readers of 1954, rather than the perhaps ideal form it had in his own mind, re-created in the Sherbrooke Street reprint.

40 Of course, a critical method emphasizing the poem's reception by a typical Canadian readership of small-press publications in 1954 would have a very different estimate of the poem's difficulty. Such a readership had been entirely unprepared by previous Canadian poetry for the degree of experiment in structure and perspective Dudek achieved in *Europe*, and their reactions to its difficulty would in no way be muted by the greater intensity of fragmentation in later work.

41 Dudek, 'Louis Dudek,' p. 138.

42 Darling, 'An Interview with Louis Dudek,' p. 2.

43 See for example his review of Olson's *In Cold Hell, In Thicket*, pp. 34–7. Fascinatingly, Dudek mocks what he calls Olson's 'theory ... that poetry is not an art form: it is a lump of coral that grows onto the living substance of life, or personality, and contains the shape and rhythm of reality. The test is authenticity' (pp. 35–6). Clearly, Dudek's own aesthetics for the later *Continuations* are criticized in this negative view of Olson. He rejects the method in 1954, the year of *Europe*'s publication, on the grounds that 'when life itself has lost all shape – as the right flank, directed by Eliot, has long ago made clear – you cannot make art out of the literal record' (pp. 35–6). The remarks suggest a greater discontinuity between Dudek's ideas in the *Europe* period and those of *Atlantis* than I shall now go on to suggest, but they are probably explained adequately by Dudek's rivalrous response to the American's impact on Robert Creeley and thence on Layton.

44 Louis Dudek, *En Mexico*, p. 15. Hereinafter cited parenthetically. In this case, citation of the original volume is imperative, since no reprint (including one Dudek authorized, in *Infinite Worlds*) has retained the original italic font or the

interspersed illustrations by Zygmunt Turkiewicz, whose contribution is noted prominently on the cover page.

45 See Bernhard Beutler, *Der Einfluss des Imagismus auf die Moderne Kanadische Lyrik Englischer Sprache.*

46 Douglas Barbour, 'Poet as Philosopher,' p. 25.

47 Louis Dudek, 'Functional Poetry,' p. 126.

48 *En Mexico* has many passages in which the traveller recognizes with humility the need of all things to find their destined form. Many of these partake of a quasi-Taoist understanding, a submission to the 'way' that is inherent in all forms of energy and life:

With tender affection
I flick an ant to the ground:
'Go along, now.'

(p. 60)

All things, all bodies:
that they should come out of nothing,
rise, as projectiles out of rock,
with spicules, with eyes, limbs,
with objects, accoutrements, skills,
amid an abundance of flora and fauna,
each to itself all –
in a jungle devouring graves.

(p. 28)

As yet undeveloped in such passages is their application to poetics: that Dudek's poetry must learn to comprehend an order as random, potentially as violent, even as impoverished, as he found *En Mexico*, the great gain being a fidelity to the reality of his experience that he had never previously envisioned.

49 Louis Dudek, *Atlantis*, p. 4. Hereinafter cited parenthetically.

50 Dudek identifies the setting as Kew Gardens in his autobiographical note 'Louis Dudek,' p. 140. Nothing in *Atlantis* makes this location clear. Kensington Gardens had been referred to twenty pages earlier (p. 112) and is probably therefore the location of the trees catalogued on page 122. That the location of these catalogued flora is so uncertain is in itself remarkable in a poem that so definitively claims 'travel' for its subject in the opening pages.

51 Dudek, 'Louis Dudek,' p. 139.

52 In Charles Taylor's formulation, 'To be moved by the [modernist] poem is also to be drawn into the personal sensibility which holds all these [fragments] together'

(*Sources of the Self*, p. 481). That Taylor is speaking of Eliot's *The Waste Land* affirms the fundamental continuity of Dudek's long search for an authentic, self-ironic subjectivism with the persistent modernist demand for new objective methods of exploring the nature of human consciousness, and thus calls into question Davey's alignment of Dudek's late poetics with (what he calls) 'the expansions and affirmations which characterize postmodernism' (p. 101).

53 The exchange continued: Page published 'Typists' in *Preview* 11 (Feb. 1943), one month after Dudek's 'Offices,' and in *Preview* 16 (Oct. 1943) she published her own 'Offices,' with an opening line that suggests a desire to claim ownership of the genre, and perhaps a defensiveness regarding her authority on the subject: 'Oh believe me, I have known offices ...' (p. 8).

54 Louis Dudek, 'Untitled ["I have seen the robin's fall ..."].'

55 Louis Dudek, 'In Praise of Sunrise,' p. 10.

56 See Trehearne, 'Finch's Early Poetry and the Dandy Manner,' or *Aestheticism and the Canadian Modernists*, pp. 95–9.

57 See Sandra Djwa, *The Politics of the Imagination: A Life of F.R. Scott*, p. 212.

58 Not to let the point drop too quickly, though, I will remark what certainly appears to be another Dudek imitation, of F.R. Scott in his 'Social Notes' period of the mid-1930s:

> Thinking of the coal shortage (brought
> on by the war) and of the
> woman
>
> In our side-street who got only two bags ...
>
> I saw the truck, a mountain of anthracite,
> Blocking up the sidewalk for me on
> Sherbrooke Street West.
>
> ('Coal Shortage')

The topicality, the ironic sense of place in relation to class, and the near-bathetic under-writing of the piece are very like Scott, though Dudek's real intimacy with the older poet would not begin until 1951 upon his return to Montreal from New York.

59 Louis Dudek, 'A Note on Isabel Ecclestone Mackay,' p. 3.

60 Louis Dudek, 'Note,' in *The Transparent Sea*, p. [6].

61 See A.J.M. Smith, 'Eclectic Detachment: Aspects of Identity in Canadian Poetry.'

62 Louis Dudek, 'At Parting,' *Unit of Five*, p. 9. Hereinafter cited parenthetically as *UoF*.

63 Louis Dudek, 'Midsummer, Adirondacks,' *East of the City*, p. 11. Hereinafter cited parenthetically as *EoC*.
64 Comfort, *Art and Social Responsibility*, p. 32.
65 The attack is quoted by Comfort himself, p. 13.
66 Louis Dudek, Review of Olson's *In Cold Hell, In Thicket*, pp 35–6.
67 Comfort, *Art and Social Responsibility*, p. 38.
68 Dudek notes, 'My "Marxist" Utopian idealist period, 3 or 4 yrs mainly inspired by Layton, lasted from 1943 or 1944 to 1947–48. It was the main cause of my first break with Layton, a silence of several years. (Stephen Spender's poetry was very much behind it; and Lionel Trilling and especially an essay by Dwight Macdonald put an end to it)' (personal communication).
69 Louis Dudek, *Infinite Worlds: The Poetry of Louis Dudek*, p. 41. Hereinafter cited parenthetically as *IW*.
70 Dudek, 'Louis Dudek,' p. 126.
71 See for example Cameron, *Irving Layton*, p. 197, and Davey, *Dudek & Souster*, p. 40; see also above, p. 292, and note 68.
72 Louis Dudek, *Twenty-Four Poems*, p. xvii. Hereinafter cited parenthetically as *24P*.
73 Dudek, 'Louis Dudek,' p. 126.
74 Louis Dudek, *The Searching Image*, p. 1. Hereinafter cited parenthetically as *SI*.
75 A.T. Tolley, *The Poetry of the Forties in Britain*, p. 63. See above re Page, p. 84.
76 Dudek, 'Louis Dudek,' pp. 126, 132.
77 Louis Dudek to Raymond Souster, 11 Dec. 1951, Lakehead University Library; qtd. in Davey, *Dudek & Souster*, p. 39, and used as epigraph to Robin Blaser's introduction to *Infinite Worlds*, p. 7.

Conclusion: The Generation of the Forties

1 Samuel Hynes, *The Auden Generation: Literature and Politics in England in the 1930s*, p. 40.
2 Page to MacLaren, undated [early 1955?], 'Floris Clarke MacLaren' dossier, *Page Papers*, vol. 8.
3 Astradur Eysteinsson, *The Concept of Modernism*, p. 28.
4 Louis Dudek to Irving Layton, 5 May 1942, *Layton Papers*, p. 5.

Bibliography

Many works of critical prose in *Preview* and *First Statement*, usually prefatory, editorial, or closing remarks, are unsigned. In *First Statement* these are certainly the work of John Sutherland, and are so entered below. In *Preview*'s case, authorship is slightly less clear, but Patrick Anderson is generally acknowledged to have written most or all of such pieces. For these reasons, and to avoid a clutter of anonymous entries, I have listed such materials under his name below (and offer my apologies to any other editor-author thus denied credit).

Primary Sources

Anderson, Patrick. *The Colour as Naked*. Toronto: McClelland & Stewart, 1953

– 'Dramatic Monologue.' *Preview* 4 (Jun. 1942): 5–7

– 'English Fantasy.' *Preview* 4 (Jun. 1942): 3

– 'An Explanatory Issue.' *Preview* 21 (Sep. 1944): 1

– Introduction. In *Preview*, pp. iii–v. New York: Kraus Reprint Co., 1980

– 'Love Poem.' *Preview* 9 (Nov. 1942): 6

– 'Night Out.' *Preview* 5 (Jul. 1942): 4

– 'Note.' *Preview* 4 (Jun. 1942): 1

– 'Note [PREVIEW FUND].' *Preview* 18 (Feb. 1944): 10

– 'Note [*The Victory Broadsheet*].' *Preview* 15 (Aug. 1943): 12

– 'Ourselves.' *Preview* 11 (Feb. 1943): 10–11

– *Patrick Anderson Papers*. National Archives, Ottawa, Ontario

– 'A Poet Past and Future.' *Canadian Literature* 46 (Autumn 1970): 7–21

– 'A Reply.' *Preview* 8 (Oct. 1942): 3–5

– *Return to Canada: Selected Poems*. Toronto: McClelland & Stewart, 1977

– 'Soldier (An Attempt).' *Preview* 11 (Feb. 1943): 11

– 'Stephen Spender and the Tragic Sense.' *Preview* 7 (Sep. 1942): 1–3

- *A Tent For April*. Montreal: First Statement Press, 1945
- 'Three Storms.' *Preview* 3 (May 1942): 5
- *A Visiting Distance*. Ottawa: Borealis, 1976
- *The White Centre*. Toronto: Ryerson, 1946

Anderson, Patrick, et al. 'Statement.' *Preview* 1 (Mar. 1942): 1

Dudek, Louis. 'Academic Literature.' *First Statement* 2.8 (Aug. 1944): 17–20. Rpt. in *Selected Essays and Criticism*, pp. 1–4

- *Atlantis*. Montreal: Delta, 1967
- 'Berger Street.' *First Statement* 1.11 (Feb. 1943): 6
- *Cerberus: Poems*. With Irving Layton and Raymond Souster, pp. 11–42. Toronto: Contact, 1952
- 'Coal Shortage.' *First Statement* 1.15 (Mar. 1943): 7
- *Continuation I*. Montreal: Véhicule, 1981
- *East of the City*. Toronto: Ryerson, 1946
- 'Emile Nelligan.' *First Statement* 2.3 (Oct. 1943): 19–20
- *En Mexico*. Toronto: Contact, 1958
- *Epigrams*. Montreal: DC Books, 1976
- *Europe*. Toronto: Laocoön [Contact] Press, 1954
- 'Functional Poetry: A Proposal.' *Delta* (July 1959). Rpt. in *Infinite Worlds*, p. 126
- 'Geography, Politics and Poetry.' *First Statement* 1.16 (Apr. 1943): 2–3
- 'The Idea of Art.' *Canadian Literature* 126 (Autumn 1990): 50–64
- *Infinite Worlds: The Poetry of Louis Dudek*. Ed. Robin Blaser. Montreal: Véhicule, 1988
- 'In Praise of Sunrise.' *First Statement* 1.12 (Feb. 1943): 10–11
- 'Layton Now and Then: Our Critical Assumptions.' *Queen's Quarterly* 63 (Summer 1956): 291–3. Rpt. in *Selected Essays and Criticism*, pp. 52–5
- 'Layton on the Carpet.' *Delta* 9 (Oct./Dec. 1959): 17–19. Rpt. in *Selected Essays and Criticism*, pp. 136–40
- 'A Letter re "First Statement" [to Michael Gnarowski].' June 1974. Rpt. in *Open Letter*, 4th ser., 8–9 (Spring/Summer 1981): 213–16
- Letter to Irving Layton. 5 May 1942. *Irving Layton Papers*. Concordia University, Montreal
- Letter to Raymond Souster. 11 Dec. 1951. Lakehead University Library, Thunder Bay
- 'Louis Dudek.' *Contemporary Authors Autobiography Series* 14, pp. 121–42
- Louis Dudek Issue. *Open Letter*, 4th ser., 8–9 (Spring/Summer 1981)
- 'The Mountains.' *First Statement* 2.5 (Mar. 1944): 4
- *1941 Diary*. Ed. Aileen Collins. Montreal: Empyreal, 1996
- 'A Note on Isabel Ecclestone Mackay.' *First Statement* 1.15 (Mar. 1943): 3
- 'Note.' In *The Transparent Sea*, p. 6. Toronto: Contact, 1956

– 'Offices.' *First Statement* 1.10 (Jan. 1943): 1
– 'On a Bridge at Pt. St. Charles.' *First Statement* 1.19 (May 1943): 1
– 'Patterns of Recent Canadian Poetry.' *Culture* 19 (1958): 399–415. Rpt. in *Selected Essays and Criticism*, pp. 94–110
– 'The Poetry of the Forties.' *Open Letter*, 4th ser., 8–9 (Spring/Summer 1981): 287–99
– 'Poetry of the 60s.' *Canadian Literature* 41 (Summer 1969): 111–20. Rpt. in *Selected Essays and Criticism*, pp. 269–81
– 'Poets of Revolt ... Or Reaction?' *First Statement* 1.20 (June 1943): 3–5
– 'Questions – Some Answers [an interview with George Bowering, Frank Davey, Steve McCaffrey, and bp nichol].' *Open Letter*, 4th ser., 8–9 (Spring/Summer 1981): 9–38
– Review of Charles Olson's *In Cold Hell, In Thicket. CIV/n* 5 (1954): 157–62. Rpt. in *Selected Essays and Criticism*, pp. 34–7
– 'The Role of Little Magazines in Canada.' *Canadian Forum* 38 (July 1958): 76–8. Rpt. in *The Making of Modern Poetry in Canada*, eds. Dudek and Gnarowski, pp. 205–12
– *The Searching Image*. Toronto: Ryerson, 1952
– *Selected Essays and Criticism*. Ottawa: Tecumseh, 1978
– 'The Theory of the Image in Modern Poetry.' E.J. Pratt Memorial Lecture, Memorial University of Newfoundland, 9 October 1979. Rpt. in *Open Letter*, 4th ser., 8–9 (Spring/Summer 1981): 263–82
– 'The Transition in Canadian Poetry.' *Culture* 20 (Sep. 1959): 282–95. Rpt. in *Selected Essays and Criticism*, pp. 122–35
– *Twenty-Four Poems*. Toronto: Contact, 1952
– *Unit of Five*. Ed. Ronald Hambleton. Toronto: Ryerson, 1944
– 'Untitled ["I have seen the robin's fall ..."].' *First Statement* 1.10 (Jan. 1943): 1
– 'Untitled ["Snow drops glistened ..."].' *First Statement* 1.12 (Feb. 1943): 11
– 'Untitled ["Out of the silence ..."].' *First Statement* 1.12 (Feb. 1943): 12
Dudek, Louis, and Michael Gnarowski, eds. *The Making of Modern Poetry in Canada: Essential Articles on Canadian Literature in English*. Toronto: Ryerson, 1967
Dudek, Louis, and Irving Layton, eds. *Canadian Poems, 1850–1952*. Toronto: Contact, 1953
Klein, A.M. 'Actuarial Report.' *Preview* 12 (Mar. 1943): 7–8. Rpt. in *Complete Poems*, pp. 607–8
– *A.M. Klein Papers*. National Archives, Ottawa
– 'Annotation on Shapiro's Essay on Rime.' *Literary Essays and Reviews*, pp. 169–77
– *Beyond Sambation: Selected Essays and Editorials. 1928–1955*. Toronto: University of Toronto Press, 1982
– 'Bread.' *Preview* 19 (Mar. 1944): 1. Rpt. in *Complete Poems*, pp. 617–18

– *Complete Poems*, 2 vols. Ed. Zailig Pollock. Toronto: University of Toronto Press, 1990
– 'Dentist.' *Preview* 20 (May 1944): 12. Rpt. in *Complete Poems*, p. 568
– 'The Hitleriad [excerpts].' *First Statement* 2.1 (Aug. 1943): 1–3; *First Statement* 2.3 (Oct. 1943): 4–7. Rpt. in *Complete Poems*, pp. 581–606
– 'The Library.' *Preview* 22 (Dec. 1944): 10. Rpt. in *Complete Poems*, p. 620
– *Literary Essays and Reviews*. Ed. Usher Caplan and M.W. Steinberg. Toronto: University of Toronto Press, 1987
– 'Montreal.' *Preview* 21 (Sep. 1944): 3–5. Rpt. in *Complete Poems*, pp. 621–3
– *Notebooks: Selections from the A.M. Klein Papers*. Ed. Zailig Pollock and Usher Caplan. Toronto: University of Toronto Press, 1994
– 'Pawnshop.' *First Statement* 2.12 (Apr./May 1945): 26–8. Rpt. in *Complete Poems*, p. 576
– *The Second Scroll*. Toronto: McClelland & Stewart [New Canadian Library], 1992
– 'Some Letters of A.M. Klein to A.J.M. Smith, 1941–1951.' In *The A.M. Klein Symposium*, ed. Seymour Mayne, pp. 1–13. Ottawa: University of Ottawa Press, 1975
– 'The Usurper.' *Literary Essays and Reviews*, pp. 195–7
Layton, Irving. 'Accept This Day.' *First Statement* 1.9 (Dec. 1942): 1
– 'After the Chinese.' *The Bull Calf and Other Poems*, pp. 30–1
– 'April.' *First Statement* 2.8 (Aug. 1944): 16–17. Rpt. (as 'Returning with an Annual Passion') in *Now Is the Place*, n.p.
– *Balls for a One-Armed Juggler*. Toronto: McClelland & Stewart, 1963.
– *The Bull Calf and Other Poems*. Toronto: Contact, 1956.
– *Cerberus: Poems*. With Louis Dudek and Raymond Souster, pp. 43–72. Toronto: Contact, 1952
– *The Collected Poems of Irving Layton*. Toronto: McClelland & Stewart, 1971
– 'Day.' *First Statement* 1.12 (Feb. 1943): 9
– 'DeBullion Street.' *First Statement* 2.5 (Mar. 1944): 3. Rpt. in *Here and Now*, n.p.
– 'The Eagle.' *Northern Review* 1.6 (Aug./Sep. 1947): 15. Rpt. in *Now Is the Place*, n.p.
– *Engagements: The Prose of Irving Layton*. Ed. Seymour Mayne. Toronto: McClelland & Stewart, 1972
– 'English for Immigrants.' *Northern Review* 1.1 (Jul. 1946): 22. Rpt. in *Now Is The Place*, n.p.
– 'First Statement Opinions.' *First Statement* 1.16 (Apr. 1943): 7–8
– 'Forecast.' *First Statement* 2.1 (Aug. 1943): 16
– *Fornalutx: Selected Poems, 1928–1990*. Kingston and Montreal: McGill-Queen's University Press, 1992
– 'Gents' Furnishings.' *First Statement* 2.3 (Oct. 1943): 16–17. Rpt. in *Here and Now*, n.p.

– 'Harold Laski: The Paradoxes of a Liberal Marxist.' M.A. thesis, McGill University, 1946
– *Here and Now.* Montreal: First Statement Press, 1945
– *Irving Layton Papers.* Department of Special Collections, Concordia University Library, Montreal
– 'Jewish Main Street.' *First Statement* 2.8 (Aug. 1944): 8–9. Rpt. in *Here and Now,* n.p.
– *Music on a Kazoo.* Toronto: Contact, 1956
– 'Newsboy.' *Direction* 2 (1943): n.p.
– '1943.' *First Statement* 2.2 (Sep. 1943): 21
– *Now Is the Place.* Montreal: First Statement Press, 1948
– 'Open Letter to Louis Dudek.' *Cataract* (Winter 1962). Rpt. in *Engagements,* pp. 175–81
– 'Politics and Poetry.' *First Statement* 2.1 (Aug. 1943): 17–21. Rpt. in *Engagements,* pp. 9–13
– 'A Poor Poet Is Grateful for a Sudden Thaw.' *Northern Review* 1.5 (Feb./Mar. 1947): 25. Rpt. in *Now Is the Place,* n.p.
– Review of A.M. Klein's *The Hitleriad. First Statement* 2.9 (Oct./Nov. 1944): 17–20
– 'Say it Again, Brother.' *First Statement* 1.19 (May 1943): 7
– *Selected Poems, 1945–1989: A Wild Peculiar Joy.* Toronto: McClelland & Stewart, 1989
– 'The Swimmer.' *First Statement* 2.10 (Dec./Jan. 1944/5): 8. Rpt. in *Selected Poems, 1945–1989: A Wild Peculiar Joy,* p. 16
– *Taking Sides: The Collected Social and Political Writings.* Ed. Howard Aster. Oakville, ON: Mosaic, 1977
– *The Uncollected Poems of Irving Layton, 1931–1959.* Ed. W. David John, with Preface by Seymour Mayne. Oakville, ON: Mosaic, 1976
– 'Upper Water Street.' *First Statement* 1.20 (Jun. 1943): 2–3. Rpt. in *Here and Now,* n.p.
– 'Vigil.' *First Statement* 2.12 (Feb. 1943): 10
– *Waiting for the Messiah: A Memoir.* Toronto: McClelland & Stewart, 1985
– 'The Way of the World.' *The Bull Calf and Other Poems,* pp. 40–1
– 'Words Without Music.' *First Statement* 2.10 (Dec./Jan. 1944/5): 22–3
Page, P.K. 'Adolescence.' *Preview* 23 ([Jan. or Feb.] 1945): 4. Rpt. in *The Glass Air,* p. 11
– *As Ten As Twenty.* Toronto: Ryerson, 1946
– 'The Bands and the Beautiful Children.' *Preview* 19 (Mar. 1944): 8. Rpt. in *The Glass Air,* p. 3
– 'Canadian Poetry 1942.' *Preview* 8 (Oct. 1942): 8–9
– *Cry Ararat! Poems New and Selected.* Toronto: McClelland & Stewart, 1967

– 'Desiring Only ...' *Preview* 2 (Apr. 1942): 4
– 'Divers.' *Preview* 15 (Aug. 1943): 3
– *Evening Dance of the Grey Flies.* Toronto: Oxford University Press, 1981
– 'Generation.' *Preview* 8 (Oct. 1942): 5–6. Rpt. in *The Glass Air*, pp. 18–19
– *The Glass Air: Selected Poems.* Toronto: Oxford University Press, 1985
– *The Hidden Room: Collected Poems*, 2 vols. Erin, ON: Porcupine's Quill, 1997
– 'Landscape of Love.' *First Statement* 1.1 (Aug. 1942): 8. Rpt. in *The Glass Air* [as 'Personal Landscape'], p. 1
– Letter to Floris Clarke McLaren [*c.* 1955]. *P.K. Page Papers*, vol. 8: Floris Clarke McLaren dossier
– *The Metal and the Flower.* Toronto: McClelland & Stewart, 1954
– 'Offices.' *Preview* 16 (Oct. 1943): 8–9
– 'Panorama.' *Preview* 14 (Jul. 1943): 5–6
– 'Photograph.' *Preview* 17 (Dec. 1943): 6. Rpt. in *The Glass Air*, p. 55
– *P.K. Page Papers.* National Archives, Ottawa
– 'Poem ["Let us by paradox ..."].' *Preview* 18 (Feb. 1944): 5. Rpt. in *The Glass Air* [as 'Poem in War Time'], p. 17
– 'Poem ["'She was dime-dead ..."].' *First Statement* 1.1 (Aug. 1942): 7. Rpt. in Hambleton, ed., *Unit of* 5 [as 'Snapshot'], p. 42
– 'Questions and Images.' *Canadian Literature* 41 (Summer 1969): 17–22. Rpt. in *The Glass Air*, pp. 187–91
– 'The Sleeper.' *First Statement* 1.7 (Nov. 1942): 6
– 'Some There Are Fearless.' *Preview* 5 (Jul. 1942): 5
– 'The Stenographers.' *Preview* 5 (Jul. 1942): 5–6
– 'Stenographers [prose].' *Preview* 11 (Feb. 1943): 1–2
– 'Summer Resort.' *Preview* 16 (Oct. 1943): 9. Rpt. in *The Glass Air*, p. 26
– 'Typists.' *Preview* 11 (Feb. 1943): 2–3
– 'Waking.' *Preview* 13 (May 1943): 5. Rpt. in *As Ten As Twenty*, p. 20
Sutherland, John. 'Convalescence and Writing.' *First Statement* 2.7 (May 1944): 18–24
– 'A Criticism of "In League with Stones".' *First Statement* 1.4 (Oct. 1942): 2
– 'Critics on the Defensive.' *Northern Review* 2.1 (Oct./Nov. 1947): 18–23. Rpt. in *Essays, Controversies and Poems*, pp. 62–7
– 'Earle Birney's "DAVID".' *First Statement* 1.9 (Dec. 1942): 6–8
– 'Editorial.' *First Statement* 1.1 (Aug. 1942): 1
– 'Editorial.' *First Statement* 1.12 (Feb. 1943): 3
– 'Editorial.' *First Statement* 2.5 (Mar. 1944): 1
– 'Editorial.' *First Statement* 2.8 (Aug. 1944): 1
– *Essays, Controversies and Poems.* Ed. Miriam Waddington. Toronto: McClelland & Stewart [New Canadian Library], 1972

– 'First Statement Opinions.' *First Statement* 1.17 (Apr. 1943): 6–8
– 'Girl in Spring.' *First Statement* 1.4 (Oct. 1942): 3. Rpt. in *Essays, Controversies and Poems*, p. 185
– 'The Great Equestrians.' *Northern Review* 6.4 (Oct.-Nov. 1953): 21–8. Rpt. in *Essays, Controversies and Poems*, pp. 76–84
– Introduction. In *Other Canadians: An Anthology of the New Poets in Canada, 1940–1946*, ed. John Sutherland, pp. 5–20. Montreal: First Statement Press, 1946
– Letter to the Editor. *Canadian Forum* 27 (Apr. 1947): 17–18
– 'Literary Colonialism.' *First Statement* 2.4 (Feb. 1944): 3
– 'The Master.' In *Essays, Controversies and Poems*, p. 181
– 'Mr. Coulter and the Canadian Landscape.' *First Statement* 1.11 (Jan. 1943): 7
– 'A Note on the Metaphor.' *First Statement* 2.4 (Feb. 1944): 9–10
– 'On a Story Published in Preview Magazine.' *First Statement* 1.1 (Aug. 1942): 4–6
– 'On Certain Obscure Poets.' *First Statement* 1.2 (Sep. 1942): 3
– 'On Thomas Wolfe.' *First Statement* 2.8 (Aug. 1944): 15–16. Rpt. in *Essays, Controversies and Poems*, p. 195
– 'The Past Decade in Canadian Poetry.' *Northern Review* 4.2 (Dec. 1950/Jan. 1951): 42–7. Rpt. in *Essays, Controversies and Poems*, pp. 70–6
– 'P.K. Page and *Preview*.' *First Statement* 1.6 (Nov. 1942): 7–8
– 'The Poetry of Patrick Anderson.' *Northern Review* 2.5 (Apr./May 1949): 8–20, 25–34. Rpt. in *Essays, Controversies and Poems*, pp. 119–28
– 'The Poetry of P.K. Page.' *Northern Review* 1.4 (Dec. 1946/Jan. 1947): 13–23. Rpt. in *Essays, Controversies and Poems*, pp. 101–12
– 'Religion, Patriotism and Poetry.' *First Statement* 1.17 (Apr. 1943): 6–8
– 'Retraction.' *First Statement* 1.20 (Jun. 1943): cover page
– Review of *The Book of Canadian Poetry*, ed. A.J.M. Smith. *First Statement* 2.6 (Apr. 1944): 19–20
– Review of *Poems* by Robert Finch. *Northern Review* 1.6 (Aug./Sep. 1947): 38–40
– Review of *Unit of Five*, ed. Ronald Hambleton. *First Statement* 2.11 (Feb./Mar. 1945): 30–1
– 'The Role of Prufrock.' *First Statement* 2.2 (Sep. 1943): 19–21
– 'The Role of the Magazines.' *First Statement* 1.15 (Mar. 1943): 1
– 'Three New Poets – Editorial.' *First Statement* 1.12 (Feb. 1943): 1–4
– 'Triumph.' *First Statement* 2.7 (May 1944):16. Rpt. in *Essays, Controversies and Poems*, p. 190
– 'The Two Schools – Editorial.' *First Statement* 2.1 (Aug. 1943): 1
– 'Wagner and Zarathustra.' *First Statement* 2.5 (Mar. 1944): 12–16
– 'Why George Left College [pseud. "Jack Hakaar"].' *First Statement* 2.6 (Apr. 1944): 15–16, 17. Rpt. in *Essays, Controversies and Poems*, pp. 198–202

– 'Why George Smokes a Pipe [pseud. "Jack Hakaar"].' *First Statement* 2.10 (Dec. 1944/Jan. 1945): 2–7. Rpt.in *Essays, Controversies and Poems*, pp. 202–6
– 'The Writing of Patrick Anderson.' *First Statement* 1.19 (May 1943): 3–6

Secondary Sources

Albright, Daniel. *Lyricality in English Literature*. Lincoln: University of Nebraska Press, 1985
Anderson, Allan. 'A Communication.' *Preview* 8 (Oct. 1942): 1–3
Anonymous. 'Correspondence.' *First Statement* 2.4 (Feb. 1944): 20
Anonymous. 'Reader's Report on *The Untouched Hills* [by P.K. Page].' *The Lorne Pierce Papers*. Queen's University Archives, Kingston, Box 12, Folder 6, Item 28 (31 Dec. 1945)
Barbour, Douglas. 'Poet as Philosopher.' *Canadian Literature* 53 (Summer 1972): 18–29
Beattie, Munroe. 'Poetry 1935–1950.' *Literary History of Canada*, vol. 2: 254–96. Toronto: University of Toronto Press, 1976
Bennett, Joy, and James Polson. *Bibliography of Irving Layton*. Montreal: Concordia University, 1978
Benstock, Shari. *Women of the Left Bank*. Austin: University of Texas Press, 1986
Bentley, D.M.R. *The Gay] Grey Moose: Essays on the Ecologies and Mythologies of Canadian Poetry 1690–1990*. Ottawa: University of Ottawa Press, 1992
– 'A Nightmare Ordered: A.M. Klein's "Portrait of the Poet as Landscape".' *Essays on Canadian Writing* 28 (Spring 1984): 1–45
Bentley, D.M.R., and Michael Gnarowski, eds. 'Four of the Former *Preview* Editors: A Discussion.' *Canadian Poetry: Studies, Documents, Reviews* 4 (Spring/Summer 1979): 93–119
Beutler, Bernhard. *Der Einfluss des Imagismus auf die Moderne Kanadische Lyrik Englischer Sprache*. Frankfurt: Lang, 1972
Birney, Earle. 'Canadian Jewish Poet.' *Canadian Forum* 20 (Feb. 1941): 354–5
– 'Struggle Against the Old Guard: Editing the *Canadian Poetry Magazine*.' In *Perspectives on Earle Birney*, pp. 9–31. Downsview, ON: ECW, 1981
Bradbury, Malcolm, and James MacFarlane, eds. *Modernism, 1890–1930*. Harmondsworth, Middlesex: Penguin, 1976
Brenner, Rachel Feldhay. 'A.M. Klein's *The Hitleriad*: Against the Silence of the Apocalypse.' *Studies in American Jewish Literature* 9.2 (Fall 1990): 228–41
Brown, E.K. *On Canadian Poetry*. Toronto: Ryerson, 1943
Buckler, Ernest. *The Mountain and the Valley*. Toronto: McClelland & Stewart [New Canadian Library], 1994
Cameron, Elspeth. *Irving Layton: A Portrait*. Toronto: Stoddart, 1985

Campbell, Patrick. 'Attic Shapes and Empty Attics: Patrick Anderson – A Memoir.' *Canadian Literature* 121 (Summer 1989): 86–99
Caplan, Usher. *Like One That Dreamed: A Portrait of A.M. Klein*. Toronto: McGraw-Hill Ryerson, 1982
Chenieux-Gendron, Jacqueline. *Surrealism*. Trans. Vivian Folkenflik. New York: Columbia University Press, 1990
Clark, Suzanne. *Sentimental Modernism: Women Writers and the Revolution of the Word*. Bloomington: Indiana University Press, 1991
Comfort, Alex. *Art and Social Responsibility: Lectures on the Ideology of Romanticism*. London: Falcon Press, 1946
Compton, Anne. *A.J.M. Smith: Canadian Metaphysical*. Toronto: ECW, 1994
Confucius. *The Analects*. Trans. Ezra Pound. *Hudson Review* 3.1 (Spring 1950): 9–52; 3.2 (Summer 1950): 237–87
Crawley, Alan. *Alan Crawley Papers*. Queen's University, Kingston
Darling, Michael. 'An Interview with Louis Dudek.' *Essays on Canadian Writing* 3 (Fall 1975): 2–14
Davey, Frank. *Louis Dudek & Raymond Souster*. Vancouver: Douglas and McIntyre, 1980
Day Lewis, Cecil. *The Poetic Image: The Clark Lectures Given at Cambridge in 1946*. London: Jonathan Cape, 1947
Djwa, Sandra. 'P.K. Page: A Biographical Interview.' *Malahat Review* 117 (Dec. 1996): 33–54
– *The Politics of the Imagination: A Life of F.R. Scott*. Toronto: McClelland & Stewart, 1987
Edwards, Justin D. 'Engendering Modern Canadian Poetry: *Preview, First Statement*, and the Disclosure of Patrick Anderson's Homosexuality.' *Essays on Canadian Writing* 62 (Fall 1997): 65–84
Eliot, T.S. 'Tradition and the Individual Talent.' In *Selected Essays* [1932], 2d ed., pp. 13–22. London: Faber and Faber, 1934
Ellmann, Maud. *The Poetics of Impersonality: T.S. Eliot and Ezra Pound*. Brighton: Harvester, 1987
Everett, Barbara. 'Eliot's "Four Quartets" and French Symbolism.' *English* 29.133 (Spring 1980): 1–37
Eysteinsson, Astradur. *The Concept of Modernism*. Ithaca, NY: Cornell University Press, 1990
Faas, Ekbert, and Sabrina Reed, eds. *Irving Layton and Robert Creeley: The Complete Correspondence, 1953–1978*. Kingston and Montreal: McGill-Queen's University Press, 1990
Fisher, Neil. *First Statement, 1942–1945: An Assessment and an Index*. Ottawa: Golden Dog, 1974

Francis, Wynne. '"The Birth of Tragedy": A Nietzschean Reading.' *Waves* 3.3 (Spring 1975): 5–8

– 'A Critic of Life: Louis Dudek as Man of Letters.' *Canadian Literature* 22 (Autumn 1964): 5–23

– 'The Expanding Spectrum: Literary Magazines.' *Canadian Literature* 57 (Summer 1973): 6–17

– '"The Farting Jesus": Layton and the Heroic Vitalists.' *CV/II* 3.3 (Jan. 1978): 46–51

– 'Irving Layton.' In *Canadian Writers and Their Works*. Poetry Series, vol. 5: 143–234. Toronto: ECW, 1985

– 'Layton and Nietzsche.' *Canadian Literature* 67 (Winter 1976): 39–52. Rpt. in Mayne, ed., *Irving Layton: The Poet and His Critics*, pp. 272–86

– 'Layton's Red Carpet: A Reading of "For Mao Tse-Tung: A Meditation on Flies and Kings".' *Inscape* 12.1 (Spring 1975): 50–6

– 'Literary Underground: Little Magazines in Canada.' *Canadian Literature* 34 (Autumn 1967): 63–70

– 'The Little Presses.' *Canadian Literature* 33 (Summer 1967): 56–62

– 'Montreal Poets of the Forties.' *Canadian Literature* 14 (Autumn 1962): 21–34

Frank, Joseph. 'Spatial Form in Modern Literature.' In *The Widening Gyre: Crisis and Mastery in Modern Literature*, pp. 3–62. New Brunswick, NJ: Rutgers University Press, 1963

Freake, Douglas. 'The Multiple Self in the Poetry of P.K. Page.' *Studies in Canadian Literature* 19.1 (1994): 94–114

Friedlander, Saul. *Probing the Limits of Representation: Nazism and the 'Final Solution.'* Cambridge, MA: Harvard University Press, 1992

Friedrich, Otto. *The End of the World: A History*. New York: Coward, McCann and Geoghegan, 1982

Gage, John T. *In the Arresting Eye: The Rhetoric of Imagism*. Baton Rouge and London: Louisiana State University Press, 1981

Gilbert, Susan, and Sandra Gubar. *No Man's Land: The Place of the Woman Writer in the Twentieth Century*, 3 vols. New Haven: Yale University Press, 1988–94

Gnarowski, Michael. *Contact, 1952–1954: Notes on the History and Background of the Periodical and an Index*. Montreal: Delta, 1966

– *Contact Press, 1952–1967: A Note on Its Origins and a Checklist of Titles*. Montreal: Delta, 1971

– Introduction. In *New Provinces: Poems of Several Authors* [1936], pp. vii–xxiii. Toronto: University of Toronto Press, 1976

– 'New Facts and Old Fictions: Some Notes on Patrick Anderson, *1945* and *En Masse*.' *Canadian Poetry: Studies, Documents, Reviews* 6 (Spring/Summer 1980): 61–8

– 'The Role of "Little Magazines" in the Development of Poetry in English in

Montreal.' *Culture* 24.3 (Sep. 1963): 274–86. Rpt. in Dudek and Gnarowski, eds., *The Making of Modern Poetry in Canada*, pp. 212–22

Goldie, Terry. 'Louis Dudek.' In *Canadian Writers and Their Works*, ed. Robert Lecker, Jack David, and Ellen Quigley. Poetry Series 5, pp. 73–139. Downsview, ON: ECW, 1985

Golfman, Noreen. 'Semantics and Semitics: The Early Poetry of A.M. Klein.' *University of Toronto Quarterly* 51.2 (Winter 1981/2): 175–91

Gordon, Mark Edward. 'Sounds and Wraiths of an Iron Fence.' *Preview* 9 (Nov. 1942): 1–2

Greenstein, Michael. 'Canadian Poetry After Auschwitz.' In *Third Solitudes: Tradition and Discontinuity in Jewish Canadian Literature*, pp. 35–53. Kingston: McGill-Queen's University Press, 1989

Halley, Paul. 'Apocalypse.' *First Statement* 2.3 (Oct. 1943): 9

Hambleton, Ronald, ed. *Unit of Five*. Toronto: Ryerson, 1944

Harrington, Lyn. *Syllables of Recorded Time: The Story of the Canadian Authors' Association*. Toronto: Simon and Pierre, 1981

Hartman, Charles O. *Free Verse: An Essay on Prosody*. Princeton, NJ: Princeton University Press, 1980

Heenan, Michael. 'Interview with A.J.M. Smith.' *Canadian Poetry: Studies, Documents, Reviews* 11 (Fall/Winter 1982): 73–7

– 'Souvenirs of Some: P.K. Page Responding to a Questionnaire.' *Canadian Poetry: Studies, Documents, Reviews* 10 (Spring/Summer 1982): 100–5

Heft, Harold. 'The Lost A.M. Klein Guggenheim Application.' *Canadian Poetry: Studies, Documents, Reviews* 32 (Spring/Summer 1993): 73–81

Holland, Normam H. *The I*. New Haven and London: Yale University Press, 1985

Hough, Graham. *Image and Experience: Studies in a Literary Revolution*. London: Duckworth, 1960

Hunt, Peter. 'Irving Layton, Pseudo-Prophet: A Reappraisal.' *Canadian Poetry: Studies, Documents, Reviews* 1 (Fall/Winter 1977): 1–26

Hutcheon, Linda. *A Poetics of Postmodernism: History, Theory, Fiction*. New York and London: Routledge, 1988

Hynes, Samuel. *The Auden Generation: Literature and Politics in England in the 1930s*. London: Bodley Head, 1976

Joyce, James. *A Portrait of the Artist as a Young Man*. [1916]. New York: Viking, 1964

Kampf, Louis. *On Modernism: The Prospects for Literature and Freedom*. Cambridge, MA: MIT Press, 1967

Kenner, Hugh. *The Pound Era*. Berkeley: University of California Press, 1971

Kertzer, J.M. 'Personality and Authority: A.M. Klein's Self-Portrait.' *Canadian Poetry: Studies, Documents, Reviews* 15 (Fall/Winter 1984): 31–47

Kilgour, Maggie. *From Communion to Cannibalism: An Anatomy of Metaphors of Incorporation*. Princeton, NJ: Princeton University Press, 1990

Killian, Laura. 'Poetry and the Modern Woman: P.K. Page and the Gender of Impersonality.' *Canadian Literature* 150 (Autumn 1996): 86–105

Kokotailo, Philip. 'The Bishop and His Deacon: Smith vs. Sutherland Reconsidered.' *Journal of Canadian Studies* 27.2 (1992): 63–81

Leahy, David. 'Patrick Anderson and John Sutherland's Heterorealism: "Some Sexual Experience of a Kind Not Normal".' *Essays on Canadian Writing* 62 (Fall 1997): 132–49

Lewis, Charlton T. *A Latin Dictionary for Schools* [1889]. Oxford: Clarendon Press, 1964

Lindberg-Seyersted, Brita. *Pound/Ford: The Story of a Literary Friendship*. New York: New Directions, 1982

Livesay, Dorothy. Review of *News of the Phoenix* by A.J.M. Smith. *First Statement* 2.6 (Apr. 1944): 18–19

– 'The Sculpture of Poetry: On Louis Dudek.' *Canadian Literature* 30 (Autumn 1966): 26–35

Madge, Charles O. 'Oxford Collective Poem.' *New Verse* 25 (May 1937): 16–19

Mandel, Eli. *Irving Layton*. Toronto: Forum House, 1969

Martin, Robert K. 'Sex and Politics in Wartime Canada: The Attack on Patrick Anderson.' *Essays on Canadian Writing* 44 (Fall 1991): 110–25

May the Twelfth: Mass-Observation Day-Surveys 1937. London: Faber and Faber, 1987

Mayne, Seymour. 'A Conversation with Patrick Anderson.' *Inscape* 11.3 (Fall 1974): 46–79

– ed. *Irving Layton: The Poet and His Critics*. Toronto: McGraw-Hill Ryerson, 1978

McCullagh, Joan. *Alan Crawley and* Contemporary Verse. Vancouver: University of British Columbia Press, 1976

McCutcheon, Sarah. 'Little Presses in Canada.' *Canadian Literature* 57 (Summer 1973): 88–96

Messenger, Cynthia G. 'Selecting P.K. Page.' *Canadian Poetry: Studies, Documents, Reviews* 35 (Fall/Winter 1994): 115–20

Morse, Arthur. *While Six Million Died: A Chronicle of American Apathy*. New York: Random House, 1968

Nause, John, and Michael Heenan. 'An Interview with Louis Dudek.' *Tamarack Review* 69 (Summer 1976): 30–43

Norris, Ken. *The Little Magazine in Canada: Its Role in the Development of Modernism and Postmodernism in Canadian Poetry*. Toronto: ECW, 1984

Olson, Charles. *Proprioception*. San Francisco: Four Seasons Foundation, 1965

O'Rourke, David. '*Preview*.' In *Oxford Companion to Canadian Literature*, pp. 682–3. Toronto: Oxford University Press, 1983

Pacey, Desmond. *Creative Writing in Canada*. Toronto: Ryerson, 1961

– 'English Canadian Poetry 1944–1954,' *Culture* 15.2 (June 1954): 255–65. Rpt. in Dudek and Gnarowski, eds., *The Making of Modern Poetry in Canada*, pp. 160–9

Pearce, Jon. 'Fried Eggs and the Workings of the Right Lobe: An Interview with P.K. Page.' *Quarry* 28.4 (Autumn 1979): 30–42

Peckham, Morse. 'Aestheticism to Modernism: Fulfilment or Revolution?' In *The Triumph of Romanticism*, pp. 202–25. Columbia: University of South Carolina Press, 1970

Pennee, Donna. 'Canadian Letters, Dead Referents: Reconsidering the Critical Construction of *The Double Hook*.' *Essays on Canadian Writing* 51/2 (1993/4): 233–57

Perkins, David. *A History of Modern Poetry*, 2 vols. Cambridge, MA, and London, England: Bellknap Press of Harvard University Press, 1976–87

Pierce, Lorne. *Lorne Pierce Papers*. Queen's University Archives, Kingston

Pollock, Zailig. *A.M. Klein: The Story of the Poet*. Toronto: University of Toronto Press, 1994

Precosky, Don. '*Preview*: An Introduction and Index.' *Canadian Poetry: Studies, Documents, Reviews* 8 (Spring/Summer 1981): 74–89

Preview. 1942–5. New York: Kraus Reprint, 1980

Purdy, Al. 'The *Collected Poems* of Irving Layton.' *Quarry* 15.3 (March 1966): 40–4. Rpt. in Mayne, ed., *Irving Layton: The Poet and His Critics*, pp. 146–50

Raine, Kathleen. *Defending Ancient Springs*. London: Oxford University Press, 1967

Ray, Paul C. *The Surrealist Movement in England*. Ithaca, NY: Cornell University Press, 1971

Relke, Diana M. 'Tracing a Terrestrial Vision in the Early Works of P.K. Page.' *Canadian Poetry: Studies, Documents, Reviews* 35 (Fall/Winter 1994): 11–30

Ringrose, C.X. 'Patrick Anderson and the Critics.' *Canadian Literature* 43 (Winter 1970): 10–23

Rooke, Constance. 'Approaching P.K. Page's "Arras".' *Canadian Poetry: Studies, Documents, Reviews* 4 (Spring/Summer 1979): 65–72

– 'P.K. Page: The Chameleon and the Centre.' *Malahat Review* 45 (Jan. 1978): 169–95

Roskolenko, Harry. Review of *Here and Now* and *Now Is the Place* [1949]. Rpt. in Mayne, ed., *Irving Layton: The Poet and His Critics*, pp. 27–9

Scobie, Stephen. 'Leonard Cohen, Phyllis Webb, and the End(s) of Modernism.' In *Canadian Canons: Essays in Literary Value*, ed. Robert Lecker, pp. 57–70. Toronto: University of Toronto Press, 1991

Scott, Bonnie Kime, ed. *The Gender of Modernism*. Bloomington: Indiana University Press, 1990

– *Refiguring Modernism*, 2 vols. Bloomington: Indiana University Press, 1995

Shaw, Neufville. 'The Maple Leaf Is Dying.' *Preview* 17 (1943): 1–3

Simpson, R.G. 'Gerontion.' *First Statement* 1.4 (Oct. 1942): 'Supplement,' 1–7

– 'Tradition in Art.' *First Statement* 1.7 (Nov. 1942): 6–8

Smith, A.J.M. *A.J.M. Smith Papers*. Trent University Archives, Peterborough

– 'Eclectic Detachment: Aspects of Identity in Canadian Poetry.' *Canadian Literature* 9 (Summer 1961): 6–14

– Introduction. In *The Book of Canadian Poetry*, 2d ed., pp. 3–31. Chicago: University of Chicago Press, 1943

– Letter to the Editor. *Canadian Forum* 27 (Apr. 1947): 18

– *Poems New and Collected*. Toronto: Oxford University Press, 1967

– 'The Poetry of P.K. Page.' *Canadian Literature* 50 (Autumn 1971): 17–27

– 'P.K. Page.' In *The Book of Canadian Poetry*, 3d ed., ed. A.J.M. Smith, p. 446. Toronto: Gage, 1957

– 'The Recent Poetry of Irving Layton.' *Queen's Quarterly* 62.4 (Winter 1956): 587–91. Rpt. in Mayne, ed., *Irving Layton: The Poet and His Critics*, pp. 43–8

– Review of P.K. Page's *As Ten As Twenty* and Patrick Anderson's *The White Centre*. *Canadian Forum* 26 (Feb. 1947): 250–2

– 'Testament.' *McGill Fortnightly Review* 2 (1927): 56

– 'To the Haggard Moon.' *Poems New and Collected*, p. 27

– 'What Strange Enchantment.' *Poems New and Collected*, p. 60

– ed., with F.R. Scott. *New Provinces: Poems of Several Authors* [1936]. Toronto: University of Toronto Press, 1976

Smith, P.K. 'Irving Layton and the Theme of Death.' *Canadian Literature* 48 (Spring 1971): 6–15

Squire, John B. 'Joyce and Mann.' *First Statement* 2.10 (Dec. 1944/Jan. 1945): 8–14

Sullivan, Rosemary. '"A Size Larger Than Seeing": The Poetry of P.K. Page.' *Canadian Literature* 79 (Winter 1978): 32–42

Surette, Leon. *The Birth of Modernism: Ezra Pound, T.S. Eliot and the Occult*. Montreal: McGill-Queen's University Press, 1993

Tallman, Warren. 'Proprioception in Charles Olson's Poetry.' *Open Letter* 3.6 (Winter 1976/7): 159–74

Taylor, Charles. *Sources of the Self: The Making of the Modern Identity*. Cambridge, MA: Harvard University Press, 1989

Teicholz, Tom. *Conversations with Jerzy Kosinski*. Jackson: University Press of Mississippi, 1993

Thomas, Dylan. *The Collected Poems of Dylan Thomas, 1934–1952*. New York: New Directions, 1971

Thornton, R.K.R. '"Decadence" in Later Nineteenth-Century England.' In *Decadence and the 1890s*, ed. Ian Fletcher, pp. 15–30. London: Edward Arnold, 1979

Tolley, A.T. *The Poetry of the Forties in Britain*. Ottawa: Carleton University Press, 1985

Tom Harrisson Mass-Observation Archive. University of Sussex, Brighton, England.

Treece, Henry. *How I See Apocalypse*. London: Lindsay Drummond, 1946

Trehearne, Brian. *Aestheticism and the Canadian Modernists: Aspects of a Poetic Influence*. Kingston and Montreal: McGill-Queen's University Press, 1989

– 'Critical Episodes in Montreal Poetry of the 1940s.' *Canadian Poetry: Studies, Documents, Reviews* 41 (Fall/ Winter 1997): 21–52

– 'Finch's Early Poetry and the Dandy Manner.' *Canadian Poetry: Studies, Documents, Reviews* 18 (Spring/Summer 1986): 11–34

– 'A Partial Correspondence.' Review of *Irving Layton and Robert Creeley: The Complete Correspondence, 1953–1978*, ed. Ekbert Faas and Sabrina Reed. *Essays on Canadian Writing* 47 (Fall 1992): 82–9

– '"Scanned and Scorned": Freedom and Fame in Layton.' In *Inside the Poem: Essays in Honour of Donald Stephen*, ed. W.H. New, pp. 139–50. Toronto: Oxford University Press, 1992

Tucker, Herbert F. 'Dramatic Monologue and the Overhearing of Lyric.' In *Lyric Poetry: Beyond New Criticism*, ed. Patricia Parker and Chaviva Hosek, pp. 241–4. Ithaca, NY: Cornell University Press, 1985

Vanneste, Hilda. *Northern Review, 1945–1956: A History and an Index*. Ottawa: Tecumseh, 1982

Van Wilt, Kurt. 'Layton, Nietzsche, and Overcoming.' *Essays on Canadian Writing* 10 (Spring 1978): 19–42

Waddington, Miriam. Introduction. In *Essays, Controversies and Poems*, pp. 7–15. Toronto: McClelland & Stewart [New Canadian Library], 1972

– 'Now We Steer.' *First Statement* 1.14 (Mar. 1943): 9–10

Waddington, Patrick. 'First Statement Opinions.' *First Statement* 1.16 (Apr. 1943): 5–7

Watt, F.W. 'Climate of Unrest: Periodicals in the Twenties and Thirties.' *Canadian Literature* 12 (Spring 1962): 15–27

Wells, Henry W. *Where Poetry Stands Now*. Toronto: Ryerson, 1948

Whalley, George, ed. *Writing in Canada: Proceedings of the Canadian Writers' Conference Held at Queen's University, July 1955*. Toronto: Macmillan, 1956

Whiteman, Bruce, ed. *The Letters of John Sutherland, 1942–1956*. Toronto: ECW, 1992

– 'Raymond Souster.' In *Canadian Writers and Their Works* Poetry Series 5, pp. 235–76. Downsview, ON: ECW, 1985

Whitney, Patricia. '*En Masse*: An Introduction and an Index.' *Canadian Poetry: Studies, Documents, Reviews* 19 (Fall/Winter 1986): 76–91

– 'From Oxford to Montreal: Patrick Anderson's Political Development.' *Canadian Poetry: Studies, Documents, Reviews* 19 (Fall/Winter 1986): 26–48

Wiens, Erwin. 'From Apocalypse to Black Mountain: The Contexts of Layton's Early Criticism.' *Canadian Poetry: Studies, Documents, Reviews* 16 (Spring/Summer 1985): 1–20

Wiesel, Elie. *One Generation After.* New York: Random House, 1970

Williamson, Alan. *Introspection and Contemporary Poetry.* Cambridge, MA, and London, England: Harvard University Press, 1984

Wilson, Milton. '*Other Canadians* and After.' *Tamarack Review* 9 (Autumn 1958): 77–92

Winters, Yvor. 'The Testament of a Stone, Being Notes on the Mechanics of the Poetic Image.' In *The Uncollected Essays and Reviews of Yvor Winters,* ed. Francis Murphy, pp. 194–215. Chicago: Swallow Press, 1973

Woodcock, George. 'On Patrick Anderson.' *Canadian Literature* 81 (Summer 1979): 162–3

Sources and Permissions

Permission to quote from writings in copyright has been generously granted by the following individuals, and I am grateful for their prompt and supportive responses to inquiries.

Extracts from published writings and private papers of Patrick Anderson reprinted by permission of Orlando Gearing.

Extracts from published writings of John Sutherland reprinted by permission of Susan Aikman.

Extracts from published writings and private papers of P.K. Page reprinted by permission of P.K. Page and The Porcupine's Quill Press.

Extracts from published writings and private papers of A.M. Klein reprinted by permission of Sandor Klein.

Extracts from published writings and private papers of Irving Layton reprinted by permission of Irving Layton.

Extracts from published writings and private papers of Louis Dudek reprinted by permission of Louis Dudek.

Extracts from the *A.J.M. Smith Papers*, Bata Library, Trent University, Peterborough, Ontario, reprinted by permission of William Toye.

Extracts from the *Lorne Pierce Papers*, Queen's University Archives, Queen's

University, Kingston, Ontario, reprinted by permission of Don Richan, University Archivist.

Index

www.ingramcontent.com/pod-product-compliance
Lightning Source LLC
LaVergne TN
LVHW020436080826
844660LV00033B/1296

9781442613232